THE CAMBRIDGE COMPANION TO
JESUS

This *Companion* takes as its starting point the realisation that Jesus of Nazareth cannot be studied purely as a subject of ancient history, 'a man like any other man'. History, literature, theology and the dynamic of a living, worldwide religious reality all appropriately impinge on the study of Jesus.

The two parts roughly correspond to the interdependent tasks of historical description and critical and theological reflection. The book incorporates the most up-to-date historical work on Jesus the Jew with the 'bigger issues' of critical method, the story of Christian faith and study, and Jesus in a global church and in the encounter with Judaism and Islam.

Written by seventeen leading international scholars, the book encourages students of the historical Jesus to discover the vital contribution of theology, and students of doctrine to engage the Christ of faith as Jesus the first-century Jew.

MARKUS BOCKMUEHL is a Reader in New Testament Studies at the University of Cambridge and a Fellow of Fitzwilliam College. He is the author of *Revelation and mystery in ancient Judaism and Pauline Christianity* (1990), *This Jesus: martyr, Lord, Messiah* (1994), *The Epistle to the Philippians* (1997) and *Jewish law in Gentile churches: halakhah and the beginning of Christian public ethics* (2000).

CAMBRIDGE COMPANIONS TO RELIGION
A series of companions to major topics and key figures in
theology and religious studies. Each volume contains specially
commissioned chapters by international scholars which provide
an accessible and stimulating introduction to the subject for new
readers and non-specialists.

Other titles in the series

THE CAMBRIDGE COMPANION TO CHRISTIAN DOCTRINE
edited by Colin Gunton
ISBN 0 521 47118 4 hardback   ISBN 0 521 47695 8 paperback

THE CAMBRIDGE COMPANION TO BIBLICAL INTERPRETATION
edited by John Barton
ISBN 0 521 48144 9 hardback   ISBN 0 521 48593 2 paperback

THE CAMBRIDGE COMPANION TO DIETRICH BONHOEFFER
edited by John de Gruchy
ISBN 0 521 58258 x hardback   ISBN 0 521 58751 6 paperback

THE CAMBRIDGE COMPANION TO LIBERATION THEOLOGY
edited by Christopher Rowland
ISBN 0 521 46144 8 hardback   ISBN 0 521 46707 1 paperback

THE CAMBRIDGE COMPANION TO KARL BARTH edited by John Webster
ISBN 0 521 58476 0 hardback   ISBN 0 521 58560 0 paperback

THE CAMBRIDGE COMPANION TO CHRISTIAN ETHICS
edited by Robin Gill
ISBN 0 521 77070 x hardback   ISBN 0 521 77918 9 paperback

THE CAMBRIDGE COMPANION TO JESUS edited by Markus Bockmuehl
ISBN 0 521 79261 4 hardback   ISBN 0 521 79678 4 paperback

Forthcoming

THE CAMBRIDGE COMPANION TO THE GOSPELS edited by Stephen C. Barton

THE CAMBRIDGE COMPANION TO ST PAUL edited by James D. G. Dunn

THE CAMBRIDGE COMPANION TO MEDIEVAL JEWISH THOUGHT
edited by Daniel H. Frank and Oliver Leaman

THE CAMBRIDGE COMPANION TO ISLAMIC THEOLOGY
edited by Timothy J. Winter

THE CAMBRIDGE COMPANION TO REFORMATION THEOLOGY
edited by David Bagchi and David Steinmetz

THE CAMBRIDGE COMPANION TO JOHN CALVIN
edited by Donald C. McKim

THE CAMBRIDGE COMPANION TO MARTIN LUTHER
edited by Donald C. McKim

THE CAMBRIDGE COMPANION TO FEMINIST THEOLOGY
edited by Susan Frank Parsons

THE CAMBRIDGE COMPANION TO POSTMODERN THEOLOGY
edited by Kevin Vanhoozer

JESUS

EDITED BY

Markus Bockmuehl

CAMBRIDGE
UNIVERSITY PRESS

PUBLISHED BY THE PRESS SYNDICATE OF THE UNIVERSITY OF CAMBRIDGE
The Pitt Building, Trumpington Street, Cambridge, United Kingdom

CAMBRIDGE UNIVERSITY PRESS
The Edinburgh Building, Cambridge CB2 2RU, UK
40 West 20th Street, New York, NY 10011-4211, USA
477 Williamstown Road, Port Melbourne, VIC 3207, Australia
Ruiz de Alarcón 13, 28014 Madrid, Spain
Dock House, The Waterfront, Cape Town 8001, South Africa

http://www.cambridge.org

First published 2001
Third printing 2002

Printed in the United Kingdom at the University Press, Cambridge

Typeface Severin 10/13 pt.   *System* LaTeX 2ε [TB]

A catalogue record for this book is available from the British Library.

Library of Congress Cataloguing in Publication Data

The Cambridge companion to Jesus / edited by Markus Bockmuehl.
    p.   cm. – (Cambridge companions to religion)
Includes bibliographical references and index.
ISBN 0 521 79261 4 (hb) – ISBN 0 521 79678 4 (pbk)
1. Jesus Christ – Biography.   2. Jesus Christ – Person and offices – History of doctrines.
I. Bockmuehl, Markus N. A.   II. Series.
BT301.2.C346   2001
232 – dc21   2001025741

ISBN 0 521 79261 4 hardback
ISBN 0 521 79678 4 paperback

Contents

Notes on contributors

STEPHEN C. BARTON is Senior Lecturer in New Testament in the Department of Theology at the University of Durham, England. He is also a priest of the Church of England and assists at St John's Church Neville's Cross, Durham. His publications include *The spirituality of the gospels* (London: SPCK, 1992); *Discipleship and family ties in Mark and Matthew* (Cambridge: Cambridge University Press, 1994); *Invitation to the Bible* (London: SPCK, 1997); and *Life together: essays on family, sexuality and community in the New Testament and today* (Edinburgh: T&T Clark, 2001).

RICHARD BAUCKHAM, FBA, is Professor of New Testament Studies and Bishop Wardlaw Professor at the University of St Andrews, Scotland. His books include: *Jude, 2 Peter*, WBC (Waco: Word, 1983); *Jude and the relatives of Jesus in the early church* (Edinburgh: T&T Clark, 1990); *The theology of the book of Revelation* (Cambridge: Cambridge University Press, 1993); *The climax of prophecy: studies in the book of Revelation* (Edinburgh: T&T Clark, 1993); *The theology of Jürgen Moltmann* (Edinburgh: T&T Clark, 1995); *God crucified: monotheism and christology in the New Testament* (Carlisle: Paternoster Press, 1998); *James: wisdom of James, disciple of Jesus the sage* (London and New York: Routledge, 1999); and (with Trevor Hart) *Hope against hope: Christian eschatology in contemporary context* (London: Darton, Longman & Todd, 1999).

MARKUS BOCKMUEHL is Reader in New Testament Studies at the University of Cambridge and a Fellow of Fitzwilliam College. His books include *This Jesus: martyr, Lord, Messiah* (Edinburgh: T&T Clark, 1994); *The Epistle to the Philippians*, BNTC (Peabody: Hendrickson, 1998); *A vision for the church: studies in early Christian ecclesiology in honour of J. P. M. Sweet*, ed. with M. B. Thompson (Edinburgh: T&T Clark, 1997); and *Jewish law in Gentile churches: halakhah and the beginning of Christian public ethics* (Edinburgh: T&T Clark, 2000).

DAVID B. BURRELL, CSC (Congregation of the Holy Cross), is Theodore Hesburgh Professor in Philosophy and Theology at the University of Notre Dame, working in comparative philosophical theology in Judaism, Christianity and Islam, as evidenced in *Knowing the unknowable God: Ibn-Sina, Maimonides, Aquinas* (Notre Dame, 1986) and *Freedom and creation in three traditions* (Notre Dame, 1993), and two translations of al-Ghazali: *Al-Ghazali on the ninety-nine beautiful names of God* (Cambridge: Islamic Texts Society, 1993) and *Al-Ghazali on faith in divine unity and trust in divine providence* [=Book 35 of his *Ihya Ulum ad-Din*] (Louisville: Fons Vitae, 2000). Luce Professor of Abrahamic Faiths at Hartford Seminary and University of Hartford in 1998, he directs the University's Jerusalem programme each spring, at the Tantur Ecumenical Institute.

JAMES CARLETON PAGET is a Lecturer in New Testament Studies at the University of Cambridge and a Fellow of Peterhouse. He is the author of *The Epistle of Barnabas: outline and background*, WUNT 2:64 (Tübingen: Mohr Siebeck, 1994) as well as a number of articles on subjects related to Christian origins. His current research projects include books in preparation on Jewish Christianity and on Albert Schweitzer.

BRUCE CHILTON currently serves as Bernard Iddings Bell Professor of Religion at Bard College, and also directs the Institute of Advanced Theology there. Throughout his career, he has been active in the pastoral ministry of the Anglican Church, and is presently Rector of the Church of St John the Evangelist. His published work includes a critical translation of the Aramaic version of Isaiah with commentary (*The Isaiah Targum*, ArBib 11 [Wilmington: Glazier, 1987]), as well as academic studies that locate Jesus within his Jewish context: *A Galilean rabbi and his Bible* (London: SPCK, 1984); *The temple of Jesus* (University Park: Pennsylvania State University Press, 1992); *Pure kingdom* (Grand Rapids: Eerdmans, 1996); *Rabbi Jesus* (New York: Bantam, 2000).

CRAIG A. EVANS is Professor of Biblical Studies at Trinity Western University. He has authored *Luke* (Peabody: Hendrickson, 1990); *Noncanonical writings and New Testament interpretation* (Peabody: Hendrickson, 1992); *Word and glory* (Sheffield: Sheffield Academic Press, 1993); *Jesus and his contemporaries* (Leiden: Brill, 1995); *Jesus in context* (Leiden: Brill, 1997); and *Mark* in the Word Commentary (Nashville: Thomas Nelson, 2001).

JOEL B. GREEN is Dean of the School of Theology and Professor of New Testament Interpretation at Asbury Theological Seminary, Wilmore,

Kentucky, USA. His extensive publications on the death of Jesus include *The death of Jesus in early Christianity*, with John T. Carroll (Peabody: Hendrickson, 1995). He is the author of *The theology of the gospel of Luke* (Cambridge: Cambridge University Press, 1995) and the New International Commentary on *The gospel of Luke* (Grand Rapids: Eerdmans, 1997).

WALTER MOBERLY has since 1985 been a Lecturer in Theology at the University of Durham, where he teaches Old Testament and Biblical Theology. He has a special interest in the responsible use of the Bible in Christian theology and spirituality today. His books include *The Old Testament of the Old Testament* (Philadelphia: Fortress, 1992); *Genesis 12–50* (Sheffield: Sheffield Academic Press, 1992); and *The Bible, theology, and faith: a study of Abraham and Jesus* (Cambridge: Cambridge University Press, 2000).

TERESA OKURE, SHCJ (Society of the Holy Child Jesus), is Professor of New Testament at the Catholic Higher Institute of West Africa at Port Harcourt, in her native Nigeria. She is currently the coordinator of Bible Studies and Mission, a networking interest group of the International Association for Mission Studies (IAMS) and Vice-President of the International Association of Catholic Missiologists (IACM). Her major works include *The Johannine approach to mission: a contextual study of John 4:1–42*, WUNT 2:31 (Tübingen: Mohr Siebeck, 1988); 'John' in *The international Bible commentary,* ed. W. R. Farmer (Collegeville: Liturgical Press, 1998); and *To cast fire upon the earth: Bible and mission collaborating in today's multicultural global context* (Pietermaritzburg: Cluster Publications, 2000).

GRAHAM STANTON is Lady Margaret's Professor of Divinity at the University of Cambridge and a Fellow of Fitzwilliam College. Recent publications include *A gospel for a new people: studies in Matthew* (Edinburgh: T&T Clark, 1992; Louisville: Westminster/John Knox, 1993); *Gospel truth? New light on Jesus and the gospels* (London: HarperCollins; Valley Forge PA: Trinity Press International, 1995); *The gospels and Jesus* (Oxford: Oxford University Press, 1989; 2nd edn 2001); *Tolerance and intolerance in early Judaism and Christianity*, ed. with G. G. Stroumsa (Cambridge: Cambridge University Press, 1998).

MARIANNE MEYE THOMPSON is Professor of New Testament Interpretation at Fuller Theological Seminary, Pasadena, California. She is the author of *The humanity of Jesus in the fourth gospel* (Philadelphia: Fortress, 1988; reprinted as *The incarnate word*, Peabody: Hendrickson, 1993); *1–3 John*

(Downers Grove: InterVarsity Press, 1992); and *The promise of the Father* (Louisville: Westminster John Knox, 2000).

PETER J. TOMSON is Professor of New Testament and Patristics at the Protestant Theological Faculty of Brussels, as well as chair of the Institutum Iudaicum of Belgium and Editor-in-Chief of Compendia Rerum Iudaicarum ad Novum Testamentum, Section III: Jewish Traditions in Early Christian Literature. His main publications include *Paul and the Jewish law: Halakha in the letters of the Apostle to the Gentiles* (Assen: van Gorcum; Philadelphia: Fortress Press, 1990); and *'If this be from heaven...': Jesus and the New Testament authors in their relation to Judaism* (Sheffield: Sheffield Academic Press, 2001).

ALAN TORRANCE is Professor of Systematic Theology at the University of St Andrews, Scotland. His main publications include *Persons in communion: an essay on Trinitarian description and human participation* (Edinburgh: T&T Clark, 1996); *Christ and context*, ed. with Hilary Regan (Edinburgh: T&T Clark, 1993); and 'The Trinity', in *The Cambridge companion to Karl Barth*, ed. John Webster (Cambridge: Cambridge University Press, 2000), 72–91. He is currently preparing the publication of *The Christ of history and the open society*, his 1997–98 Hensley Henson Lectures at the University of Oxford.

CHRISTOPHER TUCKETT is Professor of New Testament Studies and a Fellow of Wolfson College at the University of Oxford. His published works include *Q and the history of early Christianity* (Edinburgh: T&T Clark, 1996); *The revival of the Griesbach hypothesis* (Cambridge: Cambridge University Press, 1983); *Nag Hammadi and the gospel tradition* (Edinburgh: T&T Clark, 1986); *Reading the New Testament* (London: SPCK, 1987); *Luke* (Sheffield: Sheffield Academic Press, 1996), as well as many other articles and essays.

FRANCIS WATSON is Professor of New Testament Exegesis at the University of Aberdeen, having previously taught for fifteen years at King's College, London. He has published several books which seek to break down the boundaries separating New Testament studies from other theological disciplines, notably systematic theology: *Text, church and world: biblical interpretation in theological perspective* (Edinburgh: T&T Clark, 1994); *Text and truth: redefining biblical theology* (Edinburgh: T&T Clark, 1997); and, most recently, *Agape, eros, gender: towards a Pauline sexual ethic* (Cambridge: Cambridge University Press, 2000). He is currently working on the theology of John and of Paul.

ROWAN WILLIAMS is the Anglican Archbishop of Wales and a former Lady Margaret Professor of Divinity at Oxford. His most recent books include *Sergii Bulgakov: towards a Russian political theology* (Edinburgh: T&T Clark, 1999); *On Christian theology* (Oxford: Blackwell, 2000); and *Lost icons: reflections on cultural bereavement* (Edinburgh: T&T Clark, 2000). He is particularly interested in patristic theology and in the interactions between theology, spirituality and culture.

Abbreviations

The system of abbreviations in this volume follows the *SBL Handbook of Style* (Alexander *et al.* 1999), available online at www.sbl-site.org to members of the Society of Biblical Literature. It is also accessible in the 'Instructions for Contributors' of the *Journal of Biblical Literature* 117 (1998), 555–79. For ease of reference, the relevant entries are reproduced below.

GENERAL ABBREVIATIONS

ABD	*Anchor Bible Dictionary*
ABRL	Anchor Bible Reference Library
AGJU	Arbeiten zur Geschichte des antiken Judentums und des Urchristentums
ANF	*The Ante-Nicene Fathers*, ed. A. Roberts and J. Donaldson, 10 vols. (Grand Rapids: Eerdmans; Edinburgh: T&T Clark, n.d. [frequent reprints]).
ArBib	The Aramaic Bible
ASV	American Standard Version
AThR	*Anglican Theological Review*
augm.	augmented
BA	*Biblical Archaeologist*
BAG	W. Bauer, W. F. Arndt, F. W. Gingrich and F. W. Danker, *Greek–English Lexicon of the New Testament and Other Early Christian Literature*, 2nd edn (Chicago: University of Chicago, 1979)
BARev	*Biblical Archaeology Review*
BBB	Bonner biblische Beiträge
BBR	*Bulletin for Biblical Research*
BETL	Bibliotheca ephemeridum theologicarum lovaniensium
BibInt	*Biblical Interpretation*
Bk.	Book
BTB	*Biblical Theology Bulletin*

BZNW	Beihefte zur Zeitschrift für die neutestamentliche Wissenschaft
c.	*circa*, about
CBQ	*Catholic Biblical Quarterly*
cf.	*confer*, compare
ch(s).	chapter(s)
CWS	Classics of Western Spirituality
DJG	*Dictionary of Jesus and the Gospels*, ed. J. B. Green *et al.* (Downers Grove/Leicester: InterVarsity, 1992)
DSD	*Dead Sea Discoveries*
DSS	Dead Sea Scrolls
e.g.	*exempli gratia*, for example
ed(s).	editor(s), edited by
edn	edition
esp.	especially
ET	English translation
et al.	*et alii*, and others
frg.	fragment
Gk.	Greek
GNS	Good News Studies
Hebr.	Hebrew
HO	Handbuch der Orientalistik
HTR	*Harvard Theological Review*
ICC	International Critical Commentary
IEJ	*Israel Exploration Journal*
JR	*Journal of Religion*
JSNTSup	*Journal for the Study of the New Testament* Supplement Series
JSOTSup	*Journal for the Study of the Old Testament* Supplement Series
km	kilometres
L	Jesus tradition unique to Luke
l.	*logion*
LCC	Library of Christian Classics
lit.	literally
LSJ	H. G. Liddell and R. Scott, *A Greek–English Lexicon*, ed. H. S. Jones with a supplement by E. A. Barber, 9th edn with supplement (Oxford: Oxford University Press, 1968)
LXX	Septuagint (The Greek Old Testament)
M	special material in Matthew
MM	J. H. Moulton and G. Milligan, *The Vocabulary of the Greek New Testament* (Grand Rapids: Eerdmans, 1930)
n.	note
n.p.	no place, no publisher

NASB	New American Standard Bible
NB	*Nota bene*, note well
NEB	New English Bible
NovT	*Novum Testamentum*
NovTSup	Supplements to *Novum Testamentum*
NPNF	*A Select Library of the Nicene and Post-Nicene Fathers of the Christian Church*, ed. P. Schaff, Series I & II, 13 & 14 vols. (Grand Rapids: Eerdmans; Edinburgh: T&T Clark, n.d. [frequent reprints])
NRSV	New Revised Standard Version
NTOA	Novum Testamentum et Orbis Antiquus
NT	New Testament
NTS	*New Testament Studies*
NTTS	New Testament Tools and Studies
O.P.	*Ordo Praedicatorum*, Dominican Order
OT	Old Testament
p(p).	page(s)
par(r).	and parallel(s)
POxy	Oxyrhynchus Papyrus
Q	'Q', hypothetical source of Jesus sayings used by Matthew and Luke
RB	*Revue Biblique*
repr.	reprinted
rev.	revised
RSV	Revised Standard Version
SBL	Society of Biblical Literature
SBT	Studies in Biblical Theology
SJT	*Scottish Journal of Theology*
SNTSMS	SNTS (Studiorum Novi Testamenti Societas, Society of New Testament Studies) Monograph Series
SNTSU	Studien zum Neuen Testament und seiner Umwelt
SNTW	Studies of the New Testament and its World
trans.	translated by
UN	United Nations
v(v).	verse(s)
viz.	*videlicet*, namely
vol.	volume(s)
VTSup	Supplements to *Vetus Testamentum*
WUNT	Wissenschaftliche Untersuchungen zum Neuen Testament
ZNW	*Zeitschrift für die neutestamentliche Wissenschaft und die Kunde der älteren Kirche*
ZTK	*Zeitschrift für Theologie und Kirche*

PRIMARY SOURCES

Books of the Bible
Old Testament

Gen	Genesis	1-2 Chr	1-2 Chronicles	Jer	Jeremiah
Exod	Exodus	Ezra		Lam	Lamentations
Lev	Leviticus	Neh	Nehemiah	Ezek	Ezekiel
Num	Numbers	Esth	Esther	Dan	Daniel
Deut	Deuteronomy	Job		Hos	Hosea
Josh	Joshua	Ps	Psalms	Joel	
Judg	Judges	Prov	Proverbs	Amos	
Ruth		Eccl	Ecclesiastes	Obad	Obadiah
1-2 Sam	1-2 Samuel	Song	Song of Songs	Jon	Jonah
1-2 Kgs	1-2 Kings	Isa	Isaiah	Mic	Micah
Nah	Nahum	Zeph	Zephaniah	Zech	Zechariah
Hab	Habakkuk	Hag	Haggai	Mal	Malachi

LXX/Deuterocanonical Books cited

1-4 Macc	1-4 Maccabees	Wis	Wisdom of Solomon

New Testament

Matt	Matthew	1-2 Thess	1-2Thessalonians
Mark		1-2 Tim	1-2Timothy
Luke		Tit	Titus
John		Phlm	Philemon
Acts		Heb	Hebrews
Rom	Romans	Jas	James
1-2 Cor	1-2 Corinthians	1–2Pet	1-2Peter
Gal	Galatians	1-3 John	
Eph	Ephesians	Jude	
Phil	Philippians	Rev	Revelation
Col	Colossians		

Old Testament pseudepigrapha

Jub.	*Book of Jubilees*	*T. Levi*	*Testament of Levi*
Ps(s). Sol.	*Psalm(s) of Solomon*	*T. Mos.*	*Testament of Moses*

Other Jewish writings
Dead Sea Scrolls

Abbreviations for the Dead Sea Scrolls are given in the standard format indicating the number of the cave at Qumran where the documents were found, followed by a number or alphabetic siglum for the title (e.g. 1QS, 4Q246). The most widely used English translation at present is García Martínez 1996, where a listing of the scrolls and places of publication can be found on pp. 465–519. For a Hebrew–English bilingual edition see García Martínez 1998.

1QH	*Thanksgiving Hymns*	4Q521	*Messianic Apocalypse*
1QM	*War Scroll*	4QMMT	*Miqṣat Maʿaśê ha-Torah*
1QpHab	*Pesher Habakkuk*	11QT	*Temple Scroll*
1QS	*Rule of the Community*	11QMelch	*Melchizedek*
1QSa	*Rule of the Congregation*	CD	*Damascus Document*
4Q225	Pseudo-Jubilees[a]		

Josephus

Ant.	*Jewish Antiquities*	*Ag. Ap.*	*Against Apion*
J. W.	*On the Jewish War*	*Life*	*Life of Josephus*

Rabbinic literature
(1) Mishnah and Talmud

The Mishnah (*m.*) and Tosefta (*t.*) are quoted according to chapter and halakhah (e.g. *m. Sukkah* 2.3, *t. Sukkah* 2.3), the Babylonian Talmud (*b.*) according to folio, side a or b (e.g. *b. Sukkah* 17b). In quotations from the Palestinian Talmud (i.e. Yerushalmi, '*y*.'), the first two digits represent the chapter and halakhah as in the Mishnah, the third gives the folio and column, a–d (e.g. y. *Sukkah* 2.3, 17c). The tractates are abbreviated as follows:

ʿAbod. Zar.	*ʿAbodah Zarah*	*Men.*	*Menaḥot*
ʾAbot		*Moʿed Qatan*	
B. Bat.	*Baba Batra*	*Ned.*	*Nedarim*
B. Meṣiʿa	*Baba Meṣiʿa*	*Peʾah*	
Ber.	*Berakhot*	*Pesaḥ.*	*Pesaḥim*
Giṭṭ.	*Giṭṭin*	*Qidd.*	*Qidduśin*
Ḥag.	*Ḥagigah*	*Šabb.*	*Šabbat*
Ḥull.	*Ḥullin*	*Sanh.*	*Sanhedrin*
Kelim	*Kelim*	*Sukkah*	
Ketub.	*Ketubbot*	*Taʿan.*	*Taʿanit*
Meg.	*Megillah*	*Yoma*	

(2) Other Rabbinic writings

ʾAbot R. Nat.	Abot de-Rabbi Nathan
Gen. Rab.	Genesis Rabbah
Mek. deR. Ishmael	Mekhilta de-Rabbi Ishmael
Pirqe R. El.	Pirqe de-Rabbi Eliezer
Sipre Deut.	Sifre on Deuteronomy
Song Rab.	Song of Songs Rabbah
Soperim	
Targ.	Targum
Yal.	Yalqut

Early Christian writings

Apocryphal texts

Sec. Gos. Mk.	Secret Gospel of Mark
Gos. Pet.	Gospel of Peter
Gos. Thom.	Gospel of Thomas

Did.	Didache

Didymus the Blind

Comm. Ps.	Commentarii in Psalmos

Eusebius

Hist. eccl.	Ecclesiastical History

Ignatius

Ign. Rom.	Letter to the Romans

Irenaeus

Haer.	Against Heresies

Justin

1 Apol.	First Apology
Dial.	Dialogue with Trypho

Origen

Hom. Jer.	Homilies on Jeremiah
C. Cels.	Contra Celsum, Against Celsus

Other ancient writings

Pliny

Nat. Hist.   *Natural History*

Strabo

Geog.   *Geography*

Introduction

MARKUS BOCKMUEHL

Two thousand years have come and gone, but still his remains the unfinished story that refuses to go away. Jesus of Nazareth, a Jew from rural first-century Galilee, is without doubt the most famous and most influential human being who ever walked the face of the earth. His influence may at present be declining in a few countries of western Europe and parts of North America, as has from time to time transpired elsewhere. But the global fact is that the adherents of Jesus are more widespread and more numerous, and make up a greater part of the world's population, than at any time in history. Two billion people identify themselves as Christians; well over a billion Muslims revere Jesus as a prophet of God (Barrett and Johnson 2001). Unnumbered others know and respect his memory as a wise and holy man.

The followers of Jesus live in every country of the globe. They read and speak of him in a thousand tongues. For them, the world's creation and destiny hold together in him, the wholly human and visible icon of the wholly transcendent and invisible God. He animates their cultures, creeds and aspirations.

For many non-believers, too, indeed to the majority of the earth's population, Jesus is a household name, whose 'brand recognition' still far outstrips that of McDonald's, Microsoft or MTV. To be sure, that fact is today as complex as a shattered prism, refracting centuries of hopes and fears, ardour and contempt. The mention of Jesus brings to mind acts both of heroic charity and of unspeakable evil – any of which have from time to time been committed either in his name or in spite of it. Billions view the name and even the cultural symbols of Jesus as signifying either great benefits or else great torment inflicted on their collective and perhaps their personal history. Both for good and for ill, Jesus remains a household name around the world.

How ironic, then, that during his lifetime Jesus was neither exceptionally famous nor particularly influential on the lives and events in the society in which he lived. We know remarkably little about his life, and what little we think we do know is almost inevitably coated by popular loves and hates, by interpreters' wishful thinking and unbridled speculation, and of course by two thousand years of accumulated tradition.

This remarkable 'footprint' of Jesus in history, at once deeply troubling and richly life-giving, has strangely contradictory implications for an encounter with him today. On the one hand, it means that a true and adequate understanding of the man remains a vital task, even as his third millennium has dawned. And yet, the very weight of his aftermath infinitely complicates our ability to perceive and justify quite what such a 'true and adequate understanding' might be.

For all that we have learned from three centuries of so-called 'critical' (but almost exclusively western) scholarship, the simultaneous late modern globalisation and retribalisation of human culture has at last thrown us back on one basic insight: knowledge is always relative to the knower, not just to the object known. For the case in point, this means that we can never adequately know the history of Jesus unless we know our own history – and, just as significantly, vice versa. Epistemologically, Jesus and his effects in our world are inextricably intertwined: the man of Nazareth cannot be understood in isolation from the footprint he has left on our collective and individual understanding, feeling and knowing.

At least in the western world, it remains true that we can understand neither Christian faith nor much of the world around us if we do not come to terms with Jesus of Nazareth and the two millennia of engagement with his heritage. On the pages of first-century history books he was of course a mere blip, whom the journalists and historians of his day ignored or regarded as of little consequence. And yet, there is an obvious and equally 'historical' sense in which he is clearly *not* just 'a man like any other man'.

The shape of this book is significantly influenced by considerations such as these. Issues of history, literature, theology and the dynamic of a lived religious reality are of integral importance to our subject. The contributors are all accomplished scholars in their respective fields, yet all share a keen awareness of the multidisciplinary nature of any valid study of Jesus. Although committed to the highest standards of technical competence, the authors were encouraged to 'think big', to build bridges, and to view things 'in colour'.

The argument of the book unfolds in two parts, which roughly correspond to the twin tasks of the historical description of Jesus and of critical and theological reflection on him. Obviously the two tasks cannot be quite so neatly separated – as was, for example, the assumption behind the once fashionable but classically misconceived distinction between a Jesus 'of history' and the divine Christ of faith. Indeed, Part 1 demonstrates the extent to which any serious historical engagement with Jesus must face the insistent challenges of truth, hope and mercy that are inescapably raised by his life and teaching – and indeed by his abiding imprint in the life of the world. Part II in turn appropriates for theology the converse point about particularity, painfully reinforced by the century now past. The meaning of Jesus in the global story of Christian worship, life and study remains incomprehensible apart from the apostolic witness to that migrant Jew from Nazareth who walked the troubled Palestinian hills two thousand years ago, who wept for Jerusalem, and who bound his fate to that city and the people of God. The recovery of this fact is perhaps the most important achievement of the recent flurry of historical Jesus scholarship (cf. Meier 1999:486).

Part I, then, begins with 'the Jesus of history'. In a textbook like this, it is neither possible nor desirable to account at every turn for the historical-critical details of scholarly method and argument. The authors approach their task in the light of extensive and measured critical deliberation, some offering more and some less referenced documentation. And, needless to say, the resulting picture shows disagreements in emphasis and even in substance between the writers, e.g. on the importance of the sayings source known as Q, on questions of chronology, or on the place of baptism in the ministry of Jesus. The resulting narrative, however, is in every case designed as a critical synthesis of the historical evidence for Jesus, alert to the substance and implications of his message.

Craig A. Evans starts by sketching the background of Jesus' cultural and religious setting, within which a prima facie reading of his words and deeds makes historical sense. Highlights of his chapter 1 include a discussion of the social and religious setting of Galilee as well as the specific question of the influence of Scripture and its interpretation.

The next three chapters deal with different aspects of the practice and the teaching of Jesus. Peter Tomson begins with the difficult question of *what sort of Jew* Jesus was (chapter 2). Both his own fate and the history of the church acutely raise the question of how Jesus of Nazareth should be understood in relation to the Judaism of his time – and perhaps of ours. Christian interpretation has too frequently assumed that his words and actions intended a subversion, supersession or replacement of Judaism, its Temple and its law. Tracing key themes of the gospel tradition, Tomson shows that Jesus' own religious praxis and message make contextual sense only within, rather than over against, the diverse and complex reality of first-century Palestinian Judaism.

Marianne Meye Thompson then sharpens our focus more specifically on the question of Jesus' view of God (chapter 3). What, if anything, might we be able to say about the 'religion' of Jesus, and specifically his encounter of God as Father? Thompson shows that this question (which in a rather different form once occupied nineteenth-century liberals) goes to the very heart of Jesus' concerns. It also, significantly, turns out to constitute a vital bridge over the supposed chasm between 'the faith of Jesus' and 'faith in Jesus'.

Adopting a broader sweep, Graham Stanton's chapter 4 explores more fully the distinctive themes and practices that characterised Jesus' ministry: his message of the kingdom of God in its Jewish context, his parables and miracles, his highly symbolic and controversial practice of life-changing table fellowship. What was their role in highlighting, and perhaps shaping, Jesus' own identity and ministry? Stanton shows how all these different lines of inquiry about Jesus' 'messianic' words and deeds converge on the central issue of Jesus' identity, as focused by John the Baptist's question from prison (Matt 11.3 par. Luke 7.19): 'Are you the one who is to come, or are we to wait for another?'

Part I then turns its attention from the ministry of Jesus to his personal fate. The stage is set by Bruce Chilton's fast-paced narration of the relational dynamics that characterised Jesus' dealings with both friends and enemies (chapter 5). The leading cast of characters here ranges from John the Baptist's towering formative influence, via different circles of disciples, to Jesus' final confrontation with Caiaphas over his corruption of the purity of God's Temple – and with Pontius Pilate, whose slavery to political ambition made him the High Priest's willing executioner.

Joel B. Green takes this line of questioning to its logical conclusion by examining the rushed trial and Roman execution of Jesus (chapter 6). Different perspectives are possible: that of an ancient historian, of the Roman provincial administration, of the Sadducean religious leadership in Jerusalem, and so on. For the gospel writers, shaped as they are by a Jewish understanding of Scripture as prophecy, the last week of Jesus' life was so replete with biblical typology that the only way of telling the story was to show the historical and theological threads indistinguishably interwoven in the very fabric of the subject matter.

The Editor's own chapter 7 on the resurrection concludes Part I, and serves to highlight the inescapable importance of the issues raised in Part II. It stresses the importance of the historical dimension in the question of Jesus' resurrection. For all the excited confusion of the gospel narratives, whatever happened on that first Easter Sunday is an integral part of any rigorously historical account of Jesus. Beyond that, however, it seems strangely apropos, and hardly accidental, that the apostolic witness to the resurrection became the decisive reason why we have any knowledge of Jesus of Nazareth at all. The gospel writers unanimously claim that the expectation of suffering and divine vindication was part of the biblical story of the Christ from start to finish – and there is reason to think that Jesus of Nazareth thought so too. The consensus of early Christian testimony that 'God raised Jesus from the dead' turns out to be both deeply rooted in Jewish eschatological hope and at the same time a dramatic reappropriation of that heavenly hope for the here and now.

The second and somewhat longer part of the book goes on to explore some of the implications and 'begged questions' of Part I. Historical study of Jesus of Nazareth evokes a marked sense of his abiding 'footprint' in history – what Leander Keck (2000) perceptively terms 'history in perfect tense'. For any integrated critical appreciation, therefore, the past and the presence of Jesus are necessarily interdependent: each can only be fully understood and assessed in light of the other. This has implications in terms of method, of hermeneutics, and of historical and theological appropriation.

Two studies of method lead the way. The first, by Christopher Tuckett, offers a state-of-the-art survey of critical methods for the study of Jesus (chapter 8). This chapter shows the difficulties and pitfalls facing the scholarly inquiry about the historical Jesus. We are given an expert's critical assessment of the canonical gospels and the relations between them (the so-called 'Synoptic Problem'), as well as of non-traditional sources like Q and the *Gospel of Thomas*, which have been widely promoted in some recent scholarship. Tuckett then proceeds to plot a course through the strengths and weaknesses of various standard scholarly 'criteria' used to assess the historical authenticity of sayings and narratives about Jesus, highlighting especially the need to safeguard the historical and contextual 'plausibility' of the story of Jesus within first-century Jewish Galilee and Jerusalem.

While Christopher Tuckett surveys methods and criteria for the study of Jesus, James Carleton Paget offers a historical perspective on such study in chapter 9. He begins with a brief survey of ancient, medieval and early modern approaches, but then concentrates especially on developments since the Enlightenment, which he attempts to set within the broader intellectual history of their day. Ever since Albert Schweitzer's famous survey of nineteenth-century 'lives' of Jesus, the different histories of Jesus research have themselves been the subject of considerable attention; and Carleton Paget poses several critical questions to the currently dominant paradigm of 'three quests'. He concludes with some (soberingly modest) suggestions about lasting results and future desiderata of the study of the historical Jesus.

The preceding chapters necessarily raise the vexing problem of the one and the many: what, then, is the relationship between the variously reconstructed Jesuses of the historians and the 'real' Jesus, the one who stands behind all the different images and who presumably undergirds Christian faith? Three chapters address this problem from a theological point of view. First, in chapter 10 Francis Watson explores some probing questions about the seemingly adversarial relationship of Christian theology and critical historical scholarship, offering important challenges to both modes of inquiry along the way. Peter's confession at Caesarea Philippi in Mark 8 serves as an important exegetical touchstone in this respect, as it highlights the apostolic confession of Jesus vis-à-vis other possible images. Watson suggests that it is only the critical dialogue with historical scholarship that can clarify the meaning of the church's identification of the 'real' Jesus with his depiction in the fourfold gospel of Scripture.

The same plurality of witnesses, of course, faced the early church too. Stephen C. Barton addresses the fourfold gospel as the particular form in which the New Testament canon explicitly affirmed and yet limited the scope of that plurality (chapter 11). Drawing on the second-century exposition of Irenaeus of Lyons, Barton shows how the early church based its affirmation of the unity of the one gospel in the four gospels not on its ability to harmonise differences, but on the universal norm of the Rule of Faith, the substance of apostolic faith and practice.

One of the remarkable, and in Christian practice too frequently neglected, aspects of the New Testament's witness to Jesus is that it exegeted, rather than superseded, the Hebrew Bible's testimony to the God of Israel (see on this point Soulen 1996). The Old Testament is the authoritative Scripture of the New. It is against this background that Walter Moberly in chapter 12 assesses the Christian confession of the 'real' Jesus of Nazareth as the Messiah of Israel. How can that extraordinary claim be understood in light of a critical and historical reading of the Old Testament, or indeed in view of a history that appears to continue unredeemed? Moberly assesses the evangelists' handling of Scripture in light of Old Testament theology, contemporary Jewish hopes, and the early Christians' own messianism.

The next two chapters turn from the biblical negotiation of the 'real' Jesus to the place of that apostolic Jesus in theology and faith through the ages. First, Alan Torrance traces the history of Jesus in Christian doctrine, with special reference to the development of christology and soteriology (chapter 13). From ancient conflicts about the divinity and the humanity of Jesus to Enlightenment debates and the Barmen Declaration, the history of theology shows that the problem of the one and the many continued to surface in the conflict between a domesticated Jesus of human agendas and Jesus as the divine Word to humanity.

In chapter 14, Archbishop Rowan Williams provides the 'spiritual' counterpart to chapter 13: a survey of faith in Jesus in the history of Christian piety, covering a broad sweep from the beginnings of Christ-devotion via the patristic and medieval periods to more recent developments both in eastern Orthodoxy and in Catholic and evangelical movements in the west. The very vastness of this terrain provides eloquent confirmation of the historical weight of Jesus' 'presence', whose importance this *Companion to Jesus* highlights. Beyond that, however, Williams observes the uneasy relationship between the Jesus of theology and the history of his place in Christian piety: the latter's frequently relentless individualism and sentimentalism has too often hijacked Jesus in the service of favourite causes or fantasies. Devotion to Jesus is both utterly intrinsic to Christian faith and yet derives its rightful validity only from a Trinitarian framework that facilitates a movement into Jesus' relation with the Father.

The 'history of Jesus' in theology and faith must not of course be mistaken, either in principle or in fact, for a history of the west. Jesus was an Asian and an infant refugee in Africa; and after 1,500 years of western Christendom his followers are once again most numerous in those continents. Teresa Okure, a Nigerian biblical scholar and missiologist, explores this new global reality of Jesus on the threshold of the third millennium in chapter 15. She finds in the biblical theology of universal creation and salvation the framework in which to develop the global appropriation of Jesus as enfleshed and inculturated Word of God.

This global significance of Jesus will necessarily find diverse local foci. Jesus of Nazareth himself, of course, bound his own fate to that of the people of Israel – and, reluctantly but deliberately, to Jerusalem in particular. Twenty centuries later, Jerusalem is at once revitalised and deeply riven with ancient divisions. Sacred to Judaism, Christianity and Islam, it is paradoxically symbolic of a late modern world that remains both global village and tribal killing field, a place in which the rhetoric of a partisan justice is forever threatening to suffocate the truth of mercy. Against this background, David Burrell's chapter 16 sketches the city's painful history from the patristic period via Persian, Muslim and Crusader conquests to the Jewish resettlement in the shadow of gathering attempts to eradicate the Jewish people. His account leads up to the conflicts of our own day, which include the complex threat to Christianity's very survival in the Holy Land. He concludes that Jerusalem remains today 'iconic' for all three major religions, and that the work of the Spirit of Jesus will be seen in empowering each to animate peace.

After two millennia have passed, what, if anything, is the abiding significance of Jesus for the future of the world? What sense might remain in the early Christian belief that Jesus came to save the world and will return to judge and rule it? In the closing chapter 17, Richard Bauckham provides a kind of synthesis of many of the interlocking themes of this book. Documenting the early Christian hope in a future that belongs to Jesus, Bauckham argues that, despite its virtual displacement in much modern theology, Christianity needs to recover that focus in the coming Jesus who transcends his own past history and ours, and whose parousia will be seen to redeem and fulfil every present in the service of God.

It seems in the end a fitting point of convergence for this *Companion to Jesus* to note that the contingencies of history and the exalted claims of christology are at one on the subject of that ultimate horizon: the message of Jesus is a call to be transformed in the redeeming kingdom of Israel's God.

Part I

The Jesus of history

1 Context, family and formation

CRAIG A. EVANS

The so-called Third Quest of the historical Jesus has been marked by a variety of portraits. Jesus has been depicted as a rabbi, a sage, a prophet, a philosopher (perhaps even a Cynic), a holy man and a Messiah. What lies behind these discrepancies is a lack of consensus about context and differing assessments of source materials. The present chapter will treat three important areas of Jesus' background: (1) context, (2) family and (3) formation.[1] Of special interest will be the extent of the Jewishness or Hellenisation of Galilee in Jesus' day and the question of how well trained in Scripture Jesus was.

CONTEXT

Galilee of the early first century AD was profoundly Jewish, though a thin veneer of Graeco-Roman culture was present.[2] Agriculturally rich and strategically situated, Galilee was a region over which the Roman Empire maintained firm political control, alternately through client rulers (viz. the Herodian dynasty) or through the direct administration of Roman governors. Galilee measures some 69 km from north to south, and some 49 km from east to west. Although most of this territory ranges in elevation from 600 m to 1200 m above sea level, Lake Gennesaret (or popularly Sea of Galilee), some 21 km in length (north to south) and 5–11 km wide, is situated about 215 m below sea level. In the time of Jesus the lake supported (and still supports) a thriving fishing industry (cf. Strabo, *Geog.* 16.2; Pliny, *Nat. Hist.* 5.15; Josephus, *J.W.* 3.506–508; Mark 1.16–20 parr.; Luke 5.1–10; John 21.1–11).

The development of major cities at Tiberias (on the west bank of Lake Gennesaret) and Sepphoris (*c.* 6 km north-west of Nazareth), and the discovery of impressive Graeco-Roman architecture and artefacts, have led some scholars to exaggerate the extent of the Hellenisation of Galilee. Accordingly, some have suggested that the Jewish people of Galilee were for the most part not strict in the observance of their faith and that Graeco-Roman philosophies, including Cynicism, were influential even among the Jewish population.[3]

This interpretation of the archaeological evidence has contributed to the hypothesis that Jesus was significantly influenced by Cynic idiom and thought. One scholar concludes that the 'Cynic analogy repositions the historical Jesus away from a specifically Jewish sectarian milieu and toward the Hellenistic ethos known to have prevailed in Galilee' (Mack 1988:73; cf. Mack 1987, esp. 17–18), while another asserts that the 'historical Jesus was, then, a peasant Jewish Cynic. His peasant village was close enough to a Graeco-Roman city like Sepphoris that sight and knowledge of Cynicism are neither inexplicable nor unlikely' (Crossan 1991:421).

However, the archaeological data do not bear out this interpretation, especially in reference to Sepphoris. Among the faunal remains that date before AD 70 archaeologists have found virtually no pig bones, which is inexplicable if we are to imagine the presence of a significant non-Jewish population. In contrast, after AD 70 and after a sizeable growth in the non-Jewish population, pig bones come to represent 30 per cent of the faunal remains. Over one hundred fragments of stone vessels have been unearthed thus far, again pointing to a Jewish population concerned with ritual purity (cf. John 2.6). Consistent with this concern is the presence of many *miqva'ōt*, or ritual bathing pools. Coins minted at Sepphoris during this period do not depict the image of the Roman emperor or pagan deities (as was common in the coinage of this time). In contrast, in the second century coins were minted at Sepphoris bearing the images of the emperors Trajan (AD 98–117) and Antoninus Pius (138–61), and the deities Tyche and the Capitoline triad. Indeed, in the reign of Antoninus Pius the city adopts the name Diocaesarea, in honour of Zeus (Dio) and the Roman emperor (Caesar). Finally, a Hebrew ostracon and several lamp fragments bearing the image of the menorah (the seven-branched candelabra) and dating from the first century AD, along with the absence of structures typically present in a Graeco-Roman city (such as pagan temples, gymnasium, odeum, nymphaeum, or shrines and statues), lead to the firm conclusion that Sepphoris in Jesus' day was a thoroughly Jewish city.[4]

Throughout Galilee the distribution of Jewish and non-Jewish pottery is very suggestive. Whereas non-Jews purchased Jewish pottery, the Jews of Galilee did not purchase or make use of pottery manufactured by non-Jews. Accordingly, Jewish pottery that dates prior to AD 70 is found in Jewish and non-Jewish sectors in and around Galilee, while non-Jewish pottery is limited to the non-Jewish sectors. These patterns of distribution strongly suggest that the Jewish people of Galilee were scrupulous in their observance of purity laws.

Furthermore, the actions of the Jewish people in this region also do not bear out the Cynic or Hellenistic interpretation. The revolts that took place after the death of Herod the Great (4 BC), after the removal of Archelaus and the Roman census (AD 6), and the riot in Jerusalem that instigated the great revolt (66–70) all point to deep-seated Jewish resentment of the pagan presence in Israel as a whole, but also including Galilee (see Hengel 1989b). Some of the prominent leaders in these various Jewish rebellions were from Galilee (Horsley 1996:179). Thus the evidence – archaeological, literary and historical – shows that despite a Graeco-Roman presence in places, Galilean Jewry consciously and at times violently attempted to maintain its religious identity and boundaries. Moreover, there is also no archaeological or literary evidence of a Cynic presence in Galilee in the early part of the first century.

The actions undertaken by certain Jewish figures are themselves indicative of the degree of commitment to Israel's biblical heritage and future redemption. This is seen in the activity of John (c. AD 28), who urged fellow Jews to be baptised 'in the Jordan' river (Mark 1.2–8). This action, as well as reference to 'these stones' (Matt 3.9 par. Luke 3.8), may very well have been part of a Joshua motif that envisioned a reconquest of the Promised Land (cf. Josh 4.3, 20–21). Similarly, we later hear of Theudas (c. AD 45), who summoned the poor to take up their possessions and join him at the Jordan, whose waters would be divided at the command of the prophet (Josephus, *Ant.* 20.97–98; Acts 5.36), and the unnamed Jewish man from Egypt, who summoned the faithful to the Mount of Olives, that they might watch the walls of Jerusalem collapse (Josephus, *Ant.* 20.169–70; Acts 21.38). Writings produced after Rome gained control of Palestine, such as the *Psalms of Solomon* (esp. chaps. 17–18), longed for the expulsion of Gentiles from the land of Israel. These biblical typologies and calls for renewal testify to the strong desire on the part of many Jews to cleanse and restore their sacred land. It was in this thoroughly Jewish environment that Jesus developed.

FAMILY

It is conventional to date the birth of Jesus to 4 BC or a bit earlier. This date is based on the Matthean evangelist, whose narrative suggests that Jesus was born shortly before the death of Herod the Great (cf. Matt 2.1, 19). However, the evangelist's association of Jesus' birth with the final days of the reign of Herod may reflect a Moses-Jesus typology. Just as Pharaoh tried to destroy the promised saviour of the Hebrew slaves, so the wicked Herod – infamous for the execution of family members, including his elder son Alexander only days before the king himself would die – tried to destroy the saviour of Israel

(Matt 2.1–18; cf. Exod 2.1–10). It has also been suggested that Jesus may have been born near the end of the reign of Herod Archelaus (Luke 1.5),[5] at the time of the controversial census 'when Quirinius was governor of Syria' (Luke 2.1–2).[6] Given the accuracy of the Lucan evangelist in other matters pertaining to chronology and figures in office, this alternative suggestion should not be dismissed too hastily. It is therefore possible that Jesus may have been born in AD 6 and began his ministry in his mid-twenties (instead of mid-thirties).

Jesus was raised in Nazareth, though he may very well have been born in Bethlehem,[7] as the somewhat independent infancy narratives in Matthew and Luke claim. During his ministry, Jesus returns to Nazareth, where some of the residents wonder: 'Is not this the carpenter [*ho tektōn*], the son of Mary and brother of James and Joses and Judas and Simon, and are not his sisters here with us?' (Mark 6.3). To be referred to as the 'son of Mary' raises questions about Jesus' paternity. It hardly comes as a surprise then that Matthew rephrases the insulting question: 'Is not this the carpenter's son [*ho tou tektōnos huios*]?' (Matt 13.55). Jesus is here identified as the son of *Joseph* the carpenter. Not only is the stigma of his doubtful birth removed, Jesus has been distanced from his lowly occupation.

Tektōn should perhaps be translated 'woodworker' or, perhaps better, 'builder' (cf. LSJ; MM; BAG also notes an instance of 'stoneworker'). Recent archaeological excavations afford preliminary indications of very active trades at Nazareth, including pressing grapes and cutting stone. Farming terraces have also been identified. Jesus' statement that his 'yoke is easy' may in fact allude to his trade (Matt 11.30; lit. 'useful' [*chrēstos*], perhaps meaning 'fits well').

It should not be assumed that Jesus or his family were poor, or that Jesus was a peasant. The freedom with which Jesus conducted his itinerant ministry, even if requiring some support (cf. Luke 8.1–3), indicates a measure of financial means. Jesus is succeeded by his brother James as patriarch of the young church, which again points more to middle-class standing than to a peasant background. Indeed, a few of Jesus' disciples were men of means: one was a toll collector (Mark 2.14), two others were sons of a man who employed hired hands and owned at least one fishing boat (Mark 1.19–20).

There are significant indications that Jesus' family did not endorse his ministry. The open hostility between Jesus and his family is barely masked in the Marcan account (Mark 3.20–35; cf. 6.1–6; John 7.5), which the Matthean and Lucan evangelists take pains to mitigate. Although it must be acknowledged that this hostile portrait may be due in part to Marcan theology, it was in all probability the resurrection (1 Cor 15.7) that altered his family's opinion and led to his brother James's appointment to, or assumption of, authority over the movement that Jesus launched.[8]

FORMATION

The evidence is compelling that Jesus was formed in the context of Israel's historic faith, as mediated by the scriptures, as read and interpreted in the synagogue. Jesus was conversant with Israel's great story and fully embraced the redemptive vision of the Prophets. His message, 'the kingdom of God has drawn near' (Mark 1.14–15), is drawn from Isaiah (e.g. 40.9: 'behold your God'; 52.7: 'your God reigns'), as paraphrased in the Aramaic Targum: 'The kingdom of your God is revealed!'

Jesus prayed the prayers of the synagogue, again probably in Aramaic as well as in Hebrew. The closest parallel to the well-known Lord's Prayer (Matt 6.9–13 par. Luke 11.2–4: 'Our Father in heaven, may your name be sanctified, may your kingdom come ...') is the Aramaic prayer called the *Qaddish*: 'May his name be magnified and sanctified ... and may he establish his kingdom in your lifetime ...'.

These points in turn support the widely held opinion that Jesus' mother tongue was Aramaic, the language that had dominated the eastern Mediterranean for centuries. Although Greek had become widespread since Alexander's conquest, and is amply attested in inscriptions, papyri and literary sources,[9] in Jesus' day most Jews spoke Aramaic and others, perhaps in the south, spoke Hebrew.[10]

The evidence also strongly suggests that Jesus frequented the synagogue and that he was Torah-observant, even if his understanding of the oral law was significantly different from the understanding of others, such as some Pharisees. The gospels portray Jesus as frequently debating the meaning of Scripture or the legitimacy of various aspects of the oral law. How well studied in Scripture was Jesus? Could he read? Some of the members of the North American Jesus Seminar do not think Jesus could read (Funk 1998:274). The Seminar also tends to think that quotations of and allusions to Scripture are the work of the early church, not of Jesus.[11] This matter needs to be considered.

It is not easy to determine to what degree Jesus was literate. There are two passages in the gospels that suggest he was able to read, while a third may suggest that he could not. The first passage is Luke 4.16–30, which describes Jesus reading from the scroll of Isaiah and then preaching a homily. Most scholars hesitate to draw firm conclusions from this passage because of its relationship to the parallel passage in Mark 6.1–6, which says nothing about reading Scripture. The second passage is John 8.6, which says Jesus stooped down and wrote in the dust with his finger. The problem here is that in all probability this passage (viz. John 7.53–8.11) is unoriginal.[12] Even if the passage is accepted as preserving a genuine reminiscence of something Jesus did, it tells us nothing certain about Jesus' literacy. He may have been doing nothing more than doodling.

The third passage, John 7.15, is taken by some to prove that Jesus was in fact illiterate. Some in Jerusalem wonder: 'How is it that this man has learning, when he has never studied?' Literally, they have asked how he 'knows letters' (grammata oiden), 'not having studied' or 'not having learned' (mē memathēkōs). But the reference here is to a lack of formal, scribal training, not to having had no education whatsoever. Jesus has not sat at the feet of a trained, recognised rabbi or sage. We encounter the same thing in Acts, which describes the reaction of the religious authorities to the disciples of Jesus: 'Now when they saw the boldness of Peter and John, and perceived that they were uneducated [agrammatoi], common men [idiōtai], they wondered; and they recognised that they had been with Jesus' (Acts 4.13). The words agrammatoi and idiōtai should not be rendered 'unlearned and ignorant', as in the King James Version (and ASV). To be agrammatos is to lack scribal training (so LSJ), and is in fact the opposite of the grammateus ('scribe'; cf. Barrett 1994–98:2.233–34). To be agrammatos does not necessarily mean to be unable to read.

To be an idiōtēs is to be one outside of the guild, or outside of the group, as in 1 Cor 14.16, 23 and 24, where Paul refers to the 'outsider' (so RSV) or 'ungifted' (so NASB) as an idiōtēs. In contrast to professional trained scribes and priests the idiōtēs is a layman.[13] In 2 Cor 11.6 Paul says of himself, 'Even if I am unskilled [idiōtēs] in speaking…' (RSV). Idiōtēs may also refer to a commoner, in contrast to royalty.[14] The idiōtēs is the unskilled (with reference to any profession or trade) or commoner (in contrast to a ruler) and seems to be the equivalent of the Hebrew hedyōṭ, as seen in m. Moʿed Qatan 1.8 ('He that is not skilled [ha-hedyōṭ] may sew after his usual fashion, but the craftsman may make only irregular stitches') and m. Sanh. 10.2 ('Three kings and four commoners [hedyōṭōt] have no share in the world to come…').

The comments in John 7.15 and Acts 4.13 should not be taken to imply that Jesus and his disciples were illiterate. In fact, the opposite is probably the intended sense. That is, despite not having had formal training, Jesus and his disciples evince remarkable skill in the knowledge of Scripture and ability to interpret it and defend their views. These texts, more than Luke 4.16–30 and John 8.6, lend some support to the probability that Jesus was literate.

Although there is no unambiguous evidence for the literacy of Jesus, there is considerable contextual and circumstantial evidence that suggests that in all probability he was literate. At the outset, we should keep in mind the nature of Jewish faith itself. It is centred on Scripture, which narrates Israel's sacred story – a story the Jewish people are admonished to know and to teach their children. According to the *Shema*^c, which all Torah-observant Jews were expected to recite daily, parents were to teach their children Torah (Deut 4.9; 6.7; 11.19; 31.12–13; cf. 2 Chr 17.7–9; Eccl 12.9), even to adorn their doorposts with the *Shema*^c (Deut 6.9; 11.20).[15]

According to Philo and Josephus, approximate contemporaries of Jesus, Jewish parents taught their children Torah and how to read it. Philo claims that 'all men guard their own customs, but this is especially true of the Jewish nation. Holding that the laws are oracles vouchsafed by God and having been trained in this doctrine from their earliest years [*ek prōtēs hēlikias*], they carry the likenesses of the commandments enshrined in their souls' (*De Legatione* 210). It is improbable that the training of which he speaks here did not include basic literacy. Josephus, however, is more explicit: 'Above all we pride ourselves on the education of our children [*paidotrophian*], and regard as the most essential task in life the observance of our laws and of the pious practices, based thereupon, which we have inherited' (*Ag. Ap.* 1.60). He says later: '[The Law] orders that [children] shall be taught to read [*grammata paideuein*], and shall learn both the laws and the deeds of their forefathers . . .' (*Ag. Ap.* 2.204). Josephus goes so far as to say that 'most men, so far from living in accordance with their own laws, hardly know what they are . . . But, should anyone of our nation be questioned about the laws, he would repeat them all more readily than his own name. The result, then, of our thorough grounding in the laws from the first dawn of intelligence is that we have them, as it were, engraven on our souls' (*Ag. Ap.* 2.176, 178). This may not be too wide of the truth, for Augustine claims that Seneca made a similar remark: 'The Jews, however, are aware of the origin and meaning of their rites. The greater part of (other) people go through a ritual not knowing why they do so' (*De Civitate Dei* 6.11).[16]

It may be admitted that Philo and Josephus are painting idealistic pictures and perhaps have in mind affluent families that can afford the luxury of formal education for their children. But it would be a mistake to assume that the pursuit of education, including above all literacy, was limited to the upper class or to professionals. In the story of the seven martyred sons (cf. 2 Macc 7) we have no reason to imagine an upper-class family. In the version presented in 4 Maccabees the mother reminds her sons of their father's teaching: 'He, while he was still with you, taught you the Law and the Prophets. He read to you of Abel, slain by Cain, of Isaac, offered as a burnt offering, and of Joseph, in prison. He spoke to you of the zeal of Phineas, taught you about Hananiah . . . He reminded you of the Scripture of Isaiah which says . . . [Isa 43.2] . . . He sang to you the psalm of David which says . . . [Ps 34.19] . . . He recited the proverb of Solomon which says . . . [Prov 3.18] . . . He affirmed the word of Ezekiel [Ezek 37.3] . . . Nor did he forget the song that Moses taught which says . . . [Deut 32.39]' (4 Macc 18.10–19). The portrait is idealised, to be sure; but for it to have any persuasive value in Jewish society, it would have to be realistic.

Popular piety expressed in the earliest rabbinic tradition coheres with the testimonies of Philo and Josephus. The sages enjoin, 'provide yourself a teacher' (m. ʾAbot 1.16; cf. 1.6). In the saying attributed to Judah ben Tema, literacy is assumed to be the norm: 'At five years old [one is fit] for the Scripture, at ten for the Mishnah, at thirteen for [keeping] the commandments [i.e. *bar miṣvah*] . . .' (m. ʾAbot 5.21; cf. b. Ketub. 50a: 'Do not accept a pupil under the age of six; but accept one from the age of six and stuff him [with knowledge] like an ox'). Elsewhere in the Mishnah we read that 'children . . . should be educated . . . so that they will be familiar with the commandments' (m. Yoma 8.4). We find a similar injunction in the Tannaitic midrash on Deuteronomy: 'Once an infant begins to talk, his father should converse with him in the holy tongue and should teach him Torah, for if he fails to do so it is the same as if he had buried him' (*Sipre Deut.* §56 [on Deut 11.19]; cf. t. Qidd. 1.11: 'What is the father's duty towards his son? . . . to teach him Torah').[17] If a son lacks the intelligence to ask his father the proper questions concerning the meaning of Passover, his father is to instruct him (m. Pesaḥ. 10.4). There is halakhic discussion that clearly presupposes that children can read Scripture (cf. m. Meg. 4.5–6; t. Šabb. 11.17: 'If a minor holds the pen . . .'; Soperim 5.9: regulations concerning producing extracts of Scripture for children). One of the first things a new proselyte is to learn is the Hebrew alphabet, forwards and backwards (b. Šabb. 31a, in reference to Hillel). The rabbinic tradition contains numerous references to schools, to the effect that every synagogue and village had at least one school.[18] The idealistic and tendentious nature of this material is often not adequately appreciated.[19] Primarily on the basis of the rabbinic tradition, S. Safrai concludes that 'the ability to write was fairly widespread . . . [but] less widespread than that of reading which everyone possessed'.[20] Notwithstanding his uncritical use of rabbinical sources, Safrai's conclusion that literacy was widespread may be more correct than not.

Recognising the limited value of the late, idealised rabbinic literature and the apologetically orientated claims of Philo and Josephus, three general factors favour the probability of the literacy of Jesus: (1) the injunctions of Scripture to teach and learn Torah, (2) the value placed on Torah, of knowing and obeying its laws and (3) the advantage of being the first-born son. In view of these factors, it is probable that Jesus received at least some education in literacy. The probability increases when we take into account features of his later ministry.

Jesus is frequently called 'Rabbi' (*rabbi*)[21] or 'Rabboni' (*rabbouni*),[22] or its Greek equivalents 'master' (*epistata*)[23] or 'teacher' (*didaskalos*).[24] Jesus refers to himself in this manner, and is called such by supporters, opponents and non-partisans. Although prior to AD 70 the designation 'Rabbi' is informal, even vague, and lacks the later connotations of formal training and ordination, which obtain sometime after the destruction of Jerusalem and the Temple, it is very probable that at least a limited literacy was assumed.

In keeping with his designation as 'Rabbi', Jesus and others called his closest followers 'disciples', whose Greek form (*mathētai*),[25] like the Hebrew (*talmidim*),[26] derives from the cognate 'to learn' (*manthanein/lamad*). This terminology, whose appearance in the gospels betrays no hint that it was controversial or in any sense a matter of debate, or the product of early Christian tendentiousness, creates a strong presumption in favour of Jesus' literacy and that of most, if not all, of his disciples.[27] In the Jewish setting, an illiterate rabbi who surrounds himself with disciples, debating Scripture and halakhah with other rabbis and scribes, is hardly credible. Moreover, the numerous parallels between Jesus' teaching and the rabbinic tradition, as well as the many points of agreement between their respective interpretations of Scripture, only add to this conviction (cf. Riesner 1981; Chilton and Evans 1994b:285–98). Jesus' teaching in the synagogues[28] is not easily explained if he were unable to read and had not undertaken study of Scripture.

In the style of the sages and rabbis of his day, Jesus 'sat down' when he taught (cf. the discussion of when to sit or stand; *b. Meg.* 21a).[29] Moreover, Jesus' contemporaries compared him with scribes, that is, with literate people: 'And they were astonished at his teaching, for he taught them as one who had authority, and not as the scribes' (Mark 1.22). Although such comparison in itself does not prove that Jesus was literate, it supports the gospels' portrait that Jesus was a rabbi or teacher, which in turn confirms the presumption in favour of literacy.

On occasion Jesus himself refers to reading Scripture. He asks Pharisees who criticised his disciples for plucking grain on the Sabbath: 'Have you never read what David did, when he was in need and was hungry . . . ?' (Mark 2.25; cf. Matt 12.3). To this pericope Matthew adds: 'Or have you not read in the law how on the Sabbath the priests in the Temple profane the Sabbath, and are guiltless?' (Matt 12.5; cf. 19.4, where Matthew again enriches the Marcan source in a similar manner; the same is probably the case in Matt 21.16). In another polemical context, Jesus asks the ruling priests and elders: 'Have you not read this Scripture: "The very stone which the builders rejected has become the head of the corner..."?' (Mark 12.10). Later he asks the Sadducees, who had raised a question about resurrection: 'And as for the dead being raised, have you not read in the book of Moses, in the passage about the bush, how God said to him, "I am the God of Abraham, and the God of Isaac, and the God of Jacob"?' (Mark 12.26). In a discussion with a legal expert (*nomikos tis*), who has asked what one must do to inherit eternal life, Jesus asks in turn: 'What is written in the law? How do you read?' (Luke 10.26). We find in the rabbinic literature statements like 'Similarly you read' (e.g. *b. Šabb.* 97a; *Ketub.* 111a, 111b) or 'How would you read this verse?' (e.g. *b. Ketub.* 81b; *Qidd.* 22a, 40a, 81b). But Jesus' rhetorical 'have you not read?' seems to be distinctive of his style. And finally, even if we discount Luke 4.16–30 as the evangelist's retelling of Mark 6.1–6, it may nevertheless accurately recall Jesus' habit of reading and expounding Scripture in the synagogues of Galilee: 'And he came to Nazareth, where he had been brought up; and he went to the synagogue, *as his custom was*, on the Sabbath day. And he stood up to read...' (Luke 4.16, emphasis added).

Indications of Jesus' literacy may also be seen in his usage of Scripture. According to the synoptic gospels, Jesus quotes or alludes to twenty-three of the thirty-six books of the Hebrew Bible[30] (counting the books of Samuel, Kings and Chronicles as three books, not six). Jesus alludes to or quotes all five books of Moses, all three major prophets (Isaiah, Jeremiah and Ezekiel), eight of the twelve minor prophets,[31] and five of the Writings.[32] In other words, Jesus quotes or alludes to *all* of the books of the Law, *most* of the Prophets, and *some* of the Writings. According to the synoptic gospels, Jesus quotes or alludes to Deuteronomy some fifteen or sixteen times, Isaiah some forty times and the Psalms some thirteen times. These appear to be his favourite books, though Daniel and Zechariah seem to have been favourites also. Superficially, then, the 'canon' of Jesus is pretty much what it was for most religiously observant Jews of his time, including and especially the producers of the scrolls at Qumran.[33]

Similarly, the frequency and poignancy of Jesus' employment of Aramaic tradition in his allusions and interpretations of Scripture are suggestive of biblical and exegetical learning (if not literacy), regular participation in the synagogue (where the Aramaic paraphrase, or Targum, developed), and acquaintance with rabbinic and scribal education itself.[34] The dictional, thematic and exegetical coherence between the teachings of Jesus and the emerging Aramaic tradition has been well documented and need not be rehearsed here. (See Chilton 1984b; Chilton and Evans 1994b:299–309.)

The data that have been surveyed are more easily explained in reference to a literate Jesus, a Jesus who could read the Hebrew scriptures, could paraphrase and interpret them in Aramaic, and could do so in a manner that indicated his familiarity with current interpretative tendencies both in popular settings (as in the synagogues) and in professional, even elite circles (as seen in debates with scribes, ruling priests and elders). Of course, to conclude that Jesus was literate is not necessarily to conclude that he had received formal scribal training. The data do not suggest this. Jesus' innovative, experiential approach to Scripture and to Jewish faith seems to suggest the contrary.

Finally, the influence of John the Baptist must be taken into account. The admission in the gospels that Jesus was baptised by John is one of the most certain data of the tradition (Mark 1.9–11; Matt 3.13–17; Luke 3.21–22; John 1.29–34). It suggests that Jesus was for a time a disciple of John. There are important indications that this was the case. Jesus' proclamation of the kingdom of God (Mark 1.14–15) quite possibly emerged from an eschatological understanding of Isaiah 40 held in common with John, for the latter apparently appealed to Isa 40.3 ('prepare the way of the Lord') while the former appealed to Isa 40.9 in the Aramaic ('the kingdom of your God is revealed'). John spoke of 'these stones' – which, as suggested earlier, may have alluded to the twelve stones representing the tribes of Israel that Joshua placed by the Jordan. Jesus' appointment of twelve apostles (Mark 3.14, 6.30; Matt 19.28; Luke 22.28–30) may very well have held a similar meaning. Lastly, Jesus' implicit claim to be the one 'mightier' than the 'strong man' (i.e. Satan) in Mark 3.23–27 in all probability answers John's anticipation of the coming of one 'mightier' than himself (Mark 1.7). These points of coherence between Jesus and John suggest that the latter played an important role in the formation of the former.

CONCLUSION

The context, family and formation of Jesus point in every way to an extensive exposure to a Torah-observant Jewish way of life. Jesus was raised in a Jewish Galilee that embraced the faith of the Fathers and the teaching of Scripture, a Galilee that resisted non-Jewish influences, sometimes violently. Jesus was raised in an artisan family of modest but adequate means. He received some education, was active in the synagogue, where his understanding of Scripture was shaped by an interpretative and paraphrasing

Aramaic tradition, where he prayed prayers that longed for the coming of God's rule. But his education was not limited to the synagogue; at some point in his life Jesus joined the movement of John the Baptist. This movement called for national repentance and renewal in light of the approaching reign, or kingdom, of God. After the arrest of John, Jesus reignited this movement and gave it his own distinctive stamp.

Notes

1. Perhaps the finest modern assessment of this field of inquiry is found in Meier 1991–94:1.205–371.
2. See Freyne 1998 and Freyne 2000; Horsley 1995 and Horsley 1996; Strange 1997. There were present in Galilee, though mostly around its perimeter, several Graeco-Roman cities, such as those of the Decapolis. But from this it should not be inferred that the religion of the Jewish population of Galilee significantly accommodated Hellenism.
3. Early archaeological reports of the extent of urban architecture, some of it in Graeco-Roman style, as well as the great number of Greek inscriptions, led to claims that ongoing research has not supported. Batey (1991:14) describes Sepphoris as a 'burgeoning Graeco-Roman metropolis' in the time of Jesus, while Kee (1992:15) claims that the remains of Sepphoris exhibit 'all the features of a Hellenistic city'.
4. These details summarise the reports found in Strange 1997; Chancey and Meyers 2000.
5. Archelaus is not called 'Herod' in Josephus or in the New Testament, with the possibly exception of Luke 1.5. He calls himself Herod on his coins and Dio Cassius calls him 'Herod of Palestine' (cf. 55.27.6). It is true that Luke 1.5 refers to Herod as 'king', and that Archelaus never gained this title. However, Herod the Great's sons Herod Antipas and Herod Archelaus were on occasion called 'king', though neither ever had this title conferred upon them (cf. Mark 6.14 [Antipas]; Josephus, *Ant.* 18.93 [Archelaus]; cf. Matt 2.22).
6. Smith 2000. This alternate date resolves some problems but it creates new ones.
7. Most critics doubt that Jesus was born in Bethlehem of Judaea. For a recent defence of the tradition, see Smith 2000:287–91.
8. For a critical assessment of all texts that bear on the question of Jesus' relationship to his family, and especially to James, see Painter 1999:11–57.
9. On the extent of Greek influence in Palestine, see Hengel 1989a.
10. Or, what is more likely: Galilean Jews spoke an Aramaic liberally sprinkled with Hebrew, while Judaean Jews spoke a Hebrew liberally sprinkled with Aramaic. Note Matt 26.73, where the Judaean bystanders counter the Galilean Peter's claims not to know the Galilean Jesus: 'Your accent betrays you'. On the question of how influential Greek was in Jesus' day and whether Jesus may have been able to speak some Greek, see Porter 2000.
11. Funk and Hoover 1993:98: 'Citations of scripture are usually a sign of the interpretative voice of the evangelist or the early Christian community. The pattern

of evidence in the Gospels suggests that it was not Jesus' habit to make his points by quoting scripture.'

12. It is either omitted or marked off with asterisks or obeli in the earliest manuscripts. In other manuscripts it appears elsewhere in the Fourth Gospel, and in a few manuscripts it appears in Luke. However, even though the passage may not be original to the Fourth Gospel, the story itself may well be authentic.

13. According to LSJ an *idiōtēs* is a common or private person, one who lacks professional training and education.

14. Cf. LXX Prov 6.8: 'the labours to which both kings and subjects [*idiōtai*] apply themselves'. According to Josephus, Moses say to God: 'I am at a loss to know how I, a mere commoner [*idiōtēs*], blest with no strength, could either find words to persuade my people . . . or constrain Pharaoh' (*Ant.* 2.271). This nuance is also noted in LSJ.

15. Consistent with this expectation, the author of the *Testament of Levi* has the great patriarch admonish his sons: 'Teach your children letters [*grammata*] also, so that they might have understanding throughout all their lives as they ceaselessly read [*anaginōskontes adialeiptōs*] the Law of God' (*T. Levi* 13.2).

16. It is of course possible that Augustine's reference is to Josephus and not to Seneca.

17. See also ʾ*Abot R. Nat.* 6.2: 'Rabbi Aqiba took hold of one end of the tablet and his son the other end of the tablet. The teacher wrote down *alef beth* for him and he learned it; *alef taw*, and he learned it; the book of Leviticus, and he learned it. He went on studying until he learned the whole Torah.' *Gen. Rab.* 63.10 (on Gen 25.27): 'Rabbi Eleazar ben Rabbi Simeon said: "A man is responsible for his son until age thirteen".' Whatever the probative value of this tradition, the training envisioned here is probably for would-be sages and rabbis, not necessarily that of the average person.

18. On the organisation of public schools, see e.g. *b. B. Bat.* 21a; *b. Sanh.* 17b; *y. Meg.* 3.1 (73d); *y. Ketub.* 13.1 (35c) par. *b. Giṭṭ.* 58a; *y. Ḥag.* 1.7; *y. Šabb.* 119b; *y. Ketub.* 8.11 (32c). Other traditions presuppose the education of children in literacy: e.g. *b. Ḥag.* 15a–b; *b. Ḥull.* 95b; *b. Giṭṭ.* 56a; *Song Rab.* 2.5.3.

    Some have argued that the discovery of abecedaries points to the existence of schools; e.g., Millard 1985b. Abecedaries point to literacy, not to schools. For a discussion of this issue, though in reference to earlier periods in Israel's history, see Haran 1988. Townsend 1971 cautiously concludes that Jewish schools in any number did not emerge until after the Bar Kokhba war. On the whole, however, there is significant evidence for literacy in ancient Israel and in Israel of late antiquity; cf. Millard 1985a and Millard 2000.

19. As seen, for example, in Safrai 1974–76; Schürer 1973–87:2.415–20.

20. Safrai 1974–76:952. He remarks further (pp. 953–55), depending on *y. Meg.* 3.1 (73d); cf. *y. Ketub.* 13.1 (35c), that schools were connected with synagogues and that learning Torah was obligatory for boys, but not for girls.

21. Mark 9.5; 11.21; 14.45; etc.

22. Mark 10.51; John 20.16.

23. Luke 5.5; 8.24, 45; 9.33, 49; 17.13.

24. Matt 8.19; 9.11; 12.38; Mark 4.38; 5.35; 9.17; 10.17, 20; 12.14, 19, 32; Luke 19.39; John 1.38; 3.2.

25. Mark 2.15, 16, 18, 23; 3.7, 9; 4.34; 5.31; and Q. Luke 6.20; 10.23; 12.22; 14.26, 27.

26. *M. ʾAbot* 1.1, 11; 2.8; 5.12; 6.6.
27. Millard 2000 concludes that not only was Jesus himself probably literate, but so were his disciples; and that some of his followers may have written down some of Jesus' teaching during his ministry.
28. Matt 4.23; 9.35; Mark 1.21; 6.2; Luke 4.15; 6.6; 13.10; John 6.59.
29. Matt 5.1; 26.55; Mark 12.41; Luke 4.20; 5.3; cf. Matt 23.2, where Jesus refers to the scribes and Pharisees who sit on the seat of Moses (*epi tēs Mōuseōs kathēdras*).
30. See the helpful tabulation in France 1971:259–63.
31. Hosea, Joel, Amos, Jonah, Micah, Zephaniah, Zechariah and Malachi. Omitted are Obadiah, Nahum, Habakkuk and Haggai.
32. Psalms, Proverbs, Job, Daniel and Chronicles. Omitted are Song of Solomon, Ruth, Lamentations, Ecclesiastes, Esther, Ezra and Nehemiah.
33. In the non-biblical scrolls of Qumran and the region of the Dead Sea (here the *pesharim* are being excluded) the book of Deuteronomy is quoted some twenty-two times, Isaiah some thirty-five times and the Psalter some thirty-one times. See VanderKam 1998. The data of the synoptic gospels have been taken at face value. Critical assessment of the authenticity of the material would result in somewhat different tallies, but the overall impression would remain.
34. One is reminded of the rabbinic dictum: 'Scripture leads to Targum, Targum leads to Mishnah, Mishnah leads to Talmud, Talmud leads to performance' (*Sipre Deut.* §161 [on Deut 17.19]). Although this dictum postdates Jesus by centuries, it probably in part mirrors earlier concepts of scribal pedagogy.

2 Jesus and his Judaism

PETER J. TOMSON

The theme of the present chapter is more pervasive than appears at first sight. Although Jesus' Judaism seems only one among his many aspects treated in this volume, it relates to almost all of those other aspects.

Not only can the plain facts of his life be supposed to make historical sense only when seen within first-century Jewish society. More importantly, we can hope to understand how his disciples came to see him as Son of God and Messiah only if, like them, we try to interpret his life and work in the framework of Jewish history and of Jewish views of history. Jews of the period 'read' the events of history alongside Scripture, and the significance of particular happenings would be expressed and measured by their correspondence with the sacred verses. This was also the spiritual and historical context of Jesus and his disciples, and it is in this context that they must be understood.

Put the other way around, if we would isolate Jesus from Judaism to start with and see his relationship to it as something accidental, the relation between the historical and the theological perception of his person would of necessity become very problematic. Precisely this is what has happened during the past two centuries, as other chapters show in detail. Historical criticism sought a 'historical Jesus' strictly separate from the 'kerygmatic Christ', the subject of Christian faith. The corollary was that the subject of faith had nothing to do with human history. It seems to become clearer and clearer today that this asphyxiating dilemma is reduced to a historical problem of manageable dimensions if we start at the other end and consistently consider Jesus and his earliest believers within their Jewish context.

This chapter, therefore, takes the form of a summary of the description of Jesus in the gospels, while continuously examining the possible affinity to (near-)contemporary Jewish sources. The aim is not so much to demonstrate *that* he was Jewish as *what kind* of Jewish teacher he was. Simultaneously, the emerging historical construct is consistently, though not always explicitly, scrutinised for implications on the level of creed and theology.

THE SOURCES FOR JESUS' JUDAISM

The primary sources for studying Jesus' life and words are the biblical gospels. Not *per se* because these are the ones canonised by the church, but because they appear to be closest to the historical surroundings of Jesus and his first disciples – which incidentally may have also played a role in their canonisation. Among these, Mark is the oldest since both Matthew and Luke are based on it, and John on the whole makes a more remote impression (cf. also chapter 8 below). Mark also features some details that appear to be more authentic when viewed in a Jewish context. The apocryphal *Gospel of Thomas* occasionally carries a saying of Jesus in a form seemingly more authentic than in the canonical gospels, but as a whole it is far from Jesus' own surroundings.

Such sources were not created in a historical void. An event of immense import both to nascent Christianity and to Judaism was the Jewish war against Rome (66–70). In many respects it was also a civil war, which provoked great tensions both among Jews themselves and between Jews and neighbouring non-Jews. It appears that relations between Jewish and non-Jewish followers of Jesus became very tense now and in many cases broke off altogether. This development is reflected in the gospels, which were written at that time or some decades later. Especially Matthew and John are marked by a fierce conflict with contemporary rabbis and, in the case of John, with 'the Jews' as a whole. Mark carries only some traces of such a later conflict. Luke is exceptional in that it shows none at all. On the contrary, the author, who also wrote Acts, seems to stress the ties with Judaism at every possible turn.

It follows that we should first build on Mark and Luke, and then critically fit meaningful elements from Matthew and John into our construction. If we would start from Matthew and John, we would be biased by the conflict with the Jews in those texts and we could not be sure to get a trustworthy overall picture of what kind of Jew Jesus was.

Our second body of sources are the ancient Jewish writings. The Qumran scrolls are in Hebrew and definitely older than the New Testament, and the detailed information of the historian Josephus about first-century Palestine proves largely trustworthy. A special place is taken by the numerous rabbinic writings. Many scholars find difficulty in using these because they were written down centuries after the New Testament, and because they reflect an unfamiliar thought world. As it is, rabbinic literature represents a written compilation of the oral teachings of thousands of teachers over many generations. The oral creation and transmission of teachings was a cultural feature the rabbis inherited from the Pharisees. This implied both conservatism and standardisation. Exploiting such characteristics, the modern study of rabbinics has developed critical methods for discerning and evaluating ancient traditions. Furthermore this literature is much closer to the life of the common people than Josephus and the Qumran writings, which makes it most relevant for comparison with the gospels. An important example is the parables used to illustrate biblical exposition, an obvious method for teaching the common people, which we find only in the synoptic gospels and in rabbinic literature. Especially if we can find passages from Qumran or Josephus *and* from the rabbis to compare with the New Testament, we are on solid historical ground.

JESUS' APPEARANCE

The person of Jesus as he emanates from the gospels is enveloped in a cloud of enigma. He came and went with a striking personal authority (Luke 4.30; John 10.36). He had a commanding yet merciful presence; he noticed the searching soul of a tax collector hidden up in a tree or of a woman ostracised for her loose behaviour, but he was also able to present a child as a role model for future bishops (Luke 19.5; 7.44–45; Mark 9.36; 10.15). When walking amidst a crowd he sensed someone touched him and drew a force from him (Mark 5.30). He could spend hours praying up on the mountain, and yet again exhaust his forces during endless hours of healing the sick and possessed (Luke 5.16; Mark 1.34–35). His former fellow villagers could not square this person with the picture they had preserved of him: 'From where does he have all this, what is this wisdom given to him and these powerful deeds wrought by his hands? Is not this the carpenter, the son of Marya and the brother of Yakob, Yose, Yuda and Simon, and are not his sisters here with us? And they were offended by him' (Mark 6.2–3; the names reflect Galilean dialect).

This enigmatic preacher and healer emerges out of a void in our information. That he was the son of Mary, the wife of a carpenter from Nazareth (Mark 1.9), is all we know for certain. He must have been about thirty years old, Luke adds (3.23). From the teachings attributed to him we know he must have studied with Pharisaic teachers; where and when, we cannot say. We do however know one of his other teachers: the one whose message of repentance, forgiveness and baptism he accepted and made his own (Mark 1.4). John the Baptist, whose prophetic reputation is confirmed by Josephus,

probably preached in the desert of Judaea not far from Qumran, and his message of repentance and baptism was not unlike what we read of the sect that
saw for its destiny 'to prepare the way of the Lord in the desert' (Josephus,
Ant. 18.116–19; 1QS 8.13; Mark 1.3; cf. Isa 40.3). John, however, received all
of Israel who were willing to hear him, whereas the sect was very restrictive,
having 'separated itself from the majority of the people'. In this, John – and
even more Jesus – acted rather like those ancient Pharisees who taught: 'Do
not separate from the ways of the community' (Luke 3.7–14; 4QMMT 92;
m. ²Abot 2.4).

Jesus took over from John. The gospels preserve a saying of John's to the
effect that now Jesus was to be his teacher, for he himself was 'not worthy
to bow down and untie his sandal' – typically the kind of task of a Jewish
disciple towards his teacher (Mark 1.7). Some of John's other disciples now
joined Jesus, and there were other contacts between the two groups. Later,
this turned into rivalry (John 1.37; Acts 18.25, cf. John 4.1; 10.41). On his part,
too, Jesus expressed the awareness that his message represented something
completely new as compared with his teacher, although he kept him in high
esteem (Mark 2.18–22; Luke 7.24–28).

The difference is 'explained' with mysterious events. When Jesus was
baptised, Mark relates, 'he saw the heavens being rent open and the Spirit
like a dove coming down upon him, and there was a voice from the heavens:
You are my son, the beloved; in you I take pleasure' (Mark 1.10–11). It is
important to note that this is described as a mystical experience of Jesus
himself. Immediately afterwards, Jesus was transported to the desert and
there was tempted by 'Satan' (lit. the 'adversary', known from Old Testament
stories: cf. Job 2.1). 'Forty days and nights' Jesus was tried. This is the number
of days reported of Moses when on Mount Sinai receiving the model of the
sanctuary to be built on earth, and of Elijah under way in the desert to the
same mountain, also called Horeb, at a time when the prophets of the Lord
were persecuted (Exod 24.17; 1 Kgs 19.8).

We see that the scant information about Jesus' mystical experiences is
formulated in biblical terms. This is also true of the heavenly voice, which
is crucial to the story. The reference of the 'son, the beloved' is to none
other than Isaac, the 'only son, the beloved' whom Abraham was to sacrifice on Mount Moriah (Gen 22.2, 12, 16). An ancient commentary explains
that Abraham faithfully obeyed and 'brought his only-begotten son to the
altar . . . reasoning that God was able to revive him from the dead, whence
indeed he received him back again, so to say' (Heb 11.17–19). Another allusion made by the heavenly voice is to the songs of the 'Servant of the
Lord' in Isaiah, e.g.: 'Behold, my servant whom I support, my chosen one

in whom I take pleasure' (Isa 42.1). Hereupon, Jesus made his public appearance, preaching the message of God's Kingdom. He is portrayed as a remarkable Jew, distinct also from his prophetic teacher.

The heavenly voice is heard a second time, again at a crucial point in Mark's account. This is after Jesus' announcement that 'the Son of Man' is to go to Jerusalem, there to suffer and be killed, which the disciples do not understand (Mark 8.31–33). 'Son of Man' is actually a Semitism that denotes the redeemer who will come 'with the clouds of heaven *in the likeness of a man*' (cf. Dan 7.13). Six days later he takes three of them 'up a high mountain', and there his countenance becomes translucent with heavenly radiance while Moses and Elijah appear and converse with him. Then a cloud envelops them and they too hear the heavenly voice now: 'This is My son, the beloved; give heed to him' (Mark 9.2–8).

The appellations 'Son of Man' and 'beloved son' apparently reflect Jesus' self-awareness as preserved by the tradition of his disciples. However, he is also said to have been very secretive about these convictions. When Peter proclaims him to be the Messiah, he 'reprimands' him, telling him never to speak about such things (Mark 8.27–30).

JESUS' GOSPEL

Some time after Jesus' baptism and temptation, his teacher John was put in jail. Apparently it was then that Jesus began preaching, in Mark's wording: 'The moment has arrived, the kingdom of God is at hand: repent and believe in the gospel'. It is noteworthy that Jesus is said to proclaim a 'gospel', a 'good word', a message of liberation – even 'the *gospel of God*' (Mark 1.14–15). This is no slip of the pen; it is the older phrase that is sometimes also used by Paul (e.g. Rom 1.1; 1 Thess 2.2). It denotes a wider movement in Israel's history in which Jesus came to play a crucial role.

According to Matthew, Jesus proclaimed (literally) 'the kingdom of the heavens' (Matt 4.17). This is an odd phrase in Greek, too; and it must be understood from the underlying Aramaic or Hebrew. Indeed, in rabbinic literature the perfectly normal phrase is 'kingdom of heaven' – 'heaven' being a discreet appellation of God. It is quite probable that Mark, Paul and Luke 'translated' this phrase for their non-Jewish readers, a necessity which apparently did not exist for the writer of the respective passages in Matthew. It is equally likely that Jesus used the expression himself. To the question of the chief priests by what authority he acted, he replied, even in the version of Mark and Luke: 'The baptism of John, was it *from heaven* or from men?' (Mark 11.30; Luke 20.4; Matt 21.25). Thus Jesus proclaimed the nearness of the kingdom of heaven, meaning the imminence of God's kingship over the earth.

This was no non-committal announcement. In Mark's account, it required two activities: 'Repent and believe in the gospel'. The Greek word for 'repent' means literally 'change one's thought', the prior Hebrew equivalent 'turn about'. Jesus meant that one should welcome the advent of God's kingship by turning away from ways of life that stood in its way. In his perception this was difficult for 'those who have possessions' (Mark 10.23). To a rich man who faithfully obeyed all the commandments Jesus said, looking at him with sympathy: 'Sell all your possessions and give [the proceeds] to the poor, and you shall acquire a treasure in heaven; and come here, follow me' (Mark 10.21). This went much further than what the rabbis approved of, who said one should give no more than a fifth of one's possessions for charity (y. Pe'ah 1, 15b). However, it was no set recipe for Jesus. When the tax collector who climbed the tree said of his own accord he would give *half* of his possessions to the poor, Jesus proclaimed salvation for this 'son of Abraham' and his house (Luke 19.1–10).

For a number of reasons it is quite likely that Jesus' gospel also required baptism. Firstly, it seems unlikely that his disciples introduced this decisive ritual at their own initiative. Secondly, Jesus began his own career accepting the rite of repentance and forgiveness at the hands of John, which later devout Christians found hard to believe (cf. Matt 3.14; John 1.29–36; the *Gospel of the Nazarenes* as quoted by Jerome, *Against Pelagius* 3.2). Thirdly, there is explicit confirmation in the unique reports in the Gospel of John that indeed Jesus baptised (John 3.22–23; 4.1–2). Finally, joining the community of Jesus' disciples is said to have meant from the very start to 'repent and accept baptism' (Acts 2.38). Immersion was practised by the Qumran sect, not only as a regular purification but also as a rite of repentance. It is possible that new members, before being fully admitted to the community and its strict regime of purity, had to undergo immersion as an admission rite. This would then be quite similar in function to Christian baptism.

In Jesus' perception the gospel was also a physical reality. The sources affirm that his commanding yet merciful presence wrought liberation and healing in numerous sick and suffering people. Even in antiquity, the educated were of course wont to be sceptical here, given the real possibilities of mass suggestion and swindle. This is the prevailing attitude found in rabbinic literature. But as we said, rabbinic literature is also close to the people, and in spite of this dominant scepticism it contains many healing stories, some even in the name of Jesus. On this score, Jesus appears fairly remote from the centre of the Pharisaic movement.

In rabbinic parlance, the 'kingdom of heaven' has a political meaning as well, especially in prayers that include a plea for the downfall of the 'kingdom of evil' or the Roman empire. However, the Pharisees and the rabbis after them were not uniform in their attitude towards the Romans. The Pharisaic school of Shammai was more reserved towards foreigners, and apparently they were also heavily involved in the first war against the Romans (AD 66–70). Jesus was no friend of the Emperor, as he made clear in the saying about the silver denarius, but he also was wary of militarist messianic movements (Mark 12.17; Matt 24.23–28). In this he was rather more like the other Pharisaic school, that of Hillel, which was reputed for its open-mindedness and love of peace.

Nevertheless, in Jesus' own conception the gospel was addressed only to Jews. The humorous story of the Syro-Phoenician woman proves this precisely because she managed to lure him beyond that boundary (Mark 7.24–30). Another story implies the same about a Roman centurion from Capernaum (Luke 7.1–10). Hence the phrase ascribed to Jesus in Matt 15.24, 'I am only sent to the lost sheep of the house of Israel', does not seem exclusive to that gospel or its editors. Jesus appears to have set the same limitation on the mission of his disciples (Matt 10.6; and see below).

JESUS' TEACHINGS

In Matthew, we find this summary of Jesus' activities: 'He travelled the whole of Galilee, teaching in their synagogues, proclaiming the gospel of the kingdom, and healing every disease and illness among the people' (Matt 4.23; 9.35). Even if this must reflect the evangelist's pen, the summary seems to be adequate in a general sense. Jesus also taught, not only in synagogues, but also on other occasions and often in the open fields. From rabbinic literature we can deduce that this was not at all unusual for teachers. Many discussions are reported to have been carried on while under way or sitting somewhere in the open.

We already mentioned the parables as an important element of Jesus' teachings shared with the Pharisees. Many of Jesus' parables illustrate his conception of the kingdom of God: 'How shall we compare the kingdom of God or in what parable shall we render it? Like a mustard seed, which when it is sown in the earth is smaller than all other seeds on earth, but once sown springs up and grows larger than all plants, and it makes large branches so that the birds of heaven can repose in its shadow' (Mark 4.30–32). Even if imminent, the kingdom is not always visible. Faith is required. The well-known parable of the sower expresses the numerous difficulties in life that can make the seed of faith wither on the rocky grounds of persecution or suffocate between the weeds of material wealth, and only when received in good earth can it strike deep roots and make its fruit expand (Mark 4.3–9). Without 'faith like a mustard seed' (Luke 17.6; Matt 17.20), the world will remain as it is.

Another main theme is forgiveness; it is expressed in the parables of the lost sheep and the prodigal son (Luke 15.3–7, 11–32). A further parable teaches that we cannot ask God to forgive our sins if we do not forgive our neighbours (Matt 18.23–35). This is central in the prayer Jesus taught his disciples: 'Forgive us our trespasses, as we forgive those who trespassed against us' (Luke 12.4; Mark 11.25; Matt 6.12, 14–15). The same prayer also asks for the coming of the kingdom. This is a characteristic combination. We saw that repentance and forgiveness were connected with accepting the kingdom from the start.

Jewish prayers preserved in rabbinic tradition contain emphases similar to Jesus' prayer. The daily main prayer, the *Tefillah* or *ʿAmidah*, asks for bread, forgiveness and deliverance from evil; the frequent *Qaddish* prayer for the sanctification of God's name and the execution of His will. In fact the Lord's Prayer is in no way exclusively 'Christian'. At the same time, the particular combination of motifs appears to be typical of Jesus' teaching.

JESUS' INTERPRETATION OF THE LAW

Jesus' teachings on the law must be discussed separately. This subject is fraught with misunderstanding. Once relations between Christians and Jews had deteriorated to the level of pure polemics, it was thought that Jesus had abolished the commandments of the Jewish law. Worst of all, the idea also crept into the text of three of our gospels (Mark 3.6; 7.19; Matt 12.14; John 5.18). However, it is effectively contradicted by a passage in Matthew where Jesus says that he has 'not come to abolish the law but to fulfil it; . . . not one iota or stroke of the law shall pass away . . . whoever loosens one of those smallest commandments and teaches thus, shall be called the smallest in the Kingdom of Heaven' (Matt 5.17–19). These phrases closely correspond to rabbinic terminology, but they can certainly have been used by Jesus. In Luke we find that he argued with the Pharisees on a common basis. This concerns an important area of the Jewish law, the Sabbath.

Luke has more disputation stories on the Sabbath than the other gospels; but unlike the latter, his incidents never end in the Pharisaic wish to kill Jesus (cf. Mark 3.6; Matt 12.14; John 5.18). In first-century Judaism the death penalty was not applied for desecration of the Sabbath, which makes Luke's version all the more plausible. In three of Luke's dispute stories, Jesus uses arguments the Pharisees agree with. On the Sabbath one may water one's cattle or keep them alive when they have fallen into a pit; how much more must this be true for a human being! This agrees with arguments used in rabbinic literature and with the rule formulated there, that 'saving a life overrules the Sabbath' (*t. Šabb.* 15.11–16). Indeed, all of these stories in Luke end with the Pharisees remaining silent (Luke 6.6–11; 13.10–17; 14.1–6). Mark contains a unique element that confirms Luke's description. Here, Jesus uses an argument that sounds like some accepted rule: 'Man was not made for the Sabbath, but the Sabbath was made for man' (Mark 2.27). This is very similar to the rule attributed to a later rabbi: 'Man was not given to the Sabbath, but the Sabbath was given to man' – hence saving a life overrules the Sabbath (*Mek. deR. Yishmael*, ki tisa, ed. Horovitz-Rabin p. 341). Curiously, neither Luke nor Matthew copied this sentence from Mark.

Yet even in Luke there is a clear impression of tension between Jesus and the Pharisees. Though they cannot accuse him of formal transgression, his behaviour goes beyond what they think fitting. He shares important elements with them, but on a number of details he goes his own way. In this he reminds one of those whom rabbinic literature calls *ḥasidim*, 'pious'. These holy men were known for their intense prayer, their healings and miracles, but also for slight deviations from Pharisaic custom. Here tension went along with respect. In one story the leading Pharisee is reported to have said: 'If you were not Honi, I would ban you, but what can I do? You are like a spoilt son before his father!' (*m. Taʿan.* 3.8).

Another important area of the law is purity. The basic rules are in the Old Testament (Lev 11–15; Num 19), the idea being that dealing with the offerings in the sanctuary requires holiness and purification. Many Pharisees wished these rules also to be kept in everyday life, and they introduced many refinements to make them more practicable. Jesus belonged to those Jews who did not accept some of those innovations, such as purifying one's hands as a set rule for every meal or the practical distinction between defilement of the outside and the inside of a vessel (Mark 7.5; Luke 11.37–41; cf. p. 80 below).

A basic purity rule that Jesus apparently did observe was the avoidance of entering a non-Jewish home for its possible association with idolatry. This rule is not found in the Old Testament, but is evidenced in various ancient Jewish sources. Thus Jesus did not enter the home of the centurion at Capernaum, even though, as Luke explains, the man had excellent relations with the local synagogue and even anticipated that Jesus probably would not come in (Luke 7.1–10). This attitude finds corroboration in the parallel story in Acts, where Peter had great difficulty in accepting the idea of entering a non-Jewish home, as did his fellow believers back in Jerusalem (Acts 10.1–11.18). Being Jesus' foremost disciple, Peter evidently thought he had to remain faithful to his master's own behaviour. It is one important area of the law in which the disciples became more lenient than Jesus himself, once they had gained the insight that they were also sent to others than 'the lost sheep of the house of Israel'.

Christian exegesis on this topic is rather blurred, since it confuses *transferable* impurity issuing from 'sources', such as a carcass or certain bodily secretions, with *non-transferable* 'impurity' arising from the consumption of a number of animal species. The confusion is caused in part by the Old Testament, which uses the same terms of 'pure' and 'impure'. However, the kosher laws of 'unclean meats' are an axiom in Jewish life in which very little has changed since their injunction in the Old Testament (Lev 11.1–23; Deut 14.2–21). This is very different from the laws of transferable purity, which saw intensive development in ancient Judaism, especially among the Pharisees. Thus it is completely wrong to understand Peter's dream in Acts 10.10–16 as a command to abolish the biblical food laws. The fellow believers in Jerusalem correctly infer that he had eaten *with the non-Jews*, not that he had eaten unclean animals (Acts 11.3). The story is precisely about the prohibition for Jews 'to have communion with or enter with a non-Jew', and Peter says he has now learned 'to consider *no human being* impure' (Acts 10.28).

There is one area in which Jesus' interpretation of the law was notably stricter than that of the Pharisees and in this sense was adhered to even by gentile Christians. This is his prohibition of divorce. The issue was frequently debated in ancient Judaism, so that our evidence is ample here. Nor it is a surprise that Pharisees wished to know where Jesus stood in the matter (Mark 10.2). Opinions among the Pharisees were divided, the school of Hillel teaching that it could be validated on any legal grounds, whereas the school of Shammai taught that divorce was valid only in case of sexual misbehaviour (*m. Giṭṭ.* 9.10). An even stricter position was apparently held at Qumran, where it was taught that the king was not allowed to marry another wife as long as his first one lives, 'but if she dies he may marry another' (11QT 57.17–19). Similarly the priests in Jerusalem were accused that 'they take two wives while [both] are alive, whereas the principle of creation is: "[one] male and [one] female did He create them"' (CD 4.19; Gen 1.27). Literally the same exposition is also used by Jesus, arguing that Moses allowed divorce 'because of your hardness of heart, but from the principle of creation, "male and female did He create them"' (Mark 10.5–6). Jesus' radical teaching that there is no valid divorce was transmitted not only by Mark and Luke but also by Paul – the former Pharisee who on this point had switched to a *stricter* interpretation (Mark 10.11–12; Luke 16.18; 1 Cor 7.10–11). We have here, however, another example of followers of Jesus opting for a less strict interpretation. This is in Matthew, where it is twice taught explicitly that divorce is valid on the sole grounds of 'sexual misbehaviour' – the stricter Pharisaic position, though less strict than Qumran and Jesus himself (Matt 5.31–32; 19.9).

Like the Pharisees, Jesus summarised the whole law under the commandment of love: 'You shall love the Lord your God with all your heart, all your life, and all your powers', and 'You must love your neighbour as yourself' (Matt 22.37–40). Several rabbis are reported to have taught that love of the neighbour summarises the whole law. This was long thought to be inferior to Jesus' '*double* love commandment'. Whether that is correct or not, the double command also appears in a recently discovered rabbinic text dating from the Middle Ages but containing many ancient teachings (*Pitron Torah*, ed. Urbach pp. 79–80). Even if this were adopted from Christian tradition somewhere along the line, it shows that the double love command is equally at home in rabbinic tradition. The linking up of two verses by means of a common key word – 'You shall love' – is a common procedure of Jewish exposition. This makes it all the more interesting now to observe that in the versions of Mark and Luke, the law teachers variously confirm or even anticipate Jesus' exposition (Mark 12.28–34; Luke 10.25–28).

JESUS AND THE TEMPLE

There is one element of Jesus' Judaism that reveals his deepest intentions better than any other, if we study it closely in continuous comparison with ancient Judaism. This also reveals that he was extremely reticent about these intentions, even to his foremost disciples. Let us gather the evidence on Jesus' relation to the Temple.

Firstly, there are the stories to the effect that Jesus and his family were deeply attached to the Temple and even went 'every year' to celebrate Passover in Jerusalem (Luke 2). Though legendary, these stories may reflect historical truth. Frequent prayer in the Temple is also reported of Jesus' brother James by the Judeo-Christian chronographer Hegesippus (in Eusebius, *Hist. eccl.* 2.23.6). Acts 2.46 relates the same of Jesus' first disciples in Jerusalem. The Gospel of John incorporates a particular tradition following which Jesus went no less than four times to Jerusalem for a festival during his public ministry (John 2.13; 5.1; 7.10; 12.1). And the legend that depicts Jesus' temptation by the devil carries him among other locations to 'the pinnacle of the Temple' (Matt 4.5; Luke 4.9).

Secondly, there are moral teachings in which the Temple plays a significant role. A Pharisee and a publican 'went to the Temple to pray', a location essential to the narrative drama. Not the complacent Pharisee, but the truly contrite publican behaved as it is fitting in this place where God's forgiving presence is presumed (Luke 18.9–14). A similar sensitivity is expressed in the saying that 'when you are presenting your offering to the altar, but there recall that your brother has something against you... first go and be reconciled with your brother, and then come and present your offering' (Matt 5.23–24). It reminds one of the rabbinic dictum that 'transgressions between man and his fellow are not atoned for by the Atonement Day until he is reconciled with his fellow' (*m. Yoma* 8.9). A desire for true devotion in the Temple is also behind Jesus' stance on oaths and vows: 'Do not swear at all, not by heaven, for it is God's throne; ... not by Jerusalem, for it is the city of the Great King...'; 'he who swears by the Temple, swears by Him who dwells in it...' (Matt 5.34–35; 23.21).

Thirdly, Jesus expressed his attachment to the Temple when criticising its administrators. In his day, many Jews were critical of the high-priestly families and their personnel, the 'chief priests and scribes', among other reasons because they drew gross material profit from their privileged position. Rabbinic literature preserves polemics against 'the House of Baitos and their lance, the House of Katros and their pen... and the House of Yishmael ben Phiabi, for they are upper priests, their sons treasurers, and their sons-in-law administrators' (*t. Men.* 13.20–21). These families are known from other sources, and excavations in the ancient residence of the priestly elite in Jerusalem have revealed a stone weight with the inscription 'House of Katros'. Jesus shared this social indignation.

Fourthly, a strikingly emotional attachment to Jerusalem and her Temple is reported of Jesus, as also a profound anxiety that things may turn bad: 'Jerusalem, Jerusalem, that kills the prophets and lapidates those sent to her! How many times have I desired to gather your children like a hen does her chicks under her wings, but you have not willed it. Behold, your house [Temple] shall be left to you' (Luke 13.34–35; Matt 23.37). 'And when he came near and saw the city he wept over her, and he said: If only you knew this very day yourself what makes for peace! But now it is hidden from your eyes' (Luke 19.41–42). It is as though he personally identified with the city and its Temple.

Fifthly, explicit predictions of the destruction of the Temple are preserved. The last quote continues as follows: '...For the days shall come upon you in which your enemies shall besiege you with a wall, surround you . . . and they shall not leave one stone on another in you, because you did not understand the time when you were looked after' (Luke 19.43–44). This formulation probably reflects editorial embellishment, but this is much less the case with the variant tradition: 'When he left the sanctuary one of his disciples said: Master look, such stones and such buildings! And Jesus said to him: Do you see those large buildings? There shall not be left one stone on another which shall not be destroyed' (Mark 13.1–2). Predictions of the destruction were not unique in Jesus' time, as we know from Josephus; and of course there is the ancient precedent of Jeremiah (Jer 7.14).

Sixthly, the synoptic gospels report a turning point in Jesus' career, which the disciples did not understand. It is marked by the threefold announcement that 'the Son of Man' is to go to Jerusalem, there to suffer at the hands of the Temple authorities, to be killed, and to be raised from the dead in three days (Mark 8.31–38; 9.31–32; 10.32–40). While the historical value of these detailed predictions may be doubtful, the disciples' lack of understanding is not, since it shows their abiding impression that Jesus was up to something he did not explain. A more enigmatic and seemingly more authentic version of the prediction follows when Pharisees come and warn Jesus that king Herod Antipas wants to kill him while still in Galilee: 'I must travel today and tomorrow and the day after, for it is not fitting for a prophet to be killed outside Jerusalem' (Luke 13.31–33).

Finally, all these data culminate in the prophetic action in Jerusalem, which now is revealed to have been Jesus' secret goal all along. Mark's report of the so-called purification of the Temple contains some details that make this quite clear (11.11–18):

> He went into Jerusalem to the sanctuary, and having inspected everything, as it was already late, he went to Bethany with the Twelve. The next morning . . . they went into Jerusalem. When he came into the sanctuary, he began to throw out those who were selling and buying within the sanctuary; he overturned the tables of the money-changers and the chairs of the dove-sellers, and he did not allow anyone to carry an object through the sanctuary. And he was teaching and saying to them: Is it not written, 'My House shall be a house of prayer among all nations'? (Isa 56.7). But you have made it 'a robbers' den'! (Jer 7.11). Then the upper priests and scribes heard it, and they sought how they could kill him.

Jesus first went onto the Temple mount *to inspect everything*. This reveals careful preparation. His action the next day uncovers an adversary: the class of chief priests and their men who were in charge of all procedures in the Temple. Jesus also makes his intention fully explicit. His teaching, as Mark preserves it, consists of the combination of two verses by means of a common key word (at least in the full Greek version, which may well reflect some Hebrew original): *my house*, as pronounced by God. This is a procedure we encountered earlier. Instead of a centre of true devotion, the upper priests have allowed the Temple to be made into a place of greedy commerce and outright robbery.

There is one material detail that more than anything else reveals Jesus' motivations. It is in the sentence only found in Mark (another significant phrase Luke and Matthew did not care to copy): 'He did not allow anyone to carry an object through the sanctuary'. The meaning becomes evident if we compare *m. Ber.* 9.5, 'One shall not enter the Temple mount with one's stick, sandals, purse . . . and one shall not use it for a shortcut'. The rule was apparently known in Temple times but little respected, so that people carried their wares over the Temple mount as though it were just another square. In accordance with his teachings, Jesus expressed personal indignation over such patent lack of true devotion.

In the account of Mark, there now follows a series of polemical debates with various representatives of the Temple administration. These are the 'chief priests and scribes', who are once accompanied by prominent non-priestly 'elders', and another time dispatch 'some Pharisees and Herodians'. There were also some 'Sadducees' (Mark 11.18–12.28; cf. Luke 20.1–39). This concurs with Acts, where the adversaries of Jesus' apostles are the chief priests and their scribes and the 'party of Sadducees' associated with them (Acts 4.5–6; 5.17; 23.7–9). Ultimately, Jesus is condemned to death by the chief priests because he saw himself as the son of God – a way of thinking the Sadducee party utterly rejected and considered blasphemous (Mark 14.62–63; Luke 22.70–71; Matt 26.63–64; Acts 23.8). The Pharisees are not implicated in Jesus' arrest and trial at all. This is different in Matthew, where the Pharisees appear along with the chief priests among Jesus' enemies (Matt 21.45–23.36). In John, the whole account is different: the Temple purification stands at the beginning (John 2.14–25), and there are fierce polemics with 'the Jews' throughout. These different dispositions must reflect the developments after the war against Rome, mentioned earlier.

JESUS' LAST PASSOVER

After a discourse on the 'last things', there now follows the last supper, which in Mark is designated as a Passover meal (Mark 14.2). John has a different agenda, according to which the last supper fell a day or more *before*

Passover as celebrated by the chief priests (John 13.1; 18.28; 19.14). The implication is that Mark's description follows a different calendar from the one kept in the Temple, and consequently that Jesus and his disciples ate their Passover one or more days *before* the festival as observed by the priests in the Temple. The existence at that time of different calendars has been proved by texts from Qumran. Why Jesus would follow such a deviant calendar is not clear.

In any case the first three gospels describe the last supper as a Passover meal. In Luke, Jesus even says expressly that he has 'greatly desired to eat this Passover offering' with his disciples (Luke 22.15). Implied is that they have had a lamb slaughtered in the Temple for a sacrifice, have prepared it according to law and custom, and now eat it together somewhere in the city (cf. Luke 22.7–8), celebrating Israel's redemption 'from slavery to freedom, from darkness to a great light', or similar wordings (cf. *m. Pesaḥ.* 5.5–7; 7.1–2; 10.5).

In the midst of the customary table liturgy of that time (which underwent some important changes after the destruction of the Temple), Jesus, having blessed over the bread and broken it, now adds a phrase of his own to interpret the meaning of the ritual: 'This is my body'. Similarly, over the cup they drank after a blessing he said, in Mark's version: 'This is my blood of the Covenant, which is shed for many. Amen, I say to you, I shall no more drink of the fruit of the vine till the day that I shall drink it as new in the kingdom of God' (Mark 14.22, 24). Jesus thought in terms of his imminent death, which is more understandable now in view of the preceding, and also of his resurrection into the kingdom of God. Resurrection, we must remember, was a prominent tenet of faith in Pharisaic-rabbinic tradition, but not so among the Sadducees (*m. Sanh.* 10.1; Acts 23.8).

At this point, we must recall the reports of mystical visions that proclaimed Jesus as the 'son, the beloved', a phrase we recognised earlier as an allusion to Isaac. The first vision inaugurates Jesus' public appearance, the second one his journey to Jerusalem and his imminent death. It is clear that the evangelist meant us to read these connections, and also that he thought they corresponded to Jesus' own ideas. The latter is not so evident to critical scholarship. What is certain is that with these scattered reflections, the analogy with Isaac is present early on in the tradition of Jesus' words and deeds (cf. also Rom 8.32; John 3.16). However, at this point the borderline between what Jesus *himself* could have taught and what his followers taught *about* him later becomes blurred beyond distinction.

At the end, Mark tells us, the master and his disciples united in singing hymns, possibly the 'Hallel' Psalms in some form or other (Mark 14.26; cf. Ps 113–18; *m. Pesaḥ.* 10.5–7).

SUMMARY: JESUS' JUDAISM

Jesus was a devout Jew who felt intimately attached to the Temple in Jerusalem as the place of God's holy presence. He lived according to the law in a way closely related to the Pharisees, though he rejected some of their novel purity rules. His behaviour on the Sabbath resembled very liberal Pharisees, while on divorce he rather resembled the much stricter Qumran sect. Clearly he did not belong to the known movements, though he showed affinity with the ancient *ḥasidim* known from rabbinic literature. In their attitude to him, the Pharisaic leaders hesitated between sympathy and irritation. His real adversaries were the chief priests and Sadducees, the corrupt administrators of the Temple who rejected his prophetic message.

Taking over from the desert prophet John, Jesus announced the imminence of God's kingdom, calling for repentance and for baptism as a first step in accepting the kingdom. He also taught about this message in synagogues and at other occasions, and he spent endless hours healing the sick and the possessed. He saw his mission as being restricted to the Jews, a point on which his disciples later came to differ. He considered it an integral part of his mission to go to Jerusalem and to perform an ultimate prophetic sign calling the Temple administrators to repentance, even at the risk of death. However, he was secretive to his disciples about this aim and only spoke about the imminent suffering and death of 'the Son of Man'.

Although he apparently considered himself the heavenly 'Son of Man' and 'the beloved son' of God and cherished far-reaching messianic ambitions, Jesus was equally reticent about these convictions. Even so, the fact that after his death and resurrection his disciples proclaimed him as the Messiah can be understood as a direct development from his own teachings.

3 Jesus and his God

MARIANNE MEYE THOMPSON

Although Jesus of Nazareth is arguably the world's most influential historical figure, there is no agreed understanding of his aims, message and legacy. If we paint with rather broad strokes, we may divide interpretations of him into two camps. On the one hand, while traditional Christianity has described Jesus with a variety of images, it has regularly and persistently confessed him in terms of his divine identity as Lord, Saviour of the World, Son of God and, in the words of the Nicene Creed, 'very God of very God'. On the other hand, Jesus has also been characterised not so much as one to be revered and worshipped, but rather as one who taught a way of worshipping and following God. Under this rubric he has been thought of as mystic, moral teacher, religious visionary, political and social reformer, cultural critic and renewal movement leader.

Are these portrayals of Jesus mutually exclusive? If, for example, one understands Jesus primarily as a religious figure to whom worship and faith are directed, then is it also possible to speak of him as a prophet and teacher of a way of worship and faith? For some scholars who pursue historical reconstructions of Jesus, the goal of this quest is to strip away the creedal accretions and affirmations of faith that have shaped the gospels and subsequent Christian belief in order to discover the 'genuine' historical figure of Jesus beneath the layers of confession. Finding this Jesus at odds with the Christ of the church's faith, they prefer him as an example of faith to be imitated or a teacher of truth and of a way of life to be admired. So, for example, Adolf von Harnack, a German scholar of the late nineteenth and early twentieth centuries, asserted that 'The Gospel, as Jesus proclaimed it, has to do with the Father only and not with the Son' (Harnack 1957:144). Geza Vermes speaks of Jesus as a 'lover and worshipper of his Father in heaven', whose transformation into an object of worship 'would have filled this Galilean Hasid with stupefaction, anger and deepest grief' (Vermes 1983:13). More recently, Marcus Borg has written of Jesus as a Jewish mystic, a charismatic 'Spirit person', who had an intense relationship to and experience of the 'world of Spirit', and whose life serves a model of life in the Spirit (Borg 1987:50, 191). In one way or another, each of these scholars finds the Jesus of history, precisely in his character as an exemplary worshipper of God who pointed away from himself to God alone, both at odds with and more attractive than the Christ who is confessed in the creeds and by the church.

The purpose of this chapter is to investigate the gospels' portrait of what has sometimes been called 'the faith of Jesus', and to consider how Jesus believed and experienced God. Although there are important parables and sayings that come close to answering these questions explicitly, much of the data provided by the gospels for such an inquiry is indirect. What we are seeking is a credible, composite picture of Jesus' belief in and experience of God that may be culled from his parables and sayings; from practices such as prayer, healing, exorcism and table fellowship; and from events in his life such as his baptism and crucifixion. It is my contention that the gospels attest Jesus' passionate commitment and obedience to a God whom he believed to be holy, faithful, sovereign, demanding and just; graciously present and abounding in mercy, and yet also mysteriously silent, unfathomable in his purposes, and sometimes even bordering on capriciousness in his enigmatic dealings with humankind. Obviously I assume that it is appropriate to think of Jesus who spoke about God in this way, called Israel to obedience and worship of this God, and in his own life demonstrated precisely the sort of faith and trust to which he called others. But, as already noted, precisely here some have sensed a tension, perhaps a nearly irreconcilable tension, with the Jesus to whom faith and trust are directed. On this reading, the faith *of* Jesus is incompatible with faith *in* Jesus. Therefore, a concluding section of the chapter will focus on the question of the continuity between them.

STUDYING THE GOSPELS

In all study of the gospels we are faced with questions of method, and at the outset we will sketch briefly how we will proceed. First, the synoptic gospels provide the primary data for this study. Although John cannot be dismissed out of hand as a witness to the life of Jesus and to the issues at stake in his ministry, the distinctive interpretation of Jesus' words and deeds in John demands that one must treat it circumspectly in the quest of the historical Jesus. While I adopt the so-called 'two-source' theory of the origins of synoptic gospels, few conclusions reached here would be changed were one to adopt another hypothesis (for discussion of the synoptic problem as well as criteria of authenticity, see chapter 8 below). The traditions regarding Jesus' convictions about God remain relatively stable throughout various forms and sources, in all likelihood because so much of the picture of God in the gospels reflects core convictions found in the Old Testament and in early Judaism.

Second, along with a number of other scholars participating in the Quest of the historical Jesus, I deem the 'criterion of dissimilarity' or 'discontinuity' to be of limited value for the purposes of understanding Jesus in context (cf. p. 132 below). Much more useful for understanding the historical Jesus is the 'criterion of double similarity', which favours the authenticity of that material which can be credibly located within first-century Judaism, and which can credibly explain the rise of beliefs or practices in the early church, while allowing for differences from both Judaism and the early church (Wright 1996:131–32; Sanders 1985:58). Moreover, material that meets the criterion of 'multiple attestation' in more than one source (Mark, Q, M, L), and in one or more literary forms or genres (parable, saying, miracle story), has strong claims to represent what Jesus taught. But these criteria cannot be used to guarantee assured results. At times material reported only in one source, such as the parable of the prodigal, surely must be deemed authentic when that material fits with a coherent picture of Jesus and his aims, actions and words. Sometimes the whole is greater than the sum of its parts, and the total *impression* Jesus made that became embodied in the traditions of the gospels must also count in the Quest of Jesus.

Finally, it is a mistake to limit our investigation of Jesus' understanding of God to the material of Jesus' teaching. The evidence provided by the shape of his life and practices, such as his prayer, exorcisms and his death, yields material that also illumines Jesus' convictions about God. It is the whole picture of Jesus' life and practices that gives depth to Jesus' teaching about God. In trying to extrapolate from the gospels Jesus' convictions about God and his experience of God, we do not assume that we have direct access to his inner life and thought. Indeed, the gospels come to us from a culture far less fascinated by the inner life and psychological development of individuals, and far more interested in their morals and character, their exemplary deeds, and their impact upon society and culture. But we do assume that the composite picture of Jesus' practices, his teaching, and the shape of his career and life bear witness to his experience of and belief in the God of whom he spoke as father, king, judge, shepherd; holy, just, merciful and gracious; saving, delivering and judging; hiding and revealing; the one who demanded and merited love of heart, soul, strength and mind.

THE BEGINNING OF JESUS' PUBLIC MINISTRY

The gospels report that prior to commencing his public ministry Jesus was baptised by John the Baptiser, and that this event was marked by the descent of the Holy Spirit and a heavenly voice identifying Jesus as God's beloved Son. According to the synoptic gospels, Jesus was then driven by the Spirit into the wilderness, where he was tempted by Satan to test his identity as 'the son of God'. While these accounts reflect literary and theological shaping, many interpreters nevertheless regard them as recounting, in some fashion, Jesus' own religious experiences. Marcus Borg labels them 'visionary', while Peter Tomson refers to them as 'mystical', experiences (Borg 1987:42–43; cf. chapter 2 above). But whatever the current form of the accounts, their witness is that Jesus knew the Spirit of God to be a compelling force that called him to public proclamation and empowered him in his ministry.

Later accounts in the gospels testify similarly to the power of the Spirit as inspiring Jesus' proclamation and effecting victory over the powers of evil through him. Jesus' inaugural sermon at Nazareth, while arguably a Lucan construct in its present form, nevertheless testifies to Jesus' sense that 'the Spirit of the Lord is upon me'. Similarly, when his disciples report to him that crowds of people are seeking him to heal them, he speaks of the necessity of moving on to proclaim the kingdom of God (Mark 1.35–38; Luke 4.42–43). Jesus again bore witness to the power of the Spirit upon him when he spoke of his exorcisms as accomplished by 'the Spirit of God' or the 'finger of God' (Matt 12.28; Luke 11.20). The phrase 'finger of God' calls to mind the Exodus account in which the plagues are deemed to be the work of the 'finger of God' (Exod 8.19). Jesus experienced and believed that the power of God was working through him. That he experienced God's Spirit as power is also attested by the parable of the binding of the strong man: 'No one can enter a strong man's house and plunder his property without first tying up the strong man' (Mark 3.27). As an explanation of Jesus' exorcisms, the passage not only testifies to Jesus' own sense of the greater power at work within him, but also to his encounter and struggle with the power of evil: it could be compared to the struggle to bind an enemy. He distinguished between 'blasphemy of the Son of Man' and 'blasphemy of the Holy Spirit', deeming the latter as of ultimate consequence, indicating that he believed himself and his mission to be answerable to and driven by the Spirit of God (Matt 12.31–32). Without explicit reference to the Spirit, Jesus spoke of the 'constraint' upon him to accomplish the task before him; it was a 'baptism with which to be baptised', a destiny to which he would submit (Luke 12.50).

And yet the gospels show Jesus speaking of the joy of completing the work of God, and of Jesus' 'rejoicing in the Holy Spirit' when the disciples report the results of their own mission (Luke 10.21). The gospel traditions are marked by the expectation that Jesus' ministry brings joy to those who receive its blessings, both now and in the future. His disciples celebrate like guests at a wedding (Mark 2.19–20 par.; John 3.28–29). The Beatitudes contain promises of joy or commands to rejoice in the face of persecution and trials (Matt 5.12, Luke 6.23; cf. John 15.11, 16.20–24, 17.13). In the parable of the talents, those who have done the will of their master are invited to enter into his joy (Matt 25.21, 23). Similarly, in the parable of the lost things in Luke 15, there is the repeated note of joy and celebration 'in heaven' over those that have been lost and are now found (Luke 15.7, 10, 22–25). Those who truly see God at work in Jesus' ministry celebrate, as does the father, when the lost are found. The God who compels Jesus on mission is also the God who celebrates the discovery of the lost.

We may return briefly to the accounts of Jesus' temptations in the wilderness. Part of the reason for judging these accounts to have historical roots is that the experiences of Jesus recounted here converge so fully with his own teaching of his disciples and with the subsequent shape of his career and life. Tempted to turn stones to bread to satisfy his own hunger, Jesus responds that human life is to be lived in constant dependence upon God. He later taught his disciples to trust God to clothe and feed them, and to pray for their daily bread (Matt 6.25–32; Matt 6.11). Challenged to verify his calling and identity by throwing himself off the Temple to force God to act and save him, Jesus refuses to manipulate God or to ask for demonstrable proofs of God's protection. He continued steadfastly on such a course, refusing signs to those who asked to see them as proof that God had sent him (Mark 8.11–12; 11.27–33). And promised all the 'thrones and dominations' of the world, Jesus prefers to surrender the opportunity to seize such power and instead to walk the path of whole-hearted devotion to and trust in the God of Israel. He would later speak of himself as one who serves (Mark 10.45; Luke 22.27), and instruct his followers that their lives were to be characterised by self-surrender and service (Mark 9.33–37; 10.35–45). To be sure, there is mystery in Jesus' understanding of God's way for him and his followers. Why the path that God designates should be a path of giving power up in surrender of one's life and service to others, and why the way should be lived in the uncertainties of faith rather than certainties of demonstrable proofs, are mysteries that lie at the heart of Jesus' understanding of his mission and, ultimately, of the destiny that ended on the cross.

What emerges clearly from the accounts of the temptations is the coherence between the way in which Jesus meets these temptations, and the way of life that he also demanded of his followers. Jesus makes it plain that his commitment to God alone shapes his path, and that God both merits and demands whole-hearted worship, thus echoing the Old Testament note that worship ought to be offered only to the one God of Israel because the Lord is a jealous God (Exod 20.5, 34.14; Deut 4.24, 5.9, 6.15, 32.21). This leads us directly to the heart of Jesus' proclamation.

THE PROCLAMATION OF JESUS

In keeping with the insistent scriptural call to worship and honour God alone, Jesus' proclamation is characterised by its tenacious theocentricity. Jesus took the heart of the law to be the command to love God with all one's heart, soul, strength and mind (Mark 12.28–34; Luke 10.25–37). Of course at this point Jesus was not innovative. The regularly recited *Shema*ᶜ, 'Hear, O Israel, the Lord our God, the Lord is one' (Deut 6.4), expressed Israel's basic understanding of God and of its relationship to God as God's chosen and covenant people. The emphasis on God as the one who alone merits Israel's worship and obedience came to pointed expression in the slogan 'no Lord but God!' that Josephus attributes to the Zealots (Josephus, *J.W.* 2.117–18). Jesus exhorted his followers to seek the kingdom of God before all else (Matt 6.33; Luke 12.31), to commit themselves to God and not to riches (Luke 12.21). For no one, he said, can serve two masters (Matt 6.24; Luke 16.13). When addressed with the epithet 'Good Teacher', Jesus responded, 'No one is good but God alone', making God the measure of all truth and goodness (Mark 10.18). The consistency of Jesus' call to love and obey God above all demonstrates, as one scholar has put it, that Jesus' 'concentration on God and his kingdom is what was constitutive of Jesus' (Keck 1971:213).

Jesus believed God to be a holy God, and hence worthy of such commitment and worship. The opening petition of the Lord's Prayer, 'May your name be sanctified', reflects the opening petition of the Jewish *Qaddish* prayer, 'magnified and sanctified be his great name'. Like his contemporaries, Jesus used various circumlocutions, such as the Name and Power, to avoid pronouncing the holy name of God, which was deemed unspeakable in everyday discourse, as the prohibition in the Dead Sea Scrolls illustrates (1QS 6.27–7.2; cf. Josephus *Ant.* 2.275–76; *J.W.* 5.438). Jesus' most common phrase, 'the kingdom of God' or 'kingdom of heaven', stressed the sovereign and ruling character of the God of whom he spoke.

Like his contemporaries, Jesus assumed that the Temple was to be kept holy as the house of God, as he demonstrated in driving from it the money-changers and sellers. Even his prophetic warnings of the Temple's destruction reflect the belief that as the house of God the Temple ought to be a holy place, for judgement falls precisely because the Temple had become a corrupt economic centre and no longer a place of prayer and worship (see 1QpHab 8.11; 9.3–5; 12.2–10). One was not to swear an oath by heaven, earth or Jerusalem, since these represented respectively the throne, the footstool and the city of the King; in other words, they were God's and, as God's, holy (Matt 5.34–35). To use what was holy as the validation of an oath was to defile it. Similarly, Jesus' expulsion of the 'unclean spirits' and the 'cleansing' of lepers indicate his intent to demonstrate and to bring about the eschatological purity of Israel, the people of a holy God. The people of God were to honour and reflect God's holiness.

Jesus' convictions about the holy God's will for Israel came to further expression in his arguments regarding the interpretation of the law. Proper interpretation of the law and obedience to it were guided by the norms of compassion and mercy in keeping with God's character as compassionate and merciful (Luke 10.25–28; Luke 6.32–36 parr. Matt 5.43–48; Matt 9.9–13; 12.1–8; 18.23–35; 25.31–46). So Jesus argued that because 'the Sabbath was made for human beings' (Mark 2.23–28 parr.), it was appropriate to restore a human life on the Sabbath. This was no violation of honouring the Sabbath. Similarly, just as one might be allowed to pull a sheep out of a pit or water an ox on the Sabbath day – the sort of point that the Dead Sea Scrolls, for example, dispute (CD 11.14) – one could heal a man's withered hand or a woman crippled for eighteen years (Matt 12.9–13; Luke 13.10–17). Here Jesus echoes the prophetic critique against reliance on ritual and sacrifice found in many well-known Old Testament passages, asserting the priority of God's justice and righteousness as standards of conduct (Isa 58.6–7; Jer 7.3–4; Amos 5.21–24; Mic 6.8). Jesus articulates the correlation between God's character and human conduct when he tells his followers to love their enemies, 'so that you may be children of your Father in heaven; for he makes his sun rise on the evil and on the good, and sends rain on the righteous and on the unrighteous' (Matt 5.44–48; Luke 6.32–36).

This saying captures several aspects of Jesus' understanding of God as Father, the designation for God that has had the greatest influence upon later tradition, including the Gospel of John. Although the authenticity of Jesus' address to God as *abba,* an Aramaic word for 'father', has been challenged, there are good grounds for arguing that it originated with Jesus himself. A striking fact is that both Mark and Paul repeat the Aramaic term *abba* in documents (Mark, Galatians, Romans) written for Greek-speaking Gentiles a long way from Palestine, suggesting an unusual respect for the term. And although address to God as 'father' is not unique in early Judaism, the regular recurrence of both 'my father' and 'our father' in prayer, parables and sayings of the Jesus tradition does show that it is featured more centrally than in either the Old Testament or the literature of Second Temple Judaism. When taken together, these arguments suggest that the prominence of 'father' in the gospels is best understood as reflecting Jesus' own practice of addressing God (Thompson 2000:67–71).

The gospels do manifest a distinction between Jesus' address to God as 'my father' and his references, when speaking to his disciples, to God as 'your father'. The point is made differently in the Gospel of John by the use of the word 'son' (*huios*) for Jesus and 'children' (*tekna*) for Jesus' disciples. Jesus' understanding of himself as son is captured in the saying of the Q tradition that emphasises the mutual and distinctive knowledge of father and son, and the authority that the father has entrusted to the son (Matt 11.27; Luke 10.22). Although the authenticity of this saying is often disputed, it emphasises at least two aspects of Jesus' relationship to God that are amply attested elsewhere; namely, Jesus' twinned sense of authority from God and his filial dependence upon God.

Similarly, in speaking of God as Father, Jesus appropriated a biblical image for God to announce to Israel that the time for its restoration was at hand, emphasised particularly God's provision and care for his people, and called for renewed trust and obedience. The prophet Jeremiah, for example, spoke of the time of Israel's restoration, when Israel would call God 'my Father' (3.18–19). Jesus proclaimed a God who, as Father, called into being a community that would offer its allegiance, honour and love to God and live together as brothers and sisters of the one heavenly Father (Mark 3.34; Matt 18.15–18). Jesus exhorted his followers, 'Call no one your father on earth, for you have one Father – the one in heaven' (Matt 23.9). The Father could be counted on to provide for the needs of his own, just as he clothed the lilies of the field and fed the birds of the air (Matt 6.26–30; Luke 12.24–28). Taking the divine example as their own, the followers of Jesus were to be active in feeding the hungry and clothing the naked (Matt 25.34–36). Those who acknowledged God as Father were to forgive each other as they had been forgiven, and this was a central petition in the way of prayer that Jesus taught his disciples (Matt 6.12; 18.21–22). As the parable of the prodigal son so graphically illustrates, not only does God, like a compassionate father, welcome his erring children home, but he expects those in the family to receive the lost with equal joy and generous forgiveness. Hence, if through the ministry of Jesus God is now welcoming the lost home, those who have remained with the Father are to join the celebration and extend a similar welcome.

God's mercy also lay at the heart of Jesus' understanding of his mission as the one who proclaimed and enacted the kingdom of God. Jesus proclaimed that God's sovereignty and justice on earth would be manifested in healing for the sick, redemption for the captive and deliverance for the oppressed. His extensive healing ministry attests his belief that God's sovereignty was active through him to bring wholeness to people. More particularly, his exorcisms were both the evidence and experience of the powerful presence of the Spirit of God not to expel the Roman forces but to expel the demonic powers that victimised the lives of people (Matt 12.28; Luke 11.20). He put his convictions that God's reign would bring healing into practice in sharing meals with sinners, which he likened to the healing work of a physician (Mark 2.17). The captives to whom Jesus promised redemption included a woman who had been 'bound by Satan' for eighteen years, as well Zacchaeus, a rich tax collector, who had been enslaved to the power of mammon (Luke 13.10–17; 19.1–10). Jesus told his followers that 'the hairs of your head are all numbered' by the God who watched the fall of the sparrow. They were not to fear, but to trust (Matt 10.29–31; Luke 12.32).

But if Jesus spoke often of God's mercy, he also shared a common hope that God's sovereignty would be manifested in judgement on injustice and unrighteousness, that God's kingly rule over the earth would someday be fully manifested and bring about his reign of justice and peace. To establish such a rule would entail the elimination of all unrighteousness. Both the traditions of the Old Testament prophets and of Jewish sources speak of a judgement upon the nations, and particularly those that oppress Israel, as well as judgement that falls upon Israel itself (for detailed discussion see Reiser 1997). For example, one may read of the hope for vengeance upon the Gentiles in the *Psalms of Solomon* (e.g. 17.22–25). Elsewhere one finds reference to judgement upon individuals, whether Jew or Gentile, according to their good and evil deeds (e.g. *Jub.* 5). And the Dead Sea Scrolls assume a vindication of the 'sons of his truth' and a great judgement upon the 'sons of iniquity', who clearly include those within Israel who do not properly keep God's law (see 1QH; 1QM 11; 11QMelch). God's holiness and justice demand punishment upon the disobedient and wicked.

Many of the images of judgement in the gospels foresee a division between the wicked and righteous within Israel, rather than between Israel and its neighbours. In fact, noticeably absent from the gospels is the explicit hope of the judgement and punishment of the Gentiles who hold power over

Israel. Instead, Jesus spoke first of a judgement within Israel. The parables of the wheat and the weeds, the great net, and the sheep and the goats all anticipate the separation of the righteous from the wicked (Matt 13.24–30; 47–50; 25.31–48). Jesus pronounced judgement upon various cities and villages for their failure to respond to his teaching (Matt 11.21–24), and was particularly harsh in his condemnation of the leaders of the people and of the Pharisees for their failures to serve as faithful shepherds of the flock. Justice would be done. But the establishment of God's justice would bring with it a number of surprises: at times it was the 'sinners' rather than 'righteous' who found favour with God (Luke 18.9–14). God does not mechanically reward piety and punish impiety.

Indeed God's surprising action of not rewarding the righteous opens him to the charge that he is arbitrary. The parable of the labourers in the vineyard raises just this question (Matt 20.1–16). For if those who worked all day long are paid the same amount as those who laboured but a few hours, then has not justice ceased to function as the standard by which human behaviour should be regulated and judged? Similarly, if the father welcomes home the prodigal with a sumptuous banquet, does not the older son have a right to resent his father who never even gave him a goat? In both cases there is unexpected generosity to those who do not deserve it – but also apparent disregard for those who do.

Two facets of God's character come to expression in these parables. First, God is merciful, unexpectedly and abundantly generous. This was scarcely news to Israel. But Jesus was calling those who had experienced the mercy of God to make it the motivation and measure of their action as well. If God was merciful to the 'least of these', then those who wished to live as children of God were to demonstrate that same sort of mercy, knowing that they were like those who had in mercy been forgiven a large debt and who should subsequently offer that mercy to others as well (cf. Matt 18.23–35; 5.43–58 par. Luke 6.32–36). God's mercy was also made known in forgiving the sins and hearing the prayer of his people. Jesus promises that God can be trusted to listen to the prayers of his people, encouraging them to make their petitions known with boldness and persistence (Matt 7.7–11; Luke 11.5–10). He himself is pictured as entrusting himself to God in times of need, most pointedly in face of approaching death (Mark 14.36; Luke 23.34, 46).

But a second aspect of God's character also emerges in Jesus' teaching, which can best be expressed in the closing questions of the parable of the labourers in the vineyard. The owner of the vineyard asks those who did not receive what they had expected, 'Am I not allowed to do what I choose with what belongs to me? Or are you envious because I am generous?' The father of the parable of the prodigal could have asked his older son the same questions. They are questions that highlight God's sovereignty, the prerogative to do 'what I choose with what belongs to me'. Indeed, God has the power of life and death (Luke 12.4–5), and can demand an accounting of human beings at any time (Luke 12.19–20). Hence when it was reported to Jesus that Pilate had killed a number of Galileans and that the Tower of Siloam had fallen and killed eighteen pilgrims, he warned them that their lives, too, could be lost unless they were to repent (Luke 13.1–5).

Such a view of God's absolute sovereignty also lies behind Jesus' use of the enigmatic quotation from Isaiah 6.9–10 to explain the gift of the kingdom of God to some but not to others (Mark 4.10–12; Matt 13.13–15; Luke 8.10; cf. John 12.40). So also Jesus gives thanks to God 'because you have hidden these things from the wise and the intelligent and have revealed them to infants; yes, Father, for such was your gracious will' (Matt 11.25–26). God is a God who reveals and conceals as he chooses. Perhaps the parable of the unjust judge fits here as well. For alongside many passages promising God's mercy and underscoring God's faithfulness, provision and care, one finds strange, shocking elements as well, such as the comparison and contrast of God with an unjust judge who only at some delay rouses himself to assist a needy widow. Although Jesus himself proclaimed that the kingdom of God was 'at hand' (Mark 1.14–15; Matt 12.28; Luke 11.20), he also said that no one, not even he, knew the hour of God's ultimate deliverance and salvation (Mark 13.32; Matt 24.36). His entire life is marked by these twin convictions: through his ministry, the power of God was at work for the salvation of his people, but he himself waited on God.

THE CRUCIFIXION OF JESUS

Although the crucifixion is more fully discussed in chapter 6 below, for our purposes it is worth noting that the gospels portray Jesus as one who trusted in God when confronted by his adversaries, in the midst of suffering, and until he had drawn his last breath. They do so by correlating certain events of the crucifixion with several psalms of lament from the Bible, most notably Psalms 22, 31, 69. These psalms are the prayers of the righteous sufferer, either in the form of petitions for deliverance from mortal illness or from one's personal enemies. From Psalm 22 comes Jesus' so-called 'cry of dereliction', 'My God, my God, why hast thou forsaken me?' (Mark 15.34; Matt 27.46). This psalm also contains the injunction, 'Commit your cause to the LORD; let him deliver – let him rescue the one in whom he delights!' (22.8), echoed in the taunt of Jesus on the cross as found in Matt 27.43, as well as the comment, 'they cast lots for my garments' (Ps 22.18). In Psalm 69 are references to thirst in the midst of suffering, and to receiving vinegar to drink (Ps 69.3, 21; Mark 15.36; Luke 23.36; John 19.29); and in Psalm 31.5 there is the trusting prayer, 'Into your hand I commit my spirit', spoken by Jesus in Luke (23.46).

As we have them, the accounts of Jesus' death are clearly shaped by the traditional effort to connect the experiences of Jesus on the cross with the experiences of the righteous sufferer that come to expression in the Psalter. Whether or not we can ever have access, through these quotations of the Psalms, to Jesus' own frame of mind as he hung on the cross, it remains the case that the gospel writers do not shrink from presenting him as a model of obedience in the enigmatic trial of suffering, one whose life from beginning to end was marked by a passionate commitment to God who was merciful, good and faithful, and yet who could choose to hide himself and disclose his will and ways in his own time. In this faith, Jesus went to the cross:

> He died without a single sign from the God whose kingly rule he sought to effectuate in advance. His death was no less ambiguous than his life had been, though it was consistent: the God whose fidelity cannot be calculated on the basis of [human] attainments lifted not a finger on behalf of the one who trusted him utterly. By sundown, all three men on their crosses were equally dead. The God who, according to Jesus, sends sun and rain on just and unjust alike did not give Jesus preferential treatment either. Jesus died without a word or a wink from God to reassure him that, whatever the gawking crowd might think, he knew that Jesus was not only innocent but valid where it mattered. When we speak of Jesus clarifying and correcting our understanding of the character of God, we mean precisely this Jesus and no other (Keck 1971:229).

Nowhere can we speak more certainly of the faith of Jesus. And it is precisely the starkness of the portrait of Jesus as one who trusted God in his darkest hours that raises the question of the continuity between the faith *of* Jesus and faith *in* Jesus.

THE FAITH OF JESUS AND FAITH IN JESUS: CONTINUITY OR DISCONTINUITY?

Faith *in* Jesus and the faith *of* Jesus have frequently been seen as mutually exclusive options. As noted at the outset, more than one scholar has attempted to remove elements in the tradition that belong to the church's faith *in* Jesus. Robert Funk, the founder of the Jesus Seminar, contends that because Christianity is not the religion *of* Jesus, but the religion *about* him, it falls upon those who truly seek to follow Jesus to find him behind the creeds and gospels (Funk 1996:304). The implication, of course, is that there is scant continuity between the faith of Jesus and the religion about him. Luke T. Johnson (1996) argues that 'the real Jesus' is the risen Jesus of lived Christian experience and, hence, finds the 'Quest for Jesus' in historical re-construction misguided and unnecessary. Any tension between the faith of Jesus and faith in Jesus dissolves in the worship and experience of believers, and there is little attempt or need to argue a case for continuity. But while biblical scholars may have felt compelled to choose between the faith of Jesus and faith in Jesus, the earliest Christians had less difficulty than moderns do in seeing an organic continuity between these ways of understanding Jesus and his relationship to God.

It is undeniable that the earliest Christian preaching, as recorded in the letters of Paul and reflected in the speeches of Peter in Acts, can more accu-rately be characterised as proclamation *about* Jesus than as simply continuing the proclamation *of* Jesus. The shift is due in no small measure to the church's belief that Jesus had been raised to life by God, and that he had been exalted 'to the right hand of the father', to his messianic office and dignity. Early on, the resurrection is presented as God's *vindication* of Jesus: 'This Jesus, whom you put to death, God raised up' (cf. Acts 2.23–24). The preaching of the early church thus assumed the continuity between the historical figure of Jesus of Nazareth and the exalted and risen Lord. It further assumed that the exalted Lord is alive, that he is present to his disciples, and they experienced his power with them. Hence, their proclamation *about* Jesus was always a proclamation of the one who had himself preached, healed, exorcised and taught, in the name of God his father. Indeed, it was precisely because he had been faithful that he was exalted by God.

Hence, early Christians apparently moved easily between the 'poles' of offering worship and reverence to Jesus, on the one hand, and understanding him as a fellow pilgrim on the other. Put differently, they were easily able both to confess him as 'Lord' and to speak of him as 'brother'. To take one example in the New Testament, the book of Hebrews uses the image of Jesus as Son and God as Father to highlight Jesus' distinctive relationship to God as well as his solidarity with those of faith. As Son, Jesus has a unique relationship to God (1.5), is worthy of worship (1.6), and is entrusted with and carries out God's sovereign rule (1.8). As Son, Jesus represents his Father to humankind, and brings them to God (cf. 2.11–13). But because they have the same God as father, Jesus 'is not ashamed to call them brothers and sisters'. As Son,

Jesus experiences the sufferings and struggles of his brothers and sisters. Through such suffering, 'he learned obedience' and 'being made perfect he became the source of eternal salvation to all who obey him' (5.7–8). In other words, the book of Hebrews moves easily between the 'poles' of the faith and obedience of Jesus on the one hand and the worship of Jesus on the other with little sense of any tension between them. And it does so with designations, such as Son, and images, such as Jesus' suffering and temptation, that come straight from the story of Jesus himself.

This leads directly to the highly debated question of whether Jesus made 'claims' for himself and, if so, whether these claims help to draw the line of continuity from the faith of Jesus to the Jesus of faith (for further discussion of Jesus' claims, see chapters 2 and 4). The question is vast, and here we intend only to note the consistent witness of the gospels that Jesus believed himself to be acting and speaking by God's commission and in God's name. We see Jesus' most daring claims, strongest convictions and deepest trust in what he promised in the name of God. Jesus promised eternal life, entrance into the kingdom, forgiveness of sins, the blessings of salvation, healing and restoration, and he healed, ate at table with sinners, called people to repent, and went to his death believing that God would honour the promises that Jesus made in his name. In speaking of the coming of the kingdom of God through his word and deed, and of himself as Son of Man, he gave expression to his belief that through him God's sovereign rule and judgement were being proclaimed and realised. These were Jesus' convictions and his hopes. The witness of faith as enshrined in the pages of the New Testament is that God vindicated the faith and hopes of Jesus.

And herein lies the paradox of Jesus' 'self-claim'. The very terms – prophet, Messiah, Son of Man, Son – that are taken as witnessing to his distinct identity and role, show that Jesus found his identity and carried out his role precisely in service of and obedience to the one God of Israel. Jesus' public silence regarding the title 'Messiah' fits with his waiting and trusting stance that God would establish his kingdom and install the Messiah as king in his own time. In the end, Jesus waited for God to vindicate his proclamation and mission. Similarly, Jesus' references to himself as 'son' are used in the context of affirming his own obedience as well as the authority given to him by the Father. No Gospel stresses these paired realities of Jesus' life as sharply as John. While on the one hand John emphasizes the unity of Jesus with his God in terms of the Father–Son dyad, John also argues that this unity of the Son with the Father lies in the Son's *dependence* upon the Father in all that he says and does. So complete is this unity that Jesus in fact exercises the divine prerogatives of judging and giving life; but they are the divine prerogatives granted to him by the Father (esp. 5.25–27). Moreover, the unity of the Father and Son extends even to the very *being* of the Son, who is the embodiment of God's Word and God's life. What he has and gives is the very life of God. The risen Jesus was therefore not honoured as a second God, but as the one through whose word and deed God had been revealed and present – incarnate, as Jesus of Nazareth.

4 Message and miracles

GRAHAM STANTON

This chapter follows up the overview of the previous chapter by focusing on the message and miracles of Jesus. These themes may seem to be an awkward pairing: whereas the teaching of Jesus is generally considered to be readily accessible and of continuing relevance, the miracles raise problems for the modern mind. For Jesus himself, however, message and miracles were interrelated, as they were for his opponents.

When the imprisoned John the Baptist sent his disciples to ask Jesus about his role and his intention, Jesus told them to tell John what they had *heard* and what they had *seen*, and then elaborated by couching his reply with phrases taken from Isaiah. This key passage (to which we shall return) links together the message and miracles of Jesus:

> The blind receive their sight, the lame walk, the lepers are cleansed, the deaf hear, the dead are raised, and the poor have good news brought to them. (Matt 11.4–5 par. Luke 7.22–23; cf. Luke 4.16–18)

Jesus then declares starkly that both his actions and his proclamation were deeply offensive to some of his contemporaries: 'God's favour rests on anyone [or, in the more familiar phraseology, "Blessed is anyone"] who takes no offence at me'.

In his own lifetime and for several centuries later, critics of Jesus also saw that his message and miracles belonged together. His message was said to have deceived Israel, and hence not to have been delivered on God's authority; his miracles and exorcisms were seen as the result of his alliance with Beelzebul, the prince of demons, and not the result of his relationship with God. Jesus was dubbed 'a false prophet and a magician'. This standard anti-Jesus jibe was passed on from one generation to another in much the same way as religious polemic still does today in the streets of Belfast and of Jerusalem (Mark 3.22; Matt 12.24 par. Luke 11.15; John 7.12, 47; Justin, *Dial.* 69.7; *b. Sanh.* 43a, 107b).

Jesus insisted that his message of the kingdom of God was acted out in his miracles and exorcisms: 'If it is by the finger of God that I cast out demons, then the kingdom of God has come to you' (Matt 12.28 par. Luke 11.20). Message and miracles belong together.

The synoptic evangelists clearly imply that 'kingdom of God' was the central theme of Jesus' message (Mark 1.14–15; Matt 4.23, 9.35; Luke 4.43, 8.1; 9.11), so we shall start our discussion of his teaching with this topic. In the discussion of the parables of Jesus which follows, we shall consider whether they should all be seen as 'parables of the kingdom'. In the final sections of the chapter we shall turn to the miracles and exorcisms of Jesus.

THE KINGDOM OF GOD

Mark opens his account of the ministry of Jesus with a dramatic summary. 'Now after John was arrested, Jesus came to Galilee, proclaiming the good news of God, and saying, "The time is fulfilled, and the kingdom of God has come near; repent, and believe in the good news"' (Mark 1.14–15). In the parallel passage in Matthew (4.17) 'the kingdom of the heavens' is used. Matthew makes the same modification in a number of other passages, but no distinction in meaning is intended; in 19.23–4 the two phrases are clearly synonymous. Matthew uses 'kingdom of God' four times (12.28; 19.24; 21.31, 43), but elsewhere he reverts to the more traditional Jewish terminology 'kingdom of the heavens' in order to speak about God indirectly, as Jesus himself may have done.

Although some scholars claim that in his opening summary the evangelist Mark has emphasised the nearness of the kingdom at the expense of its future coming, all agree that the kingdom of God was central in Jesus' proclamation. What did Jesus mean? Rather surprisingly, the precise phrase is not found in the Old Testament, and it is not as prominent in later Jewish writings as one might have expected. Nonetheless the phrase encapsulates the declarations of God's beneficent kingship and his sovereign, dynamic rule, which are embedded in the Old Testament – especially in some of the Psalms and in some passages in Isaiah. We shall briefly discuss representative passages.

Psalm 145.8–13 is one of many passages in the Psalms that provide the backdrop to the message of Jesus concerning God's kingly rule. The Psalmist speaks of God's mercy, steadfast love and compassion (vv. 8–9). He then announces a threefold assignment for the Lord's faithful people: 'They shall speak of the glory of your kingdom, and tell of your power, to make known to all people your mighty deeds, and the glorious splendour of your kingdom'

(vv. 11–12). The Lord's kingdom is an everlasting kingdom (v. 13a); in the passage as a whole it is both a present experience and a future hope. The Lord is faithful in all his words and gracious in all his deeds (v. 13b). Words and deeds are not only juxtaposed, they are all but synonymous, as they are for Jesus himself.

Isaiah 52.7 also announces God's kingly rule, but in the more specific context of a promise to the exiles. 'How beautiful upon the mountains are the feet of the messenger who announces peace, who brings good news, who announces salvation, who says to Zion, "Your God reigns."' The four tasks given to the messenger are closely related: they are intended to interpret one another. God is mercifully forgiving and redeeming his people, and will bring them out of exile in a new exodus as they return to a purified Jerusalem. There is no doubt that this and related passages provided a script for Jesus.

Some later Jewish writings contain similar themes. Some of the *Psalms of Solomon* express the hope that God will soon reverse the disaster brought by the capture of Jerusalem by the Roman general Pompey in 63 BC. Several passages speak about God as king, and express the hope that his kingly rule will be made manifest. *Ps. Sol.* 17 opens and closes with a declaration of the everlasting kingship of the Lord (v. 1 and v. 46). The phrase 'kingdom of God' is found in v. 3.

The central section of *Ps. Sol.* 17 is even more significant, though its theme has few parallels in Jewish writings from this period. Here the Lord God is urged to raise up a king, 'the son of David, to rule over your servant Israel in the time known to you, O God' (v. 21). The hoped-for human, Davidic king will be the Lord Messiah (v. 32) who will purge Jerusalem from the gentiles who trample her to destruction (v. 22). The Messiah's kingly role as the one who will put the Romans to flight is clearly subordinate to the Lord God (v. 34).

Once again God's kingly rule is a deep-seated hope, but for the Psalmist in the middle of the first century BC it is not yet realised. In *Ps. Sol.* 17–18 there are unusually explicit references to the means God will use to manifest his kingly rule: the Davidic Messiah will exercise a political and military role on behalf of God's hard-pressed people. Although it was an option for Jesus to fulfil this particular expectation, it is clear that he eschewed violence (Matt 5.38–9 par. Luke 6.29–30; cf. also Luke 22.38) and urged his followers to love their enemies (Matt 5.44 par. Luke 6.27). Some scholars claim that Jesus saw himself as the Davidic Messiah, albeit with a very different role from the one set out in *Ps. Sol.* 17–18. On this view, Jesus was reluctant to spell out the nature of his Messiahship, but his actions and words provided plenty of hints for his followers to reach this conclusion for themselves.

These three passages (and other similar ones) affirm God's kingly rule and express the hope that he will soon act powerfully on behalf of his beleaguered people. The kingdom of God is his sovereign, dynamic rule. More often than not, there is a clearly temporal sense: the kingdom is referred to in the context of hope for the future.

The importance of this latter point becomes clear as soon as we turn to Jesus' teaching about the kingdom of God. Jesus uses such varied phraseology in his kingdom sayings that they cannot be readily analysed, though they do fall into two main groups. Many sayings refer to the kingdom in the temporal sense just mentioned. In some of these sayings Jesus announces that the kingdom will come in the future; in others, the kingdom is near, or has already come. In the other main group there are a number of sayings which have a spatial rather than a temporal reference: the kingdom is a place (or realm) to be entered, to be inherited, to be received, or to be 'in'.

Is the temporal or the spatial sense primary? There is now a consensus that in the relevant passages in Old Testament and later Jewish writings, as well as in the sayings of Jesus themselves, the temporal sense is not only more common, but primary. God's kingdom is his dynamic, kingly rule, not a geographical location with boundaries. If the primary sense is temporal, it is possible to explain the 'spatial' sayings as an implication of God's kingly rule. God's sovereign rule is not exercised in a vacuum, but among his people: so, to 'enter', to 'inherit', or to be 'in' the kingdom means to be among the people who experience God's kingly rule. However, if the spatial sense is primary, it is not easy to explain why so many sayings have a clearly temporal sense.

In Mark 10.23–25, for example, the phrase 'enter the kingdom of God' occurs three times. Jesus says twice over, 'How hard it is [for the wealthy] to enter the kingdom', and then illustrates his point with the graphic comparison: 'It is easier for a camel to go through the eye of a needle than for someone who is rich *to enter the kingdom of God*'. The context concerns discipleship, so the kingdom to be entered is not a realm with boundaries, but the people among whom God exercises his kingly rule, whether now or in the future.

Does Jesus claim that God's kingly rule is being experienced 'in the here and now' in his own message and miracles, or is the kingdom a future hope? This question has been debated keenly ever since 1892, when Johannes Weiss undermined the strong nineteenth-century tradition by insisting that for Jesus the kingdom was neither a moral cause nor a morally ordered society, but a reality to be initiated by God in the near future. Weiss correctly saw that the kingdom is never something subjective, inward or spiritual, as so often in popular piety, but God's coming kingly, dynamic rule. However,

Weiss failed to do justice to sayings that express the nearness or presence of the kingdom, a group of sayings we shall discuss shortly.

A number of kingdom sayings refer to a future coming. Once again, only a few representative passages can be noted. The second petition of the Lord's Prayer asks, 'Your kingdom come' (Matt 6.10 par. Luke 11.2): the coming of the kingdom is a future hope. In Matthew's version (but not in Luke's shorter, more original wording), there is an explanatory addition. 'May your kingly rule come' – and as a corollary, 'may your will be done on earth, as it is now in heaven'. The ethical dimension is clear, as it is also for Mark, who notes in his summary of Jesus' proclamation of the kingdom that the appropriate response is repentance and faith (Mark 1.15).

A Q tradition (Matt 8.11–12 par. Luke 13.28–29) declares that people will come from the east and west and eat in the kingdom with Abraham, Isaac and Jacob. In the eschatological banquet in heaven Gentiles (or, perhaps, Diaspora Jews) will join the patriarchs, but in the final judgement, those who reject Jesus will be rejected by God – and there will be weeping and gnashing of teeth. Here Jesus subverts the expectations of his listeners. He draws on graphic apocalyptic motifs, though in other sayings Jesus distances himself from the apocalyptic traditions popular in circles that spelled out detailed timetables and scenarios for the future (Mark 13.32–33; Luke 17.20).

In the opening beatitudes the poor, the mourners and the hungry are declared to be 'happy' or 'blessed' (Matt 5.3–6 par. Luke 6.20b-21). Why? Because the kingly rule of God reverses their present state. It is not often noted that in the first beatitude the kingdom is a present reality, while in the two following beatitudes the promise is that God *will* act on behalf of those in need. A present and a future temporal sense are juxtaposed.

Several sayings express the presence or the nearness of the kingdom, though in each case their precise temporal sense is difficult to determine. In Mark 1.15, for example, is the sense, 'the kingdom of God *has come*' or, 'is at hand', or 'is upon you'? Protracted discussion has led to the widely accepted conclusion that this verse announces the *nearness* of the kingdom: it is so near that a response is imperative.

The *presence* of the kingdom is clearer in Matt 12.28 par. Luke 11.20, Jesus' declaration that his exorcisms are confirmation of the presence of God's kingly rule. When Jesus was asked about the time of the coming of the kingdom, he refused to provide a timetable, but claimed that the kingdom was 'among you' or even, '[with]in you' (Luke 17.20–21). If the latter interpretation is adopted, it would support the popular notion that the kingdom is purely subjective, inward or spiritual, i.e. that it is 'in' the hearts of followers of Jesus. But there are no other sayings of Jesus which support this notion, and the linguistic evidence on which this interpretation of *entos humôn* in Luke 17.21 is based is now generally rejected.

Several important sayings declare that God's promises are being fulfilled *now* in the words and actions of Jesus, even though the phrase 'kingdom of God' is not used. A beatitude not included in the Sermon on the Mount runs as follows in its original form: 'Happy are the eyes that see what you see, for I tell you that many prophets and kings longed to see what you see and did not see it, and to hear what you hear and did not hear it' (Matt 13.16–17 par. Luke 10.23–24). Jesus' contemporaries are in a specially privileged position, for they have heard the words and seen the actions which are in fulfilment of ancient hopes. The similarity of this passage to the reply Jesus gives to John the Baptist is obvious (Matt 11.4–6 par. Luke 7.22–23). Once again message and miracles are inextricably linked. And once again Jesus claims that his ministry is the fulfilment of Scripture's promises and of the hopes of old.

Enough has been said in the preceding paragraphs to confirm that there are very varied emphases in the kingdom of God sayings. The kingdom sayings should not be squeezed into one mould. Both the future and the present (or nearness) sayings have good claims to authenticity, though their precise relationship is unclear.

PARABLES AND APHORISMS

Many of the parables of Jesus explain and expound the teaching of Jesus on the kingdom of God. For example, Matthew includes no fewer than six pithy parables in his collection of parables in chapter 13. They all open with the phrase, 'the kingdom of heaven is like...'; the kingdom is compared to a mustard seed, yeast, hidden treasure, a merchant in search of fine pearls, a net thrown into the sea, a master who brings out of his treasure what is new and what is old (Matt 13.31–33, 44–47, 52). Some of these parables are found in the other gospels, and Mark has a further similar one not found elsewhere: 'the kingdom of God is *as if* someone would scatter seed on the ground' (Mark 4.26–29).

Many parables throw important light on Jesus' teaching about the kingdom even though they do not refer explicitly to the kingdom of God. The parable of the sower, for example, is undoubtedly a 'kingdom' parable (Mark 4.1–20 parr.). However, it is unwise to relate all the parables of Jesus to this theme, for their scope is much broader. The Greek word *parabolē* strongly suggests that this is the case. In the Greek translation of the Old Testament (the LXX), *parabolē* often translates the Hebrew word *mašal*, which refers to a riddle, a proverb, a taunt, or even a prophetic oracle.

This broad usage is reflected in the gospels. In Luke 4.23 just three words are said to be a *parabolē*: 'Physician, heal yourself'. This is obviously a proverb, as is the *parabolē* in Luke 6.39: 'Can a blind man lead a blind man? Will they not both fall into a pit?' In Mark 4.17 *parabolē* refers to the riddle in the preceding verse; in Luke 14.7 to homely advice about proper behaviour at a feast. Hence 'parables' are closely related to aphorisms, short pithy maxims characteristic of 'wisdom' teachers. We shall return to Jesus' aphoristic teaching shortly.

While parables were not unknown in the Graeco-Roman world, they were not usually part of the stock in trade of religious teachers or philosophers, and most of them were fables or allegories. Aesop's fables were well known, but they are very different from the parables of Jesus. There are a handful of parables in the Old Testament, but only Nathan's parable of the poor man and his lamb (2 Sam 12.1–10) is usually accepted as a close parallel to the parables of Jesus. Later Jewish teachers used parables, but rarely if ever as frequently as Jesus did. In most cases their parables were used to illustrate or expound Scripture. While the parables of Jesus contain some scriptural images, very few are exegetical. It would be rash to claim that the parables of Jesus are unique, but in his extensive use of them Jesus was not following the conventions of the day.

So why did Jesus teach in parables? From the end of the second century to the end of the nineteenth century, a simple answer to this question was often given. The parables have deeper 'heavenly' meanings beneath their outward appearance as everyday 'earthly' stories. Every item in the parables was assumed to have theological significance: Jesus used parables to convey the basic principles of Christian doctrine.

In his two-volume work, never translated from German into English, Adolf Jülicher (1888) broke radically with this tradition. He insisted that the original parables of Jesus were not allegories, for each parable made only one key point – and that single point turned out to be a rather bland maxim. Most scholars now accept that Jülicher and his followers went too far. The parables are many-sided; they are much more subtle and much richer theologically than Jülicher supposed.

In particular, there is no reason to suppose that Jesus eschewed all traces of allegory in the original form of his parables. When his listeners in Galilee heard the parable of the wicked tenants (Mark 12.1–12), they would instinctively have associated the vineyard with Israel, as in Isaiah 5. Mark understands this parable primarily as an attack on the religious leaders, as the conclusion in v. 12 makes clear. It is also almost certainly an indictment of Israel for failing to produce the fruit expected by God.

So far we have noted that some of the 'parables' are riddles or proverbs, and that some are comparisons which refer to an everyday scene. The latter are usually referred to as similitudes: they are in the form of similes which give instruction about, or illustrate an aspect of the kingdom. A simile offers an indirect comparison, 'Peter fought *like* a tiger', 'the kingdom of heaven *is like* yeast' (Matt 13.33).

Even more characteristic and striking are Jesus' narrative parables. Like a metaphor ('Peter *is* a tiger') they offer a direct comparison. The narrative parables are extended metaphors which narrate something which happened just once. For example: 'There was a man who had two sons . . . ' (Luke 15.11); 'There was a rich man who had a steward . . . ' (Luke 16.1).

The narrative parables are like poetry, or like a good cartoon. They communicate in unexpected ways and often at a deeper level than statements. There is often an element of surprise which forces one to think again about God, his will and his ways with humankind.

Once we grasp that the narrative parables are extended metaphors, it becomes clear that they are far more than an unusual mode of instruction used by an exceptionally gifted teacher. The parables are not merely about the kingdom of God, they possess a vitality and a power in and of themselves: they convey something of the *reality* of the kingdom of God.

In Mark 4.10–12 there is a particularly baffling comment on the purpose of the parables. Jesus tells his followers that they have been given the secret or mystery of the kingdom, but to 'outsiders' everything comes in parables, in order that 'they may indeed look, but not perceive, and may indeed listen, but not understand; so that they may not turn again and be forgiven'. For those who reject the call and challenge of Jesus, the parables confirm them in their rejection, for they do not comprehend their point at all. But Mark makes it clear later in the same chapter that the parables were not intended to provide insight for insiders and to confirm blindness to outsiders: 'for there is nothing hidden except to be disclosed; nor is anything secret, except to come to light' (Mark 4.22). The ultimate purpose of the parables is not to hide, but to reveal. 'Is a lamp brought in to be put under the bushel basket, or under the bed, and not on the lampstand?' (Mark 4.21; cf. also 4.33).

There are about forty parables in the synoptic gospels. However, they are conspicuous by their absence from John's Gospel, where the word *parabolē* is not used at all. The synonymous word *paroimia* is used in two passages: 10.6 and 16.25, 29. It is possible that two parables have been fused together in 10.1–5. Many passages in this gospel are 'parabolic' in a broad sense, and still more are symbolic. But there is no trace at all of narrative parables. In

John 16.21, however, there is an aphorism or maxim that is referred to a few verses later as a *paroimia*: 'When a woman is in labour, she has pain, because her hour has come. But when her child is born, she no longer remembers the anguish because of the joy of having brought a human being into the world.' Here a general truth makes a powerful point in its present context, but it could also make good sense in a very different context.

There are in fact far more aphorisms than parables in the gospels – over one hundred on most definitions of an aphorism. Aphorisms are pithy, arresting sayings that are complete in themselves; i.e. they do not require a specific narrative context. They express vividly truths that are general to the experience of humankind. 'The tree is known by its fruit' (Matt 12.33b). 'The labourer is worthy of his hire' (Matt 10.10b).

Several aphorisms are in the form of admonitions. For example, 'Do not store up for yourselves treasures on earth, where moth and rust consume and where thieves break in and steal; but store up for yourselves treasures in heaven, where neither moth nor rust consumes and where thieves do not break in and steal. For where your treasure is, there your heart may be also' (Matt 5.25–26 par. Luke 12.58–59; cf. also Matt 6.19–21 par. Luke 12.33b, 34; Matt 7.13–14 par. Luke 13.23–24).

There are collections of aphoristic sayings in Proverbs, Ecclesiastes and Sirach, as well as in other Jewish writings. The aphorisms of the gospels belong to this 'wisdom' tradition. While some are (or may be) related to Jesus' proclamation of the kingdom, most are not. So this important strand of the teaching of Jesus reminds us that he was a wisdom teacher who had much in common with Jewish teachers of his time.

If Jesus' proclamation of the kingdom (and several other features of his ministry) strongly suggests that he saw himself as an eschatological prophet, his aphorisms and many of his parables suggest that he was a wisdom teacher. Is one portrait more authentic than the other? In his response to the request of some of the scribes and Pharisees for a sign, Jesus made an important implicit claim about himself, 'something greater than [the prophet] Jonah is here' and also 'something greater than [the wisdom teacher] Solomon is here' (Matt 12.38 par. 11.16, 29–32). So Jesus himself seems to have had no difficulty in juxtaposing 'prophet' and 'wisdom teacher'.

Several North American scholars, most of whom are members of the Jesus Seminar led by R. W. Funk, have recently argued that Jesus should be seen primarily as a wisdom teacher; some (most notably Crossan 1991) take a further step and claim that Jesus was a Jewish Cynic. Cynicism arose among loosely organised groups of wandering philosophers in the fourth century BC; there was a revival about the time of Jesus.

The scholars who advocate this general approach note that some of the parables and aphorisms of Jesus are non-eschatological, i.e. they are not related at all to proclamation of the coming kingdom of God. One can hardly object to this first step in the argument, though the claim that *only* these sayings are authentic to Jesus is arbitrary.

The next steps are quite implausible. The attempt to isolate a first and therefore primary non-eschatological layer of the traditions shared by Matthew and Luke (Q) is largely a case of finding what one is looking for. The appeal to the *Gospel of Thomas* as support for a 'wisdom' portrait of Jesus is even less plausible. In its present form *Thomas* is a fourth-century Gnostic collection in Coptic of 114 sayings of Jesus, some of which are related to sayings in the synoptic gospels. *Thomas* was probably written in Greek in the middle of the second century. Some of its traditions may be independent of the synoptic gospels, but it is also clear that many sayings are *dependent* on them (cf. p. 128 below). In short, reconstruction of an early non-Gnostic Greek version of *Thomas* is hazardous, to say the least.

There are some similarities between Jesus and the Cynics of his day: both moved from place to place conveying 'wisdom' teaching, some of which was socially subversive. However, it is important to note that the first-century Cynics were very diverse in their teachings and behaviour, so parallels with Jesus become less impressive. There are in fact at least as many differences as similarities. While it is possible that there were some Cynics in Galilee, there is no evidence that Jesus had direct contact with them (cf. pp. 11–13 in chapter 1 above). The Cynics were not noted for healings and exorcisms; as we shall see in a moment, miracles were a central part of the ministry of Jesus.

Those who portray Jesus primarily or solely as a wisdom teacher or Jewish Cynic have built dubious hypothesis upon dubious hypothesis. Why? One cannot help observing that once again history is repeating itself: as has often happened in historical Jesus research, the reconstructed portrait of Jesus bears an uncanny resemblance to the researcher.

MIRACLES AND EXORCISMS

In the preceding sections of this chapter we have seen that Jesus was both a prophet who called for a response to the coming kingly rule of God, and a wisdom teacher. Was he also a healer and an exorcist? There are seventeen accounts of healings in the gospels, including three of revivification; there are six accounts of exorcisms. Eight further traditions are usually referred to as 'nature miracles'. These numbers do not include parallel passages or the many references to miracles in summary passages. The bald statistics confirm the prominence of miracles in the gospels. So we cannot avoid asking whether Jesus performed miracles, and if so, why.

Miracles were not accepted without question in antiquity. Graeco-Roman writers were often reluctant to ascribe 'miraculous' events to the gods, and offered alternative explanations. Some writers were openly sceptical about miracles (e.g. Epicurus, Lucretius, Lucian). So it is a mistake to write off the miracles of Jesus as the result of the naïvety and gullibility of people in the ancient world.

In his own lifetime follower and foe alike accepted that Jesus had unusual healing powers. The question was not, 'Did Jesus perform miracles?' for that was taken for granted. What was in dispute was on whose authority and with whose power Jesus performed unusual deeds. Were the miracles the result of the presence of God's kingly rule (Matt 12.28 par. Luke 11.20) or the result of Jesus' collusion with Beelzebul, the prince of demons (Mark 3.22), or the result of his use of magical powers (cf. Justin Martyr *Dial.* 69.6–7; *b. Sanh.* 43a, 107b)?

The comments of Celsus, the philosopher and the first pagan critic of Christianity, are revealing. About the year 180 he wrote as follows (as recorded by Origen, *Contra Celsum* 1.6): 'Christians get the power they seem to possess by pronouncing the names of certain daemons and incantations . . . It was by magic that he [Jesus] was able to do the miracles which he appears to have done.'

Celsus did not doubt that both Jesus and his followers performed miracles, but he attributed them to magical powers. So was Jesus a magician? This question has been debated inconclusively by several scholars: not surprisingly, definitions are all-important. If magic is defined as the use of standard techniques, whether of word (primarily incantations) or act (e.g. touch, or the use of spittle), then there are some magical traits in the miracle traditions in the gospels.

Mark's story of the woman with a haemorrhage is the clearest example (Mark 5.24b-34). The woman came up behind Jesus and touched his cloak, confident that she would be made well if she could but touch his clothes. Jesus is aware that 'power has gone out from him' but does not know who touched him. When the woman tells him what has happened, Jesus says to her, 'Daughter, your faith has made you well'. In his redaction of this incident Matthew carefully avoids any suggestion that the woman is cured merely by touching Jesus' cloak (Matt 9.20–26).

However, there are more differences than similarities between the miracle traditions and accounts of magical practices. In the gospels there are no lengthy incantations, no lists of esoteric names, and no references to the use of amulets. Nor is there any suggestion that a petitioner can force Jesus to perform a miracle against his will. In antiquity magic was often used for purely selfish ends (e.g. to win a horse race or a lover), and normally no lasting bonds were formed between the magician and 'clients'.

While it is true that on some definitions miracle and magic are closely related, it is worth noting that in antiquity (as today) magic generally had strongly negative connotations. So magic is not a 'neutral' term that can be used without further ado with reference to Jesus.

The powers of Jesus to heal and to exorcise were not unique. He gave his own disciples authority to heal and to exorcise (Mark 6.7, 13; Matt 10.1; cf. Matt 7.22). Jesus himself refers to other exorcists who were able to cast out demons (Matt 12.27 par. Luke 11.19; cf. Acts 19.11–17). There are reports of Jewish miracle workers who lived at about the time of Jesus, though they are not common; rather surprisingly, they do not include cures of the deaf, the dumb and the lame.

Few doubt that Jesus possessed unusual gifts as a healer, though of course varied explanations are offered. Some suggest that many of the illnesses and disabilities had psychosomatic roots. While this may well have been the case, we have no ways of investigating the matter further.

The seven so-called nature miracles raise more acute problems than the healings and exorcisms: the cursing of the fig tree (Mark 11.12–14, 20–21 par. Matt 21.18–20); the miraculous catch of fish (Luke 5.1–11; cf. John 21.1–14); the walking on the water (Mark 6.45–52 parr. Matt 14.22–33; John 6.16–21); the stilling of the storm (Mark 4.35–41 parr. Matt 8.23–7; Luke 8.22–5); the changing of water into wine (John 2.1–11); the two accounts of feedings of crowds (Mark 6.32–44 and Mark 8.1–10, parr.). In terms of their structure these traditions are quite disparate, and most of them differ in several other respects from the miracle traditions. Four of them can be linked together loosely as 'gift' miracles (so Theissen 1983), for they all record the provision of food (or wine), but this observation does not take us much further forward.

In one case there is a plausible explanation. The cursing of the fig tree is the only 'destructive' miracle in the gospels (Mark 11.13–14; 20–21). Since a parable of a barren fig tree is recorded in Luke 13.6–9, the miracle story may have 'grown' out of a parable Jesus told. But it is impossible to know just what may lie behind the other so-called nature miracles. A decision on their historicity will be determined largely by one's philosophical presuppositions and by one's overall assessment of the origin and development of the gospel traditions.

Given that Jesus possessed unusual gifts as a healer, why did he perform the particular miracles recorded in the gospels? As we have noted, it was very easy to 'write off' miracle workers in first-century Palestine. So why did Jesus run the risk of ridicule and rejection? The faith of the individual is mentioned in many but by no means all cases. Although the evangelists refer to the compassion of Jesus on occasion, they do not suggest that this was the main motive for all his miracles. The evangelists record that some of the miracles attracted crowds (e.g. Mark 1.28), and this may have been one of the reasons the authorities moved against Jesus. But the attraction of crowds is unlikely to have been the main reason why Jesus performed miracles.

By paying close attention to the individuals and the circumstances involved, we can gain important insights into the intention of Jesus. Jesus healed people with many kinds of disability. The lepers healed by Jesus may have had some kind of skin disease, i.e. not what we now know as Hansen's Disease; but in the eyes of many, touching a leper was a violation of ritual regulations (Mark 1.40–45 parr.; Luke 17.11–19; Lev 13.45–6; Josephus, *Ag. Ap.* 1.279–86). As Kee (1986:78–79) has emphasised, Jesus healed persons who were considered by some of his contemporaries to be 'off-limits' by the standards of Jewish piety, by reason of their race (Mark 7.24–30), their place of residence (Mark 5.1–20, in a tomb in pagan territory), or their ritual impurity (5.25–34, a woman with menstrual flow). Although a full discussion is not possible here, many of the healings and exorcisms of Jesus were an indication of his full acceptance of those who were socially and religiously marginalised.

The healing activity of Jesus aroused suspicion and hostility (cf. Mark 3.22–27). Even John the Baptist was puzzled, for apparently he did not have healing powers. As we noted above, in his reply to John's query (Matt 11.4–6 par. Luke 7.22–23) Jesus claimed that his healing activity carried out among those on the fringes of society was in fulfilment of the promises for the coming age referred to in Isa 29.18–19; 35.5–6; 61.1. In short, Jesus saw the healings as signs of the breaking-in of God's kingly rule. He stated explicitly that his exorcisms were signs of the kingdom: 'If it is by the finger of God that I cast out demons, then has the kingdom of God come upon you' (Matt 12.28 par. Luke 11.20).

Like the parables, the miracles were 'signs' but not proof of the kingdom of God; 'outsiders' could 'see' and 'hear' but not perceive and 'understand' (Mark 4.10; 8.18). The miracles, like many of the parables, were intended by Jesus to convey to those who had eyes to see and ears to hear the reality of God's kingly rule.

TABLE FELLOWSHIP

Several traditions record that Jesus extended table fellowship to tax collectors and sinners (Mark 2.13–17 parr.; Matt 11.19 par. Luke 7.34; Luke 7.36–50; Luke 15.1–2). They provide further evidence of Jesus' strong interest in those on the margins of the society of his day. As in his healings and exorcisms, Jesus acts out his proclamation of the kingly rule of God.

Sharing a meal with a friend today is often no more than a convenient way of consuming food. In the Graeco-Roman and Jewish worlds of the first century, however, eating food with another person was far more significant socially: it indicated that the invited person was being accepted into a relationship in which the bonds were as close as in family relationships. One normally invited to meals only people whom one considered social and religious equals.

Some of the first-century conventions associated with table fellowship are sketched vividly in Luke 14.7–14. This passage concludes with a surprising reversal of the customary expectations of reciprocity in hospitality: 'But when you give a banquet, invite the poor, the crippled, the lame and the blind. And you will be blessed, because they cannot repay you, for you will be repaid at the resurrection of the righteous.' Followers of Jesus are urged to do exactly what he himself did: to extend table fellowship to those whom most would shun.

'Why does Jesus eat with tax collectors and sinners?' (Mark 2.16). This criticism is levelled at Jesus by the scribes of the Pharisees when they see whom Jesus has invited to share meals with him. In his reply Jesus insists that he has not come to invite to table fellowship those who consider themselves to be law-abiding ('righteous') but 'sinners' (Mark 2.17). In an independent tradition, Luke records similar indignant criticism (15.1–2) and links to it the reply of Jesus in the form of the parables of the lost sheep, the lost coin, and the prodigal son (15.3–32).

For our present purposes the Q tradition in which Jesus himself quotes a jibe thrown at him is even more important: 'Look, a glutton and a drunkard, a friend of tax collectors and sinners!' (Matt 11.18–19 par. Luke 7.34). Jesus accepts the legitimacy of this accusation, so his actions are quite deliberate. The accusation is the finale of a lengthy set of sayings of Jesus (Matt 11.2–19 par. Luke 7.18–35; 16.16) in which one of the central issues is the coming of God's kingly rule. When the jibe is read in context it becomes clear that the opponents of Jesus failed to see that his table fellowship with tax collectors and sinners was an implication of the coming of the kingdom.

Who were the tax collectors and sinners? The tax collectors in Galilee were despised not because they were colluding with the Romans (though that would have been the case in Judaea), but because in their abuse of a long-standing system of collecting tolls and duties they were blatantly dishonest. Strictly speaking they were toll collectors or tax farmers; they were not collecting direct taxes. As E. P. Sanders (1985) has stressed, the 'sinners' were not simply apathetic about religious observance, they were those who intentionally ignored God's commandments. So Jesus insisted on accepting openly in intimate table fellowship those who were notorious for their dishonesty or their high-handed rejection of the law.

CONCLUSION

Several threads have run through this chapter. Some readers may feel that to insist that message and miracles belong together is to labour the obvious. But that is not so, for in the first century they did not necessarily go together. Jesus may well have emerged from the circle of John's followers (cf. John 1.35–42). In several respects Jesus and John were similar: they were both perceived to be prophets; they both proclaimed God's coming kingly rule; they both attracted large crowds. But neither the gospels nor Josephus attribute miracle-working powers to John (Josephus, *Ant.* 18.116–19; cf. John 10.41). Nor was John known for his use of parables and aphorisms.

The gospel traditions portray Jesus in several guises. He was a prophet who proclaimed the coming of God's kingly rule and acted out its implications; as a 'wisdom teacher' he used parables and aphorisms to a greater extent than most other wisdom teachers; he had healing gifts; he was an interpreter of the law. The more vigorously the gospel traditions are sifted and weighed, and the more rigorously the Jewish and Graeco-Roman world of the first century is explored, the clearer it becomes that Jesus of Nazareth fits no formula. It is a mistake to try (as so many scholars have done) to portray Jesus primarily as a prophet, or as a wisdom teacher, or as a healer.

The passage with which we began this chapter underlines these points. In his reply to John the Baptist's emissaries (Matt 11.2–6 par. Luke 7.18–23) Jesus indicates that he is a miracle worker and a proclaimer of God's good news for the poor, and implies that his message and his miracles are to be seen as fulfilment of God's promises. His final comment, 'Blessed is anyone who takes no offence at me', is a beatitude or wisdom saying, so this passage also portrays Jesus as a wisdom teacher.

These verses also contain an implicit reply to John's primary concern, 'Who are you? Are you the one who is to come, or are we to expect another?'

John is not given a pat answer. Here, as elsewhere, Jesus focuses attention on God and not on himself; nonetheless, Jesus does give a clue to his own self-understanding. A recently published Qumran fragment (4Q521) also links together message and miracles by means of similar phrases from Isaiah. Like the reply of Jesus to John, it refers to Isa 61.1: 'for he will heal the wounded, give life to the dead and *proclaim good news to the poor*' (4Q521 1.ii.12). Although this fragment is difficult to interpret, it probably refers to the eschatological actions God will carry out through his anointed one, the Messiah (line 1). If so, then at the time of Jesus at least some Jews understood Isa 61.1 in a messianic sense, as Jesus probably did himself.

Who are 'the poor' to whom God's good news is being proclaimed by Jesus? They are people who are experiencing oppression and helplessness, including those living in dire poverty. They are the blind, the lame, the lepers and the deaf whom Jesus heals as a sign of the coming of God's kingly rule. They are the tax collectors and sinners to whom Jesus extends table fellowship in the teeth of vigorous opposition. The message, miracles and actions of Jesus are all focused on the socially and religiously marginalised, for God's kingly rule belongs to them (Matt 5.3 par. Luke 6.20).

5 Friends and enemies

BRUCE CHILTON

Friends and enemies have a unique power to define who we are. They locate us socially, within the world of what other people do. That localising capacity of friendship and enmity is not merely a matter of their exposing the extrinsic coordinates of who we are in terms of birth, status or education. Our relationships to friends and enemies express who we are and seek to become, as we engage or reject the kinds of behaviour, thought and feeling others represent to us.

JOHN THE BAPTIST AND HIS CIRCLE

Jesus' relationship to John the Baptist presents the strongest case in point. Certainly the most influential figure in his life, John gave Jesus the focus on purity that, in one form or another, became an emblematic feature of his activity. Jesus did not simply meet his teacher in adulthood (as a superficial reading of the gospels would suggest), but apprenticed himself to him as a youth.

Josephus' famous report about John in *Antiquities* 18.116–19 is a flashback, related to explain the opinion among 'some Jews' that the defeat of Antipas' army at the hands of Aretas, the king of Nabataea, represented divine retribution for his treatment of John. What Josephus does not say, but the gospels do attest (Mark 6.18–29; Matt 14.3–12; Luke 3.19–20), is that John had criticised Antipas for marrying Herodias, who had been married to his brother Philip. Josephus' account dovetails with the gospels, in that he gives the details of Antipas' abortive divorce from Aretas' daughter in order to marry Herodias (18.109–12). Josephus also explains that this was merely the initial source of the enmity with Aretas, which was later exacerbated by a border dispute that preceded the outbreak of hostilities (18.113).

In fact, he says that Aretas 'made this the start of a quarrel', as if it were something of a self-justification in retrospect. No explicit delay of time is indicated in the compressed narrative between the divorce, John's death and the start of the war, but mounting tension is indicated. Christiane Saulnier (1984) has argued that the divorce and the new marriage were over and done with by the early twenties AD, and a consideration of Josephus' order of presentation makes that plausible.

Saulnier proceeds on the basis that Josephus is better informed chronologically about Agrippa I than about another Herodian (pp. 365–66), and argues that the mention of Agrippa supports her earlier dating. Another consideration points in the same direction. Prior to flashing back to Antipas' various trials, Josephus has last spoken of Antipas in connection with the establishment of Tiberias in AD 19 (*Ant.* 18.36–38). Here, too, Josephus criticises Antipas, because the city was partially established on the site of tombs, and he complains elsewhere that the palace there incorporated idolatrous representations of animals, which Josephus himself undertook to destroy (*Life* 64–69). Why, then, do we see Antipas in such an uncharacteristically trenchant philo-Roman mode, flouting commandments of the Torah in a way that could only have alienated his subjects? At the opening of his section on Tiberias, Josephus provides an answer: Antipas had advanced considerably within the circle of Tiberius' friendship (*Ant.* 18.36). The foundation of Tiberias, his irregular marriage, and the execution of John (around AD 21) were part of an audacious policy of aggrandisement, which put Antipas at enmity with John himself (and at least potentially, with John's followers).

Jesus' extensive period of study and controversy with John, implied by John's Gospel, can be accommodated by this chronology. More importantly, it allows time for Jesus to remain in the land of Judaea *and practise immersion* (John 3.22). Although an attempt is made slightly later in the Gospel to take this assertion back (John 4.1–3), it is an emphatic and unambiguous description: Jesus practised a ministry of immersion comparable to John's. While Jesus remained in Judaea, John himself was immersing in Aenon near Salem (John 3.23), further north and off the Jordan River, and adjacent to the territory of Samaria. Jerome Murphy-O'Connor suggests that the division of territory between John and Jesus was deliberate: the senior rabbi took the more difficult task of dealing with Samaritans, while leaving the relatively more straightforward task of immersing those in Judaea to his disciple.[1]

The extension of purity by means of immersion to Samaritans would, of course, have been a notable development. John's Gospel itself observes that Jews do not have dealings with Samaritans (4.9). Yet Jesus in the story of the Samaritan woman deals with her extensively (John 4.4–42),[2] and without offering any particular defence, and he would later be equally matter of fact in telling the parable of the Good Samaritan (Luke 10.30–37). Both the story of the Samaritan woman and the parable of the Good Samaritan take it for granted that there is a problem about consorting with Samaritans, and that the problem can be overcome. A similar perspective is represented in a fragmentary saying of Jesus in *The Gospel of Thomas* (*l.* 60), where he comments on seeing a Samaritan carrying a lamb to Judaea (presumably, for an offering in Jerusalem). If, as Murphy-O'Connor suggests, we take the hint from John 3.23 that John was already in the process of immersing Samaritans into his generic purification, that would help us to make better sense of Jesus' attitude towards the Samaritan question. Whatever one might say of his explanation, it seems better than what is offered in John 3.23 itself, that John was immersing in Aenon near Salem 'because there was much water there'.

But any picture we might infer of easy, harmonious relations between John and Jesus is quickly upset in John 3.25:

> A controversy ensued, therefore, between the disciples of John with a Jew over purification.

Was this unnamed Jew Jesus? That emendation of the text is frequently suggested, but there is no evidence in manuscripts to support it. Yet even as the text stands, the disciples of John enter a controversy concerning purification – which, after all, is the whole point of immersion – and the argument causes them to go on to report Jesus' activity to John. They complain about Jesus' success in immersing, and John replies with a panegyric that is typical of the Fourth Gospel (John 3.26–36). Unfortunately, they do not speak of what precisely the argument over purification consisted of, nor of where John and Jesus stood within it. But that the two of them were involved in the dispute seems implicit even in the Johannine attempt to mute the controversy, and turn it into a conventional argument with 'a Jew'.

To this stage, not enough information has emerged to make it clear how John and Jesus might have fallen out over the issue of purification, but the fact of such a disagreement, difficult as it evidently is for the gospels to attest, seems plain. The relationship between John and his follower Jesus posed a crisis in two senses, each of which was largely determinative of the outcome of Jesus' activity. First, Herod Antipas' execution of John branded his movement and those associated with it as potentially seditious. Second, purification – the very centre of John's immersion – became a point of contention between the rabbi (see John 3.26) and his disciple. The consequences of each aspect of the crisis need now to be spelled out.

The synoptic gospels are quite plain about when Jesus' characteristic public ministry began: as Mark 1.14 puts it, 'after John was delivered over' (see the comparable formulations of Matt 4.12; Luke 3.19–20). One might even conclude from reading Luke's reference in context (prior to Jesus' immersion) that John did not personally immerse Jesus. But that is probably the result of a periodisation of their ministries, a treatment of the one and then the other as the key figures in separate epochs (much as Peter and Paul are presented in Acts). From the point of view of Herod Antipas, Jesus represented no immediate continuation of John's threat, because Jesus had stopped doing what John had been doing. When Herod later did react to Jesus with the threat of violence, the issue was his activity of healing, not baptism (Mark 6.14–16).

Most tellingly, Jesus stopped immersing people as his characteristic activity. Even when we allow that the Gospel according to John reflects Jesus' acceptance of John's programme of purification, and even if we surmise (plausibly, I should think) that Jesus might have reverted to that activity from time to time, the simple fact of the matter is that immersion does not become *typical* of Jesus' movement until after the resurrection (and especially in the circle of Peter). Immersion was a prominent part of Jesus' public programme before John's arrest and death and after Jesus' resurrection, but not in between, not during the time Jesus himself directed the course of his own movement. Why that was the case remains one of the most obvious – and usually unanswered[3] – questions in the critical study of the New Testament. For the moment, the point is that no source permits us to infer that Jesus was especially known for his immersing after John's death.

Josephus does not even connect Jesus with John, although it might have suited his interests to have done so. After all, he is critical of both Pilate and Herod Antipas, so that linking their innocent victims would have been effective in rhetorical terms. Moreover, his theme in discussing John is the feeling among many Jews that Antipas was justly punished for what he did to John: to have mentioned the continuation of his activity by Jesus might have been useful. Obviously, Josephus' silence does not indicate that there was no connection between John and Jesus, but the fact that Josephus mentions none does underline what we already know from the gospels: Jesus was not known as an immerser, once he entered upon his own, characteristic activity.

Nonetheless, there is an implicit connection between John and Jesus in the way that Josephus presents them (and in the way in which he does not present them). Where John is described as a good man (*Ant.* 18.117), Jesus is called a wise man, a doer of miracles, and a teacher or rabbi (*Ant.* 18.63; see Baras 1987 and cf. p. 124 below). Neither of them, it should be stressed, is styled as a prophet by Josephus, because that designation (usually amounting to a charge of false prophecy) is reserved for those who lead people against Rome with symbolic gestures on the scale of Moses or

Joshua (see *J.W.* 2.261; *Ant.* 18.85–87; 20.97–98, 169–72). But in the case of John, Josephus explains how he became a threat to Herod Antipas. In the case of Jesus, he simply says that Pilate condemned him to be crucified on the accusation of prominent men. He reports this after his report of two major controversies concerning the Temple, so we might notice some general similarity to the synoptic gospels, but Josephus' theme at this point is Pilate's careless arrogance, not Jesus' political activity. And whatever the activity that brought about Jesus' execution, it was not immersion as such; Josephus at least makes that much plain.

So desisting from immersion put Jesus in a different category from John in political terms, and to that extent afforded him some protection. The fact of his earlier connection with John, of course, could scarcely be hidden. Jesus himself, in opposition to the religious authorities in Jerusalem at one stage, would even ask them whether John's immersion came from God. Such was his teasing response to the question about his own authority (see Mark 11.27–33; Matt 21.23–27; Luke 20.1–8). By invoking John's memory, Jesus reminds his opponents of another teacher who challenged them over the issue of purity, and who could rely on considerable popular support. Even aside from his overt reference to John, over time, remembrance of the connection to John would have featured in the opposition to Jesus. Herod Antipas would hear of Jesus miracles and remark, 'This is John – whom I beheaded – raised up' (see Mark 6.14–16; Matt 14.1–2; Luke 9.7–9). Whatever exactly led Herod Antipas to that conclusion, it was not Jesus' immersion but his miracles that brought Jesus to his notice. At the very least, desisting from immersion bought Jesus time before any confrontation with Herod.

In addition to desisting from immersion, Jesus also left the geographical field of John's activity. He is now no longer in the Jordan Valley, but in Galilee. The synoptic gospels are emphatic that Jesus began to operate there after John's execution (Mark 1.14; Matt 4.12; Luke 4.14). Both desisting from baptism and removing himself to his native Galilee would have resulted in at least some estrangement from former disciples of John's, even those especially sympathetic to Jesus, such as Nathanael and Philip (see John 1.43–51). It has puzzled commentators for many years that Jesus would actually be taking up his activity in what one of them called 'the lion's den', the centre of Herod Antipas' rule.[4] But Josephus has shown us that Peraea (and particularly Machaerus), where John was killed and from which Herod's hapless wife had fled back to Nabataea (*Ant.* 18.111–12, 119), was the focus of the dispute that had made John into a fomenter of sedition. By withdrawing from that region, Jesus puts space between himself and Herod.

ENEMIES, FRIENDS AND FAMILY IN GALILEE

Small villages in Galilee became as characteristic of Jesus' activity as streams in the Jordan Valley were within John's (see Strange 1997). The shift from the wilderness to the village is obviously profound, in terms of mapping a field of purity. But in political terms, the villages provided camouflage for Jesus. They were not wilderness, and nothing to do with the Jordan Valley, the place of John's opposition to Herod Antipas. But they were also quite unlike a city (particularly Sepphoris, a garrison and seat of Antipas' power),[5] where Herod's official presence as well as the occupying Romans would be forces to be reckoned with.

Indeed, the danger of Herod Antipas' continuing enmity helps to account for what otherwise must seem rather strange. Why does Jesus, a notably popular rabbi with a diverse following, generally stay away from cities?[6] To a substantial extent, the answer to that question is to be found in Jesus' programme of purity, but as soon as we make another observation, it becomes clear that another force was also at work. The results when Jesus actually did enter the one city he did – Jerusalem – were fatal. And Jesus was conscious of the opponent he was dealing with further north (Luke 13.31–33):

> In that hour some Pharisees came forward, saying to him, Get out and go from here! Because Herod wants to kill you. And he said to them, You go, and say to that fox, Look, I put out demons and will send healings today and tomorrow, and on the third day I will be completed. Except that I must go today and tomorrow and the following day, because it is not acceptable that a prophet should perish outside of Jerusalem!

There are several indications that we are dealing with primitive material here. The Pharisees are friendly, Antipas is particularly at issue, and the Lucan Jesus does not speak in his usual, precise way about how and when he is going to die. Instead, Jesus puts himself into the general category of prophets who will be killed as a result of their prophecy.

What the saying shows us is that Jesus' geographical programme came over time to include an avoidance of Herod Antipas, and that it did so deliberately, until such time as confrontation with authorities might take place. And the only place for that was Jerusalem.

Before we consider that confrontation, however, we need to sketch how the lines of friendship and enmity developed in the years between John's death and Jesus' death. Desisting from baptism, of course, was no end in itself: in Jesus' practice, the immersion of John was replaced by fellowship at meals. This mealtime practice and activities associated with it in time both brought Jesus disciples and alienated his own family.

Meals rather than any useful work progressively became the focus of Jesus' forays from Nazareth. The Galileans understood, both emotionally and intellectually, what these meals were saying. Their land was pure and acceptable to God. They were pure and forgiven. Their bread was an emblem of God's kingdom (Mark 4.26–29). As their enthusiasm for Jesus' banquets increased, he worked less and less, and the consequences for his family steadily grew. Honour, as explained in recent social-scientific work (see e.g. Malina and Rohrbaugh 1992:309–11), demanded they acknowledge Jesus' indebtedness to his hosts at a time when he had not yet acquired the kind of wealthy friends Luke 8.2–3 refers to. They had to reciprocate by sending food or inviting the host family to eat with them. James and Joses, even if married by this stage, would still have honoured Mary's debts and the obligations of several siblings (Mark 6.3), and it was only natural for James to sound increasingly like the prodigal's older brother in Jesus' famous parable (Luke 15.11–32). To James, Jesus' activity must have seemed irresponsible. In addition, Jesus' declarations of purity – a basic assumption of his indiscriminate willingness to eat with fellow Israelites – extended to cleansing those thought unclean (Mark 1.40–45; Matt 8.1–4; Luke 5.12–16) and the exorcism of unclean spirits (Mark 1.23–28; Luke 4.33–37). His claim to act on the basis of anointing by the spirit of God was seen as so arrogant that he was seriously threatened with stoning in Nazareth (Luke 4.16–30). John 7.2–5 suggests that the tension between Jesus and his family could extend to open expressions of hostility.

Capernaum, rather than Nazareth, became the centre of Jesus' activity, owing to the hospitality and the following he enjoyed there. Two pairs of brothers, Peter and Andrew, James and John, stand out as leaders – and leading supporters, from their family holdings in Capernaum – of Jesus' movement at this stage, from around AD 24 (Matt 4.18–22; Mark 1.16–20). They commanded sufficient resources to be able to support Jesus as well as their own families, and yet kept a sufficient distance from the economic system of the Roman estates so as to enable Jesus to persist in his criticism of unjust *mammon*, as he said in Aramaic (Luke 16.1–9). This period saw Jesus taken into the home of Peter and his growing reputation as a healer (Matt 4.23–25; 8.14–15; Mark 1.29–39; Luke 4.38–44). He had been known as a visitor to the synagogue who exorcised unclean spirits (Mark 1.21–28; Luke 4.31–37), but his actual residence nearby caused a genuine following to gather around him. Indeed, journeys outward from Capernaum were to some extent undertaken, the synoptic gospels indicate, to avoid the crush of sympathisers (Mark 1.35–38; Luke 4.42–43).

DISCIPLES

The names of Jesus' disciples vary in the New Testament (see Matt 10.2–4; Mark 3.16–19; Luke 6.13–16; Acts 1.13). There are two main reasons for that. First, there was a confusion between the large group who followed Jesus around Galilee to learn his halakhah as thoroughly as they could, and the select twelve whom at a later stage Jesus delegated to speak and act on his behalf (Matt 10.1; Mark 6.7; Luke 9.1). (Luke expands the select group to include seventy or seventy-two people [Luke 10.1], but that is a symbolic number, corresponding to the traditional number in Judaism of all the non-Jewish nations of the world; Luke's Gospel manifests a particular interest in the promise of Jesus for the Gentiles. The seventy could also represent the seventy elders chosen by Moses in Num 11.24–25, but Luke's interests make that less likely.) A reasonable estimate is that twenty or thirty *talmidim* in the vicinity of Capernaum, some with wives and children, followed Jesus as best they could. But of course not all of them could follow him all the time, and the identity of the group would change. That brings us to the second reason for the variation of the names: the larger group of his disciples, from whom the delegates were chosen, came and went, some defecting because they came to disagree with Jesus' halakhah.

One typical controversy was Jesus' acceptance of the fellowship of a woman described as sinful (Luke 7.36–50). Female disciples are named, including one whom Jesus apparently exorcised repeatedly (8.1–3). The element of scandal here is probably not discussion with women (for which see *m. Ned.* 10.1–11.12), but travel with them, which could not help but prompt suspicions of impropriety. When Jesus spoke of a woman baking as an instance of divine kingdom (Luke 13.21) or referred to himself as a mother bird gathering her young (Matt 23.37), he was not just inventing arresting images. The lush fecundity of Wisdom, an emphatically feminine image of the divine world (see Prov 8.22–31), was as basic to God as sexuality was to the people created in God's image, and in one case Jesus even spoke in Wisdom's name (Luke 11.49).

Jesus acknowledged defections from his own controversial views in his parables. The parable of the sower and its interpretation (Mark 4.1–9, 13–20; Matt 13.1–9, 18–23; Luke 8.4–8, 11–15) expressly involves a theology of failure, the recognition that the word of the kingdom would not always prove productive after sowing. He could even trenchantly have spoken of someone who sowed bad seed in the midst of good (Matt 13.24–30), and of fish caught, only to be destroyed (Matt 13.47–50). These are parables of harsh judgement, directed against those once associated with Jesus, who had proven themselves useless, or even as hostile as his growing opposition.

Opposition was inevitable, from many ordinary practitioners of Judaism, including the Pharisees. In a rabbinic fashion, Jesus applied Pharisaic principles to respond to their objections. His stance reflected a teaching in the Mishnah. A rabbi named Hillel (50 BC–AD 10) had argued that the inside of a vessel, whether pure or impure, determined the purity or impurity of the whole vessel (cf. *m. Kelim* 25.6). In his criticism of the Pharisees, Jesus adhered to Hillel's principle: cleanness proceeds from within to without and purifies the whole. But if that is the case with cups, he argued with a flash insight that disarmed his opponents, then all the more so with Israelites who are pure by their intention and the way they work the land.[7] It is what is *within* that makes a person pure. His well-known aphorism conveys just this insight: it is not what goes into a person which defiles one, but what comes out of a person defiles one (Mark 7.15, see also Matt 15.11). Washing did not make the produce of rural Galilee any purer than it already was, and no amount of rinsing could cleanse the corruption of compromise with *mammon* which towns such as Capernaum permitted (Matt 6.24; Luke 16.13). Against the Pharisees, Jesus asserted that purity was a matter of the totality of one's being. One was either clean or unclean; for Jesus, there was no vacillation. The Pharisees' policy of compromise with defilement, skilfully crafted to deal with the complexities of urban pluralism, found no resonance in his mind, formed by the relative isolation of rural Galilee.

Their argument with its alternative constructions of cleanness, rooted in a common dedication to the value of purity, never matured. We shall never know whether it might have been brought to a resolution, whether some coalition of Pharisees and scribes and rural teachers such as Jesus might have found ground for agreement and common purpose, because Herod Antipas intervened and brought the debate to an abortive end. Jesus was warned by Pharisees, some of whom, although involved in dispute with him, continued to sympathise with his dedication to the purity and liberation of Israel (Luke 13.31). Jesus' exorcisms and healings – his reputation as a thaumaturge after the model of Elijah – had come to Herod's attention, and he also knew of Jesus' connection to John the Baptist (Mark 6.14–16; Matt 14.1–2; Luke 9.7–9). By the year 27, or during the 'fifteenth year of Tiberius' (Luke 3.1, the only chronological notice of Jesus' public activity), Jesus had become too well known to make Capernaum his permanent base.

The threat of Antipas accounts for Jesus' crossing into Herod Philip's territory (at first in Bethsaida, where some of his disciples had relatives). In stark relief with Jesus' acceptance – albeit at a safe distance from the danger

Capernaum now posed – of the delegation from the centurion garrisoned there (Matt 8.5–13; Luke 7.1–10), his reaction to an attempt at reconciliation by his own family was forbidding (Mark 3.31–35; Matt 12.46–50; Luke 8.19–21). When they sent a delegation of family friends to him, he would not interrupt his teaching to greet them: 'Whoever does the will of God that is my brother and sister and mother'. Still more surprising is his sojourn in Decapolis. Despite some success (Mark 7.31–37; Matt 15.29–31), the time in Decapolis proved a disaster on the whole, in that Jesus' practice of purity and the proudly Hellenistic ethos of that region were as incompatible as the pure waters of the sea of Galilee proved to be with the swine that drowned therein (Mark 5.1–20; Matt 8.28–34; Luke 8.26–39).

The fiasco of attempting to establish a base outside territorial Israel (though attesting the at least inchoate possibility of a larger Israel: see Bockmuehl 2000:49–83) led Jesus to the innovation of the Twelve, a number obviously redolent with the theological purpose of the institution. Hunted by Herod Antipas in Galilee itself, uncertain of safety within the domain of Herod Philip, repulsed by the Gentile population east of the Sea of Galilee, where exactly could Jesus go? How could he continue to reach Galilee with his message?

His response to this dilemma was a stroke of genius, which assured the wider promulgation of the kingdom: he dispatched twelve disciples as delegates on his behalf. The practice of sending a delegate (a *shaliah*), was common in the Middle East to seal a marriage or business contract. The role of 'apostle', from the Greek term *apostolos* (which translates *shaliah*), came out of the ordinary practice of sending a go-between to settle routine transactions. Jesus applied this custom of personal, business and military life to spread his own ideas and practices. He dispatched each *shaliah* to do what he did: proclaim God's kingdom and heal (Matt 10.1–16; Mark 6.6–13; Luke 9.1–5).

Those who were sent by Jesus had crossed with him into Herod Philip's territory. There was Peter, his 'Rock', the two noisy brothers James and John, Andrew, Philip, Bartholomew, Matthew, Thomas, another James (son of Alphaeus), Thaddaeus, Simon called 'Zealot', and Judas Iscariot (Mark 3.16–18; Matt 10.2–4; Luke 6.14–16). Other disciples, such as Nathanael and Cleopas, did not take on the role of a delegate, which involved more hardship than honour; it is not surprising that only twelve (rather than the seventy of Luke) took on the task.

Yet their success was such that Jesus could not avoid confronting the possibility of militant insurrection, as is reflected in the feeding of the 5,000 (John 6.1–15; Mark 6.32–44; Matt 14.13–21; Luke 9.10–17). The gospels (but for Luke, which places the incident near Bethsaida) report that 5,000 men followed Jesus into Syrian wilderness, but the precise number obviously cannot be known. The total population of Galilee was about 150,000 at this point,[8] less than half of whom were Jews living among the 204 cities and villages (Josephus, *Life* 235); even 1,000 would have represented some 4 per cent of able-bodied Jewish men, the most militant arm of Galilean Judaism. Jesus' movement had become politically significant, but militarily far short of overwhelming. Over a period of several months, what have been described as would-be zealots[9] abandoned their families, left their peasant life behind and their hillside villages, covertly making their way north and east, into the rolling countryside well outside Herod Antipas' jurisdiction. Although an overtly political programme is eschewed by Jesus in the narrative of his temptations (Matt 4.1–11; Luke 4.1–13), it is telling that he had to resist his own impulse to turn himself into the king some of his followers wanted him to be (see John 6.15).

Written as they are to support the Christian practice of Eucharist in the Hellenistic world, the gospels imbue this feeding with deeply symbolic significance. From only five loaves of bread and two fish that Jesus blessed and broke, the delegates fed the crowd, and collected remnants in twelve baskets. Twelve, the number of the clans of ancient Israel, marks the event as the promise of feeding all Israel. A different telling of the story (involving 4,000 men; Matt 15.32–39; Mark 8.1–10), had seven bushels filled, instead of twelve baskets, perhaps corresponding to the seven deacons chosen after the resurrection to give food to Greek-speaking followers of Jesus in Jerusalem from the common treasury of the movement (Acts 6.1–6). Just as twelve was the primordial number of Israel, seventy was the number of the non-Jewish nations. Even as embellished, these stories are rooted in the numerological traditions of Israel.

The thousand must have camped in shrub shelters and the odd tent, the kind of rustic base that Judas, son of Hezekiah, had used in leading his Galilean force to take Sepphoris in 4 BC (Josephus, *J.W.* 2.56). Jesus had stirred the Galileans' proud memories of resistance against Rome and of determined Galilean onslaughts on the Temple. The reference in John 6.15, to Jesus' knowledge that those he fed wanted to make him king, is an accurate indication of the line many of his followers crossed, but which he refused to transgress. He refused the prospect of enjoying the powers of all the kingdoms of this world (Matt 4.1–11; Luke 4.1–13), and the disappointment for many disciples, in the Syrian wilderness and elsewhere, must have been considerable.

CAIAPHAS AND PILATE IN JERUSALEM

His resolve was not to lead any military revolt, but to press for a programme of climactic sacrifice in Jerusalem, as is disclosed in the Transfiguration, a story whose sacrificial overtones become plain when its Old Testament antecedents are observed (Matt 16.28–17.13; Mark 9.1–13; Luke 9.27–36). Jesus is transformed before Peter, James and John – the three disciples who became pre-eminent in his movement shortly prior to and just after the resurrection – into a gleaming white figure, speaking with Moses and Elijah. Jesus' visions were not merely private; years of communal meditation made what he saw and experienced vivid to his own disciples as well. On Mount Hermon, the probable location of this event, Jesus followed in the footsteps of Moses, who took three of his followers (Aaron, Nadab and Abihu) up Mount Sinai, where they ate and drank to celebrate their vision of the God of Israel on his sapphire throne (see Exod 24.1–11). But unlike what happened on Moses' mountain, Jesus' disciples, covered by a shining cloud of glory, hear a voice, 'This is my son, the beloved, in whom I take pleasure: hear him'; and when the cloud passed they found Jesus without Moses and Elijah, standing alone as God's son (Matt 17.5). Divine 'son' was the same designation Jesus had heard during his immersions with John the Baptist (Matt 3.13–17; Mark 1.9–11; Luke 3.21–22): now his own disciples saw and heard the truth of his own vision. As in the earlier case with John, the voice that came after the luminous cloud in the Transfiguration insisted that the same spirit which had animated Moses and Elijah was present in Jesus, and that he could pass on that spirit to his followers, each of whom could also become a 'son'. In the Transfiguration, Peter offers to build 'huts' or 'booths' for Jesus, Moses and Elijah (Mark 9.5–6; Matt 17.4; Luke 9.33). In so doing, Peter in his fear is presented as stammering and foolish in the Greek gospels, but the 'huts' in question are reminiscent of those built at Sukkoth, the feast of Tabernacles. That was the sacrificial feast which, according to Zech 14, was to see the transformation of Israel and the world.

Attempting precisely this sacrifice, enacting the prophecy of Zechariah, brought Jesus into direct opposition to Caiaphas, who eventually managed to gain the consent of Pilate for the crucifixion, probably in the year 32 prior to the feast of Passover. Attempts have been made to compute the date of the crucifixion according to when 14 Nisan fell on a Friday; that yields the familiar alternatives of AD 30 and 33 (see Meier 1991–94:1.386–402). But the authorities in Mark 14.2 specifically decide to avoid any such timing, and it appears that the calendrical association of Jesus' death and Passover is a product of the liturgical practice of Christianity. Jesus' actual entry into

Jerusalem probably took place at Sukkoth; that is when waving and strewing branches at the altar was a regular part of processional practice (see Mark 11.8 and *m. Sukkah* 3.1–4.6, and the echo of 'Hosanna' in Mark 11.9 and *m. Sukkah* 3.9; 4.5). The likely year of that procession is 31, the same year that the execution of Sejanus in Rome weakened Pilate's position, and made him more susceptible to conciliation with Caiaphas (see Hoehner 1980).

The Targum of Zechariah predicts that God's kingdom (14.9) will be manifested over the entire earth when both Israelites and non-Jews present the offerings of Sukkoth at the Temple. It further predicts that these worshippers will prepare and offer their sacrifices themselves without the intervention of middlemen. The last words of the book promise that 'and there shall never again be a *trader* in the *sanctuary* of the Lord of hosts at that *time*' (*Targ.* Zech 14.21, innovative wording italicised). The thrust of the targumic prophecy brought on the dramatic confrontation that Jesus would shortly provoke in the Temple.

Enthusiastic supporters swarmed around Jesus, including his brother James. James joined his brother once Jesus' programme was defined in terms of sacrifice, rather than exorcism or military revolt. Jesus' focus on sacrifice in the Temple – which had perplexed the militant expectation of the '5,000' – was exactly what brought James to his side. Two things about James stand out from the principal sources from which we learn about him (Acts, Josephus, and the historian Hegesippus from the second century): he never participated in armed revolt and never wavered in his loyalty to the Temple. He remained devoted to the practice of sacrifice and became famous for his piety in Jerusalem, where he was ultimately killed in AD 62 by a high priest who was jealous of the reverence in which he was held.

Although the stratagem of Jesus, in converting a potential revolution into apocalyptic sacrifice, was brilliant at several levels, it ultimately misfired. Conflict with Caiaphas was perhaps inevitable, given Jesus' commitment to implementing the programme of Zechariah. But Caiaphas had newly been emboldened to change arrangements in the Temple. He had expelled the Sanhedrin from their special room and place of honour called the Chamber of Hewn Stone, within the Court of the Israelites. The Sanhedrin, consisting of priestly aristocrats, Pharisees and notables of Jerusalem, were the seventy-some-member council of the most important Jews in the city, who advised Caiaphas and Pilate on cultic and civic matters. They were 'exiled', as their own recollection of this expulsion put it, to Ḥanut (according to *b. Šabb.* 15a; *b. Sanh.* 41a; *b. ʿAbod. Zar.* 8b), the market most likely on the Mount of Olives. That expulsion permitted Caiaphas to set up vendors in the porticos of the Temple who had once been accommodated on Ḥanut (John 2.13–16; Mark 11.15–16; Matt 21.12; Luke 19.45).

Jesus' Zecharian storming of the Temple therefore challenged Caiaphas directly. It also caused Jesus to challenge the efficacy of sacrifice in that Temple, when he called the wine and the bread of his own fellowship meal the 'blood' and 'flesh' of true sacrifice (Luke 22.15–20; Mark 14.22–25; Matt 26.26–29).[10] Even some of his own disciples, Judas among them, were appalled by that implicit blasphemy, which played into Caiaphas' hands (John 6.60–71; 13.21–30; Matt 26.21–25; Luke 22.21–23). In addition, unknown to Jesus, the high priest's influence over the prefect, Pontius Pilate, was about to increase exponentially, as a result of the execution of Sejanus in Rome on 18 October, AD 31. Between then and the subsequent Passover, Caiaphas managed to convince Pilate to act, with the approval of a much-relieved Antipas (Luke 23.6–12; cf. further Hoehner 1980:224–50).

Jesus' friends and enemies locate him within his time and culture, and provide insight into his motivations, in an informative manner. Enmity came initially from Herod Antipas, in reaction to John the Baptist's attack on Antipas' marriage. As one of John's disciples, Jesus inherited the antagonism of Antipas when healings made the young teacher famous in Capernaum. Sacrifice in Jerusalem, rather than overt resistance to Antipas and his Roman sponsors, became Jesus' programme to promote God's kingdom. This sacrificial programme, inspired by the book of Zechariah, ran afoul of Caiaphas' pragmatic control of the Temple, and the violence of Jesus' expulsion of vendors from the Temple in due course aroused the mortal opposition of the Roman prefect of Judaea.

Jesus' friendships form a mirror image of this growing antagonism. His friends, like his enemies, were defined by their response to Jesus' understanding of purity. John the Baptist, Jesus' own disciples, and the Twelve, all represent commitment to a coherent teaching as well as personal sympathy. But Jesus' practice was challenging to those nearest him, as his own family's reaction to him perhaps reflects best. Even John could not endorse Jesus' treatment of non-immersed Israelites as clean, and his association with women must have perplexed many of Jesus' disciples. Most dramatically, at least one among the Twelve, forced to choose between Jesus' Zecharian sacrifice and the status quo in the Temple, chose the latter. If his friendships mirrored enmities, then the mirror was cracked, and that reflects the dynamic changes of Jesus' own life as much as the fickleness which can make a man's friends into his enemies (see Ps 41.9).

Notes

1. See Murphy-O'Connor 1990. His hypothesis involves identifying Aenon near Salem with Shechem (pp. 363–66) 'in the very heart of Samaritan territory'

(p. 365). In an otherwise very critical treatment of his work, Murphy-O'Connor receives cautious encouragement for his geographical suggestion from Ernst (1997:167–72). On balance, however, a location closer to the Jordan seems more probable to Ernst (and to me).

2. Jacob's well, which features in the story (John 4.5–6), is actually associated with Shechem in the Old Syriac Gospels, although 'Sychar' is the preferred reading. Either way, however, no link with Aenon near Salem is suggested in John, and that is one reason for which Murphy-O'Connor's suggestion is not accepted here. On the location of the well, see Stefanovic 1992.

3. See the development of a response in Chilton 1998.

4. So Schmid 1959:70. The matter is discussed in Chilton 1979:101–03.

5. See the tentative suggestion of Meyers 1997:64, within his succinct presentation of Sepphoris on the basis of the literary and archaeological evidence.

6. See Freyne 1994. On Jesus' programme of purity, see Chilton 1992.

7. The place of Hillel in the principle of purity Jesus developed was first signalled in Neusner 1976. In extending Hillel's teaching in this way, Jesus was invoking the principle of the prophet Haggai, who had once declared that just as uncleanness is contagious, so God's spirit would one day make Israel clean by its holy contagion (Hag 2.4, 10–19).

8. On the difficulty of estimating population, see Horsley 1996:44–45. Josephus would seem to imply a Galilean population of 3,000,000 (*J.W.* 3.43), but that is widely agreed to be an impossible exaggeration; see Bruce 1982:36.

9. See Brandon 1967. Although the direct application of the term 'zealot' is somewhat anachronistic, the complete elimination of what it refers to within the aspirations of Jesus' followers is even more so.

10. For a discussion of the exegetical development of these texts, see Chilton 1994; a narrative treatment of these and other findings is available in Chilton 2000a.

6 Crucifixion

JOEL B. GREEN

Why did Jesus have to die? This question is capable of multiple answers. For example, a Latin historian writing at the end of the reign of Tiberius likely would never have heard of Jesus or his execution; or if he had, he would probably have had no reason to mention it. Had he woven this crucifixion into his narrative, the most credible impetus would have been to illustrate the religio-political agitation that marked Roman–Jewish relations during this period, perhaps as an anecdote displaying how Rome dealt with those who threatened the *pax romana*. If reports of this incident were written up differently in the second century, or if already within the first century those who penned documents that would become our New Testament had relocated it from a footnote in the annals of history to its status as an epoch-making event, this is because Jesus' death had been set within different interpretative horizons.

In this chapter, my principal interest falls on setting the crucifixion of Jesus within three possible 'plots' or narrative strands that together make a tightly woven cord. That is, I will situate the crucifixion of Jesus (1) within the story of imperial Rome; (2) within the story of Israel, the people of YHWH, and especially the multiple ways of articulating that story in the Second Temple Period; and (3) within the story of the life and ministry of Jesus, to which we have access primarily by means of the Gospels of Matthew, Mark, Luke and John. Although some scholars today take the second-century *Gospel of Peter* as an independent witness to the death of Jesus (so forcefully Crossan 1988), most have concluded that this *Gospel* employed one or more of the New Testament gospels as sources and thus provides little if anything by way of independent witness (see Brown 1984:2.1317–49; Green 1987; Meier 1991–94:1.116–18). With regard to other critical issues, scholars who have explored the origin of the passion material in recent decades have tended to think in terms of a very early account or accounts that were expanded into the narratives of Jesus' suffering and death available to us in the New Testament gospels. Most analysis has focused on the traditional quality of the material shared by the Gospels of Mark and John, which are taken to be independent of one another as literary sources (e.g. Myllykoski 1991–94; Reinbold 1994) or simply argued in favour of a pre-Marcan passion narrative (e.g. Yarbro Collins 1992: 92–118). Other study has suggested that the passion account in Luke 22–23 builds both on Mark 14–15 and on a non-Marcan passion tradition (e.g. Green 1988:24–104). Although considerations of this nature are important for indicating the relative antiquity of the passion tradition, I will not be concerned here with identifying the details of the earliest tradition. Instead, I will build on three broad assumptions: (1) The earliest attempts to narrate the suffering and death of Jesus were already *interpretative* in character. One looks in vain for an interest in 'brute facts' in regard to Jesus' execution, for the event of Jesus' crucifixion was never related apart from the significance accorded it by one group or another. (2) The litmus test for any accounting of the historical Jesus is whether such an account can make sense of the question, Why was Jesus executed on a Roman cross as 'King of the Jews'? Thus, contemporary attempts to tell the story of Jesus' life must weave together as a single cloth the manner of his life and the character of his death. (3) When questions of historical veracity are put to the gospels regarding the death of Jesus (including whether or how Jesus might have anticipated and interpreted his death), such questions are best raised within the interpretative horizons to which these gospels give witness – namely, the world of Second Temple Judaism under the imperial rule of Rome. Taken together, these guiding assumptions refuse any dichotomy between history and theology in portraying Jesus' death, underscore the importance of congruence between the public ministry of Jesus and his execution, and emphasise the necessity of verisimilitude given the historical constraints within which Jesus lived and died.

One further caveat: even if the question of why Jesus was executed on a Roman cross is inexplicable apart from theological consideration, within the scope of this chapter I will note only peripherally the import of Jesus' death as this was developed in subsequent Christian theology. Narrowing the focus, I will show that the question of *why* Jesus had to die is intimately associated with two further questions: *How* did Jesus die? and *Where* did Jesus die?

THE PUZZLE OF CRUCIFIXION

Among the data available to us regarding Jesus of Nazareth, none is more incontrovertible than his execution on a Roman cross by order of Pontius Pilate. The New Testament materials testify to this event with remarkably detailed passion narratives, with references to the crucifixion especially in the speeches in Acts, and through snippets of information scattered throughout the letters and the Apocalypse. Within the first century, extra-biblical evidence is found in the writings of the Jewish historian Josephus, in the so-called *Testimonium Flavianum* (i.e. the 'testimony of Flavius Josephus'; *Ant.* 18.63–64; see also p. 124 below). Because this text speaks unabashedly of Jesus' status as Messiah and of his resurrection, and even calls into question whether Jesus might rightly be regarded as a mere human being, this paragraph in Josephus has long been suspected as a Christian interpolation. Although the authenticity of the *Testimonium* continues to be debated, it seems more likely that an original reference to Jesus in Josephus' work has been embellished than that the whole is entirely the result of Christian tampering. If one removes the most explicitly Christian material, one is left with the following:

> At this time there appeared Jesus, a wise man, for he was a doer of astounding deeds, a teacher of people who receive the truth gladly. He won a following both among many Jews and among many of Greek origin. When Pilate, because of an accusation made by our leaders, condemned him to the cross, those who had loved him previously did not cease to do so. Up until this very day the tribe of Christians (named after him) has not died out.

According to this emendation of the text (cf. Meier 1991–94:1.56–69), Josephus wrote of Jesus' crucifixion, but he did not sketch in an explicit way what we might most want to know – namely, why was Jesus executed? What was the nature of the indictment brought against him? On the other hand, it may well be that we can tease out clues from this passage. Thus, 'astounding deeds' refers to Jesus' status as a miracle worker and healer, and Josephus underscores in this short paragraph the popularity Jesus enjoyed. What is more, he makes clear that Jesus ran afoul of the Jewish elite in Jerusalem ('our leaders'). These statements cohere well with the gospel records and may be useful in framing a picture of the reasons behind Jesus' death.

In the early second century, the Roman historian Tacitus spoke of Jesus' execution as well. Writing of the persecution of Christians in Rome under Nero, Tacitus notes in his *Annals* that 'Christians' take their name from 'Christ, who, during the reign of Tiberius, had been executed by the procurator Pontius Pilate' (15.44). Still later in the second century, Lucian of Samosata wrote a sneering account of a person who had converted to, and then rejected, Christian faith. Therein, he speaks of 'the man who was crucified in Palestine because he introduced this new cult into the world', and describes

Christians as 'worshipping the crucified sophist' (*The Passing of Peregrinus*).
It is also worth reflecting on the fact that the crucifixion of Jesus was seized
upon by those antagonistic towards Christians and the Christian message so
as to discredit their claims regarding Jesus. As the second-century Christian
apologist Justin Martyr remarks, 'They say that our madness consists in the
fact that we put a crucified man in second place after the unchangeable and
eternal God, the creator of the world' (*1 Apol.* 13.4).

If we can accept the certainty of Jesus' crucifixion as an historical datum, what can we say about the manner of his death? On this, the evidence
is far more ambiguous than is generally realised. Literary sensibilities in
Roman antiquity did not promote graphic descriptions of the act of crucifixion, and even the gospels are singularly reserved at this point. They report
simply, 'They crucified him' (Mark 15.24; Luke 23.33; John 19.18). The accounts themselves are devoid of the sort of detail that apparently belonged to
the shared cultural encyclopaedia of the Evangelists and their first readers.
Literary evidence outside of the gospels makes it clear that, when it came to
the act of crucifixion, the Romans were slaves to no standard technique. In
describing the siege of Jerusalem by the Roman army, for example, Josephus
reports that 'the soldiers out of rage and hatred amused themselves by nail-
ing their prisoners in different positions' (*J.W.* 5.449–51). Elsewhere we learn
that victims of crucifixion might be fixed to the stake in order to die, or im-
paled after death as a public display. They might be fixed to the cross with
nails or with ropes. That Jesus was nailed to the cross is intimated in several
texts (John 20.25; Acts 2.23; Col 2.14; *Gos. Pet.* 6.21; Justin *Dial.* 97). Nor can
we turn to archaeological evidence for assistance. To date, the bones of only
one victim of crucifixion have been unearthed. This is not surprising when
it is remembered that the crucified were generally left on their crosses as
carrion for the birds in order to provide a public and gruesome reminder
of the fate of those who opposed imperial rule. Even if they were granted
burial, the nature of their execution would have precluded the sort of proper
burial that would provide today's physical anthropologists with evidence of
crucifixion. The crucified man from Givᶜat ha-Mivtar was found in 1968 in
an ossuary (bone box) in northern Jerusalem; his remains suggest that his
wrists were tied to the crossbeam, and that he was made to straddle the
upright beam with a single nail driven through the heel bones of one foot,
through the vertical beam, and into the other.

In spite of the paucity and ambiguity of the evidence, Martin Hengel suggests a summary sketch of the Roman procedure of crucifixion. Crucifixion
included a flogging beforehand, with victims generally made to carry their
own crossbeams to the location of their execution, where they were bound

or nailed to the cross with arms extended, raised up, and, perhaps seated on a small wooden peg (Hengel 1977:22–32). As we have seen with reference to Josephus' eyewitness account, however, this procedure was subject to wild variation.

In the context of any discussion of the material aspects of crucifixion it is crucial to remember that Rome did not embrace crucifixion as its method of choice for execution on account of the excruciating pain it caused. The act of crucifixion resulted in little blood loss and death came slowly, as the body succumbed to shock. This form of capital punishment was savage and heinous, but for other reasons. Executed publicly, situated at a major crossroads or on a well-trafficked artery, devoid of clothing, left to be eaten by birds and beasts, victims of crucifixion were subject to optimal, unmitigated, vicious ridicule.

Rome did not expose its own citizens to this form of heinous punishment, but reserved crucifixion above all for those who resisted imperial rule. In short, *that* Jesus was crucified immediately places him historically in the story of Roman rule as a character regarded as antagonistic, even a threat, to the Empire. Indeed, the inscription announcing his capital offence, 'The King of the Jews' (Matt 27.37; Mark 15.26; Luke 23.38; John 19.19–22), marks Jesus as a pretender to the throne and thus represents first a Roman (and not a Christian) point of view: *Let the cruel execution of Jesus of Nazareth be a lesson to the Jewish population that Rome will not tolerate any attempt to incite the people to rebellion.* It is hardly coincidental that Josephus documents the rise of Jewish revolutionary movements beginning at the turn of the era (e.g. *Ant.* 17.278–85; 17.271–76, 285; *J.W.* 2.55–56), and the landscape of Roman–Jewish relations is dotted with skirmishes and war until the Romans did 'annihilate, exterminate and eradicate' them from the land (Dio Cassius 59.13.3).

Historical narrative is always written from the standpoint of those who know the future of past forces and thus are compelled to ask: What led to this outcome? Hence the question: What could Jesus have done that would lead to the outcome of his death as an actual or potential adversary of Rome?

JESUS, JERUSALEM AND ROME

The gospels provide no hint that Rome – more particularly, Rome's representative, the prefect Pontius Pilate – reached any conclusion about Jesus by his own devices. Rather, Jesus was conveyed to Pilate by the Jewish leadership in Jerusalem on a capital charge. Why did Jesus have to die? This question cannot be answered satisfactorily without reference to Rome, but locating Jesus' execution only within the narrative sequence concerned with Roman interests provides an answer that ultimately is not very satisfying, historically and theologically.

Jesus, threat to Rome

In what way is it possible to conceive of Jesus as a threat to Rome? This query is resolved most directly by following the story of Jesus' relation to Israel and especially to the Jewish elite in Jerusalem. Before doing so, however, it is worth noting that, quite apart from the difficulties Jesus encountered among leading Jews, his ministry and message were on a collision course with Roman interests. Even if he was relatively unknown in the Roman world, he propagated a worldview that ran counter to official Roman ideology and encouraged others to do the same.

Neither Rome's efforts at colonisation nor its projection and maintenance of imperial rule were simple acts of accumulation and acquisition. Rather, these were supported and inspired by impressive ideological formations that included notions that certain territories and people require domination. Roman historians may debate the complex of stimuli that spawned imperial Rome, but there is no escaping the central role of Rome (the city) in defining the life-world of even the far-reaches of Roman rule (the empire). Here was the centre, the navel of the universe. Institutions like the Roman Empire are built on, belong to, and actively perpetuate a worldview that is self-legitimating. Such life-centring institutions come to believe and cultivate the belief that 'this is the way things are supposed to be' – and, indeed, that 'this is the way God/the gods would have it'. As a consequence, we must rid ourselves of the idea that Rome had political interests while the Jews had religious ones. For them, politics and religion cohabited the same space so that political infractions were inherently moral and religious, and vice versa.

With reference to Jesus and Rome, potential religio-political concerns come into focus best with regard to conflicting attitudes towards the household. As Cicero put it, the household was regarded as 'the seed-bed of the state' (*On Duties* 1.53–55); the orderliness of household relations was both a model for and the basis of order within the empire, with persons assigned a precise place in a vast network of orders, classes, tribes and centuries. At the head of the house stood the *paterfamilias*, the patriarch of an extended family, with networks of overlapping obligations proceeding from him to others of the household, and with one household mapped in relationship to others in a vast hierarchical web governed by status and social obligation. The empire itself was envisioned as a great household, with the emperor the 'father of the fatherland', the benefactor or patron of all. Relations of reciprocity thus bound slaves to masters, sons to fathers, household to household, and all to Caesar and him to the gods who had shown their favour to him.

Against such a world order, Jesus' message stands in stark contrast. On the one hand, we find evidence in the gospel narratives of 'business as usual' among Jesus' followers, as they vie for places of honour. Who is the greatest? Jesus' response to this sort of posturing for social position was to place before his disciples a little child (e.g. Mark 9.33–37). Serve these most vulnerable persons, these of lowest status, with honour; the dominion of God belongs to such persons. Here is a far-reaching inversion of Roman ideology. On the other, in the context of a world carefully managed by a system of reciprocity and patronage, Jesus insisted that people give without expectation of return. The household of Rome was built on social norms in which the giving of gifts (whether goods and services or invitations to banquets) brought with it expectations of reciprocity. Here was a systemic segregation of those of relative status from the dispossessed, since the latter were incapable either of advancing the social status of the former or even of returning the favour of an invitation to hospitality. Jesus set forth for his audiences an alternative household not characterised by concerns with debt and obligation. Services were to be performed and gifts given to others as though they were family, 'without expectation of return'. Such practices, if widespread, could only subvert the Roman world order. If Jesus were able to recruit adherents to this alternative, what then?

If Rome had reason to concern itself with the political risk posed by Jesus' mission and message, this is not to say that it was from early on aware of such a threat, and the gospel records provide little by way of suggesting that such scenarios as these were recognised for their peril. Instead, Roman interests were piqued in a more direct way by the charges brought against Jesus by the Jerusalem leadership.

Jesus and the Temple
The full interpretative force of the fact that Jesus was crucified in Jerusalem cannot be grasped without reference to the role of the Temple as the premier institutional context of the socio-religious world of Second Temple Judaism, and particularly to its central function of defining and organising the life-world of the Jewish people. Using the categories of sacred space, we can conceive of the Temple as sacred centre, the navel of the earth, an institution with two axes. The vertical axis marks the Temple as the meeting place of God and humanity, the juncture of the layers of the cosmos. Here is God's own abode; the location of service, worship, prayer and sacrifice to God; the point of divine revelation; the locus of the divine presence. The

horizontal axis emphasises the Temple's capacity to structure and orient so-cial life. Historically, the ideology of the Temple served as a binding force, relating monotheism and exclusivity: the one Temple unified the one people under the one God.

Two consequences follow that have immediate consequences for our question, Why did Jesus have to die? First, this horizontal axis signals how the Temple establishes the order of the world, providing the centre point around which human life is oriented. The architecture of the Temple – with its system of restricted spaces correlating the concepts of holiness and purity, segregating Gentile from Jew, Jewish female from Jewish male, priest from non-priest, and so on – both embodies and radiates this life-world, broadcast-ing social maps that segregate persons along lines of ethnicity and gender and, thus, with respect to relative status measured in terms of religious purity. In important ways, Jesus set himself and his ministry over against the ideol-ogy that emanates from the Temple. He flouted conventions related to food and table associates, for example, by extending table fellowship to toll col-lectors and sinners. In providing food for the multitudes he contravened tra-ditional concerns with ritual purity and status by having apparent strangers, the masses, sit and break bread together. Jesus habitually crossed the bound-aries between clean and unclean, even to the point of touching lepers and handling corpses.

Second, those whom the gospels name as centrally involved in debate with Jesus in his final days as well as those most visible in the legal pro-ceedings against him are those most intimately involved in the affairs of the Temple – that is, the chief priests, scribes, elders, Sadducees and leaders of the people. After Jesus' prophetic action in the Temple, they understandably press the question, 'By what authority do you do these things?' The piv-otal question is, Who has legitimate authority? Legitimacy is a two-pronged issue, having to do with the justification of a particular person or group of persons to wield authority as well as with the setting of limits on ap-propriate behaviour (or the determination of practices deemed acceptable). Hence, the question, 'By what authority?' points to two related questions: Who has divinely appointed authority? And, What actions can be said to fall within the parameters of divinely authorised behaviour? The point, of course, is that Jesus' antagonists drew their legitimation from their relation-ship to the Temple. They were the ones who possessed the divine right to handle holy paraphernalia, to make pronouncements on ritual cleanness, to perform sacrifices on behalf of the people, to collect tithes and maintain the Temple treasury, and, thus, to speak on God's behalf. High worship and high politics originated from the same impulse, the sacredness of the Jerusalem

Temple. If the Jerusalem leadership were thus authorised in their positions and practices by God, what was the source of Jesus' authority?

In the end, Jesus had to come to Jerusalem to press his message. His pronouncement of the kingdom of God and the practices that characterised his ministry stood in contrast to the ideology promulgated on behalf of God by these divinely legitimated spokespersons, the Jerusalem leadership. He pronounced forgiveness on God's behalf. He reinterpreted the scriptures related to the Sabbath so as to render this day a day of healing. And his final week was occupied with his prophetic act in the Temple, his teaching the Jewish people within the Temple courts, his subverting the authority of the Jerusalem elite (on their own ground, the Temple courts) through besting them in scriptural debate and calling into question their oppressive practices, and with his prophetic anticipation of calamity and destruction, including the razing of the Temple.

Adding to the portrait of hostility thus emerging is the hearing of Jesus before the Jewish council, held as a prelude to presenting Jesus before the Roman governor. For the trial accounts in the Gospels of Matthew and Mark, Jesus is charged with blasphemy and this provides the motivation for the council's seeking the death penalty in this case. The historicity of this material continues to be differently assessed. E. P. Sanders has argued against the veracity of this account, above all on the grounds of missed opportunity. That is, had Jesus been charged with speaking and acting against the Temple, he might have been indicted for blasphemy, but this is not what Matthew and Mark record; instead, the charge of blasphemy follows Jesus' statement, '[From now on] you will see the Son of Man seated at the right hand of Power and coming with [or 'on'] the clouds of heaven' (Matt 26.64; Mark 14.62; cf. Luke 22.69). For Sanders (1985:297–98), this statement is manifestly 'unblasphemous'. More recently, Darrell Bock has taken up this issue, arguing that, within Second Temple Judaism, blasphemy might involve either word or deed and that special sensitivity on the issue of blasphemy was observed where the Temple was concerned. Additionally, the evidence he garners suggests that Jesus' statement concerning the Son of Man, seated at the right hand of God, could easily have been recognised as a claim on Jesus' part to enter directly into the presence of God and, indeed, to share in God's rule. Within Second Temple Judaism, such statements as these could well have attracted the charge of blasphemy (Bock 1994; Bock 2000). Accordingly, as Matthew and Mark narrate things, from the perspective of the Jerusalem leadership, Jesus thus committed blasphemy, an offence worthy of the death penalty.

From the standpoint of the Jewish elite in Jerusalem, Jesus presented an alternative vision of God's purpose, one that did not draw its authorisation

from the Temple but that actually called the Temple into serious question. For
them, Jesus' vision of God's agenda was perverse, and by taking his claims
directly to the people, he involved them in his perversion, drawing them
away from God. Had his been a lonely voice, he might have been ignored,
but the passion accounts of the gospels are replete with testimony to his
popularity among the people. Indeed, according to the witness of the Fourth
Gospel, the Jerusalem elite even recognised the potential of Jesus' popularity
to jeopardise Rome–Jerusalem relations, a further threat to the Temple (John
11.47–53).

This is precisely the nature of the situation as it is presented in Luke
23. Jesus, the Jerusalem leadership explains to Pilate, 'perverts our nation'
(v. 2) 'stirs up the people' (v. 5); 'he perverts the people' (v. 14). With such
language, rooted in Deut 13, Jesus is charged as a false prophet – one who
lacked divine sanction for his ministry, who did not speak on behalf of YHWH,
whose attempts at reforming the Temple were treasonous against the way
of the Lord, and whose ministry of healing was nothing more than a showy
attempt to gain a following. This perspective coheres well with the parallel
allegation against Jesus as a deceiver (Matt 27.63), may be implicit in the work
of Josephus (see above), and is congruent with later, Jewish testimony that
Jesus was executed as a sorcerer who enticed and led Israel astray (*b. Sanh.*
43a; 107b).

Importantly, the language attributed by Luke to the Jerusalem elite (e.g.
'leading the people astray') is easily parlayed into a potential threat against
the peace of Rome. In its arrogance, Rome may regard Jesus' ministry and
message as harmless, but, in the end, cannot overlook the threat of civil
unrest. It is at this point that the story of Rome and the story of Israel's
leadership boldly intersect. The Jerusalem elite regarded Jesus as a threat to
their own status as those authorised to speak and act on God's behalf, and
they presented Jesus to the Jewish people as a false prophet and to Pilate as
a rebel. For all these reasons, it was necessary that Jesus be put to death.

JESUS AND HIS DEATH

If the death of Jesus is thus explicable within the narrative sequences
concerning imperial Rome and the politics of Second Temple Judaism as this
was focused on the Temple and leaders of the people in Jerusalem, what of
the place of the death of Jesus within the story of his life and ministry? Any
attempt to address this question must account for at least these factors:

(1) From the early days of his public work Jesus encountered hostility
and his ministry was embroiled in conflict. It is almost unthinkable that he

did not reflect on the possibility of his death and, thus, on its significance. In other words, how Jesus might have contemplated his own demise is a fair question to explore.

(2) As we have already begun to see, Jesus' death is related substantively to his life. His kingdom-proclamation, his emphasis on the status of little children, his associates at the dining table, his interpretation of Scripture, his practices on the Sabbath, his ministry of healing – all of these and more find their culmination, sometimes paradoxically, in the cross. In fact, it is possible to go further and to suggest that Jesus' death represents a microcosm of his life – a possibility that comes into focus in the so-called ransom-saying (Mark 10.45; Matt 20.28), in which Jesus asserts that the purpose of his coming was 'not to be served, but to serve and to give his life a ransom for many'. Here, Jesus illustrates his teaching with reference to his own mission, so that the ransom-saying functions both as an example that confirms the ethic he has proposed and as a self-disclosure of the life goal given him by God. Deep-rooted dispositions towards acquiring, claiming and maintaining relative status and power surface throughout the gospel tradition, and Jesus consistently censures them – for example, when he gives advice on dinner invitations and seating arrangements (Luke 14.1–24) and when he urges hospitality to the least impressive inhabitants of the Roman social world, little children (e.g. Mark 9.33–37; 10.13–16). In the ransom-saying, Jesus on the one hand profoundly subverts status-seeking practices by directing his disciples to comport themselves as slaves rather than despotic rulers. On the other hand, Jesus interprets the purpose of his coming, which climaxes in his death, by writing himself into the narrative of the exodus (God, it is said in the LXX, ransomed Israel, delivering the people from slavery in Egypt [Exod 6.6; 16.13]) and into the expectation of new exodus (especially as this is articulated in Isaiah 40–55 [see Isa 43.3–4]).

(3) The divine necessity of Jesus' death is woven into the fabric of the gospel passion narratives and early Christian formulae concerned with his death. This requires that we ponder the reality that, in our earliest extant records, the shameful, savage execution of Jesus has already been located within the narrative of the outworking of God's purpose for Israel. Whether in terms of direct statements that God was at work in the death of Jesus (e.g. 2 Cor 5.19) or with reference to a vibrant and dynamic intertextual association of Jesus and his passion with figures and stories at home in Israel's scriptures, the conviction that Jesus' death served the divine will inspired theological creativity in the interpretation of the cross.

We may take as axiomatic that Jesus did anticipate his death (cf. Mark 10.33–34; 38–39 parr.). In the charged environment of Roman Palestine, how could he not have done so? To admit this is to open the door to its corollary – namely, the probability that he reflected on its significance and did so in a way that intimately related it to his mission to redeem the people of God. By this I mean that Jesus was no masochist looking for an opportunity to suffer and die, but did see that his absolute commitment to the purpose of God might lead, in the context of 'this adulterous and wicked generation' (Mark 8.38), to his death. This, he discerns and embraces in prayer on the night of his arrest, was the cup given him by God (Mark 14.32–42; Luke 22.39–46).

His mission as this is known to us in the gospels is directed towards revitalising Israel as the people of God. Pursuing this aim compelled him to proclaim and embody an ethic grounded in divine dispositions, and brought him into conflict with the conveyers of Roman and Jewish ideologies and practices. It led him to a form of execution emblematic of a way of life that rejected the value of public opinion in the determination of status before God, and inspired interpretations of his death that accorded privilege to the redemptive power of righteous suffering. The way was opened for Jesus' followers to accord positive value to his shameful death, and thus to learn to associate in meaningful ways what would otherwise have been only a clash of contradictory images: Jesus' heinous suffering and his messianic status. As Ben F. Meyer (1979:218) has insisted, 'Jesus did not aim to be repudiated and killed; he aimed to charge with meaning his being repudiated and killed'.

This also means that Jesus was able to gather together Israel's history and hopes and from them forge a view of himself as the one through whose suffering Israel, and through Israel the nations, would experience divine redemption. That is, in elucidating the significance of his looming death, Jesus pushed backward into Israel's history and embraced Israel's expectations for deliverance. At the table on his last night with his followers, at a meal pregnant with the imagery of Passover and exodus, he intimated that the new exodus, God's decisive act of deliverance, was coming to fruition in his death, the climax of his mission. Moreover, he developed the meaning of his death in language and images grounded in the constitution of Israel as the covenant people of God (Exod 24.8), the conclusion of the exile (see Zech 9.9–11), and the hope of a new covenant (Jer 31.31–33), so as to mark his death as the inaugural event of covenant renewal. How could Jesus contemplate such thoughts? Taken together with his prophetic action in the Temple, the symbolic actions at the table of Jesus' last meal with his disciples suggest that he viewed himself as the focal point of God's great act of deliverance.

Where might Jesus have gone for resources to construct such a view? Attempts to find in Israel's history a 'suffering Messiah' figure have thus far proven fruitless, yet this does not preclude the possibility that Jesus could have pioneered this combination of images. Given what we know of Jesus, the issue is not whether we can allow for innovation on his part. We must ask instead whether the raw materials for innovation were at hand, as well as whether any proposed innovation could be understood by those around Jesus. With respect to this last question, the gospels repeatedly witness the obtuseness of Jesus' followers in grasping the connection between divine mission and shameful demise. This suggests that, even if the raw materials had been readily available, such a connection would not have been easy for even his closest followers.

With regard to the presence of interpretative resources, one can with relative ease sketch four interrelated traditions.

(1) The first is the tradition of the suffering of God's messengers, the prophets. The presumed destiny of divine prophets was consistently that of rejection and death (Neh 9.26; Jer 2.30; 26.20–23; *Jub.* 1.12), and it is not coincidental that Jesus both identified himself in prophetic terms and presaged his solidarity with the prophets in their having been spurned and killed (e.g. Mark 6.4; Luke 13.33; Matt 21.33–46). Importantly, within the prophetic tradition, rejection by those to whom the prophet was sent did not invalidate the prophet nor the message.

(2) The second is the tradition of the suffering righteous, with deep roots in the scriptures of Israel and ongoing development in the Second Temple period. Again, it is not coincidental that the synoptic gospels portray the death of Jesus in terms that reflect the influence of the pattern of the suffering righteous one. Indeed, the materials drawn from the Psalms of the suffering righteous are everywhere to be found on the terrain of the gospel passion narratives (see more fully Marcus 1995, esp. 206–09). See, for example, Table 6.1. Nor is it insignificant that the pattern embodied in the suffering righteous was itself shaped under the influence of Isaiah's portrayal of the suffering servant.

(3) One finds in significant strands of Second Temple Judaism the promise that the restoration of Israel as a people was related fundamentally to Israel's reconciliation to God and that Israel's deliverance would come by means of great suffering (already in Israel's scriptures – e.g. Isa 25.17–18; 66.7–8; Dan 7; 12.1–2; cf. *T. Mos.* 5–10; *Jub.* 23.22–31; 1QH 3; see further Allison 1985:5–25). Within these first three streams of tradition are the raw materials from within Israel's own story and traditions for the construction of a soteriology in which affliction might be understood not only as a condition from which to be delivered, but also as the means by which deliverance might come.

Table 6.1. *The Passion Tradition and Psalms of the Suffering Righteous*

Gospels		Psalms
Matt 26.3–4	gathered together and took counsel to kill	31.14 (LXX)
Mark 14.1 par. Matt 26.4	to kill by cunning	10.7–8
Mark 14.8 par. John 13.18	the one eating with me	41.9 (LXX)
Mark 14.61; 15.5; Luke 23.9	silence before accusers	38.13–14
Matt 27.34	offered gall	69.21 (LXX)
Mark 15.24	division of garments	22.18 (LXX)
Mark 15.29	mockery, head wagging	22.7 (LXX)
Matt 27.43	'He trusts in God. Let God deliver him!'	22.8
Mark 15.34	cry of abandonment	22.1 (LXX)

(4) Finally, the notion that the suffering of one person might have re-demptive benefit for the people has good precedent. One thinks immediately of the interpretative development of the Servant-figure in Isa 52.13–53.12 in texts related to the Maccabean martyrs (2 Macc 7.32–33, 37–38; 4 Macc 6.28–29; 17.22). Interpretations of this nature were available to Jesus and within Jesus' world, irrespective of whether one goes on to conclude that Jesus made explicit use of Isa 53 in utterances concerning his impending death.

Imagining the ensuing theology as a quilt will help to qualify this inter-pretation of the gospel material in three ways. First, as has already become clear, many pieces of patchwork from the story of Israel and its traditions have been stitched together with Jesus' career to form one whole, with the result that these two stories, Israel's and Jesus', become mutually interpret-ing. Second, this redemptive interpretation of Jesus' death does not depend on one image, one scriptural text, or one particular cord of Jewish tradition. Third, and perhaps most important, we do not need to insist that Jesus be-queathed this interpretative quilt to his followers in completed form. We may perceive creativity and innovation on Jesus' part in drawing together material stamped with the divine purpose and with suffering and repulsive death, while leaving room for Jesus' followers to add even more materials, more colours, more squares to the cloth.

It remains true nonetheless that Jesus' own disciples struggled with the nature of the life and message he lived before them and which culminated in his death. Jesus' death, however secure from the standpoint of strict historic-ity, was and is capable of many interpretations. Within the gospel tradition itself we find the story of two disciples from Emmaus who found in Jesus' crucifixion a confusing puzzle and apparent denial of their hopes that he would redeem Israel (Luke 24.19–21). The leaders of the people, the Jewish elite, must have regarded Jesus' ignominious demise as proof that he was no spokesperson for God. Jesus' disciples would find in Jesus' resurrection proof of a different sort, a validation of the message and ministry of Jesus, and, then, of the nature and significance of his death.

7 Resurrection

MARKUS BOCKMUEHL

RESURRECTION AND THE HISTORICAL JESUS

The preceding chapters of this volume have concentrated on Jesus of Nazareth as a first-century Jew – his background and beliefs, his words and works, his disputes and violent demise. Most contemporary Jesus books end here. And yet the striking fact is that without an event that occurred after his death, we would almost certainly have no information of any kind about Jesus of Nazareth. As a leading sceptic recently put it, 'The story of Jesus after his death is also part of his life, since it is only because of this history that we still know anything about him' (Lüdemann 2000:692).

Ironically, in the canonical sources the resurrection itself is nowhere described, never clearly defined, and quite diversely interpreted. Nevertheless, the New Testament writings unanimously agree on one thing: in some sense that was both inexplicable and yet unmistakable, Jesus was seen alive in personal encounters with his disciples soon after his death.

Our earliest written sources are Paul's letters to Thessalonica and Galatia. They date from around AD 50, but evidently appeal to a conviction that is already common ground (1 Thess 1.10; 4.14; Gal 1.1). Writing to Corinth five years later, Paul quotes verbatim from a fuller creedal tradition that may well date from the first decade after the crucifixion: having been dead and buried, Jesus 'was raised on the third day' and then 'appeared' in succession to Cephas (i.e. Peter), the Twelve, an unspecified group of 500, then to Jesus' brother James, and then to all the apostles together (1 Cor 15.3–7).

For the early Christians who received and passed on this tradition, it was by no means an afterthought, the requisite 'happy ending' to an otherwise heroic but sadly unsatisfactory life story. Instead, Paul and the other New Testament writers affirm the resurrection of Jesus as the defining and indispensable foundation of Christian faith:

> If Christ has not been raised, then our proclamation has been in vain and your faith has been in vain ... If Christ has not been raised, your

faith is futile and you are still in your sins . . . If for this life only we have hoped in Christ, we are of all people most to be pitied. But in fact Christ has been raised from the dead, the first fruits of those who have died. (1 Cor 15.14–20)

This paragraph is perhaps the most rhetorically forceful of such New Testament affirmations. In both form and logic, however, it merely restates what had long since become the common currency of Christian conviction – shared, as Wright (1996:658) rightly stresses, 'by all early Christians actually known to us (as opposed to those invented by modern mythographers)'.

Needless to say, 'history' and 'myth', truth and rhetoric, experience and interpretation all converge in any serious attempt to make sense of this extraordinary claim. It is therefore idle as well as inaccurate to treat it as a straightforward matter either of 'miracle', of 'myth' or of 'metaphor'. This nettle is not grasped by pseudo-scientific rationalism of either the apologetic ('who moved the stone?') or the sceptical variety (blithely poised in 'what we now know' about the power of collective autosuggestion or the like).

Nevertheless, what is perhaps most surprising is the extent to which contemporary scholarly literature on the 'historical Jesus' has studiously ig-nored and downplayed the question of the resurrection. To be sure, some authors connected with the widely publicised Jesus Seminar have obviously had a somewhat easier task in this respect, given their imaginative (but contextually most improbable) idea that Jesus' Jewish cadaver was simply discarded in the lime-pit or devoured by birds and stray dogs (so Crossan 1994:127, 154 and others). But even the more mainstream participants in the late twentieth-century 'historical Jesus' bonanza have tended to avoid the subject of the resurrection – usually on the pretext that this is solely a matter of 'faith' or of 'theology', about which no self-respecting historian could possibly have anything to say.

Precisely that scholarly silence, however, renders a good many recent 'historical Jesus' studies methodologically hamstrung, and unable to deliver what they promise. Quite what transpired on that third day after the cruci-fixion is of course a complex problem, in part no doubt beyond the remit of 'secular' historians. Nevertheless, it is a matter of historical record that *something* happened – and that this changed the course of world history like no other event before or since. In this respect, benign neglect ranks along-side dogmatic denial and naïve credulity in guaranteeing the avoidance of historical truth.

In all good historiography, there is of course a difference between an-tecedents and consequences; and it can be illuminating to study the former without constant reference to the latter. But it is only outcomes that render the mass of brute facts interpretable as history: only they make it possible to distinguish the salient from the trivial. Students of English history might be forgiven for ignoring the scruffy continental immigrant whose long and miserable Soho existence was finally laid to rest at Highgate cemetery on 17 March 1883. They might be forgiven, that is, if he had not been the author of *Das Kapital* – a work whose historical recognition and importance derives to a very large extent from developments after its author's death.

Thus also, *par excellence*, in the case of Jesus. As a humanitarian sage and political dissident, he remained a figure of negligible significance, ignored or scarcely mentioned in passing by a local historian like Flavius Josephus (see *Ant.* 18.63–4; 20.200). Judging from their own writings, even his disciples based their continuing loyalty solely on the events of that 'third day'. Without them, the apostles – like the adherents of every other first-century Jewish 'Messiah' – could only lament dashed hopes (Luke 24.21). But the effects of what transpired that first Easter were nothing less than revolutionary – in the words of one early author, 'a new birth into a living hope through the resurrection of Jesus Christ from the dead' (1 Pet 1.3).

Whatever one makes of such assertions, therefore, they merit serious investigation – not as a postscript, but at the very heart of any properly 'historical' assessment of Jesus of Nazareth.

THE RESURRECTION NARRATIVES: CONFUSION AND CONFLUENCE

The New Testament writers share a vested interest in the resurrection of Jesus, and a clear consensus on its veracity. And yet one is immediately struck by the degree of diversity and tension that characterises the Easter stories despite, or perhaps because of, that certainty. Aside from the Pauline passage cited earlier, only the four gospels offer an account of the resurrection in anything like a chronological sequence. They do agree unanimously on a few key features: after his public execution, Jesus is buried in the tomb of the Sanhedrin member Joseph of Arimathia. Two days later, this identifiable tomb is found empty by Mary Magdalene (and possibly other women disciples). Quite what happens then, however, can seem a jumble of excited claims and counter-claims that are not easily reconciled into one orderly narrative. We shall look briefly at each of the accounts.

In its earliest extant form, the Gospel of Mark has the briefest and most enigmatic narrative. Throughout the Gospel, both the resurrection of Jesus and the angel's message at the tomb are explicitly anticipated (8.31; 9.9,

31; 10.34; 14.28). And yet, the earliest attested text of Mark ends without resurrection appearances of any kind. Mary Magdalene and two others find the tomb open and encounter only 'a young man in a white robe', who asks them to tell the disciples that Jesus has been raised and will meet them in Galilee. The book ends abruptly with the women saying 'nothing to anyone' and fleeing in fear (16.8); Mark's Greek syntax reinforces that abruptness by the striking staccato of concluding on the particle *gar* ('for').

Given the evangelist's repeated anticipation of the resurrection (and of at least one appearance in Galilee, 14.28), he clearly does presuppose the truth of the angel's message: Jesus really has been raised. The story would collapse if readers either knew or suspected that the promise of 16.8 had remained unfulfilled. In view of this, some scholars accept that the astonishingly abrupt conclusion of the extant text may imply that another ending was intended, and perhaps lost. Others suspect that Mark deliberately enhances the suspense of the resurrection message at the tomb by continuing his customary secrecy theme and projecting the Easter reality into the reader's present. In the early second century, an editor added what became the canonical longer ending (16.9–20), attempting to resolve this tension by a summary of Jesus' appearances – first to Mary Magdalene (who *does* inform the disciples), then to two disciples 'walking into the country', and then before his ascension to commission the Eleven 'as they were sitting at table'. All three additional appearances are at least partly dependent on accounts in the other canonical gospels (cf. most recently Kelhoffer 2000).

In Matthew, Mary Magdalene and another Mary (the mother of James and Joseph, 27.56, 61) encounter an angel who has descended from heaven in the midst of an earthquake to roll back the stone and sit on it. He invites the women to see the empty tomb, and asks them to tell the disciples that Jesus is risen and will meet them in Galilee. On their way to carry out this instruction, they encounter Jesus in person, who repeats the same instruction. After an apologetic excursus about the chief priests buying the silence of a Roman guard placed at the tomb (28.11–15), the risen Jesus eventually appears to the Eleven on a mountain in Galilee and promises his abiding presence. In view of Peter's prominence in Matt 16.17–19, it is interesting that Matthew makes no mention of an appearance to him.

Luke 24 provides a rather fuller narrative of encounters with the risen Jesus, along with a clearer account of how they ceased. The whole account repeatedly stresses Jesus' fulfilment of Scripture, and describes appearances occurring seemingly on a single day in the vicinity of Jerusalem. Here, the women report the communication of *two* angels at the tomb as instructed. Like holy women in every age, however, these 'apostles of the apostles', as the church later called them, are at first dismissed by men as bearers of 'an idle tale' (24.11; cf. Nürnberg 1996; Theissen and Merz 1998:496–99). Peter himself then visits the empty tomb (with others? 24.12, 24). Two disciples on their walk to Emmaus hear Jesus expound his messianic fulfilling of the Law, Prophets and Writings while he walks with them – but ironically they recognise him only when he disappears during a shared meal. On their return to Jerusalem to report to 'the Eleven and their companions', they learn of an appearance to Peter that is not otherwise described (but cf. 1 Cor 15.5; John 21). Suddenly Jesus himself stands in their midst and reassures them that he is physically alive, eating fish in their presence. Disbelief gives way to joy (24.41, 52). After stressing yet again his fulfilment of the Old Testament, Jesus leads the disciples to the Mount of Olives. There he commissions them before withdrawing and being 'carried up into heaven' (24.51).

In Acts, Luke goes on to fill in some of the gaps in his earlier account. Here, the period of the resurrection appearances presents 'many convincing proofs' over a period of forty days (1.3), again explicitly confined to Jerusalem. This period terminates again in the ascension, an event described here in strikingly spatial terms: in full view of the disciples, Jesus is 'lifted up' and then taken out of sight by a cloud. A twelfth apostle is then chosen by lot as a witness of the resurrection. But while the resurrection of Jesus repeatedly features in subsequent apostolic preaching, the ascension story suspends all further earthly encounters with the risen Christ until the parousia (1.11). On each of three occasions (9.3–7; 22.6–10; 26.12–18), Paul's experience on the Damascus road is treated as a personal 'heavenly vision' (26.19), which his companions did not fully share (9.7; 22.9; 26.13–14). His subsequent ecstatic experience in the Temple is in fact the *only* time that Paul is said both to hear and to 'see Jesus' (22.18; cf. 26.14–15).

The Fourth Gospel, finally, has Peter and the Beloved Disciple racing to the tomb at Mary Magdalene's news, and finding in it only the rolled up linen grave-cloths. (For the Beloved Disciple, this is proof enough: 'he saw and believed', 20.8.) Mary Magdalene herself, lingering by the tomb, encounters the risen Jesus and initially mistakes him for a gardener. Even then, she is told not to hold on to him. Jesus later appears through closed doors to commission and bestow the Holy Spirit on the disciples – except Thomas, whose doubts he overcomes a week later by appearing again in his presence and expressly inviting him, unlike Mary, to touch his wounds. Chapter 21 provides an appendix with an added resurrection appearance at the Sea of Galilee, which involves a miraculous catch of fish and a meal, during which Jesus rehabilitates Simon Peter and appoints him as pastor of his flock.

We are thus left with considerable uncertainty surrounding the location and timing of the resurrection appearances, the persons involved and the body or form in which Jesus is assumed to appear. Tensions exist not merely between the different authors, but even *within* a given account such as Luke's or John's. On the one hand, old friends find it difficult to recognise the risen Jesus; he appears out of nowhere, passing through closed doors if need be, and just as suddenly disappears again. And yet, it is these *same* authors that stress the tangible reality of the disciples' encounter with a Jesus who talks with them at length, who walks and eats with them, and whose wounds are present to sight and touch. Some critics still typically suppose that these narrative features are gradual accretions, introduced by some sort of 'apologetic creep' to reassure doubters. But if that is the case, the evangelists seem to know nothing of it: Luke's rhetorical use of the tradition is far more overtly concerned with the fulfilment of Old Testament Scripture, and John's with the legitimacy of a faith that does *not* see (Luke 24.27, 44; John 20.29).

Matters are further complicated by the early tradition quoted in 1 Cor 15. Contrary to the consensus of the four evangelists, this text makes no explicit mention either of the empty tomb or of the women as the first to discover it – perhaps confirming the fact that women's witness tended to be discounted in an overtly male-oriented culture and legal system. At the same time, however, this tradition does list additional appearances to James (also in *Gospel of the Hebrews*, frg. 7) as well as to large numbers of people at once – 500 on one occasion and 'all the apostles' on another. The precise nature of these experiences is unspecified. It is significant, for example, that Paul's own interpretation of them allows him confidently to append his own encounter with the risen Jesus as the last, but fully analogous resurrection appearance. He 'saw' Jesus as no one after him did (1 Cor 9.1; 15.8), and he received an apostolic 'revelation' of Jesus (Gal. 1.16). The pre-Pauline tradition in 1 Cor 15 characterises the appearances by using a term (*ōphthē*) that could be taken either in a visionary or in a more concrete sense of 'seeing' (as perhaps in 1 Cor 9.1).

We are left, in the view of many scholars, with a jumble of irreconcilable differences. One popular critical view for the past two centuries has been to interpret talk of Jesus' bodily resurrection as the unnecessary and inconvenient product of a Jewish apocalyptic mind. A 'scientific' view of the world must interpret the phenomena described in the biblical accounts as individual and group hallucinations, whose context is presumed, whether for psychological or for religious reasons, to have been exceptionally prone to ecstatic and visionary experiences. Although anticipated in antiquity, this point of view came to be classically associated with nineteenth-century German critics. And it continues to attract some high-profile adherents (e.g. Goulder 1994; Lüdemann 1994; cf. Wedderburn 1999).

While harmonies of the different accounts have from time to time been attempted for apologetic purposes, none has gained widespread acceptance. Scholars have more typically tried to trace distinct source-critical 'family trees' (Catchpole 2000, Perkins 1984 and Osborne 1984 provide useful surveys). One popular reconstruction begins with 'tombless' visions, as compiled in 1 Cor 15, and the separate emergence of an initially 'appearance-free' empty tomb story, first in a pre-Marcan form and then as in Mark 16.8. The other evangelists then compile and develop the Marcan material in line with their distinctive redactional emphases. Thus, Matthew's narrative develops his Jewish apocalyptic eschatology and shows the risen Jesus as Lord of the church in its new mission to the Gentiles, while also countering Jewish opposition. Luke considerably enhances the physicality of the resurrection, and highlights Jesus' fulfilment of Scripture as well as the centrality of Jerusalem for the origin of a Spirit-filled mission of the church. John's account, marked throughout by his exalted christology, stresses the trustworthiness of the apostolic Easter testimony and its call to faith in Jesus as Messiah and Son of God, while also developing the complex relationship between the Beloved Disciple and Simon Peter. Beyond this, literary analysis traces apocryphal and Gnostic accounts with their increasingly elaborate development of the appearances and discourses of the risen Jesus. For scholarly reconstructions like this, the earliest tradition knew no empty tomb and no appearances. Once such stories had begun to accumulate, each new feature was formulated, sometimes more or less *ex nihilo*, to respond to the immediate apologetic and pastoral needs of the evangelist's respective community.

For the literary genesis of the gospel accounts, analysis along these lines can be illuminating. Historically, however, it can hardly be said to exhaust the matter at hand. Thus, for example, Paul cites the pre-formulated complex of 1 Cor 15.3–7 as a fundamental part of the catechesis he himself had received, long before his arrival in Corinth in the year 50/51 (note 15.1–3). This probably composite tradition adds to the creedal confession of Jesus' death and resurrection a list of trusted eyewitnesses who warrant the personal continuity between the dead and buried and the risen Jesus. Paul's glosses on the inherited tradition merely underscore that same continuity (15.6, 8); and as the chapter unfolds, it remains vital to his interpretation of the resurrection that both modes of existence are 'bodily'. Thus, although an affirmation of the empty tomb is not explicit, it would in any case be tautologous (cf. Wright

1999:119). Any known place of burial must have been empty: Paul's argument leaves no room for *any* form of Jesus' body to remain buried.

This tradition serves the apostle as reinforcing the indispensable importance of resurrection even for Gentile Christian faith. But he also applies it to a more wide-ranging discussion of Christian hope for the *general* resurrection, in analogy to that of Jesus. In that connection, we find a careful distinction between the perishable, 'natural' (*psychikon*; NB not 'physical') body of this world and the immortal, 'spiritual' (*pneumatikon*) one (15.42, 44) of the world to come: resurrection life here is inaccessible to 'flesh and blood' (15.50; cf. 1 Pet 3.18 and contrast Luke 24.39).

Commentaries and monographs provide a fuller account of these issues than we can offer here. We should note, however, that both the Pauline and the gospel evidence points pretty squarely to a tradition that, for all its confusion and diversity, converges on two dialectical characteristics. The New Testament writers affirm of the resurrection of Jesus both (1) that *it is an event in historical time and space*, and (2) that *it cannot be straightforwardly understood as an event in historical time and space*. The deliberate constellation of blatantly 'material' with 'spiritual' and transcendental aspects suggests a complex affirmation that is likely to resist reductionisms of any sort. To acknowledge this ambivalence is by no means 'antipathy to the crudely obvious' (cf. Alston 1997:182). Conversely, of course, it does subvert the hackneyed prejudice that notions of 'bodily' resurrection necessarily imply a preoccupation with reanimated corpses or, worse, a 'conjuring trick with bones'.

HISTORY AND WITNESS

This intrinsic polyvalence of the resurrection witness requires further comment. It is significant that the New Testament sources generally prefer a *testimonial* rather than an evidential approach. Luke, John and Paul are certainly committed to the factual nature of the resurrection, as established by 'convincing proofs' (so Acts 1.4). Nevertheless, it would be a banal misjudgement of the case to imagine the early Christians methodically compiling 'evidence that demands a verdict'.

Even on a sympathetic reading, the 'facts' are clearly far from self-interpreting. We know of many empty first-century tombs, many Messiahs who died a violent death, and many crucified men. (As was mentioned in the previous chapter, the skeleton of a certain Yoḥanan famously turned up in his tomb in the Jerusalem suburb of Givʿat ha-Mivtar with a nail still stuck through his ankles: cf. Zias and Sekeles 1985.) Ancient tomb robbery was a thriving industry; and as both Matthew (28.13) and John (20.13) already knew, an empty tomb can be interpreted in a variety of ways – not all of them self-evidently absurd.

The resurrection itself is nowhere described in the New Testament, although Matt 28.2 comes closest and apocryphal texts like the *Gospel of Peter* fill the silence with extravagant legendary embellishments. The canonical authors make no claim to be eyewitnesses – indeed it remains unclear if there *could* have been any. The Easter narratives repeatedly suggest a degree of difficulty or ambiguity in identifying the risen Jesus, even for close followers (Matt 28.17; Luke 24.16; John 20.14–15, 21.4); and the synthetic summary of the resurrection accounts in the longer ending of Mark speaks of him appearing 'in another form' (16.12). As a result, any synoptic reading of the different sources may leave us with considerable bewilderment about who saw what, where, when and how. Within the New Testament itself, too, the Easter encounters occasion both faith and doubt in the people who saw the risen Jesus and worshipped him (Matt 28.17, probably 'but they hesitated').

While the crucifixion was a matter of public record, the resurrection evidently was not. The reliability of the accounts is instead a matter of personal integrity: the early Christians proclaim not forensic 'evidence', but a trustworthy tradition based on fact and authenticated by apostolic eyewitness. As the Peter of Acts puts it, God granted Jesus to appear 'not to all the people, but to us who were chosen by God as witnesses, and who ate and drank with him after he rose from the dead' (10.41). It is the apostles, and only they, who are able and indeed 'commanded' to serve as guarantors of the resurrection tradition (10.42; cf. Acts 1.22, 25; 1 Cor 9.1; John 19.35; 21.24; 1 John 1.1–3).

This limits the tradition's public accessibility, but also the scope for unrestrained speculation and embellishment. It may be the case, as the Jesus Seminar's John Dominic Crossan (1991:426) famously opines, that 'if you cannot believe in something produced by reconstruction, you may have nothing left to believe in'. But it is hermeneutically truer to apostolic Christianity, and perhaps to life in general, that unless you are prepared to trust some faith community's embodied memory and witness, you can know nothing at all (cf. also Schüssler Fiorenza 1997:233–48). What is 'doubting' (*apistos*) about the Fourth Gospel's Thomas is not his desire for facts but his emphatic refusal to trust the apostolic testimony: '*unless* [I see and touch him], I *will not* believe' (John 20.25, 27, 29). (Even then, of course, he does not abandon the community of faith – and so is present to encounter Jesus the second time round.)

The New Testament documents are certainly in agreement on the truth and significance of the apostolic witness (note 1 Cor 15.11). In fact, it is precisely the excited confusion of their attestations, the narrative mayhem that pervades the variously redacted accounts even four or five decades after the event, which bears the most eloquent testimony to the force of their consensus (cf. Hoskyns and Davey 1981:282–84; the harmony of Mark 16.9–20 betrays the concerns of a later generation). Sanders (1993:280) captures this dimension well: 'Calculated deception should have produced greater unanimity. Instead, there seem to have been *competitors*: "I saw him first!" "No! I did."' It is in the Easter affirmation that these interpretations coalesce, suggesting a generative event of irreducibly colossal magnitude.

The apostolic writers, then, did not attempt to mount some sort of watertight 'proof' of the resurrection. But they evidently did find themselves confronted with a series of diversely experienced encounters that required interpretation and appropriation in profoundly theological terms. Their conclusions were reached not because the case was rationally unassailable or psychologically comfortable (to James and Paul, at least, it was not: cf. Catchpole 2000:210–14), but because the Jesus they encountered was now emphatically the Christ, teaching, preaching and converting them to faith. Significantly, the accounts show him appearing in almost every case to people who are as yet unbelievers, turning demoralised betrayers and defiant sceptics into empowered witnesses.

It is only on this level that we can begin to come to grips with the apostles' talk of 'resurrection'. Whatever transpired in Jerusalem on that 'first day', it was evidently so inexplicable and yet undeniable that it stretched inherited explanatory categories to breaking point – and ended up reconstituting the very centre of faith in the God of Israel.

WHY 'RESURRECTION'?

But why should first-century Jews find themselves compelled to use the distinctive language of resurrection in the first place? After all, the walking dead were a well-known phenomenon until the advent of modern medicine. Jesus, too, was credited with restoring newly dead people to life at Capernaum, Nain and Bethany (Mark 5.35–41 parr.; Luke 7.11–16; John 11.1–45). Some of his Jewish contemporaries had no difficulty believing that prophets recent or ancient might be 'raised from the dead' and walk among the living (cf. Mark 6.14–16, 8.28, 9.12 parr.; cf. e.g. 2 Macc 15.13–16; *b. B. Meṣiʿa* 59b). Apparitions of Moses and Elijah, both believed to have been bodily assumed to heaven, attended later Jewish teachers from R. Aqiba in the second century to Shabbetai Tzvi in the seventeenth (cf. e.g. Ginzberg 1909–38:4.193–235; Scholem 1973). Graeco-Roman stories, too, are familiar with the motifs of finding unexpectedly empty tombs whose occupants sub-sequently reappear alive and well (e.g. Chariton's probably second-century novel *Chaireas and Callirhoë*, Bk. 3). Similarly, various first-century heroes posthumously appeared to their followers, underwent apotheosis and even became the subjects of new and thriving cults (examples range from Roman Emperors to religious figures like Apollonius of Tyana).

Beginning no later than the second century, Christianity's critics made the most of such apparent parallels (see e.g. Origen, *C. Cels.* 2.55–58). Several of these serve as useful reminders of the extent to which popular cultural typologies of both Jewish and Graeco-Roman ruler cults would have lent themselves to the reception as well as the propagation of a resurrected and ascended Jesus (cf. Horbury 1998:109–52).

To be sure, none of these cases concerns someone publicly crucified as a common criminal. And, more importantly, none parallels the uniquely Jewish apocalyptic claim that the Easter events constitute Jesus' 'resurrection' in the sense of the inaugurated eschaton. In both Judaism and Hellenism, it was perfectly possible to conceive of the apparition or exaltation of a dead hero without needing to affirm either a bodily resurrection or the notion that this had inaugurated the life of the world to come.

Precisely the assurance of resurrection, however, is taken to authenticate Jesus as the messianic Son of David (Acts 2.31–36; 13.34–37; Rom 1.3–4; 2 Tim 2.8; Rev 22.16) and 'the firstfruits of those who have died' (1 Cor 15.20; cf. e.g. Matt 27.52–53; Rev 1.5). God has raised, exalted and established him as the Son of God empowered by the Spirit (e.g. Rom 1.4; Phil 2.19–10; Matt 28.18). To belong to this risen Lord is to share in 'indescribable and glorious joy' (1 Pet 1.8; cf. Luke 24.52; John 20.20), expectantly looking for 'the power of his resurrection' (Phil 3.10–11). It was the conclusiveness of the Easter events that made their interpretation so highly charged: 'We know that Christ, being raised from the dead, will never die again; death no longer has dominion over him' (Rom 6.9).

If nothing else, such hyperbolic theological language shows that the assertion of Jesus' resurrection departs in important respects from all known contemporary typologies for empty tombs, apparitions and apotheoses. The ancients knew full well that 'a ghost does not have flesh and bones' (Luke 24.39) and does not eat or drink, but that a resuscitated body might easily have and do all those things. And yet, neither of these perfectly familiar and acceptable categories is invoked by *any* of the diverse New Testament witnesses. The intense cultural idiosyncrasy of the resurrection claim is well worth underlining: insofar as this is history, it is history with a heavy Jewish Palestinian accent. Matthew's Roman guards, if they were indeed at the tomb and if they saw anything, would not and could not have described this in the apocalyptic language of 'resurrection' – be they adherents of the cult of the emperor, of Mithras or of Isis. Neither, of course, would 'resurrection' be a natural point of reference for their Sadducean paymasters, who are plausibly described as plotting to nip any supposed populist hocus-pocus well and truly in the bud (cf. Matt 27.62–66; 28.4, 11–15).

All of which returns us to our question: what, then, accounts for the apostolic interpretation of the events in the theologically charged and distinctive talk of 'resurrection'? The answer is, quite simply, that in the context of first-century Pharisaic and apocalyptic Judaism this was the only suitable terminology to name an astonishing reality. Here, then, unparalleled events occasioned a unique language – in principle no less striking in the first century than in the twenty-first (cf. Harvey 1994 on Mark 9.10). Rowan Williams (1996:91) rightly highlights the New Testament's 'gradual convergence of experience and pre-existing language in a way that inexorably changes the register of the language'. And for all its inalienable cultural specificity, the angelic announcement that 'He is not here, but is risen' encapsulates the only possible way in which Jewish followers of Jesus could explain the confusingly diverse and yet convergent experiences of absence and presence that followed his crucifixion.

If those experiences had been either purely visionary or straightforwardly material in nature, Palestinian Judaism had plenty of narrative and conceptual devices to signal that fact, as other cultures did. Certain Jewish visionary features do surface in the narratives, and may gain in poignancy from their Passover setting (cf. Lapide 1983:66–84, 99). But the plain sense of *all* the appearance accounts is nevertheless that the risen Jesus was *seen*, not 'visualised', as personally present (cf. Davis 1997:146; Chilton 2000b:230; cf. Lapide 1983:124–30). In the biblical sequence of post-Easter events, moreover, it is arguably the *ascended* rather than the newly risen Jesus who is properly seen in 'visions' (cf. similarly Farrow 1999:22).

The striking fact, at any rate, is that the New Testament authors do *not* resort to conventional categories. Paul and the gospel writers happily accommodate 'immanent' and 'transcendent' features side by side – perhaps because these twin modes of speaking the Easter mystery are complementary and interdependent. It is precisely Thomas's tactile Jesus who just a moment earlier has entered through locked doors (John 20.26)! In the end, the only available category big enough to fit the reality was the theocentric, eschatological affirmation of resurrection, one that is rooted in the living God, the Holy One of Israel: 'This Jesus God raised up' (Acts 2.32; cf. Keck 2000:137–44).

The Christian language of 'resurrection', then, is in the first instance the product of a specific time, place and culture. It was Jerusalem's religious conflicts and political machinations that made Jesus a victim of Roman torture and crucifixion. And it was in Jerusalem that he was first seen as risen from the dead – at once Jerusalem's victim and the vanquisher of Jerusalem's oppression (cf. Williams 1982:7–28). To translate this highly culture-specific message into another setting was always going to be a complex task, in the ancient as much as in the modern world. Luke plausibly shows Paul struggling to make himself understood to philosophers in Athens (Acts 17.18, 32), and the ancient church's pagan critics returned to this theme again and again (see e.g. Celsus in Origen *C. Cels.* 5.14; 6.29; cf. Stanton 1994a). And yet the apostles' commission and commitment to the Jewish truth of the resurrection went on to gain acceptance in the far-flung cultural and linguistic corners of the Empire.

THE HISTORY OF THE RESURRECTION AND THE MYSTERY OF THE CRUCIFIXION

We return, then, to the problem with which we began. Modern historical Jesus scholarship has had remarkably little to say about the historical dimensions of the resurrection, and about its significance for the overall footprint of Jesus of Nazareth. As we have seen, however, it is quite clearly at this point that the history of Christianity deliberately holds together the earthly identity of Jesus of Nazareth with that of the risen and ascended Christ. There are good reasons to interpret the resurrection as a theological affirmation rooted in historical fact – at a minimum, in the discovery of an empty tomb followed by variously described encounters with its occupant. Regardless of the precise view one may take on the *phenomenology* of this foundational event, its historicity was quite evidently the logical and psychological precondition for any sort of continued 'Christian' existence – a point that Pannenberg (1996) and others have often stressed. Without it, our sources would be silent: there could have been no abiding interest in either Jesus of Nazareth or the exalted Christ of faith.

This point casts doubt on the romanticism of liberal attempts, from Renan (1863) to the present day, to salvage something noble and admirable out of the plundered remains of an unresurrected Jesus. In that regard, the first-century Christian reasoning in 1 Cor is indicative of a remarkably sober realism, accessible to believer and unbeliever alike: 'If Christ has not been raised, your faith is futile and you are still in your sins. Then those also who have died in Christ have perished. If for this life only we have hoped in

Christ, we are of all people most to be pitied . . . If the dead are not raised, "Let us eat and drink, for tomorrow we die"' (15.17–19, 32).

Here, then, the conscientious historian – *qua* historian – is necessarily entangled in a matter of theological consequence. That entanglement is further reinforced by another factor, too often overlooked. The Jesus tradition itself persistently underscores the extent to which a doctrine of resurrection was in fact an important component of the historical Jesus' own eschatology, rooted in his interpretation of Scripture. One well-attested example is his refutation of the sceptical Sadducees, in good Pharisaic fashion demonstrating the resurrection from the Torah (cf. *m. Sanh.* 10.1). Here, interestingly, the state of the resurrected is said to be 'like angels in heaven' (Mark 12.25): and while the implied phenomenology should not be over-interpreted, the statement may bear out the New Testament's repeated placement of Jesus' own resurrection, ascension and parousia in the company of angels. Other eschatological sayings in different strands of the tradition either make explicit reference to the resurrection or, as in numerous Palestinian Jewish texts, presuppose it in connection with the final judgement.

At any rate, the substantive link between pre- and post-Easter Jesus tradition is a point not lost on the evangelists themselves. All four of them explicitly relate the meaning of the resurrection to the teachings of Jesus. This is perhaps most powerfully evident in Jesus' so-called 'passion predictions', which in virtually every case include an explicit reference to resurrection (Mark 8.31, 9.31, 10.34 parr.; cf. also Mark 9.9; 12.10–11; 13.26; 14.25, 28; Matt 12.40, 27.63; Luke 24.6–7, 46; John 2.20–22; 11.25).

It was at one time fashionable to dismiss these texts as late fabrications – invented out of thin air for the reassurance of doubting Christian minds, but unintelligible within the context of the earthly Jesus (see Brown 1994:2.1468–91 for a thorough survey and critique). And it is of course only plausible that such a story should gain in the telling, especially with the benefit of religious hindsight. A growing body of opinion, however, recognises in the pattern of righteous suffering and vindication an ancient and well-documented tradition of Second Temple Judaism. Suggestive Old Testament antecedents include Isaac in Gen 22, Job, Jonah, the righteous servant in Isa 53, the vindicated Son of Man in Dan 7, the murdered firstborn of the house of David in Zech 12.10–13.1, and Psalms like 22, 69 and 118. Passages like these, most of which have echoes in the gospels, suggest the outline of a theology in which the innocent sufferer's trust in God's abiding faithfulness finds approval and assurance of ultimate vindication – not just for himself, but vicariously for all his people. No one Old Testament passage fully accounts for that theology. But these biblical texts did engender a definite hermeneutical tradition, attested in literature from both the Second Temple and rabbinic periods (e.g. Wis 2; 2 Macc 6–7; 4 Macc 6, 17; 4Q225; cf. *b. Ber.* 56b; *b. Sukkah* 52a; *Pirqe R. El.* 31; cf. *Yal.* 575, 581 on Zech). The same tradition is also presupposed in a good deal of early Jewish–Christian controversy (e.g. Justin, *Dial.* 68, 89–90). And the much-queried claim that such vindication was to take place 'on the third day according to the scriptures' (1 Cor 15.3) may well find its basis in Hosea 6.2, which the Targum explicitly applies to the general resurrection.

If, therefore, the theme of a persecuted righteous person's redemptive suffering and vindication was a recognisable topic of Palestinian Jewish eschatology, then the authenticity of Jesus' resurrection predictions suddenly merits more serious discussion (cf. Bayer 1986; Evans 1999; also McArthur 1972) – especially as reinforced by his appropriation of the Danielic 'Son of Man' title (cf. Moule 1977:11–22). We may add, perhaps, that the Last Supper tradition offers further confirmation of this link in Jesus' mind. He connects his present suffering 'for many' with his future resurrection most strikingly in the Nazirite vow he takes on the eve of his arrest: 'Amen I tell you, I will never again drink of the fruit of the vine until that day when I drink it new in the kingdom of God' (Mark 14.25 parr.).

In other words, the apostolic Easter experiences actually converge with a recurrent theme in the ministry of Jesus to establish the resurrection in a curiously 'ex-centric' fashion as the key to the aspirations and the failure of the historical Jesus – both in his own view and in that of his followers. The career of Jesus of Nazareth calls for interpretation in relation to an event that in certain respects must be historical, but which nevertheless transcends history. Even before Easter, Jesus seems to have implied that his own violent demise would need to be interpreted back to front, as it were. He cast his fate deliberately within the scriptural framework of suffering and vindication. In that context, his death at the hands of his enemies could only be understood in the light of what would happen – or fail to happen – afterwards. Significantly, his followers continued to give dramatic expression to that correlation in their continued meal fellowship, meeting specifically 'on the first day of the week', the day of the resurrection, to commemorate Jesus' Last Supper and death and to participate in his presence in bread and wine (see e.g. Acts 20.7; 1 Cor 16.2; *Did.* 14.1; cf. 1 Cor 10.16; 11.23–27; Justin *1 Apol.* 65–7).

AN UPSIDE-DOWN METAPHOR

This integrative function of the resurrection of Jesus is consistently echoed and appropriated in the New Testament and patristic writings. The crucifixion is 'a stumbling block to Jews and foolishness to the Greeks' (1 Cor 1.23) – and without the resurrection, faith is known full well to be futile. Because of it, however, the cross can and does assume the redemptive significance in which Jesus envisaged it: in the words of one early tradition, 'he was handed over to death for our trespasses and was raised for our justification' (Rom 4.25). One may agree or disagree with that early Christian reasoning, but it is important to recognise it for what it is: an attempt to do interpretative justice to Jesus of Nazareth within the first-century world that he himself inhabited, and to identify the implications for his followers' life and faith. The New Testament writers needed no reminder that 'what we can *know* historically about Christ's resurrection must not be abstracted from the question of what we can hope from it, and what we have to do in its name' (Moltmann 1996b:80).

The resurrection, in other words, is indeed a metaphor, as is often said – but its function is quite the opposite of conventional metaphors. From Plato's cave to Lewis's Narnia, ordinary religious metaphors tend to employ the literal and familiar to speak (however truthfully) of an otherworldly reality. The New Testament witness to the resurrection of Jesus, by contrast, redescribes earth in terms of heaven and history in terms of eschatology.

For the early Christians, this marks the place in which God's world irreversibly invades the world of violence and corruption, planting *here* the flag of redemption. Heaven is no longer a metaphor of earthly bliss, or the world to come a pleasant postscript to mortality. Instead, Easter morning claims the redeemed cosmos as a metaphor of heaven, and transforms mortal life into the vestibule of paradise. The resurrection here constitutes the defining historical, moral and ecological reality that is the 'new creation' (cf. O'Donovan 1994; also Wright 1999:126–27). As Paul describes it, this is brought about by the self-giving reconciliation of the world in Christ, liberating forgiven sinners from bondage both suffered and self-chosen, and commissioning them as ambassadors of heaven (2 Cor 5.15–21). Similarly, the risen and ascended body of Jesus has sanctified, and promised to transform, the bodies of all those who belong to him: he will turn their humiliation and 'bondage to decay' into the freedom of divine glory, in the process destroying death itself (Rom 8.21–3; Phil 3.21; 1 Cor 15.26). This cosmic significance of the New Testament's Easter message is dramatically captured in the classic Orthodox Easter icons: the risen Jesus, ascending to heaven, reaches his hand to raise up the awaking dead.

The present chapter has highlighted the impossibility of 'bracketing out' the resurrection from any adequately historical account of Jesus and the birth of Christianity. It is only a small step from this insight to the realisation that the subsequent cultural and religious footprint of Jesus lies very much within the confines of what it might mean to understand him historically. Without the early Christian experience and proclamation of Jesus' resurrection, rooted in his own teaching, a Quest for the historical Jesus would be neither interesting nor, one suspects, even possible. As it is, however, Easter is an integral part of his story. Part II of this book must now rightly turn our attention to the study of that Quest, and to the story of prayer and praxis, mission and inquiry to which the resurrection faith gave rise.

Part II

The history of Jesus

8 Sources and methods

CHRISTOPHER TUCKETT

The aim of this chapter is to discuss the nature of the evidence available for discovering information about the 'historical Jesus' and how we might use that evidence. The phrase 'historical Jesus' is one that is potentially fraught with methodological problems (Meier 1991–94:1. 21–40). I am taking it here to mean (very crudely) Jesus during his earthly life in Palestine, without seeking to prejudge anything about the periods before or after that time. Any information we have about the historical Jesus will of course be limited by the nature of our sources. These give us Jesus as mediated through the eyes of others. Inevitably then one gets verbal portraits influenced by those who are relating them. To produce a 'real Jesus', untainted by the views of others and independent of the later pictures of him, is probably an impossible task. The 'historical Jesus' will in one sense only be 'the Jesus whom our sources enable us to reconstruct'. But that is one of the limitations within which all historical study must work.

SOURCES

The first general point to make is that our evidence for this 'historical' Jesus is almost exclusively *literary*. It consists of written *texts*. In other areas of study, ancient historians can often appeal to epigraphic or archaeological evidence. In the case of Jesus, none of this gives any direct information about Jesus himself. Such evidence can supply important information about the background of Jesus' life (e.g. on synagogues in Galilee, or on the general economic and social conditions of Jesus' environment). It occasionally supplies information about some details of early Christian history (e.g. the date of Gallio's proconsulship in Corinth [cf. Acts 18.12], which can now be dated fairly precisely via an inscription). But no such evidence has yet been found which relates directly to Jesus himself. We thus have to rely on the evidence of written texts.

Most if not all the relevant texts purport to give information about things said or done by Jesus. Further, few today would doubt that a key part of the evidence is to be found in the three 'synoptic' gospels of the New Testament. How we might use these texts, and whether we should privilege some parts of these texts over other parts, are questions I shall try to consider in the second part of this chapter. But first one or two more general remarks.

None of our extant written sources provides anything from Jesus' own hand. What we have for the most part is a number of collections of traditions about Jesus, written by other people, mostly some years after his lifetime. However, the work of Form Criticism on the gospels has shown us that individual traditions about Jesus were probably circulating orally for some time before such collections began to be formed, and indeed continued to circulate for some considerable time afterwards. We cannot therefore judge the historical value of an individual tradition simply on the basis of the date (or even necessarily the nature) of the collection in which it happens to come to light for us. Authentic traditions about Jesus may thus surface in later collections or texts.

We should also be aware of the way in which we seek to read the texts we have. Especially in relation to the New Testament evidence, there is now a plethora of different approaches on the scholarly market, including redaction criticism, 'literary' criticism, 'reader response' criticism etc. For the purposes of study of the historical Jesus, many of these may be of only indirect use at best.

The prime aim of such study is of course to try to discover reliable information about Jesus. Hence the relevant texts must be read '*historically*'. This means first that we must recognise that they come to us from a specific historical situation. (Hence some 'literary' or 'reader-response' approaches, which bypass the historical origins of the text and focus almost exclusively on the text as an independent artefact, are not appropriate here.) Second, we have to respect the fact that, for the most part, the relevant texts have the form of accounts of the activity of someone else (Jesus) prior to the time of the authors of the texts. The interests of the authors themselves (the focus of so-called 'redaction' criticism) may therefore be of importance, but often in order to discount such interests in seeking to get back behind the authors' narratives to the figure of Jesus himself. Our concern will thus be with the texts as sources for the history that lies behind them.

Virtually all the evidence we have has been preserved by Christians, all of whom clearly regarded Jesus in a positive light. That in turn makes for its own peculiar difficulties in handling the evidence, above all because it is potentially influenced by Christians' belief that the Jesus about whom they wrote had in some real sense been 'raised' from death by God and was now alive in their present. (This is not to deny that accounts of Jesus by others may be equally affected by their authors' beliefs and attitudes!)

Yet it is not quite the case that *all* evidence about Jesus is preserved for us by Christians. There is a very small amount of non-Christian evidence, and it is that which I consider first.

Non-Christian evidence
(Meier 1991–94:1.56–111; Evans 1994; Theissen and Merz 1998:63–89)

Evidence about Jesus can be found in later rabbinic sources as well as in two important witnesses, Tacitus and Josephus.

Rabbinic evidence

There are a few references to Jesus in rabbinic sources. The sources themselves are of course relatively late (fourth century or later), but they may preserve earlier traditions. One of the most famous is in *b. Sanh.* 43a which says that on the 'eve of Passover' Jesus was 'hanged' (almost certainly implying crucifixion); it goes on to say that Jesus was a magician who had 'led Israel astray'. If this is indeed a reference to Jesus of Nazareth, then it provides evidence of Jesus' existence, his execution and his 'miracle'-working activity (though interpreted here rather differently from the way it is interpreted in Christian sources).

Tacitus

The Roman historian Tacitus has one passing reference to Jesus. In his *Annals* 15.44 he records that the great fire of Rome was blamed by Nero on the 'Christians' in Rome. Tacitus notes that the name 'Christian' derives from 'Christus', a man who had 'suffered the extreme penalty during the reign of Tiberius at the hands of the procurator Pontius Pilate'. Tacitus' reference to Jesus is extremely brief, but it shows no evidence of later Christian influence and hence is widely accepted as genuine. It does then provide independent, non-Christian evidence at least for Jesus' existence and his execution under Pilate.

Josephus

The most important piece of non-Christian evidence comes from two brief references to Jesus in the work of the Jewish historian Josephus. The first is a passing reference in Josephus' account of the death of James, the brother of Jesus. In his *Ant.* 20.200, Josephus notes that James was 'the brother of Jesus who is called Christ'. Evidently Josephus thought that this helped to identify

James more readily, either because Jesus was well known to his readers or Jesus had been mentioned earlier in his work. The latter option may be relevant in seeking to evaluate the other reference to Jesus in Josephus' work. In *Ant.* 18.63–64, there is in all our extant manuscripts a short paragraph about Jesus:

> At this time there appeared Jesus, a wise man, *if indeed one ought to call him a man.* For he was a doer of amazing deeds, the teacher of persons who receive truth with pleasure. He won over many Jews and many of the Greeks. *He was the Messiah.* And when Pilate condemned him to the cross, the leading men among us having accused him, those who loved him from the first did not cease to do so. *For he appeared to them on the third day alive again, the divine prophets having spoken these things and a myriad of other marvels concerning him.* And to the present the tribe of Christians, named after this person, has not disappeared.

This so-called *Testimonium Flavianum* has given rise to enormous debate (cf. also p. 89 above). There is little doubt that it cannot have been written by Josephus in its present form: the language is too explicitly Christian for that. Many have therefore argued that the whole paragraph is a secondary addition to the text of Josephus, added by Christian scribes. However, others have argued that, if one deletes the most obviously Christian phrases (those in italics above), then the rest of the passage can be plausibly read as stemming from Josephus. If so, the text may provide further evidence from a non-Christian source for Jesus' existence and his crucifixion under Pilate (along with the witness that he had a following and was credited with performing miracles).

All this does at least render highly implausible any far-fetched theories that even Jesus' very existence was a Christian invention. The fact that Jesus existed, that he was crucified under Pontius Pilate (for whatever reason) and that he had a band of followers who continued to support his cause, seems to be part of the bedrock of historical tradition. If nothing else, the non-Christian evidence can provide us with certainty on that score.

Christian evidence outside the Synoptics

Among the Christian evidence, the prime sources of information about Jesus are usually assumed to be the New Testament gospels, those texts which purport to give 'direct' accounts of Jesus' life and teaching. We should however remember that, according to most conventional datings of the New Testament gospels, these texts are to be dated no earlier than the mid-60s of the first century. We certainly have Christian texts dating from earlier than this, viz. the letters of Paul. These letters do give us some information about Jesus, even if it emerges in an apparently less direct form than in the gospels. Nevertheless, the very early date of the evidence suggests that it should not be ignored.

Paul

Even if we had no other sources, we could still infer some things about Jesus from Paul's letters. Paul clearly implies that Jesus existed as a human being ('born of a woman' Gal 4.4), was born a Jew ('born under the Law' Gal 4.4; cf. Rom 1.3) and had brothers (1 Cor 9.5; Gal 1.19). Paul also claims possible character traits for Jesus (cf. 'meekness and gentleness' 2 Cor 10.1; Jesus 'did not please himself' Rom 15.3) and he refers to the tradition of the institution of the Eucharist at the Last Supper (1 Cor 11.23–25), taking place 'at night' (1 Cor 11.23). Above all, he refers very frequently to the fact that Jesus was crucified (1 Cor 1.23; 2.2; Gal 3.1 etc.), and at one point ascribes prime responsibility for Jesus' death to (some) Jews (1 Thess 2.15). He also occasionally explicitly refers to Jesus' teaching, e.g. on divorce (1 Cor 7.10–11) and on Christian preachers or missionaries claiming support (1 Cor 9.14).

The precise extent of Paul's knowledge of Jesus traditions is uncertain.[1] The fact that he knew some Jesus tradition is, however, indisputable. Further, the fact that this evidence is to be dated considerably earlier than the gospels suggests that it should be taken as potentially of equal importance, especially when the different witnesses disagree.[2] To take one example, Paul's version of Jesus' teaching on divorce in 1 Cor 7.10–11 is rather more open to the possibility that separation and divorce can occur than in the teaching ascribed to Jesus in Mark 10.1–12, where separation and divorce seem to be rejected out of hand.

As already noted, the New Testament gospels are often assumed to be the primary sources of information about Jesus. However, these four gospels are very different from each other. In particular, there are many differences between the three synoptic gospels and the Fourth Gospel. Few today would doubt that at least parts of the Synoptics give us some access to Jesus. What, though, of John's Gospel? How valuable is John as a witness to the historical Jesus?

The Gospel of John

It is widely believed today that John's Gospel is primarily a testimony to the beliefs and experiences of that Gospel's author (or his community) and provides at best a very indirect witness to the historical Jesus. For the most part this seems a justified conclusion. The reasons for such a view are manifold and certainly one cannot easily accept the historical reliability of both John and the Synoptics together.[3]

At the very least one must note the large number of differences between John and the Synoptics at many different levels. There are differences in terms of chronology and geography. Thus, in John, Jesus' ministry appears to last three years rather than one year; John has Jesus in Jerusalem for far longer than the Synoptics, e.g. the final period leading up to the crucifixion lasts one week in the Synoptics, six months in John. The date of the crucifixion in relation to the Jewish feast of Passover also differs: in the Synoptics Jesus dies on the feast day itself, while in John he dies on the eve of Passover.

Further, the whole style, manner and to a certain extent the content of Jesus' teaching differs when one compares John with the Synoptics. In the Synoptics, Jesus teaches for the most part in short units, making extensive use of parables, with little explicit reference to his own person and focusing on the importance of God and the coming (or present) kingly rule of God, the 'kingdom of God'. In John, Jesus teaches in much longer discourses with little use of parables, frequently focusing on himself as the true revelation of God (cf. the 'I am. . .' sayings). Moreover, virtually all talk of the kingdom of God disappears and the categories used by John's Jesus are predominantly those of 'eternal life', 'light' etc.

These differences make it very difficult to see both John and the Synoptics as equally accurate reflections of the historical Jesus. Most would agree that a focus on the kingdom of God, and extensive use of parables, are the most characteristic aspects of Jesus' teaching. Further, a move from a more original theocentric focus of Jesus' teaching (with God and God's kingly rule as central) to a later christocentric focus (on the importance of the person of Jesus himself) seems easier to envisage than the reverse process.[4] Hence the teaching of the historical Jesus is likely to be more accurately reflected in the synoptic tradition than in John's Gospel.

This does not mean that John's Gospel is historically worthless in terms of any quest for the historical Jesus. Some details of John's account appear more historically plausible than the synoptic accounts and may well be historical. For example, John's note that Jesus baptised people (John 4.1) may well be authentic and explain rather more readily why Christians adopted water baptism as their rite of initiation. Similarly, John's dating of the passion deserves serious consideration; and his picture of Jesus being in Jerusalem for considerably longer than the single hectic week implied by the Synoptics is inherently more plausible – and indeed may be implied by the words attributed to Jesus in the Synoptics themselves at his arrest (Mark 14.49: '*day after day* I was with you in the Temple teaching').

Some have also argued that, although much of the teaching in the Johannine discourses represents the evangelist's development of the tradition, there may well be potentially authentic sayings of Jesus embedded in these discourses and providing the springboard for that Johannine development (Dodd 1963; Lindars 1990). Nevertheless, it is not certain how much is gained from this in terms of additional significant information about the historical Jesus. For the most part, such potential 'nuggets' of sayings of the historical Jesus are only identified as such precisely because they cohere with the Synoptic presentation of Jesus' teaching. Hence any attempt to identify authentic traditions of Jesus' teaching in John in this way will simply reinforce the general picture already obtained from the Synoptics.

For the most part, John's Gospel offers us a profound reflection on the Jesus tradition from a particular author in a particular context. Nevertheless, the historical reliability of the gospel (in the sense of providing reliable information about the historical Jesus) may be rather limited.

Non-canonical evidence
(Meier 1991–94:1.112–66; Theissen and Merz 1998:17–62)

In addition to the New Testament texts, there is an appreciable amount of (Christian) evidence about Jesus to be found in non-canonical texts. And it has been a feature of some recent studies of Jesus to lay a considerable weight on some parts of this evidence.

Agrapha
(See Charlesworth and Evans 1994.) There are a number of (isolated) sayings of, or traditions about, Jesus recorded in a variety of places in Christian sources, e.g. in quotations from the church Fathers, as variant readings in the New Testament manuscripts, or in non-canonical texts (some of which will be considered below in this section). For example, one manuscript of Luke's Gospel (codex D) records an extra small incident of Jesus meeting someone working on the Sabbath, with the saying 'Man, if you know what you are doing you are blessed; if you do not you are cursed and a transgressor of the Law' (Luke 6.5 D). Similarly, some manuscripts of John's Gospel include at John 7.53–8.11 the story of Jesus and the woman taken in adultery. Both have no real claim to be part of the original texts of the gospels in which they now appear in some manuscripts, but they might represent 'floating' tradition with a good claim to authenticity.

However, the overall value of such sayings is uncertain. Almost all are isolated traditions; and judgements about their authenticity tend to revolve around their conformity (or otherwise) with the canonical synoptic tradition. Hence, as with possible traditional elements in the Johannine discourses, any such sayings judged authentic will almost *ipso facto* simply reinforce a picture of Jesus already gained from the synoptic gospels, and are unlikely to alter that picture significantly.

Non-canonical texts

In addition to isolated sayings, a number of non-canonical texts have been appealed to by some scholars in recent years as potentially containing material which is at least as good as, if not better than, the canonical gospels in preserving authentic Jesus tradition (Koester 1990; Crossan 1985; Crossan 1988; Crossan 1991). Among these are the *Gospel of Thomas* (*Gos. Thom.*), the *Gospel of Peter* (*Gos. Pet.*), the *Secret Gospel of Mark* (*Sec. Gos. Mk.*), Papyrus Egerton 2, and others (including the *Dialogue of the Saviour* and the *Apocryphon of James* from Nag Hammadi). There is not enough space to be able to discuss these texts in detail here. It should however be noted that most of them are very fragmentary and provide only a small amount of material. The extent of any evidence they might provide for information about Jesus is thus inevitably limited.

This applies particularly in the case of Papyrus Egerton 2, *Sec. Gos. Mk.* and *Gos. Pet.* Further, although some have argued that these texts might represent (or, in the case of *Gos. Pet.*, contain) sources earlier than our canonical gospels (so Koester, Crossan), others have claimed that they represent later, secondary rewritings of the tradition, presupposing the existence of the canonical gospels, e.g. by showing knowledge of the redactional work of the canonical evangelists (Neirynck 1991; Charlesworth and Evans 1994; for *Sec. Gos. Mk.*, Merkel 1974; for *Gos. Pet.*, Brown 1987).

The Gospel of Thomas

Potentially the most significant of all the non-canonical texts for study of the historical Jesus is the *Gospel of Thomas*. It is one of the most extensive such texts and, ever since its discovery, has generated much discussion. Fragments of the gospel had been known since the start of the twentieth century through three Oxyrhynchus fragments (POxy 1, 654, 655). The full text was discovered in 1945 as one of the texts in the Nag Hammadi library. The text consists of 114 apparently unconnected sayings of Jesus, prefaced by a bald 'Jesus said', with no narrative framework, no passion narrative and no other 'biographical' information.

Many (though not all) of the sayings in the *Gospel of Thomas* have a parallel in the synoptic tradition and there has been intense debate about the precise relationship between *Thomas* and the canonical gospels. Other sayings of *Thomas* have no parallel in the canonical gospels, raising the possibility that these sayings might provide us with possible further authentic Jesus material to supplement the canonical material.

On all these matters there has been no scholarly unanimity. Some have maintained that the *Gospel of Thomas* does indeed provide us with an independent, and early, line of the Jesus tradition (Crossan 1985; Koester 1990; Patterson 1993); others have argued that *Thomas* represents a later, post-synoptic development of the tradition dependent (at perhaps more than one stage removed) on the Synoptics (Tuckett 1988; Uro 1998). Needless to say, the evidence is ambiguous and can be interpreted in different ways.

For some, a key piece of evidence is that the order of the sayings in the *Gospel of Thomas* appears to bear no relationship to the order of the same material in the synoptic gospels. This, it is argued, tells heavily in favour of the independence of *Thomas*. On the other hand, the different order of *Thomas* might be based on thematic or catchword connections, thus simply reflecting *Thomas*' own method of composition.

Sometimes the *Gospel of Thomas* also appears to represent a more original form of a saying or tradition than that of the canonical versions. (The versions of the parable of the wicked husbandmen in Mark 12.1–9 parr. and *Thomas* 65 are often cited in this context.) However, clear unambiguous criteria for determining what constitutes a more original form of the tradition are not easy to come by. At other points it seems clear that *Thomas* shows links with material in the Synoptics that is redactional. The saying in *Thomas* 5 has a parallel in Luke 8.17 ('there is nothing hidden that will not become manifest'). Moreover, this saying is extant in one of the Oxyrhynchus fragments, so we have a Greek version available. In this case the *Gospel of Thomas* agrees verbatim (in Greek!) with Luke 8.17, which is Luke's edited version of Mark 4.22. *Thomas* thus agrees with Luke's redacted version of the saying. This seems to be clear evidence that, at this point at least, *Thomas* presupposes Luke's finished Gospel. And indeed at a number of other places *Thomas* seems to presuppose versions of the same sayings as redacted by the synoptic evangelists (Tuckett 1988).

On the other hand, we must not forget that we only have the text of most of the *Gospel of Thomas* available in an indirect form, viz. as a translation from Greek into Coptic. It may well be that, at some stage, the canonical versions of the relevant sayings influenced the transmission of the text of *Thomas*, so that some assimilation to the canonical versions may have taken place as the text was handed on and translated. Further, the nature of the evidence is such that one should probably treat each saying (or even each part of each saying) separately. What applies in one case may not apply in another. Hence one saying in *Thomas* may be independent of the canonical gospels and another dependent.

The problem posed by the *Gospel of Thomas* is probably ultimately insoluble. It seems clear that, at least in the form of the text we have, some influence of the canonical gospels has taken place. Moreover, that influence seems to have affected a substantial part of the text. I would incline to the view that *Thomas* as a whole is to be treated as a witness to the later, post-synoptic development of the Jesus tradition (without being any the worse for that); and hence in cases where the canonical gospels and *Thomas* have parallel versions, the latter is more likely to be secondary.

Nevertheless, this does not preclude the possibility that the *Gospel of Thomas* may preserve other genuine sayings of Jesus. The saying in *Thomas* 82 ('he who is near me is near the fire; he who is far from me is far from the kingdom') is independently attested in Origen (*Hom. Jer.* 20.3) and Didymus the Blind (*Comm. Ps.* 88.8). And its startling implicit claims about Jesus himself, as well as its focus on the kingdom, make it at least plausible to regard the saying as an authentic one (though there is no unanimity on this).

Traditions about Jesus are available in a wide range of sources. For the most part, our main sources remain the synoptic gospels of the New Testament, with potentially important sources provided by texts such as *Thomas* and Paul's letters. The question still, however, remains: how should we use the evidence that is available to try to discern features of Jesus himself within or behind this body of evidence? What methods should we use? What criteria should we employ?

METHODS

We have seen that almost all our available evidence for Jesus is preserved by Christians. As with all those writing about the past, such Christians were doubtless influenced by their own situations and beliefs. In particular, belief in Jesus' resurrection may have led some Christians, convinced that Jesus was still alive and speaking to the present, to put on to Jesus' lips things that they believed were being said by Jesus in the present. The extent of such activity by Christians is uncertain. However, the fact that Christians did feel free at times to rewrite parts of the Jesus tradition and make it more relevant to their own day seems undeniable, especially in the light of the evidence of the gospels themselves.

The synoptic gospels are so similar that they can be viewed alongside each other and compared, both in relation to their order of events and their detailed wording. Yet they are by no means identical. The evangelists have evidently felt free to rewrite the material in their own way. Similarly, John's Gospel indicates that the fourth evangelist acted in the same way to an even greater extent.

The synoptic problem

We must also note, however, that not all our sources are independent of each other. In particular, the similarities between the three synoptic gospels virtually demand that there is a *literary* relationship between them. There is no space here for any detailed discussion of the synoptic problem, the problem of determining the precise nature of this relationship. The most widely held solution today is some form of the 'two-source theory': Mark's Gospel was used as a source by Matthew and Luke; in addition, Matthew and Luke used another (no longer extant) source or source materials, usually known as Q. Thus our three synoptic gospels represent two primary sources, Mark and Q.[5] In addition, Matthew and Luke have further material peculiar to each Gospel, so-called M and L material.

For study of the historical Jesus, the implications of such theories should be clear. If all three gospels have a version of the same saying or story, and if Matthew and Luke have used Mark, then it is primarily the Marcan version of that saying or story that we must use as (possible) evidence for Jesus. The other two versions tell us more about how the later evangelists have adapted the tradition in the light of their own concerns. Similarly, in relation to Q material, if Matthew and Luke alone have a tradition in common, then whichever is judged to be the earlier of the two versions will be closer to the historical Jesus.[6]

Such a procedure will not necessarily lead us straight back to the historical Jesus. Earlier, I contrasted John and the Synoptics to show how John had probably changed many facets of the tradition. However, it is now clear that, in general terms, one cannot drive too much of a wedge between John and the Synoptics in this respect: the synoptic evangelists themselves also adapted the tradition in the light of their own beliefs and experiences. One can see this happening quite clearly in the way Matthew and Luke used Mark and the Q material. Similarly, Mark's Gospel is almost certainly influenced by Mark's own situation and beliefs. So too, many have argued in recent years that the Q tradition has its own distinctive characteristics, shaped perhaps by the experiences of the Christians who preserved it (Tuckett 1996; Kloppenborg Verbin 2000). In seeking to recover information about the historical Jesus, we cannot then simply repeat all the material in our sources, or even just in our earlier sources (Mark and Q), since this may reflect the authors or editors of those sources more than the historical Jesus himself. (We must also remember our earlier observation that authentic traditions may surface only in later texts.) Certainly in recent years very different reconstructions of the historical Jesus have been proposed by focusing on different parts of the synoptic evidence (and perhaps some of the non-canonical evidence) as providing the authentic core of the tradition.

Criteria

In the course of scholarly discussions about the historical Jesus, a number of different criteria have been proposed for identifying authentic material in the gospels and there has been a great deal of critical debate about these criteria. (More detail in Meier 1991–94:1.167–95; also Walker 1969; Hooker 1971; Stein 1980; Boring 1988.) Although long lists can be produced, several criteria may overlap with each other. I therefore consider here a few general headings.

Dissimilarity

One of the most famous criteria is that of 'dissimilarity'. This argues that if a tradition is dissimilar to the views of Judaism and to the views of the early church, then it can confidently be ascribed to the historical Jesus. Much has been written about this criterion. There seems little doubt that, if any tradition can pass the stringent conditions laid down, that tradition will have as good a claim as any to be regarded as authentic. Nevertheless, the criterion has some problems.

First, it assumes that we know enough about both first-century Judaism and 'the early church' to be able to say with confidence what might be 'dissimilar' to either of these two entities. In fact it has become all too clear over the years that our knowledge both of Judaism and of 'the' early church is extremely sketchy. Any over-confident use of the dissimilarity criterion thus may presuppose far more knowledge of Judaism and the early church than can really be justified.

Second, it is unclear if anything in the Christian tradition could ever in fact pass this criterion. For the very existence of a tradition indicates that it has been preserved, implying that it was congenial to someone somewhere in the early church. The very existence of the tradition may thus militate against its being regarded as 'dissimilar' to the views of 'the early church'.

Third, *if* anything can get past the barrier set by the criterion, it is uncertain how historically valuable the resulting portrait of Jesus will be. Especially if taken on its own, the criterion is in danger of producing a highly distorted, or skewed, picture of Jesus. Above all it is in danger of cutting Jesus off somewhat implausibly both from his roots in Judaism and from the Christians who followed him and his cause subsequently. One of the few things that can be doubted about Jesus is that he was a first-century Jew. Yet the dissimilarity criterion refuses to accept as authentic anything that would make Jesus similar to first-century Judaism. Similarly, it is clear that others, who claimed to be his followers, later continued Jesus' cause. To deny any common links between Jesus and his later followers, by refusing to accept as authentic anything that serves to link the two as 'similar', is equally implausible.

In a recent monograph, Theissen and Winter (1997) have argued persuasively that in fact 'the' dissimilarity criterion is really two different criteria: the questions of any dissimilarity with Judaism and with early Christianity should be separated. Further, Holmén (1999) has shown that it is really only the latter that should be relevant in any discussion about the possibility of Jesus tradition being created by later Christians. Any such activity by post-Easter Christians might wish to make Jesus similar to the concerns of early Christians, but would not necessarily be concerned to make Jesus similar to Judaism *per se*.

In the light of some of these dangers and criticisms, few today would advocate an exclusive application of the dissimilarity criterion alone. Indeed it has been a feature of the more recent studies of the historical Jesus (sometimes called the 'Third Quest'; see chapter 9 below) to situate Jesus firmly within a Jewish context. Hence traditions that make Jesus 'similar' to Judaism might *ipso facto* be regarded as more likely to be authentic than inauthentic. To say that the dissimilarity criterion has been totally discredited would be too strong. Nevertheless, scholars today are far more aware of its limitations and its dangers.

Coherence

As a result of some of the deficiencies of the dissimilarity criterion being recognised, a criterion of 'coherence' has been proposed. This proposes the authenticity of traditions that 'cohere' with other traditions already accepted as authentic (e.g. by the dissimilarity criterion).

This criterion too can be criticised. If (as was the case when originally formulated) it is coupled with the dissimilarity criterion, it is in danger of simply perpetuating the distorted picture of Jesus from which one starts. Further, 'coherence' is not necessarily easy to quantify and is inevitably rather subjective. So too one must note that what is coherent is not necessarily always historically accurate. Good fiction is often just as 'coherent' as historical fact.

Multiple attestation

One criterion always mentioned in this context is that of multiple attestation. This argues that if a tradition is attested in more than one strand of the tradition, it is more likely to be authentic. 'Strands' of the tradition must here be taken as *independent* layers of the tradition. As already noted, the three synoptic gospels themselves are almost certainly related to each other. If a tradition appears in all three gospels, this does not necessarily indicate that the tradition is multiply attested: the appearance of the tradition in Matthew and Luke is simply due to their dependence on Mark. But if a tradition appears in Mark and Q (assuming that Mark and Q are independent of each other), then this can count as multiple attestation.

As with all the criteria, this one to is open to debate, partly in relation to what it affirms, partly in relation to what it might deny.

The criterion may in fact not be very helpful in detail: for relatively few individual units of the tradition are attested in more than one strand (unless one counts the *Gospel of Thomas* as independent: see below). However, the criterion might be more readily applicable in relation to broader themes, e.g. Jesus' teaching about the kingdom of God, his use of parables, his choice of a group of twelve, etc.

Multiple attestation on its own cannot necessarily guarantee authenticity. The fact that a tradition is multiply attested may simply show that it goes back to an early stage of the tradition, prior to say Mark and Q. But that does not exclude the possibility of creation by Christians at this relatively early stage.

One must be wary too of assuming the converse of the criterion and regarding as inauthentic anything that is not multiply attested. In fact, as already noted, relatively few individual traditions may be multiply attested. For example, the so-called 'M' and 'L' material is by definition not multiply attested. Yet it would be premature to assume that this material is *ipso facto* inauthentic. Some parts may certainly have as high a claim to authenticity as any, (despite?) being preserved in just one strand of the tradition (e.g. the parable of the Good Samaritan in Luke 10.29–36).

The dangers of a possibly one-sided application of the criterion may be seen in the influential work of Crossan (1991) on the historical Jesus. Crossan effectively couples an appeal to multiple attestation with a detailed dating of the sources, and claims that the primary evidence for Jesus is to be found in material that is multiply attested in the earliest independent sources.

There is no space here to enter detailed discussion (see further Tuckett 1999). However, Crossan's method makes a number of questionable assumptions. He assumes, for example, that the *Gospel of Thomas* is an independent source. Further, he claims that behind both Q and *Thomas* are earlier layers of both sources, each of which is to be dated in his earliest period (up to AD 60). By contrast, the canonical gospels are not divided into strata or sources (apart from the Q material) and they are dated in a later period (post-60). As a result, it is the traditions attested in both Q and *Thomas* that have priority in Crossan's reconstruction, where Jesus is presented as a 'Cynic Jewish peasant'.

The datings are uncontroversial (though by no means certain: can we confidently date Q?), though the division of Q and *Thomas* into strata is debatable, as is the claim that *Thomas* is an independent source. More questionable, too, is the decision (a) to apply source-critical distinctions to some, but not all, of the texts we have; and (b) to apply considerations of date to the texts. Certainly it is not clear why traditions that were (according to our limited, extant evidence) first collected in Q should be given priority over those that were first collected in Mark or in Luke's 'L' material.[7] Further, the chronological divisions proposed are a little arbitrary: why should a great divide come at exactly AD 60 so that Q (dated prior to 60) is regarded as qualitatively different from Mark (dated post-60)? Such an approach, using multiple attestation to privilege some parts of the tradition over against other parts, probably goes beyond what the criterion can bear.

Jesus in his Jewish context

Another criterion (sometimes effectively divided into a number of separate criteria) refers to the extent to which any tradition about Jesus coheres with his Jewish context. One of the indisputable facts about Jesus is that he was a first-century Jew, living in first-century Palestine. Anything he said and did must therefore make sense within the religious, social, cultural and linguistic milieu of that context.

In practice such a criterion has been applied at a number of different levels. For example, forms of sayings of Jesus (e.g. parables) that presuppose the social conditions of a first-century Palestinian milieu are to be preferred over against those that do not. Similarly, at the level of language: Jesus (probably) spoke Aramaic, and hence Semitic features in the Greek language of the sayings recorded in our gospels are also perhaps an indication that we may have authentic material.

As with all the criteria, this one can also be criticised if applied too woodenly. The fact that a tradition reflects a Palestinian milieu, socially or linguistically, may only show that it originated in such a milieu. But we should not forget that Jesus was not the only person in first-century Palestine; nor was he the only Aramaic speaker of his day. Hence such features in the tradition are not necessarily guaranteed as authentic: they might have originated in an early (or indeed later) Christian milieu within Palestine or in an Aramaic-speaking environment.

So also we should be wary of assuming too readily that everything Jesus said or did fits neatly into a Semitic or Palestinian environment. We saw that the dissimilarity criterion is in danger of cutting Jesus off from his Jewish environment; but there is perhaps an equal danger of fitting Jesus too 'cosily' into his environment. Clearly at one level Jesus did not 'fit' his Jewish context. He was, after all, crucified: however much Jesus was a Jew and spoke and acted within a Jewish context, he also challenged many aspects of that context. So too, at a slightly 'lower' level, some of Jesus' parables may have reflected the social conditions of his time very well; but at some points the parables may have portrayed things in a way that was deliberately *not* 'true to life', and it was precisely this that enabled them to make their point.

The cross

The last point relates to the final criterion to be suggested here. One of the indisputable facts about Jesus is that he was crucified. The exact reasons for Jesus' death are notoriously difficult to determine. Nevertheless, however much we make Jesus part of his social and cultural context, one has to try to explain why Jesus was in the end rejected by at least some of his contemporaries so that he was subjected to the most degrading and cruel method of execution ever devised. It is perhaps one of the strongest criticisms to be brought against many of the nineteenth-century liberal Protestant lives of Jesus that they made Jesus into such a 'nice chap' that it becomes virtually impossible to conceive how anyone could have taken exception to him. Any proposed reconstruction of Jesus has to be a Jesus who was so offensive to at least some of his contemporaries that he was crucified.

Perhaps all these can be summed up in an overarching criterion of 'plausibility' (Theissen and Winter 1997). Any reconstruction of Jesus must show that it is 'historically plausible' in the widest sense of the phrase: it must cohere with, and make sense of, all the evidence we have. Jesus thus has to be seen as making sense within a context of first-century Judaism in Galilee and Jerusalem; but he must also be seen as standing out against at least sections of that overall context sufficiently strongly to explain his violent death. His life and teaching must be such that the written accounts which eventually emerged are explicable: hence any reconstruction which relies too heavily on one strand of the tradition only (e.g. the Q material) may be regarded as a little suspicious.

The nature of the evidence inevitably means that a variety of different portraits of Jesus can be, and have been, offered. Evaluating them, and perhaps seeking to work out one's own, remains a perennial task for all who remain fascinated by the figure who has so profoundly affected human history.

Notes

1. The situation is made complex by a number of places where Paul's language is similar to that ascribed to Jesus in the Gospels, but where Paul gives no indication that he is aware that he might be alluding to Jesus tradition: cf. Rom 12.14, 17; 13.7; 14.13; 1 Thess 5.2. See Walter 1989; Dunn 1994.
2. This is not to imply that an earlier source is *ipso facto* 'better'. But Paul's evidence here should not be ignored (as it is sometimes in danger of being, as it appears to be less 'direct').
3. By 'historical reliability' I mean the extent to which the accounts represent accurately things said or done by Jesus during his earthly ministry. How far John represents a 'theologically valid' account is quite another matter and would have to be decided on quite different criteria.
4. Without wishing necessarily to subscribe to any simplistic model of a unilinear, uniform development from a 'low' to a 'high' Christology, it still seems hard to envisage an original form of the tradition with a very open, high Christology being changed later and virtually all the openly christological elements omitted.
5. Needless to say, this solution is by no means universally held today: some would hold to J. J. Griesbach's theory (Mark came last and used both Matthew and Luke: e.g. W. R. Farmer); others would support Marcan priority but would deny the existence of Q, maintaining that Luke knew Matthew (M. D. Goulder).
6. For advocates of other solutions to the synoptic problem, the details of the argument will have to be changed, but the basic point remains the same: different versions of the same tradition in our Gospels cannot all go back to the historical Jesus. In this I would distance myself from the approach of e.g. Wright, who tends to dismiss appeals to a developing history of the tradition within the Synoptics somewhat prematurely.
7. Cf. p. 122 above on form criticism and the possibility of authentic traditions surfacing in later texts.

9 Quests for the historical Jesus

JAMES CARLETON PAGET

There are a number of reasons for giving an account of the history of the study of the historical Jesus. One is straightforwardly practical. By examining the history of the study of any subject, it is possible that desiderata in research will emerge more clearly. This is the aim of all those histories of research through which one customarily enters the body of a standard monograph. A related purpose emerges from the belief that by exposing the major fault-lines in such study, one will be better able to grasp the nature and character of the problem under discussion.[1] A third reason arises out of a desire to emphasise the historicity of the study of the subject itself. Motives for such a desire vary. Some have their roots in a certain '*pietas*' towards the work of predecessors in the field. Scholarship is a collective enterprise, and academic predecessors are part of the collective.

Other motives are less obviously positive. An appreciation of the historicity of the study of a subject can be used to question the assumption that matters have somehow progressed. Such an approach takes one of two forms. One form involves the narrator of the history demonstrating the tendency for the same problems and, broadly speaking, the same solutions to recur. The implication here is polemical, encapsulating the appropriately biblical sentiment that 'There is nothing new under the sun', with perhaps an accompanying call for a new approach that will apparently lead the scholarly world out of the perceived impasse. The other form is found in histories of research in a postmodern or (perhaps more accurately) relativistic mode. In such a procedure the aim is to show how each generation of scholars has inevitably presented solutions to the subject which themselves reflect the wider cultural concerns of the society from whence they hailed. Here again notions of progress in the study of a particular subject become questionable.

Of course, to claim that these aims are mutually exclusive would be wrong. They can combine in different ways – as they do, for instance, in Albert Schweitzer's account of the story. My hope in what follows is that some of the major issues in historical Jesus research will become apparent, and that some of its shifts of emphasis will become clear. Some attempt will be made to show that the recent tendency to divide the study of the subject into particular phases (with our present phase the so-called 'Third Quest'[2]) is too neat – and that there is a tendency for historical Jesus scholarship to repeat itself. In light of this, I shall address in skeletal form the question of progress in such research, commenting on where we have got to and what the future should and might hold.

A NARRATIVE

Any attempt at introducing a narrative of the 'Quest' has to contend with the basic problem of origins: where to begin one's story. Different authors have begun their accounts at different points. So, for instance, Schweitzer began his own story with J. S. Reimarus' essay 'On the Aims of Jesus and his Followers', published posthumously in 1778. He did so partly because he saw the roots of historical Jesus research as having their origin in anti-dogmatism, which he perceived first to be exemplified in Reimarus' essay.[3] Others who wrote before Schweitzer began at different points, although Schweitzer's starting point,[4] not without its critics, continues to have a number of supporters.[5]

Much of the problem, as implied above, lies in how one understands the subject. If, contra Schweitzer, one perceives the Quest in terms simply of an interest or a concern with the figure of Jesus as he lived and died, it is difficult to deny that it was with the Christian church from a very early stage. The presence of the gospels in the New Testament canon is in some sense evidence of this, however we perceive their authors' concern for historical accuracy (Keck 2000:3). This broad-based concern for Jesus as a historical figure is similarly exemplified in the apocryphal gospels with their desire to fill in apparent gaps in the canonical gospels' account of Jesus' life. It recurs in a slightly different way in pilgrimage to Palestine, evident from at least the second century, and increasing in the fourth and fifth, in which pilgrims showed a strong interest in the geographical references of the gospels. More abstractly, the church's firm commitment to the fact of Jesus' earthly life was evidenced in many Christians' opposition to docetism, a lurking presence from earliest times, and given verbal expression in a variety of definitions of Jesus' person, culminating in Chalcedon (see chapter 13 below).

Of course, what we lack in the previous discussion is evidence of some kind of critical engagement with the gospels as reliable witnesses to the 'brute facts' of Jesus' life. Antiquity hints at such a thing. Papias' comments about the order of Mark's Gospel (in Eusebius *Hist. eccl.* 3.39.15) imply the existence of some critical engagement with that Gospel. The second-century Tatian's *Diatessaron* can to a limited degree be regarded as a response to the discrepancies between the gospels, as can observations of certain church writers on the differences between John's Gospel and the Synoptics, in particular in their opening chapters.[6] But if by 'critical' we mean 'doubting' or 'negative', then there is some evidence of this from the second half of the second century. So in this respect we might point to the pagan Celsus' harshly critical discussions of the gospel accounts of Jesus' birth, baptism, death, resurrection, miracles and teaching, and his accompanying revisionist account of Jesus' life preserved in Origen's *Against Celsus* (Wilken 1984:108–12), as well as the late third-century Porphyry's even more fragmentarily preserved attack upon the gospel's historical integrity. The latter in particular emphasised the disharmony between the gospels and was keen, it appears, to point up the unreliability of the disciples' witness to Jesus. It is possible that Augustine's lengthy *De Consensu Evangelistarum*, which was in the main an extended attempt to defend the gospels against the charge of disagreement amongst themselves, was partly a response to Porphyry's criticisms (Wilken 1984:144–47). Certainly Augustine's work, which took further a project begun by Tatian, makes clear the importance Christians ascribed to these historically based attacks upon their faith.

The medieval period saw less interest in defending or attacking the gospels as legitimate historical sources, and a greater concern with sometimes elaborate retelling of the gospel tale.[7] Continuing a tradition first exemplified in the apocryphal gospels, such works, sometimes written in poetry,[8] had as their primary purpose Christian instruction of whatever kind.[9] The Renaissance's growing concern with linguistic and textual study, classically exemplified in Lorenzo Valla's study of the Vulgate, Erasmus' edition of the Greek text of the New Testament and an ever increasing interest in Hebraica, offered initial stimuli to the more technical study of biblical documents. Something of this same concern emerges in the Reformers' interest in the writing of biblical harmonies, now with the innovative use of parallel columns, which allowed the reader better to evaluate both the discrepancies between the gospel accounts and the proposed solutions of the harmonists.

Increased interest in Hebraica, and in particular rabbinical commentaries and other ancient Jewish writings, also produced a growing sense of the importance of such works for the study of the gospels. Sebastian Münster, for instance, who was professor of Hebrew and theology at the University of Basle from 1528 to 1553, wrote a commentary on Matthew's Gospel, published in 1537 as *Evangelium Secundum Matthaeum in Lingua Hebraica*, which had as its assumption the view that the world out of which

Jesus emerged was best understood as Jewish, and that, therefore, the use of rabbinical works and other Judaica was a desideratum of any commentary on the gospels. Indeed Münster went so far as to translate Matthew into Hebrew, as the title of his work states. While scholars like Münster or the harmonists of a similar time did not see their studies as calling into question the historicity of the gospels, their work assumed the historically contextualised character of the world of Jesus and his followers (Friedman 1993).

It is probably in the seventeenth and early eighteenth centuries that the seeds of what we might call the modern study of the historical Jesus study are to be found. A number of factors account for this. Some have to do with a growing conviction amongst a minority of Christians that the Bible's witness to truth could not be sustained by a simple appeal to the idea of revelation, but rather by an appeal to reason. Allegiance to rationalism and a deep discontent with established religion were perhaps caused, amongst other things, by the wars of religion.

In this new worldview, the Bible's claim to be an inspired document that spoke in some privileged way about divine truth was undermined. It became instead a collection of books whose primary meaning should be located in what its author intended.[10] Anything found in it that smacked of the miraculous or the particular was suspect, and only what could be shown to be universal and reasonable (by the standards of rationalism) was deemed acceptable.

Out of this atmosphere, the English deists,[11] men like Toland (1670–1722), Collins (1676–1729) and Woolston (1670–1733), emerged as particular critics of the gospels. These individuals, while never producing lives of Jesus or indulging in a recognisable form of literary or source criticism, sowed the seeds of much subsequent historical Jesus research in their conviction that the Jesus of the gospels who performed miracles, rose from the dead and was the central subject of Old Testament revelation, was a figment of the imagination, and was to be replaced by a human Jesus who preached a warm-hearted, universal morality (Brown 1984:36–55, esp. 50–55).

Against this background, J. S. Reimarus' (1694–1768) essay on the aims of Jesus and his disciples, to which reference has already been made, should not be viewed as the bolt from the blue that Schweitzer claimed it to be (Kümmel 1973; Brown 1984:50). Reimarus had travelled in England and was familiar with the works of English deists, many of which had been translated into German.[12] Much of what he states in his essay, at least in general terms, bristles with deistic assumptions and assumptions of the Enlightenment in general: a scepticism about the possibility of miracle, a firm rejection of the view that Jesus could be seen as in some sense a fulfilment of Old Testament scriptures, an accompanying tendency to see him in purely human terms, and a robustly sceptical view of the resurrection. What distinguished Reimarus from his predecessors was his commitment to giving a complete account of Jesus' life that focused in particular upon his aims, seeing those aims against a Jewish background, and engaging in greater detail with the aims and motives of Jesus' disciples – in part harking back to views like those of Celsus or Porphyry.[13] For Reimarus, Jesus was a Jew in essential continuity with his culture. Central to his ministry was the preaching of the kingdom of God, a kingdom which, when viewed in its appropriate Jewish context, was to be seen in political terms. Jesus had messianic pretensions and saw himself as a future king of this new kingdom. His failure to bring this into being in a revolution led to his death, and it was only thanks to his disciples, who turned him into a universal saviour due to return in glory, that Christianity came into being. Far from being the universalist of the English deists, Jesus emerged as an enthusiast unable to transcend the political limitations of his own time and place.

By questioning the gospels' account of Jesus' life in such radical terms, and seeing Jesus' real character in terms of a construal of his aims against a Jewish background, Reimarus had given pungent and polemical expression to problems that were to be central to the Quest. The posthumous publication of this and other essays inspired a number of responses. J. S. Semler (1725–91), for instance, while accepting the imperfect character of the gospels' witness to Christ, challenged Reimarus' view of Jesus, and, in particular, his attribution to Jesus of a 'this-worldly' view of the 'kingdom of God'. Semler argued strongly for a Jesus who transcended, rather than conformed to, the tenets of Judaism. It was G. E. Lessing (1729–81) who had published Reimarus' *Fragments*; and although critical of aspects of his reconstruction, he endorsed Reimarus' essentially human view of Jesus, in particular describing John's christology as without historical basis (cf. Brown 1984:16–29). Others, like H. E. G. Paulus (1761–1851), sought to soften the impact of Reimarus' observations by arguing for the veracity of the accounts of the miracles of Jesus, contending that they gave evidence of natural events which had been falsely but sincerely understood as miraculous. F. Schleiermacher (1768–1834), more on theoretical than historical grounds, sought to defend a form of orthodox christology by concentrating upon Jesus' God-consciousness as the key to presenting a christology acceptable to the age.

Scholars such as Semler, Paulus and especially Schleiermacher represented types of mediating theologies, in which a variety of truces were negotiated between scientific study (*Wissenschaft*) on the one hand, and traditional belief (*Glaube*) on the other. These appeared to have met their nemesis in D. F. Strauss' *Leben Jesu kritisch untersucht* (ET *The life of Jesus critically examined*), the first edition of which was published in 1835. Strauss saw his work as part of a history of criticism that he felt had reached an impasse. While he rejected supernaturalist defences of the gospels out of hand, he attacked with equal vigour those like Paulus who had sought to explain the miracles in naturalistic ways, and those like Schleiermacher who appeared to be arguing for a christology that was philosophically meaningless. For Strauss the gospels were dominated by an idea, namely the messianic identity of Jesus, and the disciples' acceptance of the truth of this idea had led them unconsciously to give voice to that conviction by constructing what Strauss saw as mythological stories about Jesus. The disciples were not deceivers in the sense Reimarus imagined them, or those who had misunderstood natural events, as Paulus and others had thought. They were simply believers who had unconsciously allowed their beliefs about Jesus to become the guiding and necessarily distorting force in their retelling of his story. What emerged after Strauss had wandered through the gospels applying his mythological criteria looked more like what Reimarus had found: a messianic pretender who bore no relationship to his dogmatic successor. (See Strauss 1972:296. It is fair to say, however, that he had only a limited interest in reconstructing any detailed picture of the historical Jesus.) Strauss' Hegelian attempt to derive something theologically positive from his account seemed abstract and unacceptable to the ears of the mediating theologians, let alone the orthodox: he offered an idea, the God-man, which pointed to a possibility realisable in all humans, but bore no substantive relationship to the figure who had by chance been its originator.

Strauss' significance was considerable. He had criticised the views of those who had preceded him. His mythological solution not only introduced the idea of myth into the interpretation of the gospel in a *thoroughgoing* and absolute way, but made it plain how different was the world that the earliest Christians inhabited from what he termed 'our own enlightened age' (Strauss 1972:83). He was the first scholar seriously to reflect upon criteria for the establishment of historicity, or in his case the lack of it;[14] and he was the first categorically to deny any historical claims that might be attributed to John's Gospel. Perhaps more importantly, he made it clear that scholarship and faith were at daggers drawn (cf. Frei 1985); and in that sense he became, as Barth was to put it, the guilty conscience of nineteenth-century theology.

Strauss had shown what the full effects of apparently close historical study could be. The effect of what he wrote was more devastating than that of Reimarus precisely because it was so closely and monumentally argued and so obviously 'critical'. Those who followed him adopted a variety of approaches. Some did embrace in a perhaps dramatic way the sceptical implications of his work.[15] Others were less pessimistic and wrote lives of Jesus that were humanistic in their flavour and sought in an imaginative and bold way to re-create Jesus' mental and social outlook.[16] Still others turned their attention to an examination of the gospels themselves, either to identify their tendencies and give them their place in a preconceived understanding of the development of Christianity,[17] or to try and establish the literary relationship between them. By the 1860s, a consensus on this point seemed to have emerged: according to this, Mark was seen as the first gospel – and to some, therefore, as the most historically reliable text for reconstructing the life of Jesus. It was on the basis of Mark's Gospel that the so-called 'liberal lives' of Jesus were to emerge, in particular associated with such figures as H. J. Holtzmann, T. Keim and A. Harnack.

It is important to remember that the scholars who wrote 'liberal lives' of Jesus were deeply influenced by the attack upon orthodox christology, which Schweitzer identified as a significant factor in historical Jesus research. Few of them were willing to countenance the possibility that Jesus of Nazareth thought himself to be the second person of the Trinity. The essence of the Christian message was that Jesus had lived and died a human being and any attempt to diminish that fact was wrongheaded. Underpinning all of this was a type of historical metaphysics that saw history as the realm in which God revealed himself, and human personality as the ultimate domain of that revelation. Against such a background, the reclaiming of the historical Jesus was not an optional extra, but a necessary and almost divine task. Many of these assumptions manifest themselves in an understanding of Jesus' importance primarily in terms of his teaching – a teaching that was distinct from the Jewish culture out of which he emerged, and at whose core was a message about the brotherhood of man and the fatherhood of God. Harnack's popular lectures of 1900–01 in Berlin (*Das Wesen des Christentums*; ET *What is Christianity?*) gave eloquent voice to the assumptions of this movement, assumptions that arose from German idealism (Hurth 1988:93–94).

Of course, what I have outlined above can only be called 'tendencies' in research, and perhaps even tendencies in *German* research. British and American scholars, admittedly much less influential and creative than their German counterparts,[18] resisted the broadly sceptical attitude towards the gospels which German theologians tended to endorse. Moreover, they were less willing to give in to what might be perceived as German theology's acceptance of the incompatibility of orthodox conceptions of faith with historical research.[19]

The type of Jesus research that reached its popular apotheosis in Harnack's *What is Christianity?* was based upon a certain qualified confidence in the critic's ability to sift fact from fancy – a confidence that the results of such study about the human Jesus would provide the Christian with a liberating and practical truth. The end of the nineteenth and the beginning of the twentieth century, however, were to witness a collapse of confidence in the truth of such assumptions.

Aspects of the weakness of the liberal position were revealed by Martin Kähler. He described the Quest as a dead end. While one of his principal points in this regard lay in asserting the distance between the liberal Jesus and the Jesus who had sustained Christian communities through the generations, he made telling historical and methodological observations along the way. The gospels, he argued, did not consciously make a distinction between the preached Christ and the Jesus of history – they remained inevitably and absolutely intermeshed in their pages, making the process of sifting historical truth from fancy almost impossible. The corollary of this was a type of historical scepticism that lent itself to conservative conclusions. But Kähler did not stop there. He went on to argue that the Quest was in the end a subjective exercise, in which scholars created fifth gospels that had more to do with themselves than with the gospel proper; and he attacked what he took to be the implicit prioritising of the findings of scholarly research over faithful response to the text. Johannes Weiss' publication in 1890 of *Jesus' proclamation of the kingdom of God* (ET Weiss 1985) seemed to advocate in an admittedly non-political garb a return to an understanding of Jesus as a failed eschatological prophet; and William Wrede's publication of *The messianic secret* (1901, ET Wrede 1971) questioned the notion that Mark was in any sense a reliable source for knowledge of the historical Jesus.

Albert Schweitzer, who owed much to Weiss and Wrede, but surprisingly did not mention Kähler, further undercut the portrait of Jesus found in the 'liberal lives'. Not only did he show up its subjectivity (it simply reflected the religious assumptions of the scholars who had created it), but he presented an alternative picture of Jesus the eschatological enthusiast and messianic pretender who died in dramatic fashion on the cross trying to force God to bring in his longed-for kingdom. Schweitzer's Jesus research had much in common with that of Weiss; but his tone in the critique of his predecessors, and the way in which he sought to ram home the difference between his Jesus and the Jesus of the liberals, were striking. The liberal hermeneutic, with its assumption of the human Jesus' universal relevance emerging out of careful historical engagement, seemed beyond repair. As Schweitzer wrote: 'He will be to our age an enigma and a stranger' (Schweitzer 2000:479).

The early twentieth-century crisis in historical Jesus research manifested itself in a variety of ways. One was seen in the proliferation of books questioning whether Jesus had even existed.[20] Others emerged in a type of theological attack upon the historicist enterprise, witnessed in the work of Karl Barth, and later in Rudolf Bultmann. Barth argued that 'the reliability and communality of the knowledge of the person of Jesus Christ as the centre of the gospel can be none other than that of God-awakened faith'; critical-historical study signifies the deserved and necessary end of those foundations of this knowledge that are no foundations at all, since they have not been laid by God. In this, he seemed to give no place to a historical Jesus in Christian faith. Indeed, insofar as history had any ongoing relevance, it was simply to prove that we no longer knew Christ after the flesh.[21]

Bultmann's position distinguished itself from Barth's in the fact that it was allied to a technical commitment to the study of the New Testament. Following the work of K. L. Schmidt, and taking up an observation of Kähler, he argued strongly for the kerygmatic or proclamatory character of gospel traditions about Jesus, and their lack of historical content or interest in history. Such scepticism, exemplified in the oft-quoted but sometimes misused statement that 'we can know almost nothing about the life and personality of Christ' (Bultmann 1934:8), fed into theological convictions that were strongly opposed to a desire to base faith upon established facts. To a Lutheran, this seemed like justification by works.

Of course, there was resistance to such conclusions. Some of these came from Germany itself, where the ageing Harnack battled to fight the reflections of his miscreant pupil Barth. But objections also came from the English-speaking world. Scholars in Britain and the United States continued to resist the historical scepticism of Bultmann and his school as well as their theological contentions.[22] Soon Bultmann's own pupils began to question what appeared to them as an apparent embrace of the ancient Christian heresy of docetism. Ernst Käsemann's essay of 1953 marked a start (ET Käsemann 1964). He boldly asserted that the very fact of the existence of the gospels in the New Testament canon, which stood out in such stark relief when compared with the other contents of that canon, demanded that the scholar take the historical Jesus seriously. Pursuers of what some have wanted to call the New Quest did not advocate a return to the broadly biographic approach of a previous age. In fact, Käsemann's essay is laced with all sorts of denials of such an approach;[23] and Günther Bornkamm's *Jesus of Nazareth*, thought by some to be a remarkable break with the past, seemed at times to be more sceptical than positive in tone.[24] In many ways Bultmannian presuppositions still stalked the land, however much some would continue to insist that they were involved in a new quest.[25]

The so-called New Quest produced a number of criteria for determining the historicity of gospel traditions about Jesus. To say that an interest in establishing such criteria was something new would be wrong. The implicit and sometimes explicit use of such criteria had always existed.[26] But perhaps the quest for these was pursued more self-consciously now. One of the most important was the criterion of dissimilarity, which asserts that a statement attributed to Jesus in the gospels is genuine if it has no parallel either in the Judaism from which he hailed or in subsequent church traditions. In a sense this flawed criterion summed up two tendencies or assumptions in historical Jesus research during the period we have just discussed (Holmén 1999). (1) The first of these was a general scepticism, dominant in Germany, about the extent to which the church and Jesus were in any kind of continuity. Such scepticism reached its full flowering in the work of Bultmann, but had been a part of historical Jesus research from before Reimarus. (2) The second, and perhaps more important assumption, lay in the view that genuine traditions associated with Jesus would often be marked by what distinguished them from the Judaism out of which he emerged. This in turn gave voice to the view that the essence of Jesus' career could be construed in terms of an opposition between his teaching and aspects of his Jewish heritage. The 'de-Judaisation' of Jesus, implicit in these assumptions, reached its zenith in the occasional assertion that Jesus had not been born a Jew.[27]

I mention these two tendencies (and we should regard them as no more than that, since some significant scholars beginning with Reimarus failed to endorse the second one) because the so-called 'Third Quest' of recent times has subjected them to severe scrutiny. The first tendency has come to be reassessed in the light of a growing conviction amongst many scholars that the gospels tell us more about Jesus and his aims than we had previously thought. This 'growing conviction' is in part explained by reference to certain features of the so-called New Quest. More particularly, however, it derives from a dissatisfaction with some of the assumptions of Form Criticism, not least the bold belief that the gospels are kerygmatic literature and, as such, simply reflect the convictions of the church that produced them. Growing out of this, somewhat inevitably, is the notion that subsequent Christianity may be in greater continuity with Jesus than was previously thought.[28]

Linked in with this growing conviction, and related to a revision of the second tendency outlined above, is a belief that the key to making sense of our sources lies in a greater appreciation of Jesus' Jewish identity. This in turn calls for a deeper immersion on the part of scholars in the Jewish sources associated with the Second Temple period (Wright 1992b:800), along with a revision of negative preconceptions about Judaism and a greater sense of the continuities between Jesus and Judaism.

To be sure, we cannot return to the positivistic and quasi-biographical inclinations of an earlier age. Nevertheless, the revision of two central assumptions in the New Quest has led to the conviction that we can say something clear about Jesus' aims and even his self-understanding, by interweaving assured gospel material about Jesus with known information about the Judaism that formed the backdrop for his ministry. In such a quest even the miracles, for so long a bugbear in the study of the historical Jesus, come to play a significant role in understanding his purposes (see Meier 1991–94:2.509–1038).

Of course, the term 'Third Quest' can give a false sense of uniformity to present-day Jesus scholarship – despite the fact that it is no longer dominated by scholars of the Protestant tradition, but includes a strong presence of Catholics and Jews (cf. Meier 1999:461–64). Scholars apparently operating in the same field can reach quite different conclusions. So, for instance, Allison's and Sanders's portraits of Jesus, which both in different ways place an eschatological Jesus at the heart of their research, differ considerably from Wright's Jesus who can broadly be called eschatological but whose hopes for the future might be seen in largely metaphorical terms.

Some scholars, moreover, do not appear to be operating in the 'Third Quest' at all, in particular the members of the so-called Jesus Seminar.[29] Individual members of this seminar, as well as its collective publications, present a Jesus altogether different from anything associated with the so-called 'Third Quest'. The seminar is not only more sceptical about the gospels' claims to historicity, but its reconstructions of Jesus' teaching draw heavily on extra-canonical sources, in particular a stratified Q and the apocryphal *Gospel of Thomas*. As a result, Jesus emerges as primarily a non-eschatological preacher, somehow at odds with the prevailing Jewish culture of his day. Harnack and his ilk stalk the land in the garb of late twentieth-century American liberals.[30]

And we need not only refer to the Jesus Seminar to gain a sense of the less than ordered character of the field. Liberation theologians and feminists are often omitted from conventional accounts of the Quest. Scholars from these traditions are difficult to categorise straightforwardly as historical critics: their hermeneutical assumptions do not quite allow them to endorse historical-critical methods. But they do still claim to be recovering radical and liberating traditions connected with Jesus.[31]

THE RESULTS

The final paragraph of the preceding section hints at one of the great difficulties of writing a historiography of the study of any subject. Whom to include and whom not to include? In the history of the quest for the historical Jesus, New Testament scholars have never quite escaped the tendency to create a Germano-centric portrait whose patterns are perhaps more in the eye of the beholder than self-evidently real. So, for instance, the currently fashionable categorisation of Jesus research in terms of 'Old Quest, No Quest, New Quest, Third Quest' supposes a periodisation that is difficult fully to justify. The 'Old Quest' was far more complex than is ever indicated in such accounts, since at many points it hinted at things to come. Similarly, the account of a period of 'no quest' fails to take into consideration the situation in the English-speaking world.[32] In its strong emphasis on the *preached* word as the locus of our understanding of Christ, moreover, it has a good deal in common with the liberalism against which it rebelled and in which Jesus' teaching played so central a role. The 'New Quest' in turn shows much continuity with the supposed 'no quest'; and the 'Third Quest', whose very definition is problematic, includes within its membership a great diversity of portraits of Jesus.[33]

What is more, this narrative of linear progression is undercut not only by pointing to the ways in which the supposedly different phases merge. It is also weakened by the cyclical and repetitive nature of research in this area. I have already referred to the similarities of the conclusions of the Jesus Seminar to a scholar like Adolf von Harnack. But we can go much further than that and talk about the Jesus Seminar engendering a similar response to that engendered by the nineteenth-century liberal lives, whether it be in terms of Luke Timothy Johnson's Kähleresque rebuttal of the whole 'historical Jesus' enterprise (Johnson 1996), or Dale Allison's Schweitzeresque reaffirmation of the millennial Jesus (Allison 1998). And this is only to name a few 'repetitions'.

A further note of caution is added when we realise that contributors to the Jesus debate have invariably employed their accounts to further a particular cause or idea close to their heart.[34] It can make a difference that Reimarus wrote with certain Enlightenment presuppositions; that Strauss was a Hegelian; that Harnack was a liberal Protestant; that Schweitzer had read Nietzsche and had already decided when he wrote *The Quest* to give up his present way of life for one of self-abnegation; and that members of the Jesus Seminar operate in a country where Christian fundamentalism of an apocalyptic colour is so influential. Many other examples could be given.

Attempts to deconstruct the Quest date back at least as far as Kähler. They have a certain value,[35] but cannot *ipso facto* render the Quest worthless. Scholars are still in the main attempting to engage 'honestly' with texts from another age. They cannot be objective in some idealised Platonic way. But our increasing knowledge of the world of Jesus does enable them to give their readers a sense of the difference of that world from our own, even if they disagree about how that task should be undertaken.

THE QUESTION OF PROGRESS

But where, then, in this complex area of study might we locate points of progress? Or should we endorse the implications of the last few paragraphs and dismiss the exercise *in toto*?

The obvious way of addressing this question is to ask whether we know more about the historical Jesus than our forebears. In one sense the answer is 'No': that is, we cannot claim beyond reasonable doubt to have access to more reliable primary material *about* our subject matter. The jury remains out, for instance, on the relevance for the study of Jesus of the *Gospel of Thomas* and the *Gospel of Peter*, although the consensus is now broadly negative. On the other hand, the answer is 'Yes' in the sense that archaeology and chance finds of texts have indeed increased our knowledge of the Second Temple Judaism out of which Jesus emerged. It has often been chance discoveries that have moved the Quest forward,[36] none more so than that of the Dead Sea Scrolls in 1947. New Testament scholars are still digesting their significance, but already they have contributed greatly to our understanding of contemporary Jewish messianism, scriptural and legal interpretation, prayer, and a heap of other subjects, all directly relevant to historical Jesus research (cf. Fitzmyer 2000).

These brief comments point to another area in which progress is clear. As we noted earlier, one of the features of much recent historical Jesus study is a strong conviction that Jesus should be seen in a Jewish context. This is not of course a novel observation, and both Jewish and Christian scholars have long insisted on its importance. It has, however, come into sharper focus under the influence of Christian self-reflection following the Holocaust, and in the light of greater appreciation of the diversity of Second Temple Judaism. As a result, scholars are now much less willing to paint a bleak picture of that faith, or to see Jesus only in contrast to it.[37] A sometimes polemical insistence on the exceptionality of Jesus vis-à-vis a stereotyped and monolithic Judaism is no longer the order of the day. Of course, most scholarly accounts do consider atypical aspects of Jesus, but this is not in the interest of unfavourable comparisons with his religious and social heritage. Some may want to view this as moral progress. It has also, I would suggest, been beneficial to scholarship.

The 're-Judaisation' of Jesus does of course raise complex questions. First, there is the question of its appropriate context. Given the diversity of Judaism at the time of Jesus, against *what type* of Judaism should we see Jesus (Harrington 1987) – Galilean Hasidism (Vermes 1983)? Jewish hopes of restoration (Sanders 1985)? A more socially radical background? Secondly, there is the problem of our limited knowledge of Second Temple Judaism. For example, A. E. Harvey's otherwise helpful idea of the 'historical constraints' upon the ministry of Jesus arguably assumed a deeper knowledge of Judaism than we can attain (Harvey 1982).

Thirdly, there is the prescriptive use of our limited knowledge of Judaism in assessing the historicity of Jesus material. If, for instance, words or actions attributed to Jesus by the evangelists seem to go beyond anything we know about in Second Temple Judaism, should we regard them as historically reliable precisely because of their distinctiveness – or as suspect for the same reason? This pertains, for example, to problems of christology,[38] and can be understood in terms of a dialectic between constraint and creativity. It also bears upon the difficult question, first posed by J. Klausner, of how it could be that Jesus lived within Judaism and yet became the origin of a movement that eventually broke with it?[39]

Such comments indicate that Jesus research is a multiply complex affair, and that establishing cast-iron approaches or methods for it is impossible. Scholars have become increasingly aware of this fact, and find themselves keen to attack positivistic approaches. As Crossan (1991:426) has noted, 'there is only reconstruction'; and most would accept this. Of course, scholars adopt a variety of methods that inevitably affect their conclusions, and lead them to precisely the positivist language they would like to disclaim. But at least there is now an open recognition of the complexity of the task. This is progress of a kind.

THE FUTURE

What, then, of the future? Scholars can hope for a discovery of the importance of Qumran. The field is in need of something new and primary to nudge it along. Such discoveries give clear reminders of the provisionality of scholarly conclusions. We may hope, too, for a continuing engagement with the question of Jesus' place within Judaism, and a resistance to the creation of alternative contexts. An ongoing concern with the eschatological character of Jesus' message is equally desirable, together with a greater sense that this may explain a whole variety of aspects of his ministry (Allison 1998).

We cannot perhaps hope for consensus, a coming together of minds in the subject. The chaos of opinions ('*Meinungswirrwarr*') of which Kümmel (1994:695) spoke will be a continuing reality. In some respects this is healthy: the banging together of different opinions is essential to any academic study. But in a subject where so much of the argument is taken up with distinguishing fact from fancy, and where we appear to be arguing again and again about the same issues in the same texts, the exercise can look almost futile to both participants and onlookers. And yet, to dismiss the exercise as futile would be wrong precisely because Jesus is a figure of ongoing significance to so many people. And this brings me to my last point, the place of theology in the ongoing debate.

We have seen that theology was central to the historical Jesus discussion. To some, the Quest seemed to free Jesus from the straitjacket of Christian dogma; to others, the enterprise was suspect for precisely that reason and should be abandoned. The matter, therefore, has always been controversial, but at least the need has been felt to argue about it.

Nowadays, however, despite the proliferation of historical Jesus studies, theological reflection on the matter is non-existent or perfunctory in tone. Certainly it is true that the Jesus Seminar has a theological agenda of sorts, but it smacks of a historicist fundamentalism that leaves too many questions unanswered – as does the Kähleresque riposte of L. T. Johnson, by another way. Serious discussion of the role of Jesus research in the construction of a New Testament theology is rarely evidenced.[40]

There are many reasons for this phenomenon. Some have to do with the often fiercely secular environments, in particular in North America, in which this work is carried out. Some have to do with the sectionalised character of the larger subject known as theology or religious studies, where specialisms multiply and few, whether *Neutestamentler* or others, have the time or energy to interact with disciplines other than their own. And yet, precisely because Jesus as he lived and died is claimed as the saviour figure of the Christian faith, the subject must be discussed. The Jesus of history is of course an elusive figure, but he is an identifiable figure nevertheless; and Christians affirm his humanity as well as his divinity. Jesus was a Jew living in a culture different from our own, with presuppositions that may appear to us jarring. That is a starting point for discussion, a discussion that ought to take seriously the scandal of particularity at the centre of the doctrine of the incarnation. That scandal encapsulates the difficulty and the creative potential of appropriating such a figure for our time.

Notes

1. This was the aim of Schweitzer 2000 (enlarged ET) and Schweitzer 1912. He attributed the origins of such an approach to his reading of Aristotle's *Metaphysics* (Schweitzer 1949:119). Of course, it is important to note that Schweitzer developed his own narrative in such a way as to make himself appear the endpoint of such research.

2. The term 'Third Quest' is attributed to N. T. Wright in Neill and Wright 1988: 379. It has now become a standard term in the field. See Telford 1994: 55–61.

3. Schweitzer (2000:6) writes that most lives were written 'out of hate . . . not so much hate directed against the person of Jesus as against the supernatural nimbus with which he had come to be surrounded'. For further comments on this see Hurth 1988:17–18.

4. Hase (1876:110–11) began with Tatian; Nippold (1880–1906:3.207) began with Strauss – who incidentally had begun his own account on a thematic basis with a discussion of the differences between the Antiochene and Alexandrian schools of scriptural interpretation.

5. See Wright 1992b. Pals 1982 and Kissinger 1985 begin with the early church, as in broad terms does Hurth 1988. Kümmel 1973 and Brown 1984 are openly critical of Schweitzer's decision to begin with Reimarus.

6. See Grant 1961:62–70, here highlighting Origen's attempt to solve the difficulty.

7. On this see Pals 1982:6–7. For a general discussion of why such lives became so popular in the medieval period see Georgi 1992.

8. See Sedulius' *Carmen Paschale* (fifth cent.), Cynewulf's *Christ* (ninth cent.) and Ezzo of Bamberg's *Cantilena* (eleventh cent.).

9. See Pals 1982:7 and his discussion of the *Meditationes Vitae Christi*, sometimes attributed to Bonaventure, along with its English translation and reworking in Nicholas Love's *Myrrour of the Blessed Lyf of Jesus Christ*. These works aimed to promote a type of devotional realisation of the life of Christ.

10. See e.g. Spinoza's *Tractatus Theologico-Politicus* (1670), excerpted in Dawes 2000:5–26.

11. Dr Johnson's definition in his *Dictionary of the English language* (1755) is helpfully concise: it is 'the opinion of those who only acknowledge one God, without the reception of any revealed religion'.

12. On the reception of English deistical works in Germany see Brown 1984:51–52, and the accompanying bibliography in his endnotes.

13. 'Reimarus went beyond the English deists in developing a comprehensive alternative account of the origins of Christianity' (Brown 1984:53).

14. Strauss 1972:83–84. Note especially his attempt to introduce negative and positive criteria for the establishment of myth, and also his genuine belief that the establishment of precise criteria in this instance was very difficult: 'The boundary line . . . between the historical and unhistorical, in records in which, as in our Gospels, this latter element is incorporated, will ever remain fluctuating and unsusceptible of precise attainment' (Strauss 1972:91).

15. So e.g. Bauer 1851–52, who denied the existence of Jesus.

16. See most famously Renan 1863 and the discussion of its importance in Pals 1982:32–39.
17. Most important in this respect was F. C. Baur and his introduction of so-called *Tendenzkritik*. See Brown 1984:204–19.
18. For helpful explanations as to why this was the case see Pals 1982:125–63.
19. See Pals 1982. He notes that some British scholars did write more sceptical accounts of Jesus' life, but these accounts were normally derivative and rarely influential in the way that their more conservative alternatives were. Morgan 1980 shows how Anglican commitment to the doctrine of the incarnation was a significant factor in the critical reception of more sceptical German works.
20. These books are associated in particular with the names of Arthur Drews and John M. Robertson, discussed by Weaver 1999:49–62. Interestingly, a large part of Albert Schweitzer's 1913 revision of *The Quest* was taken up with a discussion of Drews *et al.*
21. See the fourteenth point of Barth's exchange with his former teacher Harnack, published in the journal *Die Christliche Welt* in 1923, and translated in Rumscheidt 1972:35. Equally instructive for the position Barth was opposing is Harnack's fourteenth point in Rumscheidt 1972:31: 'If the person of Jesus Christ stands at the centre of the gospel, how else can the basis for reliable and communal knowledge of this person be gained but through critical-historical study so that the imagined Christ is not put in place of the real one'.
22. This becomes clear in Weaver 1999. He also notes the work of Shirley Jackson Case and William Manson who both, in their different ways, opposed form-critical scepticism. R. H. Lightfoot was a more enthusiastic advocate of this scepticism.
23. Note Käsemann's strong attack upon Jeremias' insistence upon the conjunction of history and faith.
24. Bornkamm 1960. On the sometimes confused character of this book, see Keck 1969.
25. See Fowl 1989:329 n.13, who cites Van Harvey's judgement that Bultmann and his opponents had more in common than is usually admitted.
26. Note, for instance, our comments on Strauss; and Schmiedel 1907, who sought to establish a bare minimum of nine 'pillar' passages whose historicity could not be doubted.
27. See Grundmann 1940. The tendencies to de-Judaise Jesus may be said to reach their zenith in Grundmann's work, although there are clear continuities between some of the things Grundmann wrote and some of the things liberals like Harnack asserted about the essence of Jesus' message. It should be noted that Harnack was not an anti-Semite, whereas Grundmann was a signed-up member of the Nazi party.
28. So, for instance, see Sanders 1985, who argues that any account of the historical Jesus should explain how the church that worshipped him came into being. See also Meyer 1979.
29. See Meier 1999:459; he places the Jesus Seminar within the 'Third Quest', whereas Wright (1996:28–82) puts it in the 'New Quest'.
30. See especially Harnack (1908:250–51), who announces after a painstaking reconstruction of Q, 'Above all, the tendency to exaggerate the apocalyptic and

eschatological element in our Lord's message, and to subordinate to this the purely religious and ethical elements, will ever find its refutation in Q'.

31. Particular note in this regard should be taken of Schüssler Fiorenza 1986, which is strongly historical in its orientation.

32. See Weaver 1999:xi–xii; and for a more nuanced periodisation Marsh 1997: 408–13.

33. Wright (1992b:800) appears to concede this point when he observes: 'The closer we get to our own day, the harder it is to plot patterns and movements'.

34. Schweitzer's observation (2000:6) about lives of Jesus being written with love or hatred is relevant here.

35. On this see Marsh 1997:417–18 who seeks a partial deconstruction of more recent writings on the Quest.

36. See Morgan 1993:94–95, who notes how the discoveries in the nineteenth century of such texts as 1 *Enoch, Assumption of Moses* and 2 *Baruch* contributed to the debate about the eschatological Jesus.

37. A list of polemical quotations about ancient Judaism found in books about Jesus can be found in Sanders 1985:23–24 and Keck 2000:23–31.

38. Anyone, for instance, who has followed the recent debate about the Son of Man will note how so much of it is taken up with evidence, or lack of it, of pre-Christian messianic uses of the term. More often than not, scholars' decision on this matter determines whether they believe that Jesus could have used the term in a messianic way. There are obvious problems with such an approach.

39. Klausner 1925:369, posed again by Sanders 1985:3. See Fowl 1989 for an intelligent discussion of this point.

40. Morgan 1987 is an exception. His view that Christian theology must primarily reflect upon the Christ of faith but that historical research can act as a kind of *Hilfswissenschaft*, correcting or modifying the one-sidedness of the individual Gospels' account of Jesus, is problematic but interesting. Keck 2000 is the most recent scholar seriously to engage with the problem.

10 The quest for the real Jesus

FRANCIS WATSON

There are many 'images' of Jesus, whether verbal or visual. Each canonical gospel presents one such image, but the process of image-making does not stop there. There are non-canonical, 'apocryphal' images, and there are images of Jesus in theology and literature, high art and popular religious culture. These images derive from many times and places, and will always reflect something of their own time and place, within which they will meet a perceived need. Does this constant manufacture of images testify to Jesus' extraordinary impact on western and global cultures? Or is Jesus little more than a blank screen onto which individuals and cultures may project their own aspirations and fantasies? Is Jesus (like Mary, perhaps) the origin and pretext for an entire myth-making industry? And if so, is the 'real' Jesus of any significance? There was, no doubt, a first-century Jew of that name who came from Nazareth and was crucified in Jerusalem, but the 'reality' of Jesus' impact on history is simply the reality of the images: or so it might be argued. Perhaps even the two centuries of scholarly endeavour to get behind the images to the 'real', historical Jesus have merely produced a further profusion of images, similar in kind to the ones they sought to displace?

The contemporary sense of the irreducible multiplicity of images is so potent that it is difficult to speak of a singular 'reality' preceding the images and determining their adequacy and appropriateness. Yet it is precisely the 'reality' that each image claims to represent – and to do so more adequately and appropriately than alternative images. The Christian community is the site not just of the manufacture of images but also of controversy about them. Images of Jesus are always *contested*. Can the claim of a particular image to represent the real be substantiated? And if not – if it is the product of fantasy and myth-making – should it not be eliminated? In Christian history and theology, images are constantly subjected to critical scrutiny, and themselves arise out of that process; and the basis for that scrutiny is the perceived need for the image to correspond to the reality. According to the image, we are to imagine Jesus in a particular way because this most adequately represents who the real Jesus was and is, in the full range of his significance for us. The process of image-making is always contested and controversial, for the image is always vulnerable to denunciation as an idol, a false and arbitrary rendering of the reality. To be Christian is, among other things, to *care* about the way that Jesus is represented, and to do so because the reality is so supremely important that misrepresentations are bound to be deeply damaging. To celebrate the limitless proliferation of images of Jesus, not caring about their adequacy as representations of reality, is only possible on non-Christian premises. It is an expression of commitment to a polytheistic worldview, in contemporary 'postmodern' guise.

Christian faith shares with historical research a commitment to the pursuit of the 'real' Jesus, who may very well be quite different from many of the images currently in circulation. But any construal of reality will depend not simply on the object in itself but on the perspective or interpretative framework within which it is set. Christian faith and secularised historical research view the reality of Jesus very differently. Christian faith finds the real Jesus in the four canonical gospels, in which the early church's believing reception of Jesus as the Christ attained normative form. The real Jesus is the Jesus mediated by the believing reception that he himself evoked, and the gospels are therefore documents of faith from beginning to end. In contrast, historical research typically seeks a real Jesus prior to and apart from the reception he evoked; and this 'real' Jesus is said to expose the images of Jesus in the four canonical gospels as, in important respects, 'unreal'. Much that is found in them and attributed to Jesus is in fact 'late' and 'inauthentic'. Among other things, the gospels present Jesus as miraculously conceived without sexual intercourse, as acclaimed at his birth by angels and humans, as performing surprising feats with water (turning it into wine, walking on it, calming it in stormy weather), as illuminated with heavenly splendour on a mountain-top, and as appearing physically to his followers shortly after his death and burial. None of this can qualify as 'real' within the historian's normal frame of reference; rather, it is 'legend' – a common enough phenomenon in pre-modern narrative texts. The real Jesus only begins to emerge after the beginning and end of the story the evangelists tell has been removed, together with a considerable amount of the intervening material as well. The real Jesus of the historian is, typically, a greatly reduced Jesus, since somewhere between about 50 and 95 per cent of the gospel material is regarded as too problematic to be useful historically.[1] The discarded material becomes useful again when we turn to the historical reality of the early church; but by then a gulf has been set between the church and the historical Jesus. Whatever the differences between the various versions of the historical Jesus (differences that are often much exaggerated), they tend to agree at this point: that the real Jesus differed significantly from the composite image of him created by the evangelists.[2]

Those for whom the real Jesus is the figure of the fourfold gospel narrative may be tempted simply to reject the historian's version, thus reinforcing the divide between the two accounts from their own side of it. On this view, the methodological flaws of the so-called 'Quest of the historical Jesus' are so fundamental that its results are of minimal value. Its criteria for distinguishing authentic from inauthentic material are difficult either to formulate or to apply, and the resulting images of Jesus are clearly marked by the cultural pressures of our own time. Historical scholarship gives us little or nothing of the reality of Jesus as acknowledged by Christian believers, and we would be well advised to bypass this entire scholarly enterprise and to regard the composite image of the canonical gospels as sufficient.[3]

This rejection of historical accounts of the real Jesus is understandable. The figure they present is not the Jesus acknowledged in Christian faith. Yet the historical approach to the reality of Jesus should not be so quickly dismissed. In what follows, I shall argue that *only a critical dialogue with historical scholarship can clarify what it means to identify the real Jesus with his representation in the fourfold canonical gospel.* Ultimately, this historical scholarship can be put to positive and constructive theological use; but everything depends on how this is done.[4]

One possibility is to question whether there need be such a sharp difference of perspective between the historian and the Christian believer. Is it really necessary for the historian to eliminate all references to miraculous events, on the grounds that such events are simply inconceivable within the 'real world' of historical investigation? If the first Christians claimed that certain highly unusual events accompanied the beginning and followed the ending of Jesus' life, should the historian dismiss their claims without further reflection? The first Christians knew as well as we do that human life begins with sexual intercourse between an adult male and female, and that it ends irreversibly with death, burial and decomposition. They were aware how strange it would seem to claim anything different for Jesus. Yet they made such claims. An open-minded historian will weigh these claims dispassionately, and will not reach too quickly for the obvious alternative accounts – that Joseph or some other male was Jesus' biological father, that the disciples' visions of the risen Jesus were subjective in origin, and that the genesis of early Christian beliefs to the contrary can be explained by reference to their cultural context. To reject these beliefs as a matter of principle is (it is said) a sign not of methodological rigour but of a closed mind, a negative dogmatism.

Perhaps it is precisely the open-minded historian who is able to confirm, beyond reasonable doubt, that Jesus really did rise from the dead?

In my view, there is little or no merit to this argument. It may seem to be on slightly stronger ground in the case of the resurrection than in that of the virgin birth, since Jesus' resurrection was much more central to the earliest Christian proclamation. Even here, however, critical historical research serves only to expose the fragmentary and ambiguous nature of the 'evidence'. Historical research can confirm that belief in Jesus' resurrection goes back to the earliest days of the Christian community, but it also shows that the content of that belief may have changed over time. It is not clear that Paul knew of the empty tomb story that occurs first in Mark and subsequently in the other canonical gospels, or whether for Paul resurrection entailed the reanimation of Jesus' corpse. It is not clear that stories of resurrection appearances were in wide circulation at the time when Mark composed his Gospel, for he seems not to have included any such stories. The diversity of the appearance stories in the later gospels indicates that even towards the end of the first century there was no normative account of the Easter events and their aftermath; indeed, the stories may not predate the literary contexts in which they are found. In the case of an alleged event as extraordinary as the resurrection, historical research can make very few confident assertions on the basis of texts dating from the second half of the first century. For that very reason, historical research may not result in a dogmatic *denial* of the claim that Jesus rose from the dead. But it may well appear to plunge the whole subject into acute uncertainty. Historical research gives no credence to the traditional apologetic claim that only the resurrection can account for the disappearance of Jesus' corpse (which is quite wrongly regarded as an unquestionable historical fact). The Christian affirmation that God raised Jesus from the dead neither needs nor receives the support of the historian *qua* historian.[5]

Attempts to minimise the differences between the historian's image(s) of Jesus and the canonical gospels are in the end bound to fail. They may be of some value in challenging a dogmatic scepticism that proclaims almost everything in the gospels to be 'inauthentic', congratulating itself on its superior methodological rigour as it does so. A scepticism of this kind often originates merely in hostility to the Jesus Christ of the church's faith, in a determination to wrest Jesus out of the hands of the church and to reclaim him for those on or beyond the margins of Christian faith. Yet, granted that there may be a great deal of common ground between the historian's image of Jesus and that of the gospels, and that historical research often explains and clarifies much that would otherwise be obscure, doing its utmost to be helpful to those whose Christian faith motivates their concern to get their image of Jesus right, the fact remains that the two images of Jesus are in their totality significantly different from each other. From the standpoint of Christian faith, the historian's image of Jesus may seem to be a *truncated* one.[6] The difficulties that the beginning and end of the gospel narrative pose for the historian are symptomatic of a great omission in the historian's account. The life of Jesus is not a piece of history like any other, for this life, uniquely, is the act of God for the reconciliation of the world to God (cf. 2 Cor 5.19): and history cannot speak of this transcendent meaning of the life of Jesus, although it is just this that makes Jesus' life so important for Christians. For the historian, on the other hand, the images of Jesus found in the canonical gospels are *secondary*. The gospels derive from a process of accretion in which an original image of Jesus was overlaid with all kinds of later material which expresses the faith of the early church but does not go back to Jesus. For Christian faith, the reality of Jesus is identical to the reality of God and God's action; the reality of Jesus is theologically construed, although without detriment to its historical actuality. For the historian, the reality of Jesus is what comes to light when later accretions are removed and the surviving, 'authentic' material is restored to its 'original context'. From that perspective, one *cannot* speak of God; from the other perspective, one *cannot but* speak of God. The common ground between the two perspectives – which is sometimes very striking – should not be allowed to mask this fundamental difference. The difference is no less fundamental when the historian and the believer coexist in the same person. It is of course possible for the same individual to affirm both that Jesus suffered death by crucifixion in Jerusalem around AD 30, and that God raised him from the dead, but these are two very different kinds of affirmation. To affirm God's action in Christ is to assert that statements about Jesus which do not refer to God are incomplete and potentially misleading.

In due course, we shall ask how this difference of perspective can be made fruitful and productive. The next step, however, is to look more closely at the *roots* of this difference. It does not merely originate in a post-Enlightenment worldview, according to which much that was previously credible is now deemed to be incredible. The difference may be traced back to the gospels themselves, and to the manner in which they tell the story of Jesus. According to the gospels, the fact that the life of Jesus is at the same time the definitive act of God for the salvation of the world cannot merely be read off the surface of the story that they tell. The God who determines the life of Jesus is also the God who determines its *disclosure* as what it truly is, the definitive divine saving action in which God's own being is revealed and constituted.

God determines the life of Jesus and the disclosure of its significance, and these are not two separate divine acts but one: for God's action in Jesus is to be seen as *communicative* action, an action in which a communicative intention is constitutive and primary, not secondary and incidental. Yet, if *God* determines the disclosure of the significance of Jesus' life as God's own action, this disclosure remains within the sphere of God's determination. Jesus' life is not *transparent* to God's action, as though its basis in the divine action were universally accessible. It might have taken such a form, in which case it would have been immediately and universally recognised; but it did not. On the contrary, all four gospels assume both that God acts to ensure the recognition of the divine action in Jesus, and that this recognition may be withheld. Where recognition of the divine basis of Jesus' life is withheld, that life will inevitably seem to possess some quite different significance. Thus, the gospels themselves allow space for a plurality of perspectives on the figure of Jesus. The possibility of other perspectives – even if one-sided or false – is integral to the particular faith-perspective that the evangelists adopt.

A reading of the Marcan account of Peter's confession at Caesarea Philippi will help to clarify this point.

'Who do people say that I am?' (Mark 8.27). It is assumed at the outset that Jesus' identity is not an unproblematic datum but that it is an *issue*, raised by Jesus' own activity. Before he puts this question to his disciples, his public ministry is already a question demanding an answer, though not compelling any particular answer. At this point in the narrative, the word made flesh takes the form of the interrogative, *who?* (cf. Mark 4.41: 'Who then is this...?'). It is assumed that various answers to this interrogative are being given, and that this is a matter on which most people can be expected to hold an opinion. The opinions cited – 'Some say John the Baptist, others Elijah, others one of the prophets' (Mark 8.28, cf. 6.14–16) – are in fact quite similar to each other. All of them judge Jesus favourably, as an authentic messenger of God, and (strangely) all of them see in him not a new prophet but the return of one of the prophets from the recent or distant past. In reporting these favourable opinions, however, the disciples suppress the unfavourable opinions to which Mark elsewhere refers. Not everyone identifies Jesus as a prophet. Some are saying, 'He is out of his mind'; others are saying, 'He is possessed by Beelzebul, and by the prince of demons he casts out the demons' (Mark 3.21–22). Others still claim that the onus is on Jesus to make his identity unambiguous by means of a sign (8.11). Jesus' life-story unfolds within this polarity of popular enthusiasm and more or less definite rejection. He is a *controversial* figure, the focal point for a plurality of perspectives both positive and negative. The Christian perspective, which Peter is shortly to enunciate, is beyond this polarity, but it does not eliminate or suppress the play of opinions. Jesus allows himself to be viewed as a prophetic figure, one who brings an authentic word of God in continuity with the prophetic traditions of the past. He also allows himself to be viewed as a deranged fanatic who leads the people astray. In both cases, he allows himself to be viewed as a *relative* phenomenon, not as embodying something unique, unsurpassable and definitive. Jesus' public ministry imposes itself on the populace of Galilee in the form of a question rather than an answer, and it permits a range of answers. It does not overwhelm perspectives on itself other than the true one with a display of force, on the analogy of the acts of judgement leading to the exodus from Egypt. In that sense, Jesus' public ministry is an exercise in tolerance and a manifestation of the divine patience. Where Jesus is intolerant and impatient, the objects of his wrath are often the disciples themselves. 'Do you not yet perceive or understand? Are your hearts hardened? Having eyes do you not see, and having ears do you not hear? And do you not remember?' (Mark 8.17–18, cf. 9.19). It seems that an intolerance of blindness and stupidity within the community of Jesus' followers can coexist with an attitude of ironic equanimity towards both admirers and detractors outside the community.

What is it that creates this difference between the outside and the inside? It is Jesus' question together with Peter's answer: 'But who do *you* say that I am?' – 'You are the Christ!' (Mark 8.29). It will shortly become clear that Peter's understanding of the title 'Christ' is quite different to Jesus'; for Peter is denounced with extraordinary harshness for questioning whether suffering, rejection and resurrection can really be the destiny of the Christ (Mark 8.31–33). Despite this, Peter's confession is a genuine acknowledgement of the truth, which is that Jesus does not belong to a small, select class ('one of the prophets') but that he is in a class of his own. There are many prophets, but there is only one Christ. The Christ sums up everything that has preceded, and is its goal and meaning. He is the definitive turning point in the world's history, since in him the purposes of God find their culmination. In him God is no longer hidden but is finally manifest as the one who ensures the ultimate well-being of God's people, so that their sorrow and penitence give way to gratitude and praise. The prophet looks ahead to this event as future, and interprets a particular present in the light of it; but the Christ *is* that event. The prophet's significance is relative; but the significance of the Christ is absolute and unsurpassable, for in this event God's own being attains its definitive form. At the end, in the advent of the Christ, God most truly is who God is. In unfolding the history of 'Jesus Christ the Son of God'

(Mark 1.1), the evangelist narrates the history of God's own self. And if *that* is the story that is told, then every attempt to tell the story of Jesus apart from the confession that he is the Christ will be profoundly mistaken. To speak of Jesus as someone other than the Christ is to miss precisely the factor that gives him his absolute and unsurpassable significance, and to replace this with a merely relative, inner-historical significance. Yet, because the recognition of Jesus as the Christ is itself grounded in a divine action that may be withheld, space is ceded within which alternative accounts of Jesus' identity can come into being. Not everyone confesses that Jesus is the Christ; some think that he is one of the prophets, or that he is deranged. The question *who?* intends the answer, 'You are the Christ!', yet it does not impose this answer but remains a genuine question to which an alternative answer may be given.[7]

All this has a number of important implications, by no means purely negative, for the 'Quest of the historical Jesus'.

(1) If Jesus is confessed as the Christ, the only serious alternative is that he is not the Christ. There may perhaps be disputes between those who say that he is Elijah and those who say that he is some other prophet, and both groups will be at odds with those who think that Jesus is merely deranged. For Christian faith, however, these hostile or friendly views both occupy a single space in which Jesus is regarded as *not-Christ*, and thus as something other than what he truly is. (Later historical analogies to the contemporary judgements reported by the gospels are not hard to come by: a negative judgement about Jesus has been a significant element in orthodox Jewish identity, whereas Islamic tradition represents a more positive assessment.)

It is this pre-existing space into which the 'Quest of the historical Jesus' has more recently entered – insofar as it omits to acknowledge Jesus as the Christ, the turning point and meaning of history, thereby proceeding from an assumption other than Peter's. Within the self-imposed limits of the 'quest', it is possible to argue that Jesus *claimed* to be the Christ, and to discuss in what sense he might have done so, just as it is possible to attempt to explain the rise of early Christian faith in Jesus as the Christ. Yet such an investigation stops short of the confession that Jesus is the Christ. As 'the historical Jesus', Jesus is not yet the object of Christian faith and confession. As in the Jewish and Islamic examples, he is understood within the framework of a non-Christian worldview which is taken for granted. In this case, it is the adjective 'historical' that identifies the worldview in question (although there are admittedly shifts in the connotations of this term, so that a late nineteenth-century 'historical Jesus' will be significantly different from a late twentieth-century one). In contemporary usage, 'history' is construed as a single, neutral, homogeneous space, itself without origin, *telos*, limit or meaning, which constitutes the field within which particular trains of events occur in a manner that is neither predictable in advance nor entirely devoid of a coherence and rationality which the historian may retrospectively identify. 'History' is a kind of container for particular histories, including the one that occasioned the rise of Christianity as a historical phenomenon. Christians may claim that in this particular history lies the key to the meaning of history as a whole, but the historian can no more make use of this key than can the orthodox Jew or Muslim; for in each case Jesus has been set within the framework of a worldview which makes the christological confession impossible. Even Christian historians, who at a 'personal' level accept that Jesus is the Christ, will be subject to the constraints of this methodologically atheistic worldview – unless they are prepared to rethink what 'history' is, on the basis of theology.[8]

It is inevitable that the question that Jesus poses and is should be answered in ways other than Peter's. It is inevitable that attempts should be made to detach Jesus from his disciples' confession and to ascribe to him some other, purely relative significance, whether negative, positive or merely neutral. All this is inevitable because the question is genuinely a question, whose answer is given but not imposed. So there is no occasion here for ill-tempered polemics or earnest apologetics: what is required is simply to clarify the point at issue.

Yet this disjunction between a 'historical Jesus' and the Jesus who is confessed as the Christ cannot be the last word on the subject. In the discussion that follows, we shall explore the possibility of a more positive account of the relationship between the two.

(2) 'History' might be understood as something other than the neutral, homogeneous space within which particular histories occur. There might be a theologically informed approach to the 'historical Jesus' that operates *within* the ideological perspective of the gospels, according to which Jesus is the Christ, the final meaning of history. Instead of discarding that perspective in an attempt to make Jesus equally accessible to people of diverse convictions and commitments, we might learn from the gospels what history really is. Modern historical study tends to understand ancient historiographical texts as 'sources', disregarding their ideological biases and other 'unhistorical' elements and using the residue as raw material for independent historical reconstruction (which will naturally display ideological biases of its own). That is also the approach taken to the gospels when the object of study is 'the historical Jesus'. An alternative approach is also possible, however: one

in which the textuality of the gospels is preserved and the integrity of the evangelists' attempts to write the history of Jesus as the Christ is respected. In their own way, the gospels are genuinely historiographical texts. If they fail to conform to some of the conventions of this genre, the reason is not so much that the evangelists were not trained historians (a point which is anyway debatable in the case of Luke) but that the event whose history they narrate is qualitatively unique: for this is not one historical event among others but the particular history in which the goal and meaning of history is disclosed. Narrating *this* history requires a recourse to material and methods that a historian might otherwise find problematic. If the significance and density of this event are to stand out clearly, the legends that give expression to fundamental Christian convictions will have a place alongside empirically trustworthy material. Even the sayings of Jesus may be totally recast (as in the case of the Gospel of John), in order to give clearer expression to what is being said in these sayings.

The story that is told in the gospels is the story of Jesus as the Christ, and not that of a neutral Jesus. According to the gospels, however, it is not enough for Jesus to *be* the Christ, he must also be *confessed* as the Christ – a point that is made within the narratives in the confessions of Peter (Mark 8.29), the centurion (Mark 15.29), Martha (John 11.27), Mary (John 20.18), Thomas (John 20.28) and others. The believing reception of the event of Jesus as the Christ belongs to the story that is told, and the telling of the story therefore reflects both the event and its reception; for the event itself *includes* its own reception.[9] If the perspective of Christian faith has shaped or formed the contents of the gospels at every point, that is fully consistent with the story they tell – the story not of a neutral Jesus but of Jesus who is and is confessed as the Christ. That is why, in the Lucan birth stories, the divine act that initiates the life of Jesus immediately evokes the human (and angelic) response of praise. The same Holy Spirit through whose creative action Jesus is conceived also inspires the songs that celebrate this event (Luke 1.35, 41, 67, 2.26–27), for God's action in Christ is *communicative* action which does not reach its intended goal until it evokes a responsive human recognition and acknowledgement. The traditions about Jesus that underlie the gospels were developed in the context of the early Christian acknowledgement that what takes place in Jesus is *God's* definitive and unsurpassable action, and the free creativity with which these traditions were shaped is the expression of that acknowledgement. It is precisely in the material that is most problematic to the secular historian (for example, the birth and resurrection stories) that this acknowledgement of the true scope and significance of the event of Jesus' life is most clearly manifested.

Conventional historical work on the gospels finds itself unable to accept the evangelists' assumption that the Jesus of history is identical to the Jesus who is confessed as the Christ. Nevertheless, this work performs a valuable service in making clear the extent to which early Christian reception of Jesus as the Christ has actively shaped the material that eventually took canonical form in the gospels. In identifying certain types of material as 'legendary', for example, historical research makes that active shaping and reshaping *visible*. In its own way, it reminds us that the event the gospels narrate is the event of Jesus who is the Christ *and who is acknowledged as such* – in such a way that the acknowledgement belongs within the scope of the event itself. Even the rationalistic, anti-supernaturalist assumptions that often underlie the identification of 'legendary' material can have a positive role, compelling us to ask how far the theological point of the story in question is really dependent on the factual occurrence of the event it ostensibly narrates. It enables us to see that the truth of the story is to be sought somewhere in the relationship between Jesus, God and the world, in the broad space opened up by Christian faith rather than in the cramped space of factual occurrence or non-occurrence. If historical research regards this material as untruthful in labelling it as 'unhistorical', then Christian faith can only reject this conclusion. Yet it is a positive theological gain to recognise that the relationship between story and reality may be more or less direct or indirect, and that the nature of the reality in question requires this complex mode of narration.[10]

(3) Modern historical scholarship shares with the Christian faith articulated in the gospels a concern with the full humanity of Jesus. In Christian piety, practice and thought, it has proved all too easy to create a 'Christ' who has little or no connection with the particular historical figure of Jesus of Nazareth. For example, in circles where there is talk of a 'personal relationship with Christ', the 'Christ' referred to appears to be the purely present figure of an exalted, divine Lord whose *prehistory* is to be found in the gospels but not his full reality. The christophanies of Acts 9 or Revelation 1 would then be primary sources for our knowledge of this figure. According to the gospels, however, the full reality of Jesus is rendered precisely by way of the story they tell of a human life and its outcome in a divine vindication that overturns human rejection. Jesus *is* his own life-story; his identity is not detachable from his history. If in earlier contexts we have had to emphasise that, for the evangelists, Jesus is the Christ, it must now be emphasised that the Christ is no one other than Jesus: '*You* are the Christ!' (Mark 8.29).[11]

Historical research can help to make the full humanity of Jesus imaginable and plausible, especially by filling out the picture provided by the gospels of his geographical, historical and cultural context. The gospels refer to Galilee and Judaea, Nazareth and Jerusalem, but they do not tell us where these places are; nor are we told what a synagogue or a Pharisee is. The realities of Roman power and the role of high priest and temple are presupposed but not explained. The 'implied reader' of the gospels already possesses a broad understanding of Jesus' context, and to supplement this understanding from elsewhere should in principle lead to new insights into the story the evangelists tell. These insights will not be confined to relatively trivial aspects of this story, but will contribute to an understanding of matters that lie at its heart. When Peter confesses, 'You are the Christ!', it is presupposed that this term and the role it designates have already been made available to him through his primary linguistic and cultural formation (cf. John 1.41). 'Christ' is not presented as a uniquely Christian coinage; historical research must therefore trace its pre-Christian Jewish antecedents in other surviving texts, so as to clarify the distinctively Christian appropriation of this term. The canonical status of the four gospels does not mean that they should be read in isolation from other texts, any more than the church that recognises their canonicity should live in isolation from the wider world. Although the reality of Jesus is mediated to us in the irreducibly textual form of the fourfold canonical gospel, and is not available to us outside that textual embodiment, historical research can help to ensure that the reality of Jesus is not simply *identified* with the figure in the narrative, as though he were a fictive figure with no prior reality of his own.[12] To isolate Jesus from his wider historical context is to risk losing his reality, and thus to confess as the Christ an essentially fictive character, wholly contained by the narratives in which he is the protagonist. If the impetus to theology is 'faith seeking understanding', then that quest for understanding must include the study of Jesus' historical context if the reality of Jesus is to be made intelligible and plausible.

If the reality of Jesus is the reality of the Jesus as the Christ, then no simple judgement for or against the scholarly enterprise known as the 'Quest of the historical Jesus' is possible or desirable. If the 'historical Jesus' is distinguished from the figure who is confessed as the Christ, then the reality that is ascribed to this Jesus is at best a truncated, minimal reality. Yet this reduced reality has a certain limited legitimacy, since acknowledgement of Jesus as the Christ is by no means universal. It can also perform a positive service in ensuring that the figure confessed as the Christ really is Jesus and not a fictive surrogate. The differentiations it offers between the 'historical' and the 'unhistorical' have the effect of tearing apart the seamless garment of the gospel narrative, subjecting it to a methodologically atheistic view of history. Yet these differentiations also serve to make visible the fact that the Jesus of the gospels is the Jesus who was *received as* the Christ in early Christian faith and confession. They make it impossible to read the gospels as purely factual accounts of a Jesus who just *is* the Christ, the Son of God, in abstraction from his reception as such. Without this reception, Jesus *is not* the Christ; it is integral to who he is to evoke the confession that finally achieves normative form in the fourfold canonical testimony. Even in its much-maligned 'prejudice against the supernatural', modern historical research serves to illuminate the nature of that testimony and so contributes towards a genuinely evangelical hermeneutic.

All this suggests that the relationship between Christian faith and historical research is to be seen as an ongoing critical dialogue about Jesus and his significance. There is no pre-established harmony between the two sides, and the hope for an eventual consensus is in current circumstances utopian. But neither is this a purely negative relationship of absolute antagonism or indifference. The dialogue may at least serve to clarify why it is that for some Jesus is one of the prophets, whereas for others he is the Christ. Each side in the dialogue remains an unresolved problem to the other – and, as such, an opportunity to learn something new.

Notes

1. A figure towards the higher end of this spectrum is suggested in Funk and Hoover 1993, which prints the sayings of Jesus that Funk's 'Jesus Seminar' regarded as certainly authentic in red, and those regarded as probably or partially authentic in pink.
2. See e.g. Fredriksen 1988:18–61, 94–126, who distinguishes 'Images of Jesus in the Gospels and Paul' from the 'Historical Image of Jesus', which is located in 'the World of Judaism'.
3. For a recent statement along these lines, see Johnson 1996. His work is largely a polemical critique of the 'Jesus Seminar' and of scholars associated with it, such as Robert Funk, Marcus Borg and J. D. Crossan. But the real intellectual and theological substance of the best work in the 'historical Jesus' genre over the past two centuries should not be overlooked; Albert Schweitzer was not entirely mistaken when he wrote of the nineteenth-century quest that 'the greatest achievement of German theology is the critical investigation of the life of Jesus' (Schweitzer 2000:3).
4. In arguing this case, I develop further the position outlined in Watson 1994:223–31, 241–64, and Watson 1997:33–93.
5. Contrast the view of N. T. Wright, for whom the historian poses the dilemma: 'Either solve the historical puzzle [of the emptiness of Jesus' tomb] by agreeing that Jesus' body was transformed into a new sort of life, or leave it in essence unsolved by coming up with flights of fancy, which themselves create far more problems . . . [D]o we in fact have good grounds for ruling the straightforward solution out of court a priori?' (Borg and Wright 1999:124). This use of the word 'straightforward' is idiosyncratic.

6. Here and elsewhere in this chapter, references to 'the historian' reflect my assumption that representatives of the more sceptical tendency in New Testament scholarship have, overall, a better claim to be doing what secular historians would readily accept as 'history' than those who argue for the maximal 'historicity' of the canonical gospels. Other contributors to this volume might well wish to dissent from this.

7. The phrase 'Jesus as the Christ', used repeatedly in the discussion that follows, is derived from Tillich 1951–63:2.98, as is the focus on the Caesarea Philippi story.

8. The classic account of the relationship between modern historical research on the gospels and the modern view of history in general is still that of Troeltsch 1972. Troeltsch is still prepared to contemplate the possibility that history as a whole has a goal, and therefore a meaning; this appears to be one of the points at which modern and postmodern philosophies of history divide.

9. 'Jesus as the Christ is both a historical fact and a subject of believing reception. One cannot speak the truth about the event on which Christianity is based without asserting both sides' (Tillich 1951–63:2.98). 'Without this reception the Christ would not have been the Christ, namely, the manifestation of the New Being in time and space . . . He would not have been the Christ even if he had claimed to be the Christ. The receptive side of the Christian event is as important as the factual side. And only their unity creates the event upon whch Christianity is based' (p. 99).

10. If this point is accepted, then an argumentative rhetoric such as the following becomes redundant: 'Of course if one rules out the supernatural *a priori*, there is much here that will have to be dismissed or radically reinterpreted. For those open to a God who occasionally intervenes miraculously into his universe, however, several arguments favor the trustworthiness of the material' (Blomberg 1997:208, where the reference is to the Matthean and Lucan birth stories). But the gospels everywhere testify to the fact that Jesus is the Christ, and to his reception as such; that is, they present the life of Jesus as, from beginning to end, God's definitive self-disclosive action for the reconciliation of the world. To speak of this God as 'a God who occasionally intervenes into his universe' is a piece of untheological reductionism.

11. Contrast L. T. Johnson's claim that 'Christians direct their faith not to the historical figure of Jesus but to the living Lord Jesus . . . [T]heir faith is confirmed, not by the establishment of facts about the past, but by the reality of Christ's power in the present' (Johnson 1996:142–43). But that is to detach the risen Jesus from his history – the true story of his life, death and resurrection, which is also the true story of how God was in Christ reconciling the world to God's self. All that is relegated to the past, where it represents the prehistory of the risen Christ, and the emphasis is placed on a post-history that is also present occurrence. But the past in question is the past of God's definitive eschatological action for the reconciliation of the world, and it can therefore become present in the encounter with the risen Jesus without losing its pastness.

12. Hans Frei's important and influential claim that the identity of Jesus Christ is rendered only by way of the fourfold gospel narrative is insufficiently attentive to this danger; see Frei 1974; Frei 1975; Frei 1993:45–93.

11 Many gospels, one Jesus?

STEPHEN C. BARTON

One of the most striking features of the history of the early church is the decision to include four gospels in the canon of Christian Scripture. The aim of this chapter is to explore the significance of the fourfold gospel for our knowledge of Jesus. The main argument will be that the four gospel texts bear witness in distinctive ways to the one gospel message at the heart of which is the one person, Jesus of Nazareth. That there are four gospels standing side by side in the canon, none of which has been subordinated to another, is an invitation to recognise that the truth about Jesus to which the gospels bear witness is *irreducibly plural* without being either incoherent or completely elastic. The fourfold gospel points to the profundity of Jesus' impact on his followers, the inexhaustibility of the truth about him, and the way in which knowledge of Jesus is necessarily self-involving.

WHAT IS THE PROBLEM?

The fact of four gospels in the canon – themselves a selection from a larger number mostly now lost – obviously raises questions about our knowledge of Jesus. These questions push in opposite directions. On the one hand, there are questions arising from the fact of having *more than one* account of Jesus in the canon. Are the four gospel testimonies so diverse that we can have no confidence that they bring us into contact with the one Jesus? On the other hand, there are questions relating to the *restriction to four*. Given that, at a very early stage in the church's history, a decision was made to accept only four gospels as canonical, and that other (i.e. the apocryphal and gnostic) gospels were not included, are we left arbitrarily with the traditions which happened to be prized by people who knew no better or who happened to be the party in power at the time?

Both sets of questions are legitimate and important. Why? Because they have to do with the *grounds for our knowledge of Jesus*. Since, according to Christian teaching, human identity and salvation are bound up inextricably with our knowledge of Jesus, the authority of the fourfold gospel or of some alternative (one gospel only? an unlimited multiplicity?) deserves considered attention.[1]

THE SHAPES THIS PROBLEM TAKES IN THE (POST-)MODERN WORLD

Perhaps surprisingly, this issue is alive and well in current scholarly and popular debate. Take feminist criticism, with its central concern to critique and reinterpret the tradition in ways that overthrow patriarchal domination in church and society in order to bring about the liberation of women. Given that questions about the New Testament canon are *normative* questions relating directly to issues of authority, identity and church polity, and given also that the canon is a product of decisions by a patriarchal hierarchy in the early church, may it not be the case that the fourfold gospel canon is too restrictive, denying to women the 'lost coins' of inspiration and authority available in the (so-called) apocryphal gospels? In brief, is the fourfold gospel canon an instrument of male domination? The assumption that this may well be the case has led in one of two directions: some *expand* the canon to include apocryphal works (including apocryphal gospels), while others *go behind* the canonical gospels to see if the Jesus who can be found there is amenable to interpretation in feminist terms as (implicitly or explicitly) an advocate and practitioner of women's liberation. (See further Schüssler Fiorenza 1995b; Kwok and Schüssler Fiorenza 1998, esp. 29–36.)

The status of the fourfold gospel canon is also at issue in another area of scholarly and popular debate: the 'Quest of the historical Jesus'. Arising in part out of a suspicion that, in the interests of early church orthodoxy, the fourfold gospel *conceals* the truth about the 'real' Jesus as much as it reveals it, the attempt is made to reconstruct the 'historical' Jesus independently of the canonical shape of the gospels. Again, as in the case of feminism – another form of ideological criticism whose historical and philosophical genealogy it shares to some extent – this leads in one of two directions with respect to the fourfold gospel: either the expansion of the canon (sometimes to the point of doing away with the idea of a canon altogether) in order to draw upon whatever sources allow an historical reconstruction of Jesus, or going behind it by means of source, form and redaction criticism.[2] In passing, it is worth noting that, if a more certain knowledge of the 'real' Jesus is the goal of those engaged in this Quest, the results are not all that promising. What we are given is Jesus the Jewish Prophet, the Cynic Jesus, the Zealot Jesus, Jesus the Mediterranean Peasant, Jesus the Sage, and so on (cf. Witherington 1995;

Moxnes 1998). In other words, dispensing with the fourfold gospel does not necessarily solve the problem of a plurality of portraits of Jesus. Instead it gives us a different plurality.

A third example is less mainstream but no less interesting. It arises occasionally in journalistic and media-inspired debates, and has as its focus an interest in what we might call the 'esoteric Jesus'. In this context, *conspiracy theories* tend to thrive: there is a truth to be known about Jesus which church authorities (such as the Vatican) are only too keen to suppress. The fourfold gospel does not give us Jesus-as-he-really-was: but new finds are making possible the discovery of the 'real' truth about him. The Dead Sea Scrolls are sometimes enlisted in the debate here (e.g. typically in Thiering 1992). So also are the gnostic texts from Nag Hammadi. The underlying assumption is that, interpreted with enough ingenuity and with a willingness to question the vested interests of the Establishment (whether academic or ecclesiastical), these texts offer the possibility, not only of filling in historical gaps in our background knowledge, but of revealing a different and more authentic Jesus altogether. In the context of these debates, the fourfold gospel is as irrelevant as the canon as a whole. New gospels and a new canon take their place. The Jesus who surfaces is the Jesus previously hidden but now brought to light by the wit of the investigative journalist.[3]

Curiously, these basically liberal or radical attempts to establish our knowledge of Jesus by looking beyond or behind the fourfold gospel canon are mirrored to some degree by strategies that come from the other end of the religious and theological spectrum altogether. That is to say, in religiously conservative circles, there is a tendency to accept the fourfold gospel (on scriptural or traditional grounds) while at the same time playing down the inherent plurality of four gospels in one canon. There is a tension here, at the heart of which is a set of beliefs about revelation and salvation. If revelation comes through Scripture (and tradition), and if assurance of salvation comes through receiving that scriptural revelation as true, then it is vital that the testimony of the gospels to Jesus as Saviour and Lord is uniform and stable. One way to ensure this is to ignore the differences between the gospels and concentrate on the important 'purple passages'. Alternatively, rather than ignore the differences, the attempt is made to *harmonise* them in order to allow the plurality of gospels to speak with a single voice. Sometimes, that voice is provided by giving precedence to just one of the four gospels, for example, the Gospel of John, as if Matthew, Mark and Luke 'really say' the same as John but John says it better. Whichever of these alternatives is followed, this approach adopts (implicitly or otherwise) a canon 'within' the canon, and, in that sense, it is like those approaches already described which go behind or beyond the canon to something accepted as more important.

What these brief case-studies show is that the question, 'many gospels, one Jesus?', is not only alive and well, but also of central importance in a wide variety of areas of study and of religious and secular life.[4] Before proceeding further, however, it needs to be demonstrated that, at the level of the actual gospel narratives, there is a significant issue: *the plurality is there* and has to be reckoned with. Any unifying moves have to take this plurality into account.

A DEFINITE PLURALITY

The first point to make is that, not only are there four gospels in the canon, but each differs from the other. It is not just the case, for example, that the synoptic Gospels of Matthew, Mark and Luke – called 'synoptic' because they share traditions in common and therefore can be 'seen together' – are like each other and different from the Gospel of John, even if their literary interdependence gives the Synoptics greater homogeneity. Indeed, the gospels themselves provide strong evidence that, at least to some extent, one of the motives for their creation was the desire to improve upon (i.e. to give a more compelling account of Jesus than) their predecessors. In other words, there was an impetus towards a multiplicity of gospels from the beginning. Thus (assuming both the chronological priority of Mark and that Matthew used Mark), Matthew 'improves' Mark by incorporating and massively expanding his narrative of Jesus' life, death and resurrection and by making minor modifications of many kinds. Luke states, as one of his specific reasons for writing, his desire to give his addressee Theophilus a life of Jesus that goes further than the '*many*' previous accounts, '. . . so that you [Theophilus] may know the truth concerning the things about which you have been instructed' (Luke 1.1–4). And the Gospel of John shows a clear awareness of having been selective in the use of the Jesus tradition and of using the tradition in a creative way: 'Now Jesus did *many other signs* in the presence of his disciples *which are not written in this book*. But these are written so that you may come to believe . . .' (John 20.30–31; cf. also 21.24–25).

But having said just now that the Synoptics themselves represent a genuine multiplicity, it is nevertheless also the case that John is distinctive in comparison with the Synoptics taken together (cf. usefully Smith 1980). First, they differ in their accounts of Jesus' origins. Mark begins with the appearance of John the Baptist at the River Jordan and Jesus' baptism by him. Matthew and Luke take us a stage further back and provide us with genealogies, birth and (at least in the case of Luke) infancy narratives. John shows no interest in the birth and boyhood of Jesus, and instead focuses all our attention on his identification of Jesus as the incarnation of the pre-existent *Logos* (Word) of God (John 1.1–18).

There are also major differences in the accounts of Jesus' miracles. Whereas in the Synoptics the demon exorcisms bulk large, in John there are none at all. Nor is there any account of the Transfiguration, an event which is so pivotal in the Synoptics and which would have lent itself so readily to John's interest in demonstrating the divine 'glory' (*doxa*) of Jesus as the Son of God. Of the healing miracles, John has no precise parallel to any of the Marcan healings, and he reduces the number to just four, a fraction of the number in the Synoptics. When it comes to the interpretation of the miracles, there is another contrast. In the Synoptics, they are pointers to the in-breaking of the kingdom of God in Jesus (cf. Matt 12.28 par. Luke 11.20). In John, they are 'signs' (*sēmeia*) whose purpose is much more explicitly christological: to reveal the identity of Jesus as the divine Son (e.g. John 2.11). Jesus, the proclaimer of the kingdom in the Synoptics, becomes Jesus the king in John; and the miracles are signs of his kingship (cf. John 6.15; 18.33–38a).

But it is perhaps in the teaching of the Johannine Jesus that John's distinctiveness comes most strongly to the fore. For example, although he speaks in figures and allegories, he does not teach in 'kingdom' parables in the way that is so characteristic of the Jesus of the Synoptics (e.g. Mark 4; Matt 13; Luke 15). Instead, and in contrast with the pithy aphorisms of the Synoptics, there are long convoluted discourses in which a theme is taken and developed at length in a rather homiletic style. And in relation to the content of Jesus' teaching, it is generally true to say that most of the synoptic teaching is not in John, and most of the Johannine teaching is not in the Synoptics. Again, the synoptic proclaimer of the coming of the kingdom of God becomes the Johannine revealer of himself as God's 'I am' (e.g. John 4.26; 6.35; 8.12, 58; 10.11; 11.25; etc.).

There can be no question, therefore, of denying either the differences between each of the four gospels or the difference between John and the Synoptics. The undoubted evidence of literary interrelationship between the Synoptics demonstrated by source criticism – for example, the overwhelming likelihood that Matthew and Luke used Mark – make these differences all the more remarkable. That is to say, the respective gospel writers had an evident sense of freedom – of *obligation* even – to retell the story of Jesus in ways significantly different from (and, from their respective points of view, implicitly better than) their predecessors. Likewise, the evidence of a likely interrelationship between the Synoptics and John, as demonstrated by traditio-historical analysis, shows the extent to which John, claiming the inspiration of the Spirit-Paraclete (cf. John 14.25–26; 16.12–15), felt obliged, nevertheless, to take the Jesus tradition in new directions.

FOUR PORTRAITS OF JESUS, NOT ONE

To reinforce the point that the plurality of canonical accounts of Jesus is real, it is worth attempting a thumbnail characterisation of each of the four portraits of Jesus, following the canonical order (see further Kingsbury 1981; Stanton 1989; Barton 1992). For Matthew, Jesus is Immanuel, 'God with us' (cf. Matt 1.23; 28.20): the one who as God's Son authoritatively reveals the life of the kingdom of heaven and invites into discipleship all who accept his invitation, follow his example and obey his teaching. With the coming of Jesus as the Messiah of the end-time, God has drawn near to bring salvation and judgement to Israel and the nations through the revelation of his will, above all in the death of his Son 'for the forgiveness of sins' (Matt 26.28). This brings into being a 'new covenant' community, the *ekklēsia* ('church') of disciples of Jesus drawn from people of every nation, Gentiles as well as Jews. The ending of Matthew ties all the main threads together: the pre-eminent and universal authority of Jesus as the crucified and risen Son who comes to his people; the command to the disciples to go on mission to all nations, baptising as Jesus himself was baptised and teaching as Jesus had taught them; and the reassuring promise of his sovereign presence 'to the end of the age' (Matt 28.16–20).

The Jesus of Mark's Gospel is a figure of mystery and paradox who evokes incomprehension and awe-struck 'fear and trembling'. He is the Spirit-empowered Son of God and heavenly Son of Man (cf. Dan 7.13–14) who teaches and heals 'with authority', but who nevertheless '*must* suffer many things' (Mark 8.31; 9.31; 10.33) and whose life ends with a cry of forsakenness on a Roman cross. In this fundamental paradox is the 'messianic secret' for which Mark is famous. It is the 'secret' of the hiddenness of the saving power of God in the weakness of the Son of God who, in obedience to the divine will, gives his life as 'a ransom for many' (Mark 10.45). To this secret, only those with faith are given access: they are portrayed in the narrative as a woman with a chronic illness, a Gentile woman with a demonised daughter, children brought to Jesus, a blind beggar by the roadside, and the like. It is a mystery of cosmic significance sustained right through to the end, an ending whose difference from that of Matthew could hardly be greater: 'So they [the women] went out and fled from the tomb, for terror and amazement had seized them; and they said nothing to anyone, for they were afraid' (Mark 16.8).

In Luke's writing, there is a profound innovation. Luke tells the story of Jesus in, not one part, but two: what we call the Gospel according to Luke and the Acts of the Apostles. The two-part narrative represents a deliberate authorial decision. What was at stake for Luke was a way of seeing history. (It is there in Matthew and Mark also, but not so emphatically.) In brief, God's saving purposes for humankind are being fulfilled (1) in the mission of Jesus the Messiah to Israel in the power of the Spirit (the Gospel), and (2) in the mission of Jesus' apostles 'to the ends of the earth' in the power of the same Spirit (Acts). 'Today' is the day of salvation (cf. Luke 2.11; 4.21; 19.9; 23.43), a message which Jesus takes all the way to Jerusalem, and which Paul takes all the way to Rome. The coming of Jesus inaugurates the new age of eschatological (end-time) fulfilment of God's promises to Israel. This is an age of unbounded grace in which salvation is offered to all who repent and come with joy to Jesus' eschatological banqueting table. For the self-righteous this is a scandal; for the 'poor, maimed, blind and lame' it is joy and peace and issues in praise to God. Once again, the Gospel's ending is paradigmatic of the evangelist's distinctive picture as a whole. There is the exaltation of Jesus, the empowerment of the apostles, the central role in salvation history of Jerusalem and the Temple, and the joyful doxology of eschatological fulfilment: 'While he [the risen Jesus] was blessing them, he withdrew from them and was carried up into heaven. And they worshipped him, and returned to Jerusalem with great joy; and they were continually in the Temple blessing God' (Luke 24.51–53).

What, finally, of John's portrait of Jesus (of which something has been said already)? Perhaps most striking is the cosmic scale of the drama of salvation in which the Jesus of John plays the main part. Somehow, to call Jesus 'Messiah', if by that is meant Israel's saviour, while it is true, is not enough (cf. 6.15). Rather, Jesus is recast as the incarnate Son of the heavenly Father who shows God's love to the whole world. Above all, he is identified with the divine *Logos* (Word) of God, pre-existent with God. Like the Wisdom figure of biblical and Jewish tradition, he is the agent through whom God created the world. He is the bearer of the divine glory. And he is the One who descended from heaven and took flesh as Jesus of Nazareth (cf. John 1.1–18 and *passim*). His incomparability as the giver of 'eternal life' is revealed in the gigantic sign-miracles he performs before the people in the first main part of John's Gospel (chs. 1–12), culminating in the raising of Lazarus his friend, 'dead *four days*' (John 11.39). In the second part of the Gospel (chs. 13–21), his incomparability is also revealed in his ascent back to the Father via the cross and resurrection to prepare a place in heaven for 'his own', an ascent which shows that he (and no other) is, indeed, 'the way, the truth and the life' (John 14.6). Indeed, so incomparable is Jesus that traditional Christian belief in the coming of salvation and judgement in time *future* reflected in the Synoptics is transposed in John into an assurance that salvation and judgement have come *already* with the coming, in Jesus, of the heavenly Son of Man.

These thumb-nail sketches lead to only one conclusion. The accounts of the life of Jesus in the four canonical gospels are irreducibly diverse. Each has an integrity of its own. As redaction criticism and (more recently) narrative criticism have helped us to see, we *have* to speak of 'the Jesus of Matthew', 'the Jesus of Mark', and so on. Harmonisation (i.e. trying to make all four gospels say the same thing), at least at the level of what the gospels actually say, is not possible. Nor, given the evident sense on the part of the gospel writers that no single account could do full justice to its sublime subject matter, is harmonisation even desirable. This does not mean that nothing coherent can be said about Jesus, nor that it is a matter of 'anything goes'. What it does mean is that our knowledge of Jesus will always be partial, always open to correction, always a matter of listening to the diverse testimonies of those who claim to know or to have known him. That will include the testimonies of the gospel writers themselves.

PRECEDENTS AND ANALOGIES: PLURALITY IN THE BIBLE AND EARLY JUDAISM

In passing, it is worth observing that this clear plurality in the gospel accounts of the life of Jesus is not unprecedented from the viewpoint of the canon as a whole and developments in early Judaism. In the Old Testament, there is a very significant amount of narrative repetition at both micro- and macro-levels (cf. Alter 1981:88–113), the most striking examples of the latter being the parallel accounts of the Davidic dynasty in the books of Kings and Chronicles. If we cast our net wider to include the literature of early Judaism (cf. Nickelsburg 1981), we note there that stories from the Bible are retold and multiple traditions about the patriarchs and prophets take shape. For example, the *Book of Jubilees* elaborates the narrative running from Gen 1 to Exod 12; the story of Joseph is retold and elaborated in *Joseph and Asenath*; patriarchal death-bed scenes provide the occasion for the account of the *Testaments of the Twelve Patriarchs*; and the *Testament of Moses* retells the events described in Deut 31–34.

This implies something important about the nature of biblical and related literature: that its main concern was not to give a single, fixed account of the past, but to provide authoritative, scriptural resources to enable Israel (and subsequently the Jews) to live *from the past in the present and with a view to the future.* For this to be possible, multiple retellings and ongoing elaborations of the oral and literary inheritance were essential.

Given that the transmission and inscribing of the gospel traditions about Jesus took place in a primarily Jewish milieu and was shaped heavily by scriptural precedents, it is very likely that similar dynamics were at work. The story of Jesus, told and retold, provided authoritative, scriptural resources enabling believers in Christ to 'follow' him, as the first disciples had done, in subsequent generations. The remembrance (*anamnēsis*) of Jesus was not a way of 'fixing' him in the past, but of encountering now, in the present, the one who had been with the disciples then (cf. 1 Cor 11.23–34a; see further Dahl 1976).

WHAT IS A GOSPEL?

As well as observing scriptural precedents that make the plurality of gospels in the canon understandable, we also need to ask *what a gospel is.* For it may be the case that the phenomenon of 'many gospels' is only a problem if the nature and purpose of the gospels are misunderstood.

The first point to be made here has to do with the word 'gospel' itself (see further Talbert 1981). In earliest Christian usage, 'the gospel' (*to euaggelion*) referred to the message of salvation and judgement proclaimed by Jesus (cf. Mark 1.14–15) and, subsequently, by the apostles (cf. 1 Cor 1.17–25; Rom 1.1–5). The gospel, in other words, was *an announcement of hope and warning* in view of the drawing near of God. Because God's presence was believed to have been displayed pre-eminently in Jesus himself – in his life, death and resurrection – the message of the gospel came to focus on Jesus.

This message was communicated primarily in oral form by those who could claim to be witnesses (cf. Acts 1.15–26, esp. vv. 21–22; 1 Cor 9.1; 15.1–11). But from very early days, the ongoing oral proclamation was accompanied and supplemented by written forms of communication (cf. Luke 1.1–4; John 20.30–31). Some of these took the form of letters, as in the case of Paul; and here, the extent to which the letters represent personal testimony to the living Lord is noteworthy. Other written communication took a form most like what the ancients would have called *bioi* ('lives') of Jesus (see Burridge 1992). They are called 'gospels' because their content is *the* gospel of the drawing near of God in Christ. Hence, in the opening of Mark ('The beginning of the gospel of Jesus Christ, the Son of God'), 'gospel' designates *both* a literary work for which this first sentence is the opening *and* a proclamation whose source and content is 'Jesus Christ, the Son of God' (Mark 1.1; cf. 1.14–15; 8.35; 10.29; 14.9).

Understanding the nuances of the term 'gospel' in this way is important because it allows us to see that *multiple and diverse* testimonies to Christ, in forms both oral and written, were an inevitable expression of the revelatory impact he made on those who came to know him before and after the resurrection. This impact was *personal.* That is implicit in the gospel superscriptions, which take the form 'the gospel according to so-and-so' (see now Hengel 2000:48–52): in other words, the *one* gospel from and about Jesus Christ *in the version of* Matthew or Mark or Luke or John. It was also *deep and ongoing*: no single narrative could convey it adequately. More than one gospel was not only inevitable but also necessary.

WHY FOUR?

This question invites answers at the historical level and at the theological level – though, as we shall see, the two are closely intertwined. We begin with the historical, noting what was said earlier, that developments generally took two directions: towards multiplication (why *only four* and not more?) and, alternatively, towards reduction (why not *just one* gospel in the canon?). (See further Cullmann 1956, Stanton 1990 and Hengel 2000.)

Initially, the trend was towards multiplication, not only with the writing of the four gospels, each seeking to improve upon or supplement its predecessor, but also with the writing of other 'gospels', some of which were no more than collections of the sayings (*logia*) of Jesus, like the *Gospel of Thomas*, others of which were elaborations, using legendary material to fill in the silences about Jesus left by the earlier gospels. Examples of the latter are birth and infancy 'gospels', like the *Protoevangelium of James* and the *Infancy Gospel of Thomas*. There are also 'gospels' that elaborate the other end of Jesus' life. *The Gospel of Peter* is an apocryphal reworking and expansion of the passion and resurrection, while other works contain apocryphal post-resurrection revelations, like *The Apocalypse of Peter*, the *Epistle of the Apostles* and the *Gospel of Mary*.[5]

At the same time, and perhaps in part as a reaction against this multiplicity, there was a trend towards reducing the number of gospels, even to the point of accepting just one. We know from Irenaeus that there were docetic circles that preferred the Gospel of Mark, and that the Ebionites recognised only the Gospel of Matthew. As is also well known, Marcion (died *c.* 160) accepted as valid (by virtue of its link with Paul) only an edited version of the Gospel of Luke, and dispensed with the rest. In the Syrian church, Tatian took a different line. Rather than accepting as valid only one of the four, he synthesised or 'harmonised' the four into one, in a work (*c.* 170) that became known as the *Diatessaron* (i.e. 'the [one] from the four').

How, then, did a fourfold gospel gain acceptance over these alternatives? At the mundane level, one reason probably has to do with an important innovation in the early church: the use of the codex rather than the scroll. The codex allowed more than one gospel to be bound together side by side; and there is early evidence of Christian codices containing all four gospels. Indeed, it may be the case that the fourfold gospel presupposes the four-gospel codex and vice versa: the fourfold gospel was made a practical possibility by the codex, and, conversely, the development of the multiple gospel codex was an expression of the acceptance of the fourfold gospel (see Stanton 1990:326–29, 336–40).

But the main reason is more profound: it concerns the preservation of the unity and catholicity of the church in the shared remembrance of Jesus, by bringing together in a single, fourfold collection the most authoritative testimony to him. The most famous ancient defence of this fourfold gospel is that of the second-century Bishop of Lyons, Irenaeus (*c.* 130–200). His argument reflects the concern of the early church to show, among other things, that the fourfold gospel was not arbitrary. The relevant passage from his work *Against Heresies*, written *c.* 180, is worth quoting at length[6] (3.11.8–9, in Richardson *et al.* 1953:1.382–3):

> The gospels could not possibly be either more or less in number than they are. Since there are four zones of the world in which we live, and four principal winds, while the Church is spread over all the earth, and the pillar and foundation of the Church is the gospel, and the Spirit of life, it fittingly has four pillars, everywhere breathing out incorruption and revivifying men. From this it is clear that the Word, the artificer of all things, he who sits upon the cherubim and sustains all things, being manifested to men gave us the gospel, fourfold in form but held together by the Spirit. As David said, when asking for his coming, 'O sitter upon the cherubim, show yourself.' For the cherubim have four faces, and their faces are images of the activity of the Son of God. For the first living creature, it says, was like a lion, signifying his active and princely and royal character; the second was like an ox, showing his sacrificial and priestly order; the third had the face of man, indicating very clearly his coming in human guise; and the fourth was like a flying eagle, making plain the giving of the Spirit who broods over the church. Now the Gospels, in which Christ is enthroned, are

like these . . . Again, the Word of God himself used to speak to the patriarchs before Moses, in a divine and glorious manner, but for those under the Law he established a priestly and liturgical order; after this, becoming man, he sent out the gift of the Holy Spirit into the whole earth, guarding us by his own wings. As for the activity of the Son of God, such is the form of the living creatures; and as is the form of the living creatures, such is also the character of the Gospel. For the living creatures were quadriform, and the gospel and the activity of the Lord is fourfold. Therefore four general covenants were given to mankind: one was that of Noah's deluge, by the bow; the second was Abraham's, by the sign of circumcision; the third was the giving of the Law by Moses; and the fourth is that of the Gospel, through our Lord Jesus Christ. Since this is the case, they are foolish and uninstructed, even audacious, who destroy the pattern of the gospel, and present either more or less than four forms of the gospel – the former, because they claim to have found more than the truth, the latter because they annul the dispensation of God . . .

Irenaeus' arguments clearly presuppose ways of thinking that do not fit well with modern notions of rationality. But they are instructive nonetheless. In this case, he starts from what he takes to be the *givenness* of the fourfold gospel and argues in *post hoc* fashion for a deep concurrence between their fourfold character and God's providence in creation and salvation. Thus, by theological and scriptural arguments of a partly numerological kind, reinforced by appeals to the scriptural texts on the 'four living creatures' around the heavenly throne (cf. Ezek 1; Rev 4), Irenaeus shows that, far from being arbitrary, the fourfold gospel is miraculous and providential, the very manifestation of God's will and character.

For present purposes, what is of lasting importance here is Irenaeus' implicit recognition that a defence of the fourfold gospel has to come *from outside but not independently of* the gospels themselves, that the validity of the subsequently canonised fourfold gospel has to be judged against a canon (or 'rule') *of another kind*, namely, the 'Rule of Faith' (*regula fidei*).[7] The Rule of Faith, the earliest references to which come from Irenaeus himself, is understood as the basis in universal (i.e. catholic) belief and practice on which the church orders its common life and distinguishes truth from error. On this basis, the fourfold gospel is not canonical because it is in the (literary) canon of Scripture; but rather, it is in the canon of Scripture because it is canonical.[8] That is to say, in the life and worship of the early church claiming the guidance of the Holy Spirit, the four gospels, and only these four, were found to bear *true and sufficient* (even if partial and incomplete) witness to the coming of God in Christ for the salvation of the world. The *gospels* bore witness to the *gospel*.

This helps to explain why more strictly historical matters about the gospels, important to us, were relatively unimportant to the leaders of the church in the first two centuries. Originally, for example, the gospels may have had no authorial attribution.[9] The important thing was not so much who wrote the gospels, but whether or not the gospels themselves were judged to be true and sufficient witnesses to Jesus. The authors were not 'authors' in our modern sense of the word. Rather, they saw themselves as 'servants of the word' (to use Luke's phrase in Luke 1.2), whose responsibility and calling was to pass on and interpret the oral and written tradition concerning Jesus and the gospel. In other words, of overriding importance was the desire to affirm the *apostolicity* of the gospels, the conformity of their contents with the gospel message. Attribution to an actual apostle or to the follower of an apostle was important primarily in serving that end.

FOUR GOSPELS, ONE JESUS AND CHRISTIAN FAITH

In the light of the preceding, we may conclude that Christian theology and spirituality would be seriously impoverished if, instead of having four gospels for our knowledge of Jesus, we had only one. For instead of receiving an invitation to encounter, through patient attention to multiple apostolic testimonies, the mystery of salvation revealed in Jesus, we might be tempted to think that whatever 'mystery' there was could be grasped in a single account, which left no questions unanswered and asked for none. With four gospels, we are challenged by the possibility that the reality to which they bear witness is too sublime to be encapsulated in any one account.

Thus, we do not need to see a plurality of gospels in a negative way at all – as if all it does is throw up damaging 'contradictions' that it is our duty to explain away, in case a single crack in the static edifice of Christian revelation were to bring the whole edifice down. On the contrary, what a plurality of gospels offers is a complex repetition and multiple elaboration that *intensifies and complicates*. The Jesus of whom the gospels tell is not fully known in the first encounter. We have to return again and again, not just to one gospel but to all four, and not just to the gospels but to the whole scriptural witness. And theological wisdom suggests that we will gain most out of successive encounters if we come to the gospels, not just on our own, but in good company: the good company of the communion of saints past and present, who embody in their lives and in their worship what true knowledge of Jesus, mediated by the gospels, is all about (cf. Matzko 1996).

Notes

1. This is the thrust of Childs 1984:143–56, esp. 153.
2. A recent example of 'historical Jesus' research that works with an expanded canon is represented in the Jesus Seminar. See Funk and Hoover 1993. The work of the Seminar is described by Borg 1994:160–81, who is one of its members. The 'fifth gospel' incorporated with the four canonical gospels is the *Gospel of Thomas*, a gnostic work discovered at Nag Hammadi in Egypt in 1945. For a lively critique of the Jesus Seminar and related works, see Johnson 1996, esp. 1–56.
3. See for this Loughlin 1995, on Baigent and Leigh 1982 as well as Baigent and Leigh 1991.
4. There is also a significant inter-religious dimension to this subject, which cannot be pursued here. I refer to the difficulty that the fourfold gospel canon poses for Muslims. In a personal correspondence of 7 December 2000, Dr Hugh Goddard, an expert in Muslim–Christian relations at Nottingham University, writes: 'Compared with the (relatively) simple and homogeneous Qur'an, therefore, the fact that there are four accounts of the Gospel of Jesus Christ is pretty perplexing to Muslims, since the Qur'an itself refers to the Gospel (singular) and Muslims' expectation is that that Gospel will be pretty like the Qur'an – i.e. a record of Jesus' message, the words which God told him to recite. In fact, of course, it isn't . . . Later Muslims thinking on this question therefore came up with the idea that the four Gospel accounts as they exist today are not a faithful record of the original Gospel given to Jesus, but versions made up by later generations of Christians which are therefore corrupt by virtue of not being original. Jesus' original message, therefore, according to most Muslims, has been lost, and that is one reason for the later coming of Islam – to restore the true message of Jesus.' For more on this see Goddard 1995.
5. Such sources are readily available in translation in Schneemelcher 1991, vol. 1. For an introductory survey, see Bauckham 1992.
6. Not least because of the influence of the symbolism of the 'four living creatures' on subsequent Christian art, including illuminated manuscripts of the fourfold gospel like the Book of Kells, in which Matthew is symbolised by the man-like creature, Mark by the lion, Luke by the ox and John by the eagle. For a lively exploration of the gospels that draws upon these characterisations, see Burridge 1994.
7. See further Hanson 1962:75–129. The contents of the Rule of Faith, beginning with passages from Irenaeus' *Against heresies*, are set out on pp. 86–91.
8. For a discussion of 'the relation of the Rule of Faith to Scripture' in the teaching of the Fathers, see Hanson 1962:102–17.
9. The matter is disputed. For the argument that the gospel superscriptions were original and that the gospels did not circulate at first anonymously, see Hengel 2000:50–56.

12 The Christ of the Old and New Testaments

R. W. L. MOBERLY

The belief that Jesus is the Christ has been fundamental to Christian faith down the ages. So basic a belief is it that it has become incorporated into essential Christian vocabulary. Already within the New Testament what is initially a Jewish title and role, 'the Christ/Messiah',[1] as commonly in the gospels, becomes a proper name, Jesus Christ, as commonly in the letters of Paul and in Christian usage subsequently;[2] and the followers of Jesus have been known as 'Christians' since earliest times (Acts 11.26).[3]

It is a belief that can also be seen to encapsulate what came to be the Christian conviction that the Bible should be composed of two testaments, the scriptures of Israel in conjunction with the apostolic writings of the early church. For Christians the Bible contains both an Old Testament, where the Jewish category of 'Christ/Messiah' is formulated and becomes an important category for expressing hope in God's action especially through the house of David, and a New Testament where Jesus fulfils and transforms Israel's existing categories. Thus, major issues of biblical interpretation as a whole centre on the affirmation that Jesus is the Christ.

The importance of this belief is readily seen in the four gospels, where the applicability of the title 'the Christ' to Jesus is centre stage. John's explicit statement of purpose in writing his gospel could in many ways stand for all the evangelists (and has been so taken in Christian history): 'These are written so that you may believe that Jesus is the Christ, the Son of God, and that through believing you may have life in his name' (John 20.31). Belief in Jesus as the Christ is primary, and it is life-giving.

HOW SHOULD WE PROCEED? ONE COMMON CRITICAL STORY

How should such a belief appropriately receive scholarly scrutiny? The way one tackles such a question is a major issue in its own right. For the answers one receives depend on the questions one asks. And the questions one asks depend upon the wider context within which one situates oneself.

The predominant approach in modern biblical criticism has been to utilise the sharper sense of historical awareness and critical historical method that developed in the Enlightenment. Anything inherited from the past must now be refracted through a critical historical prism. Thus the questions have predominantly focused on the origins and development of messianic beliefs in Israel and the early church. This has involved dating key texts in chronological sequence (which more often than not differs from the canonical sequence) and contextualising them within the likely beliefs and practices of their time of composition (which often gives them a meaning different from that which Christians subsequently came to hold). Thus the common context has been modernity's ability to subject received religious tradition to critical scrutiny and, if it finds it wanting, to say so.

One widespread way of telling the scholarly story (not, of course, the only way) would be to tell of a traditional belief that has been exploded by modern critical awareness. According to this story, Christian faith held that the Old Testament predicted a coming Messiah, a king and saviour – predictions which, while found throughout the Old Testament, are especially present in famous passages in Isaiah and the Psalms. Jesus came as the fulfilment of these, and the marvel of his matching the predictions is an argument for the truth of Christian faith.

This pattern is well displayed in the beautiful chapel of King's College, Cambridge. On the one hand, the chapel windows depict Old Testament stories with their New Testament counterparts directly adjacent to them. On the other hand, in the annual Christmas Eve service of Nine Lessons and Carols one can expect to hear read out an Old Testament passage such as Isa 9.2, 5, 'The people who walked in darkness have seen a great light ... For to us a child is born, to us a son is given ...', where the premise is that this is about Jesus, whose coming the New Testament relates.

Traditional. Beautiful. But unfortunately (though one may be permitted a nostalgic sigh) unbelievable, because it is based on what we now know to be mistakes.[4] On the one hand, the Old Testament does not predict a Messiah, let alone Jesus as that Messiah; if some of Israel's apparently 'larger-than-life' depictions of its king do have wider resonances, then these resonances are with exotic royal ideologies common in the ancient Near East (and so why should special significance be attributed to Israel's ideology?). On the other hand, Jesus' messianic claims within the gospels can no longer be confidently ascribed to him, for they may be put into his mouth as expressions of the convictions of the early church. Since, moreover, Caesar was still as securely on his throne in Rome after Jesus' life in Palestine as before, Jesus made no real difference anyway; the wider claims for Jesus in the New Testament are interesting evidence for ancient mythology and psychology which had a long afterlife but which now can, and indeed should (for our own good), be firmly dispensed with.[5]

IS THE CRITICAL STORY SUFFICIENTLY SELF-CRITICAL?

Such a story is hard to evaluate, for it is a complex mixture of insight and misrepresentation. One point that should be noted is that many of the key elements in the story are not in fact modern insights at all (however much modernity may have developed, emphasised, and found a wide audience for them), for they were anticipated by Jewish criticism of Christian faith already in antiquity and the Middle Ages. From the outset Christian belief in Jesus as Messiah was fiercely contested by many Jews who rejected such a belief. The heart of the Jewish critique is simple: if Jesus is the redeemer, why is the world still so unredeemed? The question is given particular poignancy by the extensive suffering of Jews within Christian cultures over the centuries.

Biblical interpretation is a corollary of the Jewish critique. On the one hand, if biblical texts speak of a king who establishes justice and peace – as in the famous Isaiah passage (9.6–7), 'To us a child is born, to us a son is given . . . of the increase of his government and of peace there will be no end, upon the throne of David . . . with justice and with righteousness, from now and for always' – then the plain sense of the text requires that justice and peace be permanently established before one can believe that the text has been fulfilled. On the other hand, it was regularly argued that biblical texts often appealed to by Christians as predicting Jesus do not in fact do so. The most famous text in this regard is the Immanuel prediction of Isa 7.14, cited in Matt 1.23. Jews regularly contended that this referred to a king in the time of Isaiah, probably Hezekiah (and modern scholarship has generally supported this, though the specific identification with Hezekiah remains open to debate).

Nonetheless, Christian belief in Jesus as the Christ was not formulated in ignorance of the problems of the world. The Jesus in whom Christians believed was executed by the Romans with the torturous execution reserved for the most abject – slaves and failed rebels; and his resurrection, in which they also believed, did not entail Jesus confronting his executioners with their mistake or his returning to adopt a more 'successful' programme than that which led him to the cross. The continuing might of the Roman Empire was not news to early Christians, who themselves were often persecuted and martyred for their faith. Nor were Christians unaware of conflict with the *prima facie* sense of certain Old Testament passages; otherwise, apologetic efforts to demonstrate the scriptural congruence of Christian faith would not have taken the form they did.

So the most interesting questions, which the critical story tends to over-simplify or marginalise, are surely: What does such a startling belief as that of Jesus as the Christ really mean? How might one appropriately determine whether or not such a contested belief could appropriately be believed to be true (or be falsified) at any time from its initial formulation up to the present day?

JESUS AS THE CHRIST IN THE SYNOPTIC GOSPELS

This chapter will try to suggest at least one way in which a scholarly story might be retold. The general context for this is that of 'postmodernity' – and the realisation that 'modernity' operated with assumptions that may be nei-ther as self-evident nor as generally true as was once supposed. This is not to retreat from the insights of modernity (for example, critical historiography). It is, rather, to question whether such insights really possess the kind of finality often ascribed to them, and to suggest that other insights may be no less significant.

We will look first at some of the gospel material, where the applicability of 'the Christ' to Jesus is at stake. In terms of method, serious imaginative engagement with the overall portrayal within the biblical text is primary. To be sure, critical historiography starts here too. However, a widespread consensus that various elements within the gospels are later additions to the tradition, and that the most 'original' elements are most important, has meant that interest in most modern discussions tends to be redirected from the portrayals as a whole to selected elements within them (with Mark con-sistently preferred to Matthew on the grounds that Mark is earlier than, and a source for, Matthew). A developmental history of messianic belief is then regularly offered. A common assumption is that the earlier and more 'original' a text is, then the better it is for understanding the truth about Jesus. Purity of origins is preferred to maturity of insight; methodological rigour is preferred to penetrative grasp of content. These are characteristic judgements whose status needs rethinking.

Within the gospels, there is a definite sense of Jewish expectation of a coming figure. It is perhaps best expressed in the words of John the Baptist, which his disciples put to Jesus: 'Are you the one who is to come, or should we wait for another?' (Matt 11.3 par. Luke 7.19–20). Interestingly the question is not 'Are you the Messiah?' but is expressed in a more general way, as though the expectation that a significant figure would appear and act on God's behalf was not necessarily tied to the category 'Messiah'.[6]

Within Matthew and Mark a key episode, which is a turning point in their narratives, is Peter's confession of Jesus at Caesarea Philippi.[7] Here the identity and significance of Jesus is explicitly at stake. It is Matthew's account which down the ages has been most significant and will be our focus here.

Matthew 16.13–28

A question that was probably being asked by his contemporaries ('Who does he think he is?') – and has certainly been asked by subsequent interpreters ('Who did he think he was?' 'What was Jesus' self-understanding?') – is turned around by Jesus ('Who do people generally, and you disciples specifically, think I am?'), perhaps because evaluation of Jesus' significance is inseparable from response to him. The disciples make clear that people are turning primarily to Israel's scriptures to try to find an answer, and they themselves do the same when Peter says: 'You are the Christ, the Son of the living God'. Jesus accepts Peter's words, seeing in them God-given insight, such that here is the foundation upon which the community of Jesus' followers will be built, a point Jesus reinforces with a memorable word play: 'And I tell you, you are Peter [Gk. *petros*], and on this rock [Gk. *petra*] I will build my church, and the gates of Hades will not prevail against it'.[8] Indeed in some way Peter's recognition of Jesus will admit or exclude people in relation to that divine kingdom of whose coming Jesus regularly speaks. One could hardly ascribe greater significance to Peter's recognition (hence the aptness for all the gospels of the Johannine summary that here is a belief which brings life). Jesus, however, perhaps surprisingly, then tells his disciples *not* to tell this truth to others.

If Jesus is the Christ, as Peter says, what does this really mean? Jesus takes the initiative and gives a first prediction of his coming suffering, death and resurrection. To Peter this seems incomprehensible, a contradiction of what had just been established; for how could the agent of God's kingship be removed by hostile human actions? Yet his attempt to correct Jesus on this point leads to a stinging rebuke and the reproach that he thinks in human categories which lack God's perspective. Jesus goes even further and generalises what he has just said about his own coming suffering and death – for only those who would 'be a disciple of Jesus', who will 'take up their cross' (so that the disciple is as one whose life is forfeit, being on the way to brutal Roman execution) and 'lose their lives', will gain life. The meaning of the Messiahship of Jesus, both for himself and for others, is being spelled out, and it is related to the climax and goal of all the gospel narratives, the crucifixion and resurrection of Jesus.

The other two prime passages relating to Jesus as the Christ come (unsurprisingly) in the passion narrative. In the trial before the Jewish authorities Jesus is asked 'Are you the Christ?' (Matt 26.63; Mark 14.61; Luke 22.67). It is clear from all accounts that Jesus does not deny it, but regards the term as inappropriate or misleading,[9] at least in that context. For if (as the evangelists make clear) the concern of the authorities is to find a sufficient reason for condemning Jesus, then 'the Christ' is little more than a convenient label, a pretext, and it would not be understood by those using it in any life-giving kind of way.

At the crucifixion the charge affixed to Jesus' cross is 'the king of the Jews', i.e. 'the Christ' (Matt 27.37; Mark 15.26; Luke 23.38; John 19.19).[10] Further, Jesus is mocked as a failed Christ or king – an impotent saviour, a king who will only get a kingdom by coming down from the cross (Matt 27.39–42; Mark 15.29–32; Luke 23.35–37). The evangelists, of course, are writing with heavy irony: the truth (that Jesus is king) is before people's eyes, yet they fail to see it; they think they know what words like 'salvation' and 'kingdom' mean – they mean escaping the cross, saving life, and on that basis winning adherents – when in fact it is only by Jesus' remaining on the cross that they can be realised.

The rightness before God of Jesus' dying thus is confirmed by God's raising Jesus from death, which becomes the definitive vindication of the way of Jesus. In Matthew's account the risen Jesus can speak of 'all authority in heaven and on earth given to him', with a consequent Christian mission without limit of person or place or time (28.18–20). That is to say, the way of Jesus, centred on his death and resurrection, has become the definitive way for humanity, and is a truth that must be made known so that people can enter into it. Or in Luke's account the risen Jesus says to two uncomprehending disciples on the way to Emmaus, 'How foolish you are and slow of heart to believe all that the prophets have declared! Were not these things necessary, that the Messiah should suffer and enter into his glory?' (24.25–26). That is to say, Jesus' mission is fully in accord with God's will as revealed in Israel's scripture, and his way of the cross is the key to his being the Messiah and entering divine glory. Thus Jesus' identity as the Christ is as central as it could be to the gospel portrayals of Jesus in his life, death and resurrection (even if many other categories are also used to depict him).

JESUS AND JEWISH EXPECTATIONS OF A MESSIAH

The texts that describe Jesus as 'the Christ' or 'king' all see these titles as applicable only in the context of a particular and distinctive understanding of what either term means. How is this to be understood?

A common, and natural, move is to set the gospel portrayal alongside contemporary Jewish hopes and expectations and to contrast it with them. Thus, for example, the Jews of Judaea were unwilling subjects of imperial Roman power (which was interested in Judaea primarily to safeguard the granaries of Egypt from which Rome was fed) and longed for another King David, the most successful military figure in Israel's history, to free them from Rome. A well-known Jewish text, the *Psalms of Solomon*, especially *Psalm* 17, probably written soon after Jerusalem came under Roman power in 63 BC, expresses such a hope clearly:

> See, Lord, and raise up for them their king, the son of David, to rule over your servant Israel in the time known to you, O God. Undergird him with the strength to destroy the unrighteous rulers, to purge Jerusalem from Gentiles who trample her to destruction.[11]

Jesus' Messiahship, by contrast, is not of such a military (or political) kind; difficulties over Jesus' Messiahship are the difficulties of persuading contemporary Jews, even his disciples, to abandon cherished hopes of armed deliverance from Rome (when Jews did attempt to fight against Roman rule in the wars of 66–70 and 132–35, the results were disastrous for them).

While such an account has value, at least three caveats are necessary. First, Jewish hopes and understandings at the time of Jesus are extremely diverse, in line with the diversity of their scriptures. While there is an un-doubted militancy in some first-century Jewish circles, this is one, not the only, Jewish position. Certainly Jesus opposes some contemporary under-standings, but his is at heart a position within, not over against, Jewish debate as to the meaning of their scriptures. The distinctiveness of Jesus' Messiahship lies in the profundity of his construal of certain self-giving el-ements within Israel's scriptures, and aspects of his construal appear also within rabbinic writings.

Secondly, if there is an obvious contrast between Jesus' kingship and that of the Davidic king in a text such as *Psalms of Solomon* 17, there is no less of a contrast with *any* conventional understanding of kingship. This is particularly clear when Jesus says to his disciples:

> You know that among the Gentiles those whom they recognise as their rulers lord it over them, and their great ones are tyrants over them. But it is not so among you; but whoever wishes to become great among you must be your servant, and whoever wishes to be first among you must be slave of all. For the Son of Man came not to be served but to serve, and to give his life a ransom for many.[12]

Any king (in any society prior to the modern west) is someone who by definition exercises power over others. Yet the gospels depict Jesus 'suffering'; the Greek verb is *paschein*, whose aorist infinitive is used of Jesus in such key passages as Matt 16.21, Luke 24.26. In Greek *paschein* ('to suffer') functions as a kind of passive to the verb *poiein* ('to do'). That is, the prime sense is not the endurance of physical or mental pain, but rather 'to be done to', to be acted upon by others (and without positive intent, as in actions of love). This gives a sense of paradox, indeed mystery, to Jesus' kingship: rule over others through being acted upon by others, dominion through service, life through death.[13]

Thirdly, when Jesus' kingship is contrasted with a military or political understanding, there remains a problem as to which positive categories should be used to depict it. There is a history of Christian depiction of Jesus as a 'spiritual' Messiah or king in a way that wholly removes his kingship from the public realm of human life and privatises it – thus effectively leaving earthly powers to pursue their course without let or hindrance. This is *not* what the gospels depict, for Jesus is rather concerned to redefine and re-enact human life as a whole in such a way that life becomes responsive to the reality of God, and able to embody God's priorities.[14] Ultimately, however, it is only God's action in raising Jesus from the dead which decisively shows that his is indeed the truly royal way, rather than a well-meaning hope doomed to disappointment in the brutal *Realpolitik* of Roman imperialism.

UNDERSTANDING JESUS AS AN INTRINSIC DIFFICULTY

Another issue, which follows from the previous point, concerns a recurrent emphasis of the gospel texts: that recognition of Jesus as Messiah is in no way obvious or straightforward. If Peter does recognise, then it is a gift of God (Matt 16.17), and even so he directly goes on to misunderstand the import of his recognition (Matt 16.21–23). If even the leading disciple misunderstands his own use of the word, it may become at least partially comprehensible why Jesus as Messiah is not something simply to be spread abroad – for that would risk encouraging an uncomprehending bandying around of the title or its equivalents, which the evangelists show happening in the mockery which characterises both the trial and the crucifixion. The texts thus imply that recognition of Jesus as the Christ is a demanding act of discernment, which becomes impossible to those who behave in a manipulative or abusive way.

An entirely different interpretation of this feature was given a century ago by William Wrede in one of the most influential modern studies of Mark,

The messianic secret (1901).[15] In a complex and multi-faceted argument, Wrede thought that Jesus became Messiah, and was recognised as such, only at the resurrection. Therefore all references to Jesus as Messiah within the gospels are retrojections of the convictions of the early church, while injunctions to silence in the gospel are apologetic early Christian devices to explain why Jesus' contemporaries failed to respond positively to him (i.e. because Jesus did not want to be recognised).

What is striking is the way Wrede transposes a practical problem (likely misunderstanding of 'the Christ') with moral and spiritual dimensions (complacency or hostility towards Jesus make misunderstanding inevitable) into a complex religio-historical hypothesis to do with tendentious rationalisations on the part of early Christians. Wrede (and many of those writing in his wake) never engages with the intrinsic meaning of the recurrent biblical portrayal of possible moral and spiritual obstacles to perceiving the work of God. Yet unless one takes with full seriousness the possibility that truth may be before people's eyes and yet they may be rendered incapable of perceiving it by their preconceptions and attitudes and actions, one is unlikely to understand something central to all the gospels in their portrayal of Jesus as the Christ.

OLD TESTAMENT USES OF 'MESSIAH' AND 'KING'

Thus far we have focused on the gospel portrayal of Jesus as 'the Christ' with some reference to the question of Jewish messianic expectations, but without considering the larger historical and scriptural context that the gospels presuppose. To this we must now turn.

However, when we look for antecedents to Jesus' Messiahship, we should remember that it is primarily Jesus' highly distinctive Messiahship, as portrayed in the gospels and affirmed by Christians, which makes this an issue. Despite the tradition that Rabbi Aqiba acclaimed Bar Kochba as Messiah in the second century AD, we do not know of another Jewish figure of the period who was seriously acclaimed as Messiah. Without Jesus, most of the texts that are closely scrutinised for incipient messianism would lose much of their interest and become mere footnotes in a rather different history of rabbinic messianism.

Within the Old Testament the term 'anointed' is not reserved for any one person, but is applied to those whose role in life was marked, perhaps initiated, by a solemn ritual of anointing. Thus Leviticus depicts rituals regularly performed by 'the anointed priest' (*ha-kohen ha-mashiaḥ*: Lev 4.3, 5, 16; 6.22 [Heb 6.15]). However, the term is used most commonly of kings.[16] Although the traditional associations of the term are specifically with depicting the house of David, the densest cluster of uses is in fact on the lips of David with reference to Saul, expressing David's reluctance to strike Saul (even when Saul was at his mercy) because Saul was 'YHWH's anointed'.[17] Nonetheless the phrase 'YHWH's anointed' is used of David in the same way as of Saul,[18] and clearly comes to be used of other kings in the line of David, especially in psalms which became important within Israel's worship.[19]

This terminology raises various technical issues. On the one hand, the Hebrew text of the Old Testament nowhere uses 'the anointed/Messiah' (*ha-mashiah*) on its own to denote a specific title or role; successive priests and Davidic kings were 'anointed ones'. Even the one undoubted reference, in the book of Daniel (9.25–26), to a future anointed figure (whoever he is) is to 'an anointed one' (*mashiah*) not 'the anointed one' (*ha-mashiah*). On the other hand, the background to New Testament usage lies within the context of Jewish reflections upon their scripture. Already in the second century BC the wording 'the anointed one/Messiah' was in use, perhaps originating as a popular abbreviation for the well-attested biblical phrase 'YHWH's anointed'.[20] In any case, the Greek of the Septuagint sometimes uses the definite article (*ho christos*), as in its rendering of Dan 9.26, while Hebrew usage of 'the anointed one' (*ha-mashiah*) can be found at Qumran.[21]

IMPLICATIONS OF THE OLD TESTAMENT AND ITS ANCIENT JEWISH INTERPRETATIONS

The preceding outline of Old Testament usage can be enlarged upon in various ways. First, because of the close association of 'anointed one' with 'king' (which could be used in poetic parallelism with each other, 1 Sam 2.10), continuing Jewish reflection on 'anointed ones' became inseparable from wider questions about the future and significance of the royal house of David. Thus one must look beyond specific words to the whole concept of kingship and its role within God's purposes, where the king is in significant ways analogous to a prophet as a person with responsibility to enact God's purposes on earth. The undoubted linkage between 'anointed one' and 'king', and its importance for Christian theology, should not obscure, however, that there was also considerable Jewish reflection, again in line with biblical usage, on priestly anointed figures, whose role was usually envisaged as complementing that of the royal figure; this is well attested at Qumran.

Secondly, a fundamental text for the house of David is 2 Sam 7 where God, through Nathan, promises David a royal dynasty in perpetuity: 'Your house and your kingdom shall be made sure for ever before me; your throne shall be established for ever' (v. 16). Yet with the fall of Jerusalem to the Babylonians in the early sixth century BC, the rule of the house of David over Judah came to an end and was never restored. This fact posed a difficult problem for Jewish belief in the reliability and faithfulness of their God whose promises about the house of David seemed called in question.

This issue is starkly faced in Psalm 89, a text whose depth and religious intensity is formative for early Jewish messianism. An initial hymn to a faithful God (vv. 1–18) leads into an account of God's promises to David (vv. 19–37, recalling the language of 2 Sam 7), in which God's promise is depicted in the most solemn and binding language in the whole Bible (vv. 34–37); yet what has happened seems fundamentally to call God's promise in question (vv. 38–45), and all the Psalmist can do is appeal to YHWH's steadfast love (*ḥesed*, vv. 46–51). The Psalmist refuses to deny either divine promise or contemporary calamity but insists on affirming them both in unresolved tension, while looking to the God who has caused the anguish as the one who is also its resolution.

Thirdly, the time when Jews sought to discern which of their religious texts were of enduring, indeed definitive, value – i.e. the time of the canonising of Hebrew Scripture – was most likely primarily in the post-exilic period. This was a time when there was no longer a Davidic king and, after a brief flurry around the figure of Zerubbabel in *c.* 520 BC, little prospect of any restoration: Judah became a small province under successive Persian and Greek dominion, and the senior Jewish figure became not a king but a high priest. Such evidence as we have suggests that royal texts were seen to have enduring significance in a variety of ways, both grounding the present in the past and also giving rise to new hopes for the future. What this means, in most general terms, is that the interpretation of the texts is likely to have developed in various kinds of metaphorical and symbolic modes (which did not exclude continuing literal interpretations also).

This process is perhaps clearest with the Psalms. It is one thing to recognise (as modern biblical interpretation has characteristically done) that psalms depicting a king probably arose in the First Temple period when Jerusalem had a Davidic king. Thus, for example, Psalm 2, which depicts God saying 'I have set my king on Zion, my holy hill', presupposes a ceremony of royal enthronement. But the question must also be asked how such texts were understood when there was no longer a king and when Psalm 2 was made with Psalm 1 into an introduction to the Psalter as a whole. There is, for example, some evidence that the Septuagint translation of the Psalms already attests a future messianic hope (see Schaper 1995, esp. 107–26, 138–64).

All this greatly enriches and complicates (depending on one's point of view) the interpretative task. The most characteristic approach of modern biblical scholarship has been to trace a history of texts and ideas. Thus, with texts such as royal psalms and Isaiah, one can work backwards to likely original context and meaning, and perhaps also forwards from that reconstructed original to the text in its present form and canonical context. Then one can trace the history of interpretation and usage beyond the biblical context. Extant non-biblical Jewish texts – such as *Jubilees, Testaments of the Twelve Patriarchs, Psalms of Solomon,* and the texts from Qumran – have been intensively scrutinised for their biblical interpretation in general and their 'messianic' interpretations in particular; a task which for Christians can be background to scrutinising the messianic interpretations contained within the New Testament. (Collins 1995 is a valuable guide.)

Yet one may ask not only how the Old Testament was used by the writers of the New Testament but also how far the Old Testament should continue to inform Christian understanding. Two extreme approaches must be eschewed: that which says that the Old Testament can only mean what the New Testament says it means, and that which says that the Old Testament can only mean what the original writers of particular texts thought those texts to mean. One must recognise that meaning to some extent depends on context, and that many texts went through various recontextualisations already within the time of the formation of the Old Testament. Likewise the New Testament appeal to the Old Testament, in a key passage such as Luke 24.25–27, should not be conceived narrowly or mechanistically in terms of particular messianic proof texts, though various kinds of proof texts of course play a not insignificant role from the New Testament onwards. Rather, 'fulfilment' is a broad and variable concept. Luke, for example, portrays Jesus' grasp of his own vocation primarily with reference to non-messianic texts in Deuteronomy about trust and obedience (4.1–13), before portraying Jesus as the specific fulfilment of Isa 61.1–2 (4.16–21); while the enduring moral and spiritual challenge of 'Moses and the prophets' is not negated or displaced by resurrection from the dead (16.19–31), even when it is the Messiah who is resurrected (24.25–27).[22]

CONCLUSIONS

One recurrent issue in twentieth-century gospel debate (courtesy especially of Wrede) was whether Jesus thought of himself as the Messiah. The crucial question, however, is surely whether or not Jesus genuinely *was* and *is* the Messiah. To establish what Jesus said and did (not least as expressions of what he thought) matters; for if Jesus was not concerned to enact God's purposes of salvation, then to recognise him as Messiah would be inappropriate. Yet to depict Jesus' ministry in the general terms of 'enacting God's purposes of salvation' is hardly controversial. To recognise him as 'a messiah' thus may be, on one level, relatively straightforward. Nonetheless, the validity (or otherwise) of belief in Jesus as 'the Messiah' crucially depends on many other factors beyond any reconstruction of his ministry. These include the resurrection and its implications for understanding Jesus' death; the nature of the church whose existence is in part to direct attention to the gospels as continuingly truthful about God, Jesus and humanity; willingness to confront human power-seeking; and the moral and spiritual dynamics of repentance and faith.

A final reflection may be drawn from John's Gospel, which is highly suggestive for continuing engagement with Jesus as the Christ. On the one hand, John (like other New Testament writers) adds categories other than 'the Christ' by which Jesus should be understood, so that a multi-faceted reality can be better depicted. Famously, his gospel begins with 'the Word' who was in the beginning with God, through whom all things were made, and who became flesh as Jesus (1.1–3, 14). Such language about the Word as agent of creation means (among other things) that faith in Jesus the Christ (the enabling of which is the purpose of the gospel) is not some optional extra, or arbitrary imposition. Rather Jesus enables people to encounter, and to realise in practice, their true nature, that for which they are made; for human nature is constituted according to that divine reality which is Jesus. John presents faith in God through Jesus as giving access not only to the true God but also to the truth of our humanity.

John 18.33–19.16

On the other hand, a dramatic climax of the gospel is the trial of Jesus before Pilate, and their conversation, where the central issue is Jesus as 'king' (18.33–19.16; cf. Hengel 1995:333–57). Jesus is uneasy with the term in the same way as in the other gospels (18.33–35, 37a), but characteristically accepts it in terms of his own definition, a definition with two crucial elements.

First, negatively, it is emphatically 'not from this world . . . not from here' (v. 36). This is part of the key Johannine polarity between that which derives its nature and meaning solely from human concerns in misunderstanding or heedlessness of the Creator, and that which is 'from above', i.e. receives its nature and meaning from God (as spelled out programmatically in 1.12–13; 3.1–8, 31–36). Thus Jesus' followers do not resort to violence (or should not, though Peter in Gethsemane misunderstands, 18.10–11), as would be appropriate if his kingship fitted conventional categories.

Secondly, positively, Jesus' kingship is defined in terms of 'witnessing to the truth' (v. 38), a witness to which those who are 'of the truth' will respond. This recalls the earlier account of the purpose of Jesus' life (3.16–21), which itself recalls the Prologue (esp. 1.5, 9–13). The truth is like the light – a searchlight that shines into the darkness of the world, and, when it shines on people, compels a choice: either to shrink back into the darkness, lest what they do be exposed; or to come forward in glad response to the light, and so realise the true God-derived nature of those good intuitions and practices they already had (3.19–21). This true light, this kingship, however, comes in the unobvious form of the man Jesus who can be ridiculed and rejected in favour of conventional understandings of kingship (19.1–16).

John's Gospel thus portrays Jesus' Messiahship as the vocation of presenting to the world the truth about its ways of living, a truth that embodies the perspectives of the creator God as articulated in Scripture. It is a vocation whose goal is to enable human life to become what it is made to be, and which the risen Jesus commissions and enables the disciples to continue (20.21–23); thus the vocation of the church becomes a continuation of the work of Jesus, a vocation to make known through word and deed the truth of human existence through a faith that is life-giving.

To sum up: what we find in Scripture is a searching account of the problematic condition of God's world and people, and of what can be done about it (i.e. 'salvation through the Messiah'). The gospels presuppose that life is characterised by such a pervasiveness of human self-will, self-seeking and self-deception that no one – not even the one through whom all was made – can straightforwardly 'put it right'. The gospels thus show the hope of a 'fix it' solution to the problems of the world to be a dream that must be relinquished. But this does not mean that nothing can be done, or that God is impotent in the face of humanity. The Old Testament understands Israel to be set in the world by God's call to live out God's truth, whatever the rest of the world may do; though since Israel can be as self-willed and self-deceiving as the rest of the world, this vocation is rarely straightforward and often takes paradoxical forms (as also for the church). What Jesus does, according to the New Testament, is to take to its fullest extent what that living of God's truth entails: a confrontation with human self-will and self-deception whose demands are total, and whose climax in death and resurrection is never neatly 'explained' but remains a mysterious reality which, like love, begins to be understood and to reveal its true nature as people enter into it.[23]

Notes

1. 'Christ' is a slightly modified transcription of a Greek noun, *christos*, which means 'anointed one' (from the verb *chrio*, 'anoint'), while 'Messiah' is a slightly modified transcription of a Hebrew noun, *mashiaḥ*, which also means 'anointed one' (from the verb *mashaḥ*, 'anoint'). Thus 'Christ' and 'Messiah' are identical in meaning, one a Greek word and the other Hebrew. When the Hebrew Old Testament was translated into Greek in the third and second centuries BC (the translation known as the Septuagint), *mashiaḥ* was consistently rendered by *christos*. It is only the religious assumptions and practices of the Jewish context, however, which make the term meaningful.

2. There are, of course, exceptions. The introductions to three of the gospels use the developed name form (Matt 1.1; Mark 1.1; John 1.17), for the gospels tell the story of how Jesus' role (then) has become central to his identity (now) for Christians; while Paul's practice of sometimes writing 'Christ' before 'Jesus' (i.e. 'Christ Jesus', 'Messiah Jesus') suggests that he is still aware of the titular significance of the term (e.g. Phil 3.7–8).

3. The form of the Greek word *christianoi* shows it to be a transcription of a Latin word, presumably coined by a Roman official in Antioch, the seat of Roman administration in the eastern Mediterranean. It designates a group with a particular allegiance, analogous to the Herodians (*Hērōdianoi*, Mark 3.6).

4. One can still, however, find Christians who defensively resist many aspects of modern critical approaches and who present the story just outlined in one form or other; e.g. Kaiser 1995. Kaiser's account is, however, as distinctively modern in its own way as the alternatives he resists.

5. Significant elements of this story can be found in Casey 1991.

6. Comparable is the interrogation of John himself in the Fourth Gospel, where the categories 'the Messiah', 'Elijah' and 'the prophet' are all utilised, with no sense of 'the Messiah' as the sole meaningful category of expectation (John 1.19–28).

7. Luke also contains the episode (9.18–22), but does not identify the location as Caesarea Philippi, and does not give the episode the same pivotal function as do Matthew and Mark.

8. The word play presumably originates in Aramaic, most likely the language spoken by Jesus, where both 'rock' and 'Peter' would be *cepha* (in Greek, *Cephas*, John 1.42; Gal 2.11).

9. Jesus' wording is most explicit in Mark 14.62, 'I am', but he instantly switches into his own preferred self-designation 'son of man'.

10. From the perspective of the Roman authorities 'king of the Jews' need not be a messianic title, but it seems clear that from the evangelists' perspective 'king of the Jews' and 'Messiah' are synonymous.

11. *Ps. Sol.* 17.21–22, ET by R. B. Wright, in Charlesworth 1983–85:2.639–70, quote p. 667.

12. Mark 10.42–45 (NRSV), closely paralleled in Matt 20.25–28, and with more difference, and a different setting, in Luke 22.25–27.

13. The paradox is well captured by Paul in his account in 2 Cor of authentic apostolic life, a life which must replicate (non-identically) the suffering of Jesus the Christ (esp. 4.7–12; 6.3–10; 11.21–33). Climactically, when Paul sought to escape the

thorn in his flesh, the risen Christ said to him, 'My grace is sufficient for you, for power is made perfect in weakness' and Paul had learned from this that 'when I am weak, then I am powerful' (12.9–10).

14. A fresh account of Jesus' ministry and Messiahship, which strongly protests against any privatising spirituality, is Wright 1996.

15. ET Wrede 1971. Twentieth-century academic debate about Jesus as Messiah took much of its shape and direction from Wrede. This debate is neatly described and summarised by Hengel 1995:1–72. There is also a collection of essays in Tuckett 1983, and an extended dialogue with Wrede in Räisänen 1990.

16. Even the Persian ruler Cyrus can be called God's 'anointed' (Isa 45.1a), because God uses Cyrus to deliver the Jews from captivity in Babylon and return them to Jerusalem (Isa 44.24–45.7) – though such a designation and use of Cyrus seems to have aroused controversy among the prophet's audience (Isa 45.9–13).

17. 1 Sam 24.6, 10 [Heb. 24.7, 11]; 26.9, 11, 16, 23; cf. 2 Sam 1.14, 16.

18. 2 Sam 19.21; cf. 23.1; Ps 89.20 [Heb. 89.21].

19. Ps 2.2; 89.38, 51 [Heb. 89.39, 52]; 132.10.

20. This is interestingly discussed in Horbury 1998:5–35, esp. p. 7.

21. 1QSa 2.11–12 (where the context is prescriptions for community seating arrangements in formal assembly) has the phrase 'until God engenders [?] the Messiah'. The verb is problematic, but the noun and article are not in doubt.

22. I have discussed this more fully in Moberly 2000:45–70.

23. I am grateful to David Day and Jimmy Dunn for their comments on a draft of this chapter, and to Markus Bockmuehl for his fine editorial direction.

13 Jesus in Christian doctrine

ALAN TORRANCE

In AD 325 the Council of Nicaea affirmed the divinity of Jesus in the creed of Nicaea. This led to the emergence, over fifty years later, of the Nicene Creed, which defines the faith of the Christian church world-wide. At the heart of both stands the affirmation that Jesus Christ is 'God from God, light from light, true God from true God, begotten, not made, of one being [*homoousios*] with the Father, through whom all things were made...' The intention of both is clear. They wish to affirm with unambiguous clarity that Jesus is to be identified as God incarnate – God has not merely come *in* a human being but *as human.* What is less obvious is that the issue at stake here concerns the very possibility of Christian God-talk. Without this decisive affirmation, it is questionable not only whether the Christian church would have continued to exist, but whether its existence would have been warranted. The whole *raison d'être* of the church is the recognition that Jesus is not simply a good person, or an inspired prophet, or a person with spiritual insight but, rather, the very presence of God identifying with humanity and revealing himself to humanity in a reconciling act of pure and unanticipatable grace.

If Nicene orthodoxy is still the official definition of the faith of the Christian church, its critics are more vocal than ever. Indeed, it sometimes appears that the defining character of much modern theology is a shared determination to distance itself from the Nicene affirmations. There is a widespread insistence that the ancient affirmations of the Nicene creed constitute pre-scientific mythology from which an enlightened and inclusive Christian faith come of age is obliged to liberate itself.

The tone of much contemporary debate can be traced to the eminent historian of Christianity, Adolf von Harnack, who, at the end of the nineteenth century, argued that the Nicene doctrine of the incarnation was the result of a Hellenising process through which Greek metaphysical concepts and categories were imposed inappropriately on the claims of the New Testament. The implication was that the christological claims of the New Testament should be regarded – as is often suggested nowadays – as essentially 'functional' rather than 'ontological'. Indeed, the last two hundred years have been characterised by a widespread desire – exemplified in Albrecht Ritschl, the father of 'liberal theology' – to get behind these supposedly 'metaphysical' claims to the 'simple' faith of the New Testament.

Over the last thirty years, this claim has been reiterated together with the charge that the 'Hellenisation' of Christianity has served to engender an exclusively 'Eurocentric' faith bound to European thought forms which are no longer appropriate in a 'post-Eurocentric', multicultural, multi-ethnic and multi-lingual world – a world characterised by diverse and disparate spiritual and philosophical homes. Consequently, a new generation of 'indigenous' and 'contextual' christologies have emerged which have sought to distance themselves from what are perceived as the abstruse categories of Nicene orthodoxy and attempting to reinterpret Jesus' significance in the light of the spiritualities characteristic of their specific contexts. Notable examples of such an approach have been found emerging in south-east Asia, from within the very different contexts of Sri Lanka, India, China, the oppressed workers (*Minjung*) of South Korea, the peasant farmers of Japan and Thailand and those involved in political struggles in the Philippines.

A 'contextual' critique of a different but related kind has emerged in recent feminist debates, which have viewed the affirmation of the *homoousios* as serving to divinise the 'male'. As Elisabeth Moltmann-Wendel has asked, how is it possible that identifying God with a male human being could be liberating for more than 50 per cent of the human race? Mary Daly famously insisted that if God is male, then male is God. Nicene Christianity, it is suggested, serves to elevate maleness and precisely this has been enshrined in the life and practice of the church ever since. The tendency of contemporary feminist theologians has been, therefore, to advocate 'theologies from below', side-stepping the incarnational affirmations characteristic of the Nicene tradition in order that God-talk can be allowed to unfold from women's experience and spiritualities.

Underlying and enforcing these trends, however, has been a suspicion of the doctrine of the incarnation that has haunted Christian theology since the Enlightenment. This is exemplified in modern times in the influential collection of essays entitled *The myth of God incarnate* (Hick 1977). In this volume a group of influential biblical scholars and theologians argued that it was time to recognise that the doctrine of the incarnation was a piece of mythology more appropriate to the thought-patterns of ancient civilisation than to those of contemporary society. A similar agenda has found expression in discussions of the incarnation not only as 'myth' but also as 'metaphor', 'story', 'fable', 'parable' and 'saga'. The underlying supposition throughout is that Christian doctrine should free itself from the 'mythological' projections which have characterised traditional Christian orthodoxy.

In the light of all this, it is of critical importance to note that the concern to distinguish theology from mythology is by no means new. Certainly, it informed the agendas of Rudolf Bultmann earlier in the twentieth century, and of David Friedrich Strauss a century before him; but, as we shall see, it lay at the very heart of the Nicene debates of the fourth century. For this reason, it is necessary that we consider in some depth the theological concerns and insights that led the Fathers to establish the doctrine of the incarnation as the cotter-pin of Christian doctrine and the key to interpreting who Jesus is.

THE DEBATE BETWEEN ATHANASIUS AND ARIUS

The Nicene debates resulted from a disagreement between Arius and his bishop, Alexander, whom Arius regarded as holding confused views concerning the status of the Son. Alexander, Arius believed, failed to distinguish between the Father and the Son and was in danger of introducing a 'Sabellian' fusion of the two.[1] Fundamental to Arius' approach stood a dichotomy between God and the world, where God is identified as 'that which has no cause or source outside itself' and the world as that which does. To be confused about this distinction was to commit a fundamental philosophical mistake, namely, to undermine the absolute qualitative difference between God and that which is not God. This supposition became wedded, in Arius' mind, to a confusion between two similar but entirely different Greek concepts, that is, between the word *gennétos* which means 'begotten' and *genétos* which means 'has come into being'. As a result, Arius believed that to describe the Son as '*genétos*' (begotten) involved his being '*genétos*', that is, his having come into being. If he had come into being, he could not be eternal and thus could not be God.

Consequently, Arius sought to drive home the dichotomy between God the Father and the Son by insisting that there was never a time when the Father did not exist, but that there *was* a time when the Son did not exist: 'The Son has a beginning, but God is without beginning'.[2] Consequently, he argued, the Son neither was nor could be 'of one being' with the Father but was *created* by him. For Arius, therefore, the Son was not God but belonged to the contingent, creaturely realm – albeit as the 'first creature' (*prôton ktisma*). Created first, he was the one through whom *everything else* was made.[3]

The debates surrounding Nicaea were stormy, political and politicised. At stake, however, were theological questions of crucial importance, the ramifications of which were perceived by Athanasius with remarkable clarity and profundity. So how is it that such a seemingly abstruse metaphysical dispute could be of such decisive significance? And why was the struggle between Arius and Nicaea over the word '*homoousion*' so unavoidable? As Alasdair Heron (1981:67) points out, it was not the word itself (*homoousion*) that was important for Athanasius, but what it affirmed. And what it affirmed was quite simply that the reality of God himself is present with us and for us in Christ.

But if this was to become the very keystone by which the Christian faith would stand or fall, what did the *homoousion* safeguard that was not equally preserved by Arius' interpretation of the Son as the 'first creature'? Heron (1981:68) replies,

> To this eminently reasonable question Athanasius had a single shattering answer. What was missing in Arius' entire scheme was, quite simply, God himself. True, he was there – after a fashion. He was there, but he was silent, remote in the infinity of his utter transcendence, acting only through the intermediacy of the Son or Word, between whose being and his own, Arius drew such a sharp distinction. The God in whom Arius believed had no direct contact with his creation; he was for ever and by definition insulated and isolated from it in the absolute serenity of an unchanging and unmoving perfection. God himself neither creates nor redeems it; he is involved with it only at second hand.

What emerged from the debate is an issue that has haunted Christian doctrine right through to the present day, namely, the basic and fundamental incompatibility between the God of the biblical witness and the Hellenised God of Arianism. As Athanasius saw with such clarity, the biblical interpretations of Jesus only have theological significance if they refer to a God who is present and who acts in and for the world he has created. The Christian faith lives, therefore, from the recognition that God's presence and activity are uniquely concentrated in the person of Christ who is recognised through the Spirit to be Immanuel, God-with-us. For Athanasius, therefore, the incarnation constitutes the hinge between God and humanity. Without it all our 'God-talk' loses its grounds and can only collapse into the unwarranted projections onto the transcendent of the self-understandings of creatures who were literally without knowledge (*agnôsis*). If God has not *given himself to be spoken of* by creatures within the contingent order, 'theology' can amount to no more than confused mythological speculation of a kind which only 'insanity' (*mania*) could identify with truthful God-talk. In short, for Athanasius, Arianism's Hellenic suppositions impelled it to dismiss *a priori* the very possibility that God could identify himself with human history and thus the very grounds of the Christian faith. To the extent that the Arians made any statements whatsoever about God's relationship to the contingent order, they were hoist on their own petard. Any such claims must be regarded, on their own terms, as entirely without warrant.

Heron (1981:70) again offers a neat summary of the situation:

> If one takes seriously Arius' conception of the divine being, it is hard to see how anyone could know anything about God at all. By a curious irony, on which Athanasius was not slow to remark, Arius seemed to possess a good deal of privileged information. But where had he got it from? Athanasius was in no doubt about the source: the Arians had fabricated this concept of the divine being out of their own minds, thus making their own intellects the measure of ultimate reality, and assigning to Christ, the Word-made-flesh, the place which their minds could make for him.

For Athanasius, it was the fact that Jesus was the eternal Word of God made flesh that constituted the ground of Christian God-talk. Jesus mediated knowledge of God because he was 'Immanuel'. If he were not, then it is entirely unclear how he can be relevant for God-talk in any way at all. This, however, appears to pose a problem for Athanasius. To affirm that Jesus is 'of one being with the Father' does not of itself solve the problem! Knowledge of God is not mediated by Jesus unless, first, he is identified with the being of God and unless, second, he is, and can be, *recognised* to be such. Without the latter condition, the incarnation in no way facilitates knowledge of God. The incarnation of God as Jesus would no more communicate knowledge of God than the incarnation of God as a fish in a mountain stream!

This was not lost on Athanasius, who was clear that the New Testament does not bear witness simply to God's identification with humanity in Jesus but, simultaneously, to God's presence with humanity in the person of the Holy Spirit. It is through the Holy Spirit that human beings are given the eyes to perceive who Jesus is – and thus enable the incarnation to become an event that actually reveals God. For Athanasius, to affirm the *homoousion* of the incarnate Word was inextricably bound up with affirming the *homoousion* of the Holy Spirit – a point insufficiently appreciated throughout history when it came to the theological assessment of incarnational claims. The transforming presence of the Holy Spirit who was 'of one being with the Father', was the necessary subjective condition for the recognition of Jesus as the incarnate Word. What this makes clear is that Jesus' place in the doctrinal affirmations formative of the Christian church is grounded in the irreducibly *Trinitarian* structure of the church's faith. If God is not present as the Holy Spirit in and with the 'mind' of the church, then there is no possibility of that 'mind' recognising or being informed by the presence of God in Jesus. As Jesus made plain to Peter following his recognition of who Jesus was, 'flesh and blood has not revealed this to you . . .'.

THE RELATIONSHIP BETWEEN JESUS AND GOD'S CREATIVE AND SALVIFIC PURPOSE

So far, we have focused on the significance of the *homoousion* for the knowledge of God and the warrant for God-talk intrinsic to Christian faith. Although these issues were and are fundamental to the church's interpretation of the place of Jesus in Christian doctrine, there are further and much more wide-ranging issues at stake here. The debate between Athanasius and Arianism in all its forms has profound ramifications for the interpretation of God's relationship to creation and, indeed, for the whole grammar of salvation. It is to these questions that we must now turn.

The Synoptic accounts of Jesus' healing and restoring presence identify him with the creative agency of God – an implication formulated more explicitly in the Johannine and Pauline accounts. Just as in the event of creation God imposed form on the forces of chaos (symbolised, for example, by wind and water), so Jesus exercised parallel power over those same symbols of chaos – calming the storm, driving out evil spirits and delivering people from physical and spiritual dysfunction. The implication was that, as Paul argued, Jesus represents the reconciling presence of God, the 'fullness of the Godhead dwelling bodily', 'the one through whom and for whom all things were created' reconciling an alienated creation to God and recapitulating God's purposes for it.

For Athanasius, none of these claims can make any sense at all without the recognition that in the person of the Logos we meet the creative energy of God himself, that same energy without which nothing at all would exist. In radical contrast to this, however, for Arius and his disciples (as these are to be found right through to the present day), we do not (and cannot) meet the Creator in the person of the Word since, in the final analysis, Jesus himself is simply another creature and object of God's creative act – and, as such, not to be confused with God.

The problems with the Arian approach are further compounded when we come to consider the soteriological role of Jesus. Central to the biblical witness is the recognition that only God can redeem his people. This is because sin is perceived as a violation of the Creator and his purposes by his creatures. To the extent that sin is sin against God (and not merely some problem internal to creation), only God can be the Agent of reconciliation and forgiveness. Furthermore, the very nature of the alienation of the created order is such that it is not able to restore itself. It is precisely because the contingent order cannot reconcile itself to God that, as Paul emphasised, God comes, in Christ, to reconcile the world to himself. It was this that lay behind Irenaeus' emphasis that in Jesus, God the Son took what was ours (namely, our alienated and confused condition), and healed it so that we might have what is his (the communion with God which was God's creative purpose for humanity from the very beginning). This insistence, conceived as a summary of the gospel, was central to patristic orthodoxy. Indeed, we find Gregory of Nazianzus emphasising its negative implications, namely, that the unassumed is the unredeemed – that which God has *not* taken to himself in the person of Jesus *is not* healed and *cannot* be healed.

In stark contrast to this, to describe Jesus as 'saviour' from an Arian perspective suggests that salvation is nothing more than a minor adjustment internal to the contingent order – something which one creature can perform in relation to others. It is to suggest, moreover, that God is not the object of sin, that he is not offended by sin and, ultimately, that he is entirely uninvolved in dealing with sin. Reconciliation and atonement, far from being events that take place between God and humanity, take place exclusively between creatures. For Arius and those who stand in his tradition, the gulf between God and creation is axiomatic – an essential presupposition of Hellenic thought. For Athanasius, the only separation between the creation and its Creator is that generated from the human side by sin – an alienation that God determined to overcome in Jesus (cf. Heron 1981:70–71).

What becomes unambiguously clear from this, therefore, is that the decisive doctrinal formulations in the christology of the early church show that, far from being 'Hellenisers' of the gospel, Athanasius and the Nicene fathers set out to affirm its content precisely *over and against* Hellenistic disjunctions – between the divine and the contingent, between the eternal and the spatio-temporal, between mind and body, and between the intelligible and the sensible realms. For Athanasius, Christian faith was grounded in recognising God to be a God of grace, thoroughly and profoundly involved in (and committed to) the world he had created – a God whose purpose from the beginning of all things was to bring creatures into dynamic communion with himself. The contrast between this God and the remote, metaphysically transcendent and monadic God of Arianism could hardly be more stark.

Modern theological debates have continued to be influenced by the same tendency to assume an Arian and, indeed, Hellenistic dichotomy between the divine and the contingent. The inclination to operate on the basis of *a priori* assumptions as to the actuality, possibility and boundaries of God's engagement with the contingent order have been at least as influential in modern theological debates as they were in the theology of the fourth century. The fundamental question at issue, right through the history of the interpretation of Jesus in Christian doctrine, concerns not only whether God is involved – or is capable of involvement – in the contingent order, but whether the gospel narratives and the New Testament writings provide warrant for God-talk of any kind whatsoever. The alternative, as Athanasius saw, is that we are simply obliged to withdraw into *agnôsis* and the irrational projection of our prior philosophical or cultural epistemic affiliations on to the transcendent – a form of activity better described as 'mythology' than 'theology'. As should be quite clear by now, the grounds of this age-old debate concerning doctrinal claims about Jesus revolve not around the *word 'homoousion'* but around that to which it *refers* – what the Nicene fathers were seeking to affirm when they used it. The challenge which Nicaea issues to modernity, postmodernity and the various forms of context-driven theologies (to which we referred at the start of this chapter) is whether, if they are to dismiss the language of the incarnation, they can provide alternative justification for Christian theological statements which possesses as much coherence, rigour and cogency as that which stems from the incarnational and pneumatological affirmations of the Nicene fathers.

THE HUMANITY OF JESUS

So far, we have sought to consider the strengths of the Nicene affirmation of Jesus' divinity. It is also the case that the Nicene tradition left the door open to more problematic tendencies. An unfortunate and unintentional consequence of the Nicene debates was the emergence of a one-sidedness in christological interpretation. In his monumental study, *The place of Christ in liturgical prayer*, Joseph Jungmann (ET 1989) has explored the distorting impact that fear of Arianism was to have on the interpretation of the significance of Jesus for Christian worship. Concern to avoid any Arian diminishing of the divinity of Christ led the church to emphasise the divinity of Jesus to the detriment of the all-important stress on his humanity. Jesus was therefore seen to be an *object* of prayer and worship but with the result that recognition of his role as the *agent* and *mediator* of prayer and worship suffered. Prayers were directed *to* Christ rather than *through* Christ with a resulting loss of emphasis on the priesthood of Jesus – the recognition that he prays with and for his people, as our Intercessor (cf. John 17 and

Rom 8), as our human Advocate and the Priest of our confession, in the language of the author of Hebrews. Whereas the Fathers had emphasised that in Christ we have God coming to humanity *as God* (what T. F. Torrance 1965: 131–32 refers to as the *anhypostatic* or God-humanward movement), their integral and attendant emphasis that the incarnation simultaneously denotes the incarnate Son's presentation of humanity to the Father *as fellow-human* (the *enhypostatic*, human-Godward movement) was weakened. Without this twofold movement, the essential grammar of the New Testament, namely, that Jesus represents both God's coming to humanity *as God*, and God's reconciliation and representation of humanity to himself as the true human (*eschatos Adam*, the 'Last' or 'Second Adam'), is lost.

In short, fear of an Arian denigration of the divinity of Christ opened the door to the church's failing to take sufficiently seriously the full *humanity* of Christ. Whereas the church had wrestled with Arian tendencies, it also had to wrestle with the opposite (albeit related) 'Apollinarian' tendency. Like Arius, Apollinarius also failed to hold together the divinity and humanity of Christ, but took a different turn. He suggested that the eternal Logos expropriated the human soul of Jesus such that any 'human source of initiative' (in G. T. D. Angel's phrase [1978:56]) was replaced by God. The mind of Christ was identified with the eternal Logos, and was not therefore to be regarded as human. The effect of this was to suggest, on the one hand, that the human life of Jesus was something of a charade and, on the other, that human beings do not have a fully human saviour, advocate, representative or 'priest' and that the temptations and suffering of Jesus were not ultimately 'human' at all. Jesus ceased, on this account, to be one who, in every respect, has suffered and been tempted *as we are* (cf. Heb 4.15; 5.7–8). The soteriological implications of Apollinarianism, moreover, were equally clear. If the unassumed is the unredeemed, then God has not redeemed the human mind in Christ. It is thus neither possible for human beings to have 'that mind which was in Christ Jesus' nor, indeed, to participate in his knowledge of the Father – since his knowledge of the Father is not a human knowledge. The effect of Apollinarianism was to reintroduce the Hellenic dichotomy between mind and body, between the divine and human. Thereby, in parallel with Arianism, it undermined the patristic dictum that the Son took 'what was ours' (our full humanity) and redeemed it *in toto*, that we might have what is *his*, namely, participation *as human beings* in the divine life. Like Arianism before it, Apollinarianism was condemned by the church in the 'Tome of Damasus' (382) which emerged out of the Council of Rome.[4]

Although condemned, an Apollinarian tendency tinged with the fear of Arianism had a profound influence on the grammar of Christian worship.

If worship denotes the full and all-embracing response of humanity to the loving faithfulness of God, it is not something that sinful human beings are capable of offering. The logic of the New Testament, however, is that the faithful human response of gratitude to God – that all-embracing corresponding to God's unconditional faithfulness which is required of us (and which knows no dichotomy between worship and 'ethics', i.e. 'worth-ship') – is provided *by God* on behalf of humanity in Jesus. He alone offers that true human response, that faith and faithfulness, worship and *koinonia*, which humankind cannot offer. In other words, God provides for us by grace the Amen to God and God's purpose required of us. This is offered by Jesus *as human* and in our place as our kinsman-redeemer, as the Second Adam. This same risen Lord, then, comes to unite women and men with him by the Spirit so that they come to live in the light of the response that he has offered on their behalf and continues to offer as their High Priest. The existence of the Body of Christ, the New Humanity, is thus characterised by Paul as participation 'in Christ' – a phrase he uses over 150 times! Worship (conceived in this all-embracing manner) requires to be seen in the first instance not as something that human beings provide in and of themselves, but as something that Jesus fulfils on their behalf. Both worship and ethics (conceived as lived gratitude) are to be regarded, therefore, as the gift of participating, by the Spirit, in *his* life of worship and communion with the Father.

When fear of Arianism, combined with Apollinarianism, played down the humanity of Jesus, its effect was to undermine this vision of the full extent of the grace of God. Worship became a 'task' which human beings are expected to perform in relation to Jesus rather than the gift of participating in his humanity, in his risen life and in his continuing priesthood. The impact on the history of the church was that worship became a 'legal' obligation placed on humanity rather than the 'filial' gift of participating in the divine life – and which lies at the very heart of the gospel.

IN WHAT WAY HUMAN?

A further and related tendency that characterised the early church's attempt to articulate who Jesus was, concerned the interpretation of his suffering. There was a deeply ingrained assumption in the philosophy of the time, that what is truly Real could not change. Unchangeability, incorruptibility and impassibility went hand in hand. If any of these were questioned, it would imply that God could change. This in turn would amount to claiming either (a) that God had acquired some kind of 'reality' that was previously lacking, or (b) that God was losing some form of 'reality' he previously possessed. Either was deemed unacceptable since it questioned the ultimate Reality and 'Godness' of God. Consequently, there was extreme nervousness about implicating the divine too closely in any 'change' deemed appropriate to the humanity of Jesus.

Thus, fear of confusing Jesus' divinity with a humanity conceived as transitory, changeable, corruptible, mortal and capable of suffering generated a tension. To affirm the *homoousion* involved the insistence that Jesus was 'of one being with the Father'. Consequently, it was clear that the divine and human 'natures' should not be separated. At the same time, the incarnation could not mean the collapse of the divine into the human. The strategy adopted by the Council of Chalcedon was to safeguard the divinity and the humanity of Jesus by repudiating any confusion of the two, on the one hand, and any separation of the two on the other. Reaffirming that Jesus Christ is *homoousios* with the Father, the Council stated,

> We confess that the one and the same Lord Jesus Christ, the
> only-begotten Son, must be acknowledged in two natures, without
> confusion or change, without division or separation. The distinction
> between the natures was never abolished by their union but rather the
> character proper to each of the two natures was preserved as they came
> together in one person [*prosôpon*] and one *hypostasis*. (Neuner and
> Dupuis 1983:615; Denzinger and Schönmetzer 1953:302)

Thus a series of perceived safeguards were simply laid down without any attempt to clarify how precisely they were to be held together.

What were the implications of this thinking for the interpretation of Jesus' suffering and death? If the Passion narratives were taken at face value and it were suggested that 'God' was subjected to suffering at the hands of sinful humanity, this would, as we have seen, threaten to impugn, if not vitiate, the 'Godness' of God – with the result that faith in God's capacity to deliver humanity from suffering would be undermined. As Jürgen Moltmann (1974:228) summarises these concerns: 'where can transitory and mortal man find salvation if not in intransitoriness and immortality, that is, in participation in the divine being . . . ?' In short, the church was torn between, on the one hand, affirming a God whose full presence in the sufferings of Christ was placed in question and, on the other, placing their faith in a pauper God so helplessly caught up in the exigencies of human history that his ability to redeem was placed in question. Fear of the latter meant that 'patripassianism', the doctrine that the Father shared fully in the sufferings of the Son, was rejected outright. Canon 14 of the 'Tome of Damasus' states, 'If anyone says that in the passion of the cross it is God himself who felt the pain and not the flesh and the soul which Christ, the Son of God, had taken to himself – the form of servant which He had accepted as Scripture says [cf. Phil 2.7] – he is mistaken' (Neuner and Dupuis 1983:147; Denzinger and Schönmetzer 1953:166). As Moltmann (1974:228) comments, 'If one considers the event on the cross between Jesus and his God in the framework of the doctrine of the two natures, then the Platonic axiom of the essential *apatheia* of God sets up an intellectual barrier against the recognition of the suffering of Christ, for a God who is subject to suffering like all other creatures cannot be "God"'.

The legacy of this was that the whole history of Christian doctrine was characterised by a struggle to hold together the divinity and the humanity of Christ in interpreting the crucifixion and death of Jesus – a challenge which has only adequately been taken up in more recent times. As Richard Bauckham points out in the conclusion of his book, *God crucified*, 'That God was crucified is indeed a patristic formulation, but the Fathers largely resisted its implications for the doctrine of God. Adequate theological appropriation of the deepest insights of New Testament christology . . . was not to occur until Martin Luther, Karl Barth and more recent theologies of the cross' (1998:79). That process of appropriation, however, posed conceptual challenges to which we must now turn.

FROM THE 'WHO' QUESTION TO THE 'HOW' QUESTION

The Reformation period was characterised by some fraught debates as to how precisely Christ was present in the elements at the Eucharist or Mass. The most significant effect of this was the resurrection of the Chalcedonian debates concerning how we might hold together the divine and the human in the interpretation of Jesus. This resulted from the Lutheran claim that Jesus Christ is present in the elements at the Eucharist, since his divinity involved the communication to his humanity of the divine properties (the *communicatio idiomatum*) – such as omnipresence. This, it was believed, served to explain how Christ's human body could be present within the elements at the Mass.

This attempt to solve a problem besetting eucharistic theology led the Lutheran theologians, Johann Brenz and Martin Chemnitz, to promulgate that there took place in the event of the incarnation a fusing of the divine and human properties – an argument developed specifically by Johann Gerhard. This suggested that Christ's humanity possessed omnipotence, omniscience and omnipresence by virtue of its union with the Logos. Any apparent limits attaching to Jesus' life were to be attributed, therefore, to the self-limitation of the God-man, rather than to the Logos. These were renounced not by virtue of the incarnation of the Logos but, rather, by the decision of the *incarnate* Jesus to take upon himself the form of a servant until his ascension and exaltation. This is emphatically not to suggest a humiliation of the Logos (in the sense of a lack or absence of the divinity and majesty communicated to the flesh), but, rather, a free commitment, on Jesus' part, to either a 'retraction' or 'intermission' with respect to their use (cf. Ritschl 1872:175). Jesus elected either for a concealment (*krypsis*) of his divine attributes, as Brenz suggested, or for an emptying (*kenosis*) of them, as Chemnitz argued.

In the nineteenth century, Thomasius and his successors reversed the argument. Instead of modifying the humanity to take into account union with the distinctively divine, the divine attributes were modified in order to take seriously the human nature of Jesus – an approach E. L. Mascall would describe as monophysitism in reverse. Thomasius interpreted the affirmation in Phil 2.7 ('he emptied himself...') in metaphysical terms as denoting a self-abandonment on the part of God and his divine attributes to the human. On this account of the incarnation, Barth comments, God does not simply give himself but 'gives himself away' – an approach Donald Baillie would similarly dismiss as 'a gratuitous piece of mythology', requiring a period of 'cosmic absenteeism' and leaving insoluble the problem as to how this emptied God could resume the distinctively divine attributes. The most radical form of such an approach (arguably, its *reductio ad absurdum*) is to be found in the modern 'death of God' theologies of William Hamilton and Thomas Altizer. Theologically, such an approach risks not only undermining the divine attributes of the Logos, but also placing in question the real human nature of Christ.

In England, a less radical form of kenotic theory emerged. Bishop Charles Gore formulated a moderate kenoticism which sought to resurrect Irenaeus' suggestion that the Logos was filled with as much Godhead as the humanity could bear. Determined to emphasise the real humanity of Christ, he spoke of the incarnation as an event of self-sacrifice as viewed from God's side and as some form of kenosis viewed from the human side. Whereas Cyril of Alexandria (c. 375–444) had suggested that what the Logos possessed he retained and that what he did not possess he assumed in the incarnation, Gore modified the first clause hovering between a theory of divine self-abandonment and a theory of self-limitation. Frank Weston, bishop of Zanzibar, offered a more consistent theory suggesting that the self-limiting Logos assumed a complete, 'ensouled' human nature but one which progressively grew and developed, in such a way that it came to accommodate or 'encapsulate' more and more of the Logos. Adopting an approach not dissimilar to Weston, P. T.

Forsyth argued for a theory of 'retraction'. The Logos is eternally present in the Trinity and there is a progressive *plérôsis* (filling) of the humanity by the Logos throughout Christ's life. One apparent benefit of such an account was that it seemed to help make sense of the temptations of Christ. Although Christ could not sin, he did not know this and therefore his temptations were totally real for him.

The problem with accounts suggesting a temporary retraction is that one is left asking whether the incarnate Son is the retracted deity (a diminished God – something less than the 'God' in whom we live and move and have our being) or a simultaneously self-retracting deity (which suggests that God is *both* the retracting Agent *and* the One retracted). The latter does not seem to constitute an advance on traditional 'two natures' accounts and the former leaves open the question as to how such a retraction can be reversible and 'what was happening to the rest of the universe during the period of our Lord's earthly life?' (cf. Temple 1925:142–3). Furthermore, these moderate accounts would still seem to be vulnerable to the argument famously presented by Donald Baillie, namely, that such a 'pagan metamorphosis' undermines the real presence of *God* in the incarnation. Although, in defence, H. E. W. Turner (1976:60–85) argues that the Logos stands at the heart of the Incarnation for moderate kenoticists and thus his ultimate importance is never in doubt. The underlying problem, however, as Baillie observes, is the apparent metaphysical incompatibility between the divine and human conceived as conjoined in one person. This presents a particular challenge to the modern emphasis on psychology and personality in anthropological accounts which kenotic theories have attempted to interpret from the perspective of a 'worm's eye view' (Turner 1976:81) of the situation. As Emil Brunner was to point out, the really significant question raised by such debates concerned the extent of our entitlement to embark on the kind of speculation characteristic of the kenotic debates.[5]

It was Karl Barth who, more than any other theologian in recent times, liberated christology from the confines of such debates. For Barth, the condescension of God as human is an act of God's free and sovereign love. As such, its recognition and acknowledgement should not lead to pragmatic metaphysical speculation by those lacking a God's-eye view, but rather to an approach to theology which gives primacy to the 'Who' question over the 'How' questions. The Christian faith lives from the perception of *who* Jesus is, not *how* God can become human – a question that is not ultimately our concern. Such a refusal to be distracted from the 'Who' question was arguably one of the strengths of the classic christological accounts. And pertinent to this, perhaps, is the central emphasis of the kenoticists' favourite text – Phil 2.7. Exhorting Christians to adopt the self-emptying life of service witnessed in Christ the Suffering Servant, it seems to place in question the kind of pride which can all too easily characterise the refusal of theologians to stop with the 'Who' question preferring, rather, to explain God's actions from their 'worm's eye view'. Whereas the Christian witness is to the Self-accommodation for humanity of the Eternal God in a humanly inconceivable and unanticipatable act of grace, kenotic christology all too easily found itself re-engaging the kind of *metaphysical* interpretation which it originally sought to counteract.

FROM 'HOW CONCEIVABLE' TO 'HOW RECOGNISABLE'

The attempt to resolve metaphysical quandaries of this kind immediately brings us back to the more fundamental methodological and epistemological concerns raised by attempts to evaluate the significance of Jesus for Christian doctrine. The primary question posed since the Enlightenment has concerned the role of history in doctrinal formulation. To what extent is historical inquiry capable of recognising the presence of God in history?

One of the most influential writers to exemplify this tension here was the father of 'myth theory', David Friedrich Strauss (1808–74). His approach, together with much historical investigation since the Enlightenment, was profoundly influenced by the epistemology of Leibniz (1646–1716) with its dichotomy between the necessary truths of reason (to which epistemic access is *a priori*) and contingent truths (mediated *a posteriori* through sense perception). Leibniz's approach chimed with Spinoza's (1632–77) insistence that the truth of a historical narrative cannot provide knowledge of God. The latter must derive exclusively from general (that is, timeless) ideas which possess demonstrable, epistemic certainty. These two approaches led Gotthold Lessing (1729–81) to insist that events and truths belong to radically different and logically unconnected categories. Epitomising the Enlightenment's approach to religion, he argued that historical evidence provides an insufficient basis for religious belief, for 'the accidental truths of history' can never provide proof of the 'necessary truths of reason' (Lessing 1777). There is thus an 'ugly, broad ditch [between theological and historical claims] which I cannot get across, however often and however earnestly I have tried to make the leap' (Lessing 1957:55).

The effect of Lessing's ditch was to question whether engagement with 'contingent' historical truths could ever provide access to the kind of 'universal' truth appropriate to the transcendent. Religious knowledge, Lessing contended, must be concerned with 'eternal truths of reason' and thus the historical is simply unsuited to be the proper object of knowledge of God (cf. Evans 1996). If this is accepted, the implications for christological claims are obvious. The only kind of theological value that historical claims could have would be 'illustrative'. History could do no more than provide illustrations or examples of religious truths already known in advance and accessed quite independently of engagement with the historical. When Lessing's dictum is accepted, the inevitable consequence is that theological inquiry is directed back into the self, to those universal ideas 'internal' to human self-understanding and experience which are deemed to possess 'religious' value. The consequence in New Testament scholarship has been the profound influence on it of idealism, in either its Hegelian or Neo-Kantian forms. The necessary conclusion is that any identification of God with one particular human individual must be regarded as 'mythological'. Accordingly, in David Friedrich Strauss, the founder of myth theory, we find precisely such a synthesis of the influences of Leibniz and Spinoza, on the one hand, with those of (Hegelian) idealism on the other. Jesus was simply one example of 'the *idea* of God and man in their reciprocal relation'. Does this mean that we must attach exclusive value to that particular piece of history which is the life of Jesus, Strauss asks? Emphatically not! Exemplifying the implications of the Enlightenment's association of the divine with the universal and its consequent *dissociation* of the divine with the particular or historical, he argues that the 'key to the whole of Christology' is that we place, 'instead of an individual, an idea...', an idea universalised to the extent that it is identified with the idea of the race.

> In an individual, a God-man, the properties and functions which the church ascribes to Christ contradict themselves; in the idea of the race, they perfectly agree. Humanity is the union of the two natures – god becomes man, the infinite manifesting itself in the finite, and the finite spirit *remembering* its infinitude... It is Humanity that dies, rises and ascends to heaven, for from the negation of its *phenomenal* life there ever proceeds a higher spiritual life... This alone is the absolute sense of Christology... The phenomenal history of the individual, says Hegel, is only a starting point for the mind.[6]

What should be clear, is that if the control on theological interpretation is the prior set of 'rational' criteria immanent within the human subject, then theology can do none other than interpret the Jesus of history as 'exemplifying' and 'illustrating' our prior ideas and ideals which are thereby absolutised in the process. If these are universalised, the result is a selective process of value-transfer of the 'divine' from Jesus (or any other 'example' of the criteria one chooses to endorse) to the human race as a whole. The inescapable conclusion (as also the starting point), which is made explicit in Strauss, is the deification of universal humanity and the consequent denigration of the particular, the creaturely, the material, the spatio-temporal, the historical – to what Strauss and, later, Bultmann termed the 'phenomenal', i.e. that which has no ultimate reality. As Søren Kierkegaard saw with unparalleled clarity, this whole approach reposes on Socratic *anamnēsis* – that form of 'remembering' (see the quotation above) which recognises the divine because it already knows it.[7] On such an account, faith can never discover anything new, we can only 'recognise' what we already know through our innate participation in the divine. The implication of this is that whatever we suppose to be eternal within the human spirit acquires the status of theological criteria. And as Kierkegaard argued so forcefully (ET Kierkegaard 1987), what this ultimately means is that God's Word becomes identified not with Jesus but with the prior prescriptions of our own self-understanding.

Ironically, if not surprisingly, what informs idealist approaches to the interpretation of Jesus can now be seen to be a specific form of the doctrine of the *communicatio idiomatum* (the communication of the divine properties to the human). Here, however, the divine properties are not communicated to the particular humanity of the historical Jesus but to the universal humanity of the human race. In short, we find ourselves back with the Greek philosophical assumptions which lay behind the Arian debate with which we started, namely, the dichotomy between the *kosmos noētos* (the world of ideas) and the *kosmos aisthētos* (the 'unreal' world of space and time) – and the supposition that God is to be identified exclusively with the former, but incapable of being tainted with the latter, with the particular or the historical. Human self-understanding becomes the control and criterion in christology, resulting in the material identification of God's Self-communication with the universalisation of our own prior interpretative criteria and self-understandings.[8] The impact of this on the diverse attempts since those of Strauss to proffer theological interpretations of Jesus has been widespread. All have been characterised by the Delphic oracle's injunction invoked by Socrates, 'Know thyself!' – the conviction that knowledge of self constitutes the sole source, criterion and means of access to religious truth in its totality.

Equally diverse conclusions characterised the attempts of modernity to uncover the 'real' Jesus of history. Unsurprisingly, these conclusions have too easily been determined by the socio-cultural, political and religious agendas of those engaged in the task, be they romantic, pious, ethical or self-consciously 'contextual'. Too often one is left asking whether these searches and their 'discoveries' have been historical at all (cf. Heron 1980:53). As

George Tyrrell, the Catholic Modernist, famously remarked, the biographers of Jesus 'looked into the deep well of history, and saw there only the reflection of their own faces' (cited in Heron 1980:53–54). What we have sought to argue is that, if Jesus does not represent the concrete Self-revelation of God, not only will the biographers of Jesus inevitably generate a human figure who ratifies their own agendas, but the discovery of their own self-understanding will be the only theological 'datum' possible, as Athanasius saw with such clarity.

All interpretations of who Jesus is are, by the nature of the case, interpretations from a particular perspective. They are interpretations through the lenses of our contextual and cultural affiliations. At the same time, to recognise and to acknowledge that it is the incarnate Word that one is seeking to interpret is to allow that same Word to transform and place in question all our categories of interpretation. The pressure of interpretation must transform our affiliations lest we find ourselves simplistically using revelation to offer divine ratification for our prior allegiances.[9] The risks of failure here – that is, of allowing the direction of interpretation to be from our prior supposition to the Word and not the other way round – do not need to be rehearsed following a century in which two world wars have emerged from within the home of the Reformation and where the evils of apartheid and ethnic cleansing have been perpetrated by other 'Christian' nations. Two key twentieth-century figures stand out as challenging with unambiguous clarity the self-referential forms of christological interpretation and the destructive political agendas to which these give rise, namely, Karl Barth and Dietrich Bonhoeffer. In August 1914, a group of ninety-three intellectuals issued a declaration in support of the Kaiser's war policy, as necessary to the defence of Christian civilisation. The discovery that this included most of his former theological teachers convinced the young Barth of the theological inadequacy of the attempt to allow christological interpretation to be conditioned by cultural or any other prior allegiances. All too easily it leads to 'the rebellious establishment of some very private *Weltanschauung* [worldview] as a kind of papacy'.[10] For Barth, the theological significance of Jesus lies precisely in the fact that, as God's decisive and once-and-for-all Word to humanity, he cannot and must not be commandeered by our prior human allegiances and affiliations (be they cultural, political, religious or philosophical). Rather, the Jesus recognised by the eyes of faith and attested to us in Scripture as Lord is God's personal Word of grace to humanity and thus 'the One Word of God which we have to hear, and which we have to trust and obey in life and in death'.[11] As such he requires to be heard, recognised and interpreted in his own light and within his own space as God's all-inclusive claim upon it. This claim is grounded in God's all-inclusive 'Yes' to humanity in the One in whom there is neither Jew nor Gentile, black nor white, slave nor free, male nor female. Barth's many volumes constitute, accordingly, the attempt to interpret the significance of this Word for every facet of human, social, political and ecclesial life. And it was this same commitment that gave rise to the Barmen Declaration, as it served to define the allegiance of the Confessing Church over against Hitler and the 'German Christians'.

In 1933, during the intensification of anti-Semitism in Germany and the ultimate commandeering of Christianity by culture, Dietrich Bonhoeffer gave a series of lectures on christology. In these he argued that Jesus Christ should not be regarded as the 'Logos' in the sense of the one 'idea' interpreted as the ratification of our own prior 'logoi'. Nor was the christological question to be reduced to a 'How' question ('How is it possible for Christ to be both man and God'). Both involve the prioritisation of the logos of the inquiring subject. Rather, to the extent that Jesus Christ is the Logos of God, he is to be regarded from our perspective as the Counter-Logos. And then he adds (Bonhoeffer 1978:30),

> When the Counter-Logos appears in history, no longer as an idea, but as 'Word' become flesh, there is no longer any possibility of assimilating him into the existing order of the human logos. The only real question which now remains is: 'Who are you? Speak for yourself!'

In assessing the place of Jesus in Christian doctrine, one is confronted with an 'either–or'. Either God is uniquely and concretely present in Jesus and thus the identity of God is irreducibly bound up with this particular person – or he is not God. If the latter is the case, then – as Athanasius and the Nicene fathers saw with such clarity back in the fourth century – there is no sense in which Jesus has any decisive contribution to make to the business of God-talk and we would do well to abandon him to the sands of history. If, however, the former is the case, he constitutes the reference point in the light of which we must interpret and continually reinterpret every area of Christian doctrine (be it creation, anthropology, soteriology or eschatology) as also every facet of human life. What should hopefully now be clear in considering this 'either–or', is that no historical inquiry nor theological inquiry nor, indeed, any other kind of inquiry – 'neither flesh nor blood' – can ever establish or be expected to establish the presence of God in Jesus. There is no Archimedean point, no other foundation from which we can answer the question posed by this volume and which was Jesus' question to Peter: 'Who do you say that I am?'

Notes

1. In the following discussion I am indebted to Heron 1981.
2. Integral to Arius' thinking here was the supposition that if the Father and the Son were conceived to be co-eternal, they must be identical with each other – thereby destroying the foundational doctrine of divine simplicity.
3. To deny this and to conceive of the Son as consubstantial (*homoousios*) with the Father, was, on Arius' view, to destroy the divine simplicity such that the Father becomes 'compound and divisible and alterable and a body...' This is taken from a fragment of Arius' *Thalia*, cited by Athanasius, *De Synodis* 15. Cf. Heron 1981:62 and n.5a.
4. Canon 7 runs as follows: 'We condemn those who say that the Word of God dwelling in human flesh took the place of the rational and spiritual soul, since the Son and the Word of God did not replace the rational and spiritual soul in His body but rather assumed our soul (i.e., a rational and spiritual one) without sin and saved it' (Neuner and Dupuis 1983:147; Denzinger and Schönmetzer 1953:159).
5. Brunner 1946:349n.1: 'A secret, and indeed unfathomable, essential secret – the mystery of revelation itself – means the co-existence of this psychological-historical and this eternal-divine personality. To try to fathom this means from the very outset to draw the Divine Person in the human sphere.'
6. Strauss 1972:780. Whether Hegel would have been happy with Strauss' interpretation of his thought is a matter for debate. There is clearly, however, more than sufficient continuity to illustrate the point we wish to make here.
7. Platonic participation *methexis* of the inherently divine by nature supplants the Pauline participation *koinonia* of the inherently creaturely and particular by grace.
8. It is not surprising that Strauss 1972 (ET) would so influence Feuerbach in his concern to explore further human consciousness and the psychological mechanisms underlying myth-making.
9. Paul argues in Rom 12 that our minds require to be transformed (*metamorphousthe*) and not schematised (*mē suschēmatizesthe*) by our secular contexts, if there is to be discernment of the truth.
10. Karl Barth, '*Nein!*' ET in Brunner and Barth 1946:87.
11. Barmen Declaration, Thesis 1, ET by D. S. Bax repr. in Jüngel 1992:xxiii.

14 A history of faith in Jesus

ROWAN WILLIAMS

There is little or no trace in the first Christian decades of a Christianity unmarked by devotion to Jesus as a living agent. Even allowing for the most sceptical reading of the Gospels and Acts, we can say that within about twenty-five years from the likeliest date of Jesus' crucifixion, he was being invoked by Christians as a source of divine favour and almost certainly addressed in public prayer at Christian assemblies. The concluding verses of Paul's first letter to the church at Corinth (16.22–23) illustrate both things, with the ambiguous Aramaic formula, *maranatha*, strongly suggesting a direct address to the glorified Jesus as Lord, and the reference to 'grace' stemming from Jesus identifying him as a bestower of the kind of favour that is normally to be looked for from God. Without entering into the very involved question of how far Jewish piety at the time accepted a cult of angelic powers,[1] we can at least say with certainty that Jesus was, within a generation of his death, regarded as *present* to and in the believing community, the object of personal devotion, the recipient of personal address. He is coming again to act as judge; but in the meantime, he is not absent, and his future judgement can in some ways be anticipated or affected by the present decisions of the church and especially of its charismatic leaders, acting 'in' the Spirit of Jesus (e.g. 1 Cor 5.4–5). By the end of the first Christian century, this presence of Jesus and anticipation of his return and judgement have become both pervasive and pictorially vivid in Christian literature. Luke depicts the first martyr Stephen commending his spirit to Jesus (Acts 7.59) as Jesus had commended his to the Father (Luke 23.46); the writer of the Revelation depicts Jesus as bearing the title and the attributes of the God of Israel (Rev 1.11, cf. Isa 44.6; and compare the pictorial details with the divine manifestations e.g. in Dan 7 and Ezek 1), and issuing sentences upon the Christian communities of western Asia Minor.

If we are to speak of 'devotion' to Jesus in the first days of the Christian church, this is where we must start. It is not helpful to speculate about some supposed primitive phase in which a dead leader was remembered with warmth, 'devotion' in the loosest sense; our primary literary sources show something more robust, a conviction that human destinies are decided by a heavenly Lord who may be spoken to, prayed to, even adored as God is adored (Rev 1.17). Those who receive his Spirit are able to understand something of the judgements that he will pronounce when he comes in glory, and to transmit these judgements to the church (the seer of Revelation, like Paul, is 'in the Spirit' when he sees the glorified Jesus, and hears his messages to the churches; Rev 1.10). It may seem a sombre picture in some respects; but it is softened by the pervasive association of 'grace' with the figure of Jesus, primarily but not at all exclusively in Paul. Jesus' appearing in judgement is longed for rather than feared (cf. 2 Tim 4.8); the favour, light and love now experienced by the believer are themselves the anticipation of an encounter that will not end in condemnation (Rom 8.1; cf. 1 John 3–4, *passim*). In this sense, devotion to Jesus is an eager looking towards him in the expectation of seeing in him not simply the decisive judgement of God but the beauty or splendour of God (2 Cor 4.6).

We know from Pliny's celebrated letter to the emperor Trajan in AD 112 that Christians at their meetings addressed hymns to Christ 'as to a god' (*Letters*, 10.96). Not many early exemplars of such hymnody survive, though those that do are of great interest. The *Odes of Solomon*, which emanate from a Syriac milieu in the second century, build up a sophisticated and rich repertoire of metaphors for Jesus and his work: he is the 'crown' that saved humanity is to wear, the 'mind' or 'thought' of God, the 'name' given to Christians to put on or receive (a common theme in early Christian writing, echoing the very ancient prayers of the *Didache*). Around the end of the second century, we have a hymn by Clement of Alexandria, attached to the end of his treatise on the Christian teacher (*Paidagogos*), addressing Christ as a horse-tamer, bridling the wild passions of the human soul. One of the most ancient and durable hymns, the *phôs hilaron*, which may go back to the second century, addresses Jesus in terms strikingly close to the language of 2 Cor: he is 'the joyful radiance of the immortal Father's glory'.

Some of the language of early Alexandrian theology in particular similarly emphasises the role of Jesus as the visible manifestation of the invisible God, the mediator, not so much of salvation or forgiveness as of true perception of the divine nature. The earliest theologian to stress this theme, however, is not an Alexandrian, but an émigré from Asia Minor, Irenaeus, who became bishop of Lyons in France; and for him Jesus' role as revealer immediately connects with a further and more profound set of considerations. Jesus reveals because of his own relation to the Father; because his face is wholly turned to the Father, it reflects his glory. For us to know and recognise that glory, we must be brought into that relation – a fundamental theme of Paul and John in the New Testament (Rom 8, John 17, among much else), which Irenaeus develops extensively.[2] Jesus is an *example*, not only in the sense of being a model of behaviour we ought to imitate (again a New Testament theme, as in Matt 11.29; 1 Cor 11.1), but as a paradigm of relation to God as Father. Our attention or devotion to him is a kind of tracing the contour of his life so as to see its conformity to the Father's character and purpose; we are to pick up the essential clues as to how to recognise what it is to be a child of the heavenly Father by looking single-mindedly at him (cf. Heb 12.2). Being in the Spirit is not only or even primarily a gift of prophetic alignment with the ultimate judgement of Jesus, but entails the gift of sharing Jesus' relation with the Father, beginning to love God as parent with the same confidence as Jesus shows.

It is important when looking at the earliest days of Christianity to re-member that Jesus is seldom if ever presented primarily as any kind of *moral* exemplar, someone whose values and priorities (in contemporary terms) we are encouraged to share or reproduce. Certainly there is a pattern of behaviour that grows out of the contemplation of the narrative of Jesus (e.g. John 13.14–15; Rom 15.7; Phil 2.5–11, etc.), but it is not quite a simple matter of choosing to follow an example. The central theme is the notion of a gift bestowed which equips us to speak to God in the voice of Jesus, as it were; Jesus is indeed a spiritual paradigm for us, but we cannot of ourselves reproduce the quality of his life or prayer; we must receive a particular sort of inner freedom first, concentrating not on our will and effort but on his grace, the clear experience of divine favour and welcome made possible by his death and resurrection. When we do 'imitate' Jesus in our choices and actions, this is more an outflowing from the inner gift than the result of a systematic effort to conform our behaviour to his.

There is, however, a sort of exception to this. The Christian has to cultivate the freedom to die for the sake of Jesus and in imitation of Jesus. From Ignatius of Antioch (*c.* 110) onwards, the martyr's death was seen as a sharing in the cross of Christ: 'Let me become an imitator of the passion of my God' is Ignatius' prayer (*Rom.* 6.3). The earliest accounts of Christian martyrdom stress repeatedly the parallels between these deaths and Christ's. The story of Polycarp's execution in Smyrna in about 156, with its themes of betrayal and mob denunciation, its depiction of Bishop Polycarp offering a sort of eucharistic prayer over his own condemned body, and its echo of the anxieties of the Jews in Matt 28 about the disposal of a particularly sacred corpse, illustrates the point amply. More tersely, the record of the death of the slave-girl Blandina, crucified at Lyons in 177, speaks of the believing spectators seeing Christ in her body on the cross (Eusebius *Hist. eccl.* 5.1.41, 55–56). As martyrdom becomes less common, the theme develops of an interiorising of the martyr's death through detachment from the present world, or, in a way that has still deeper theological resonance, through a participation in the *kenosis*, the self-emptying of the divine Son, building upon the famous hymn of Phil 2.[3] The conviction that monastic life is fundamentally an imitation of Christ rests on this theological base (cf. Williams 1990: 49–70, 92–117). Jesus is here above all the model of dying to the self, abandoning security and self-concern for the sake of God and neighbour. Even here, though, the emphasis is regularly on such behaviour as the making visible of a gift already given – the life of the eternal Son lived out in the believer's life, so that the process of incarnational involvement enacted by the eternal Son is also realised in us. The disciplining of the passions and the emptying-out of self-regard may properly be thought of as matters in which we can dispose ourselves by asceticism and effort to become better aligned with Christ's action; but once again the focus is not *finally* on effort but on the revealing of the life that has been given.

Martyrdom became less common, of course, as the church became a legitimate body in Roman society; and this process had its own effects on how Jesus was imagined. The fourth century, during which Christianity won widespread social and cultural acceptance, witnessed far-reaching developments in art and worship, reflecting the new situation. For the first time, it was possible to display in public unmistakeable images of Jesus as the visual focus of corporate devotion (in contrast to the anonymous images of the teacher or the good shepherd found in the pre-Constantinian period); Christian churches were purpose-built, normally on the pattern of the Roman imperial basilica, the great public hall for audiences and trials, and the image of Jesus occupied the dominant position as once the imperial portrait or statue would have done. But this has led to some confusion in the textbook accounts of the period. It is not true that these early artistic depictions simply borrow the conventions of imperial portraiture: Christ's dress is sometimes purple in colour, but he never wears a recognisable imperial costume. With the possible exception of the rather unusual sixth-century mosaic in the archiepiscopal chapel at Ravenna, in which he wears military uniform, he is always robed as a philosopher, in tunic and shawl. Recent research has shown that these pictures probably depend on two classical types: some, intriguingly, seem to be based on Late Antique pictures of Homer, some on depictions of the gods Zeus or Serapis – sombre figures with untrimmed hair, heavy brows and full beards, quite unlike the conventional images of secular authority.[4] In other words, Jesus is being 'seen' as a sage or poet (and there are instances where scholars have suggested that we should interpret pictures of Orpheus as intended to represent Christ as well), or as a ruler among the gods; but never simply as an inflated version of the earthly monarch.[5] And the crucifixion is already being depicted on fourth-century sarcophagi; a further counter-instance to the assertion that early Christian art simply takes over the imagery of a cultus of imperial power.

These early images of Christ (mostly from about AD 400 onwards) do, however, emphasise what we might call the element of holy dread in the approach of believers to their Lord. As the art of the Byzantine Empire develops in the next few centuries, the depictions of Christ in the dome of the church building are often clearly meant to be overwhelming rather than just comforting. The very well-known instance at Daphni in Greece (from about 1100) is the culmination of a long and vigorous artistic tradition; such images also reflect the effects of liturgical language during these centuries in the Christian East. Scholars of Christian worship have often noted how, from the fourth century onwards, the rhetoric of eucharistic worship in particular is characterised by expressions of awe and the building up of extravagant epithets, as if to induce a sense of 'extremity' in the experience of worship: in the Eucharist, Jesus is present in the fullness of his divine activity, taking up and transforming the bread and wine, and the only possible reaction is abasement, wonder and a visionary, incantatory recital of the mysteries of the divine life that is in Christ ('wisdom, life, sanctification, power, true light', in the words of the fourth-century liturgy of St Basil). Although the eucharistic prayer itself is almost always addressed to God the Father (the major exception is the very early Syrian liturgy of Addai and Mari), the actual *practice* of the Eucharist naturally encourages devotion to the presence of Christ in the consecrated elements as the concrete embodiment of the sacred in our midst. The great prayer of thanksgiving over the bread and wine is seen as a sharing in Christ's prayer to the Father. But, from the fourth century onwards, there is a growing interest in the idea of a climactic point of transforming consecration in the Eucharist; and this naturally intensifies a sense of adoration directed to the present Christ – 'the one who is to come' already among us, in anticipation of the end of the world.[6]

Thus, after the fourth century, two significant themes in Christian devotion begin to develop in full vigour: the adoration of Christ as cosmic Lord, depicted in the intense visual idiom of the Byzantine icon, and devotion to Christ sacramentally present in the Eucharist. In the Byzantine world, these two elements came into direct collision in the 'iconoclast' controversies of the eighth and ninth centuries. Faced with the competitive pressures of an Islam that rejected all visual representations of the divine, a school of thought in

Byzantium argued that the only defensible image of Christ was the sacrament itself, the image actually ordained by Jesus. The response to this drew on the doctrinal formulations of the fifth and sixth centuries: if Christ is genuinely and wholly both divine and human, and if the 'energies' of his divine nature permeate and transfigure his humanity without altering its nature, then a depiction of Christ's humanity (which is obviously possible in principle, if he is a human individual in some sense like others) is a theologically intelligible and licensed depiction of his divinity, represented in its action and effect. By analogy, the icon of a saint shows the divine 'energy' by showing how a human person is transfigured by it. The sacrament is not in this sense an image: it is *more* than an image in that it actually conveys transfiguring grace, the seeds of immortal life. It is, you could say, part of the process whose endpoint is depicted in an icon. And the more this concrete conveying of grace is articulated in the liturgy and the theology of the liturgy, the more overt become the gestures of adoration directed towards the consecrated elements.[7]

Western Christianity shared both these themes up to the beginning of the Middle Ages; subsequently, though, both art and liturgy began to move in somewhat different directions. Before about 1100, most (though not all) of the public and canonical images of Christ in the west are broadly comparable with the Byzantine conventions. After this date, there is an increasing interest in the human vulnerability of Jesus, shown in increasingly realistic depictions of the crucifixion. The physical and mental anguish of Christ on the cross is more and more invoked and explored both visually and verbally, in a process that reaches a climax in the immediate pre-reformation period. Behind this development lies, on the one hand, a general 'humanistic' interest in the specific psychology of Jesus, at a time when fascination was growing with the nuances of diverse human experience, and, on the other, a pious concern to foster in the believer a proper sense of indebtedness and gratitude towards Jesus for 'all the pains and insults you have borne for us' (in the well-known prayer of St Richard of Chichester, 1197–1253). The intensifying of a sort of grotesque hyper-realism in the artistic portrayal of the effects of scourging, beating, crowning with thorns and crucifixion, the appearance by the fifteenth century of a specific 'Man of Sorrows' image in art, the production of meditative texts designed to stir the imagination to the point of some sort of empathetic identification with these extreme physical tortures and the proliferation of lyrics of lament or complaint[8] – all this serves to intensify the believer's grief and shame for sin. From being simultaneously the terrifying judge and the bountiful, life-giving patron, Christ has become the petitioner at our gates, appealing for our sympathy.

And in a curious parallel movement, the eucharistic presence comes to be seen in new ways. Rather than being the fire from heaven celebrated in Byzantine and Syrian hymnody,[9] it is seen as a concretising of the suffering and crucified humanity in an object that is here and now presented for our adoration. The process was aided by the definition of the Lateran Council of 1215 which declared that the substance of the bread and wine was replaced by the substance of Christ's body and blood at the Eucharist – not a doctrine in itself wholly alien to earlier formulations, but undoubtedly encouraging a greater focus on the tangible 'thereness' of Christ's human identity. Legends of the later Middle Ages often distorted this into a crudely local and physical presence: hosts bleed, visionaries see the bread as a lump of dripping flesh, and, worst of all, stolen hosts are 'tortured' by Jews (the supposed enemies of the 'social' Body of Christ, who are also accused of the literal torture and murder of Christian children[10]).

The general effect is to give to western medieval devotion to Christ a more blatant pathos than is found in eastern literature, and to enshrine images of dramatic suffering as the focal visual expressions of Christian faith (in a way that contrasts sharply with the classical iconographic tradition). The *Revelations of divine love* recorded in the early fourteenth century by Julian of Norwich begin with some alarmingly intense visualising of the suffering of the crucified, but modulate into an extraordinary colloquy between the visionary and a Jesus giving rich assurances of faithfulness and ultimate healing, with an unexpected use of maternal imagery not only for God in general but for Jesus in particular. A text like this shows how the passion-oriented spirituality of the medieval west had its positive side.[11] It can be seen, first, in a refusal to absorb the cross into the resurrection, and an insistence upon the utter 'ordinariness' of the flesh of Jesus by (paradoxically) stressing the extraordinary intensity of his suffering; and, second, by means of this to leave a door open for the idea that the death of Jesus might suggest a critique of human conceptions of power and security, making compassion the basic element in Jesus' transfiguration of the human world – a crucial theme in Julian. If we turn to the perennially popular *Imitation of Christ* ascribed to Thomas à Kempis, we find a slightly more 'moralised' and individualised rendering of the theme that imitation of Christ is imitation of his passion by means of our own inner detachment and mortification. There is not so much as in Julian a sense of *surprise* at the methods of God's workings, so at odds with human assumptions.[12]

There is a problematic side to this devotion to Jesus, faintly discernible in Thomas a Kempis, more obviously visible in the words and pictures of more popular devotion. It shows itself in a tendency to sentimentalise the death of Jesus and to make paradigmatic for Christian devotion a sense of individual reproach, the covertly resentful guilt provoked by accusations of ingratitude and unresponsiveness. It is perhaps not too much to say that this tradition profoundly *eroticises* devotion to Jesus; our relation to him is the kind of thing found in a stormy love affair, or even in the dangerous territory where pain is close to orgiastic delight.

But of course, it will be said, erotic metaphors for the believer's relation to Christ are not a peculiarity of the late medieval West. Their foundation charter is in New Testament texts like 2 Cor 11.2, Eph 5.23–32 or Rev 21.2 and 22.17, where the whole community is seen as Jesus' bride (just as the relation between ancient Israel and its God was repeatedly cast into the language of marital fidelity and infidelity). The earliest application of this imagery to the relation between Christ and the individual soul seems to be Origen's Commentary on the Song of Songs, in the early third century, where the great Alexandrian commentator writes of how we are 'wounded' by the touch of divine love so that we long to experience the embrace of 'our bridegroom, the Word of God' without the mediation of any other human agency.[13] Here as in the comparable commentary of Gregory of Nyssa in the fourth century, the reference shifts between the particular soul and the corporate experience of the church; but it is clear that direct erotic yearning for union with Christ is understood as something that a mature Christian should grow into. In the early Middle Ages, the genre of commentaries and homilies on the Song of Songs became one of the richest in monastic literature,[14] and the sense of Christ as erotic partner finds powerful and uninhibited expression particularly in the great cycle of sermons on the text written by Bernard of Clairvaux for his monks mostly in the 1130s and 1140s (ET Bernard of Clairvaux 1976). The last great flowering of this style of meditation is to be seen in the poetry of St John of the Cross in sixteenth-century Spain, and his prose reflections on the poems; here it is no longer precisely a matter of commentary on the Song, but of poetic *paraphrase*, deploying the imagery and the emotional tonality of the biblical text to produce a strikingly new composition.[15] For John, the most important aspect of the Song's imagery is clearly that which deals with agonising loss, the search for the renewal of an encounter that has 'injured' or interrupted the soul's life. Both John and his contemporary and friend Teresa of Avila will also use the conventions of popular vernacular love lyrics – the forlorn shepherd despairing of a response from the beloved and so on. There are close parallels with the themes of English devotional lyrics of the Middle Ages, the songs of complaint or desolation already mentioned.

However, John's poetry is more complex in its implications. 'Erotic' union with Christ, the union in difference of the soul with its beloved, is only an element in the soul's assimilation to the deeper union in difference, which is the eternal Son's oneness with the Father. Creation exists in its entirety to be a 'bride' for the Son, to share and reflect his joy; but that joy is fundamentally and inescapably the joy of his relation to the Father, so that creation, in sharing the joy, shares the relation.[16] The twofold dynamism here takes us a step beyond the straightforward erotic passion of the soul for Jesus and points back to older and more basic themes of the believer's assimilation to Christ as beloved and intimate child of God. Later and more 'routinised' forms of the spousal imagery of contemplative writers, particularly in the marital ceremonies surrounding monastic profession for women,[17] seldom make the connection with growth into the full measure of adoptive intimacy with the Father. And outside monastic circles and the writings of a few visionaries, the post-Reformation era saw little development of the image of Jesus as erotic partner; a more fragmented Christian world had become more nervous of this language, with its risky intensities.

But, as Michel de Certeau pointed out in his groundbreaking research on early modern spirituality, the erotic pathos of medieval and Counter-Reformation mysticism left a significant trace on the whole history of later western culture. It defined the soul as 'homeless', always in search, always on the move; when God has retreated over the cultural horizon, what remains is simply the drama of restlessness (Certeau 1992:197–200, 292–93, 298–99). In late medieval or sixteenth-century Spanish spirituality, the sense of loss and excruciating pain in the soul's journey could be christologically grounded: along with the yearning for fulfilment in the embrace of Christ went the conviction that this entailed sharing in the dereliction of Christ. The darkness and sense of absence classically treated by John of the Cross can be seen both as the abandoned lover's pangs and as a sharing in the crucified Christ's sense of abandonment by the Father. Faith means to walk Christ's way, expecting no easier path. This looks back to the whole theme already noted in relation to patristic spirituality of the imitation of Christ's self-emptying; monastic literature had often related this to the monk's call to follow Christ's nakedness and poverty,[18] and the Franciscan movement had placed this decisively at the centre of its vision. St Francis's receiving in his body of the wounds of the crucified[19] is a particularly strong externalising of the theme of imitating the crucified (it is referred to by John of the Cross as reinforcing his model of advance in spiritual maturity). Without the element of relation to Christ in all this, we are left with the characteristic drama of the 'modern' self, searching for its own truth, self-martyred.

Perhaps the most recurrent problem in the history of devotion to Jesus is the sense in which he, as a specific individual, is or remains the terminus of prayer and meditation. Several very diverse responses can be traced in the tradition. Origen, in the commentary already referred to, speaks of the human identity of Christ as a protective shadow to shield our eyes from the full glare of the divine life; as we grow spiritually, we move away from the contemplation of the humanity until in heaven (whence, in Origen's system, we fell before the world's creation) we return to the vision of the divine Logos and, in the Logos, of the Father. It is thus important not to become attached to the humanity of Jesus as an object of love or adoration.[20] This attitude is shared widely in the patristic and medieval tradition, and it is found even in St Bernard of Clairvaux, whose warmth and enthusiasm in writing of the humanity of Jesus is so evident. *Ultimately*, the humanity of Jesus is the path to contemplation of his divinity, however intensely we are drawn by that humanity as we set out on the path. By the sixteenth century, the issue has become further complicated. The Franciscan writer Osuna takes the classical line that meditation on the specifics of Jesus' human life has to be left behind as we mature (and John of the Cross largely echoes this). Teresa of Avila, for all her indebtedness to Osuna and her closeness to John, spiritedly repudiates the idea that Jesus ever becomes superfluous in our spiritual pilgrimage. Ignatius of Loyola builds on medieval precedent to provide an exceptionally full and rigorously structured scheme of meditation on Jesus' life in his *Spiritual exercises*; and his *Spiritual diary* notes how in his personal prayer he was aware of some activity 'terminating' in Jesus, some in the Father or the Spirit, and some in the Trinity as a whole. His consciousness of this variety leads him, however, not to any attempt to 'grade' devotional activities but to a deepened sense of the oneness of the divine persons: when one is addressed or focused upon in prayer, the others are at once implicated, evoked alongside.[21]

Perhaps, like Teresa, he has shaken off the residual Platonism still found in Osuna and John which considers the humanity of Jesus a less worthy object of pious attention because it is, after all, a phenomenon of the material and historical world. But there can be some confusion in interpreting all this. As we have seen, John of the Cross gives central significance to the actualities of Jesus' fleshly life and death as paradigms for our spiritual history; what he, like others, questions is whether sustained meditation on the narrative is desirable beyond a certain point. The problem is less the concentration on a material phenomenon than the characteristic issue in John of how we liberate ourselves from the trap of binding God to one set of images, whether material or otherwise. Purely theologically, there is less difference between Teresa, John and Ignatius than a first reading might suggest.

This issue is, of course, rather different from the related set of problems associated in the early church with the name of Origen and centring on the appropriateness of addressing prayer to Jesus. It is difficult to untangle precisely what Origen did or did not commend on this matter, but it is fairly clear that he discouraged prayer not simply to Jesus, as the incarnate form of the Logos, but to the Logos as such, since our prayer is ultimately a sharing in the Logos's prayer to the Father (*On prayer* 15.1–4; 16.1; ET Oulton and Chadwick 1954). This position has impeccable theological logic at one level, since this is exactly the dynamic of most of the New Testament; but it pulls against almost universal practice (we have noted how early on we find hymns addressed to the Son in Christian usage). It also gave hostages to fortune in the early church, since the refusal to pray to the Logos was interpreted as a refusal to recognise his full divinity. Paradoxically, in the fourth century, the critics of the creed of Nicaea, which affirmed the unequivocal divinity of the Logos, seem to have maintained the common liturgical practice of addressing hymns and prayers to him. Athanasius of Alexandria, writing against these dissidents, makes much of this contradiction and appeals to New Testament examples of worship being given to the glorified Christ (e.g. in *Against the Arians*; ET in *NPNF* vol. 4).

The problems here are inevitable. Jesus is manifestly the focus of the renewed sense of God that constitutes the distinctive news Christianity brings; it is through his life and death and resurrection as an historical individual that change occurs in our standing in relation to God. But that change is precisely a movement into the relation Jesus always and already has to God: he is and is not the 'terminus' of devotion, and there is (as Christian writers from Gregory of Nyssa to John of the Cross to Michel de Certeau have recognised) an *absence* at the centre of the Christian imagination, a space opening up to the final otherness and final intimacy of encounter with the Father. To move into this space, in prayer and imagination, is to move into the new identity Christ makes possible – to become, as the eastern Christian tradition has always put it, 'deified' by coming to 'embody' Jesus' own prayer. The history of modern understandings of devotion to Jesus shows the difficulties that arise when the person of Jesus is separated from this further space of encounter, from the gift of adoption and participation in divine life and relation that is central in the New Testament and the patristic tradition. What develops is a bifurcation of the older styles into a cult of Jesus as individual on the one hand and a series of attempts to domesticate Jesus as teacher and exemplar on the other. One remarkable survival or revival of a more classical balance between intense personal love towards Jesus and a robust theology of deification can be found in the best of classical Protestant hymnody in the seventeenth and eighteenth centuries. You have only to listen to the greatest hymns of a Paul Gerhard (especially in their sublime use in the Passions and Cantatas of J. S. Bach) or a Charles Wesley to see how the governing themes of patristic and medieval theology can be made vivid and accessible to the body of worshippers (see e.g. Kimbrough 1992). But by the end of the eighteenth century, much of this 'classical' energy is giving way to a more individualised feeling, in Catholic and Protestant devotion alike.

These developments must be held partly responsible for some of the bewilderment and agnosticism about the figure of Jesus that characterises a good deal of twentieth-century theology, sitting uncomfortably alongside a hugely popular devotional idiom that focuses uncomplicatedly on the worship of Jesus. The late twentieth century has witnessed an extraordinary explosion of devotional song, whose popularity seems to cross an unprecedented range of cultural and linguistic boundaries; in a way curiously reminiscent of the Middle Ages, there is now an international language for worship – not literally a single tongue, but a strongly unified style. Its roots are evangelical and charismatic, but it has conquered great tracts of the Roman Catholic world as well. Some of it, perhaps much of it, has a solid theological basis, and can be strongly evocative of the paradoxes of 'meekness and majesty' (to allude to the refrain of a well-known example); much of it is utterly unadorned and often deeply moving adoration of Jesus. But there is a disquieting element in a good deal of this literature; it is not just that devotion to Jesus can often be expressed in a way that detaches it from the Trinitarian dynamic of the New Testament, it is also that the erotic idiom of medieval and Counter-Reformation spirituality can reappear with fewer checks and nuances than in earlier centuries. Jesus as object of loving devotion can slip into Jesus as fantasy partner in a dream of emotional fulfilment. To avoid sentimental solipsism, there needs to be either a strong and self-critical theological environment or (which is often the same thing in other guises) a clear orientation to the world's needs and the action of Christ in the whole social and material environment. Some songs will sound very different depending on whether they are sung in an atmosphere of social comfort or in a *favela* in the Two-Thirds World.

The role of actual 'lives of Jesus' in devotion is a many-sided story. Reflective summaries of the life of Jesus were fairly common in the Middle Ages, and the Reformation continued the tradition. Jeremy Taylor's *The great exemplar* of 1649[22] is a late flowering, marked, as we might expect, by a less 'mystical' and more 'moral' emphasis than some medieval works, yet aiming at the same goal of narrating the earthly life of Jesus so as to lead the reader to contemplation of the eternal truths of divine and human nature. But the new historical methods of reading Scripture had a powerful impact from the mid-eighteenth century onwards: the story could no longer be told with the same 'innocence'. When David Friedrich Strauss published a 'life' of Jesus in 1835, it was a composition of a wholly different kind from anything earlier, an attempt to reconstruct a neutral record by reading the gospel texts with an eye to their likely distortion by confessional interest (by devotion, indeed). Later in the century, Ernest Renan's essay in the genre helped to create what was almost a new devotional language, but one of an entirely humanistic character: Jesus becomes a 'beautiful soul', a poetic genius who can be appreciated (and best appreciated) by the aesthetic response. The gospel record is a pastoral fantasia, moving us to higher sensibility – neither strictly an ethic, nor a dogmatic. Jesus becomes a culture hero for the educated and enlightened.[23]

More starkly ethical readings were also being proposed in the nineteenth century, building (with greater or lesser degrees of acknowledgement) upon Immanuel Kant's seminal *Religion within the limits of reason alone* (ET Kant 1934, esp. 119–21, 145–51). Jesus is here transformed into the teacher of enlightened common sense, tolerant, generous, appealing to the highest in human nature, not to supernatural revealed authority. This became a popular trope in American writing, from Jefferson to Emerson and beyond (its distant echoes may be heard in the quirky and relaxed peasant guru favoured by many members of the 'Jesus Seminar' within the American Society of Biblical Literature); but its fiercest and most consistent exposition is in the late work of Leo Tolstoy (esp. Tolstoy 1961), for whom Jesus 'teaches us not to commit stupidities' and sets out to undermine the entire system of law-governed social authority in the name of radical trust and love between human beings.

In a justly famous essay, George Steiner (1959) argued that the two great Russian novelists, Tolstoy and Dostoevsky, represented two basic and irreconcilable attitudes to faith in general and the figure of Jesus in particular. Tolstoy regards Jesus, ultimately, as a fellow-worker in the same cause of emancipation; Dostoevsky sees him as mercilessly other, mysterious, silent, practically powerless, as in his unforgettable fantasy of the 'Grand Inquisitor', which forms a decisive episode in *The brothers Karamazov*. Tolstoy was excommunicated by the Orthodox Church; Dostoevsky was regarded as a faithful apologist for it. The point as Steiner sees it is that Dostoevsky begins from the sense that the figure of Jesus disturbs the human agenda, social, political and religious, and is therefore appropriately the focus not of the faintly patronising commendations of Tolstoy but of both love and terror (he goes on to suggest, plausibly, that some of Dostoevsky's Christ-images should have disturbed his ecclesiastical allies more than they did). It is possible to see Dostoevsky's Jesus, especially in the *Inquisitor*, as a figure in visible continuity with both the language of the New Testament and the Byzantine iconographic tradition, for all that he represents – in a very typically Russian idiom – a self-emptied and helpless deity (cf. Gorodetzky 1938). The salient thing is that he stands in judgement on the personalities and events of his environment, and also realises radically different possibilities for and in that environment. Twentieth-century Russian novels, especially Pasternak's *Doctor Zhivago* and Bulgakov's *The master and Margarita*, work with some of these themes, in a continuing and lively dialectic with the Orthodox theological tradition.

It seems that there are two things that continue to connect the representations of Jesus, verbal and visual, in devotion with the theological enterprise. There is first the sense that encounter with the figure of Jesus can bring about radical questioning and change; and second the conviction that the outcome of such change is a relation with God as source and parent, fully realised in Jesus but in some degree shared with the believer. Divorced from this, the image of Jesus becomes somewhat problematic. The visual representations of Jesus canonised in the nineteenth century – from the German 'Nazarene' painters to the British pre-Raphaelites, along with the abundance of popular devotional art, including Roman Catholic icons of the Sacred Heart – show a figure of androgynous charm, characterised by a rather exhausted tenderness of aspect. They can be read as the long-term fruit of that late medieval tendency already described, to show Jesus as primarily requiring compassion, understanding and response from us (Holman Hunt's *Light of the World* is a magnificent case in point); as such, while they are not without power, they risk leaving unanswered the question of why this figure should be seen as bringing about conversion or renewal. In a nutshell, these are images that leave Jesus as object for us and not subject beyond us. Most of the strategies designed to assist devotion to the 'Sacred Humanity' seem to have run this risk – the cultus of the Sacred Heart (whose origins lie in the seventeenth century), the concentration in Baroque and later eucharistic piety on the Host as the concrete presence of the crucified, the 'prisoner of love' in the tabernacle, the nineteenth- and early twentieth-century Protestant passion for historically and geographically 'authentic' illustration of the gospel text (William Hole's watercolours shaped generations of young British Christian imaginations).

In such a light, the revolt against the focus on Jesus as an historical figure becomes intelligible – from Kierkegaard's proclamation in the *Philosophical fragments* of the incarnation as the wreckage of a certain kind of historical inquiry (ET Kierkegaard 1987) to Rudolf Bultmann and beyond.[24] The imbalances of this have been more than adequately discussed in the theology of the last quarter of the twentieth century. But the issue remains: Jesus cannot but figure in Christian devotion, cannot but be the object of pious attention and imagination; yet Jesus is not the terminus of Christian experience and prayer, and when he becomes so, something is lost and confused in the Christian mind. Current controversies over the status of a male saviour for female selves raise many complex issues; but some of the literature suggests (on both conservative and radical sides) a muddle over the way in which Jesus should and should not be the focus of all spiritual attention and aspiration for the Christian. As more than one feminist has noted, the problem looks very different in the perspective of patristic christology (see e.g. Hampson 1990:53–58). Is it possible, chastened by the modern history of sentimental and emotionally oppressive representation of Jesus in art and worship, to find a contemporary idiom for expressing relation to Jesus that will revive the primitive Christian seriousness about judgement and change? The theologies and spiritualities of the developing world represent a significant challenge already to individualistic and historicist readings of the believer's relation to Jesus (see especially Míguez Bonino 1984 and Schüssler Fiorenza 1995a). There are bridges to be built here with the substantial historical resources we have sketched – if we can overcome both western and modernist snobberies.

Notes

1. A very reliable guide to the discussion is Horbury 1998.
2. See especially his *Proof of the apostolic preaching* 6, 7, 31 (ET Irenaeus 1952) and *Haer.* 4.7, 24, 28, 34.
3. The theme comes into some prominence in the fourth century in texts like Gregory of Nyssa's commentary on the Lord's Prayer (ET Gregory of Nyssa 1954), and is developed extensively in the later Greek tradition by the seventh-century Maximus the Confessor.
4. See Hanfmann 1980 and the ground-breaking study of Mathews 1993:92–141.
5. Mathews 1993:3–22 authoritatively dismantles the notion of a simple 'imperial mystique' in the art of the period. For a possible representation of Christ as Orpheus, see Murray 1977; the assimilation of Christ to Orpheus can already be found in Clement of Alexandria at the end of the second century.
6. The celebrated essay of Dix 1945 was the first major work to point out the 'slippage' from the understanding of the Eucharist as anticipation of the end of the world towards a stress on the concrete presence of Christ here and now in a more static sense; but he tends to ignore the strong link in the Byzantine liturgical tradition between the presence and the anticipated judgement. Cf. Schmemann 1988 for an excellent modern statement of this.
7. On the controversy over images, see (amongst a great deal of scholarly literature) Herrin 1987:307–43; for a more overtly theological treatment, though in informal style, see Ugolnik 1989. A fuller technical study of the interrelation between

Christology and the icon controversy is Schönborn 1994. Dix 1945:268–302 remains helpful for understanding the evolution of devotional practice.

8. See e.g. Davies 1963, Nos. 22, 24, 41, 46, 47, 62, 63, 106.

9. As e.g. in some of the hymns of Ephrem the Syrian; see Murray 1970.

10. See FitzPatrick 1993:221–25; and, for a wider social survey, Rubin 1991, a seminal text on the connections between eucharistic practice and social inclusion/exclusion.

11. The *Revelations* were translated into modern English by C. Wolters (Julian of Norwich 1966); the original text is edited by Glasscoe 1986. See chs. 4, 7–8, 10, 16–24 in particular for the evocation of the physical details of the passion of Christ; 51 for the 'parable of the lord and the servant', a sustained meditation on the whole story of fall and incarnation; 59–61 for Jesus as mother.

12. The *Imitation* is widely available in translation. See especially 2.12 on the following of the crucified; the fourth book is of great interest in showing how eucharistic devotion has become a vehicle for individual colloquy with Jesus.

13. *On the Song of Songs* 1 (Origen 1925:331 is the standard Greek text). See Crouzel 1989 on the spiritual centre of Origen's exegesis.

14. See the excellent survey in Turner 1995.

15. See especially 'Songs of the Soul in Rapture' and the 'Spiritual Canticle' – more properly, 'Songs between the Soul and the Bridegroom' (many translations, including Campbell 1951:10–27 for the texts referred to here).

16. This is spelled out in the *Romances*, John's sequence of ballad-like lyrics on creation and incarnation, see Campbell 1951:48–77.

17. St Thérèse of Lisieux provides a vivid commentary on this tradition in ch. 27 of her *Histoire d'une ame* (ET Thérèse of Lisieux 1958:164) by composing a 'Letter of invitation to the wedding of Sister Thérèse of the Child Jesus and of the Holy Face' written on behalf of God the Father and the Virgin Mary as parents of the bridegroom.

18. 'Naked to follow the naked Christ' (*nudus sequere Christum nudum*) is a typical early medieval formulation; the theme is prominent in several eleventh- and twelfth-century writers including Peter Damian and the obscure but very interesting Stephen of Muret, who claimed to have no monastic rule but the gospel itself. More radical groups like the Waldensians and the followers of Arnold of Brescia in the same period echo the same concern for Christlike poverty, and it becomes, of course, a matter of fierce controversy among the Franciscans in the early fourteenth century (the 'Spiritual' Franciscans were condemned by the pope in 1322–23 for teaching that Christ possessed no property, and thus that the perfect imitation of Christ was impossible for those who owned property).

19. On 14 September (Holy Cross Day) 1224, as recorded in the *First life of St Francis* by Thomas of Celano, ch. 94 (ET in Habig 1973).

20. See e.g. Origen's Commentary on John 1.7–8, and the famous twenty-seventh Homily on Numbers; for a brief discussion, cf. also Williams 1990:40–43, with further references.

21. Osuna 1981:17.1–5 on the differences between the contemplation of Jesus' humanity and the contemplation of his divinity. Book II ch. 12 of John of the Cross's *Ascent of Mount Carmel* (ET Peers 1943) is a *locus classicus* for cautions about meditation on imagined physical details of the life and death of Jesus. Teresa

touches on the question both in her early *Life* (ch. 22) and in the masterpiece of her maturity, *The interior castle* (VI.7–8); for ET see Avila 1976–80. Among many pertinent references in Ignatius, see particularly entries 63, 83–87, 129, 138, 140, 156 in the *Spiritual diary* (ET Ganss 1991).

22. Properly *The history of the life and death of the holy Jesus* (*The great exemplar* is the subtitle); reprinted in Taylor 1990.

23. Renan's work appeared in 1863. There is much helpful discussion of these and other nineteenth-century approaches in Pelikan 1985. For a vigorous short overview of the whole period, see Wright 1996:16–21.

24. See Wright 1996:21–27 on the Bultmann legacy (with bibliography).

15 The global Jesus

TERESA OKURE, SHCJ

The perennial question of Jesus' significance for humanity has occasioned much discussion and assumed new dimensions in recent years. It is accentuated by the UN Declaration on Human Rights that no human being may be persecuted or discriminated against on the basis of religion. There is a growing tendency to see Jesus as one among the many prophets of world religions: Moses, Mohammed and Buddha, to name but a few. At the same time, Jesus has always been recognised and is increasingly being accepted by peoples of every tribe, language and nation as God's unique agent of human salvation, 'the Savior of the World' (John 4.42). Others again contest this Christian claim, holding that the teaching of their prophets is equally a good road to God. Thus, as prophesied by Simeon, Jesus continues to be a sign that is contradicted, as out of many hearts thoughts are revealed (Luke 2.34–35). What is it that makes him so attractive to people of every race and nation, across cultural, sex and religious boundaries, and yet such a bone of contention?

The answers to this question and the approaches adopted vary according to the historical and social-cultural location and religious affiliation of the one who answers it. One's standpoint in viewing a particular object determines to a great extent what one sees or understands of the object or person viewed.

Our approach in this presentation is biblical and historical. The biblical perspective calls for awareness that the question of the global Jesus needs to be situated first and foremost within the context of biblical history and faith where it rightly belongs, and from which it derives its fundamental identity. Put differently, all efforts to understand and appreciate the global nature of Jesus are to be located within biblical history. More specifically, it relates to the biblical accounts of creation and fall (protology) as well as salvation and redemption (soteriology), seen comprehensively as God's work of love and mercy for humanity.

Taken out of this biblical context of protology and soteriology, the discussion of Jesus in his global significance for humanity and his consequent reception by every age, loses much of its meaning and causes irresolvable problems, for then the question becomes a square peg in a round hole. The biblical history of creation and salvation provides the only authentic (in the etymological sense of 'that which is proper to itself') context for asking and answering the question of the global Jesus. If one situates the question in the context of other creation stories, soteriologies and ideologies, one cannot expect to obtain adequate answers to the question. We must apply the common philosophical principle, 'That which is, is itself and not something else'. New wine requires new skins so that both the wine and the skins are preserved.

This does not necessarily imply an unquestionable acceptance of the biblical view of the global Jesus, or that the question has no relevance to the prophets of other religions. In its biblical context the question is essentially a matter of faith, rather than of logical or philosophical reasoning. The significance of Jesus' biblical identity stands on its own right, with or without reference to the secondary question of a comparison with prophets of other religions. Comparisons tend to blur realities and deprive them of their unique identity. Where the biblical view of Jesus has an intrinsic bearing on other world religions and their prophets, it does so not comparatively, but because these prophets are part of God's creation. Appreciation of this relationship also requires faith based on a correct interpretation of Scripture. This study invites us to contemplate the global Jesus within the biblical context, as the primary revelatory setting in which his meaning and identity can be (and historically has been) understood. That biblical history begins from Genesis and ends in Revelation. It is essentially a history that calls for a faith-based understanding.

The following discussion begins with this primary biblical context for the global Jesus. Then it briefly examines how peoples of different tribes, languages, nations and religions have successively interpreted and appropriated this biblical revelation, as a testimony of their faith in God's word and work. Lastly, this chapter invites us to consider our own personal and communal response to the global Jesus.

The term 'global Jesus' needs closer attention. Is it a way of 'globalising' Jesus, to make him an acceptable commodity of globalisation? Or does the terminology refer to the essential nature and place of Jesus within God's universal work of creation and redemption of humanity and the cosmos (which existed long before the advent of capitalist globalisation)? Put this way the answer is somewhat self-evident. Though the term 'global Jesus' suggests a relation to globalisation, it is not a construct of this modern monster-friend. Instead, our question rightly understood may serve as an asset for a sound evaluation of globalisation.

Traditionally, this issue has been discussed in terms of 'the uniqueness of Jesus' for human salvation and his nature as the cosmic Christ. These 'traditional' terms derive more directly from the biblical tradition than does 'global Jesus' (cf. Acts 4.12; 17.31). Globalisation refers primarily to the process of making universal or spreading worldwide what is by origin particular and local. Thus, information technology and the Internet, the multi-national companies (e.g. Coca-Cola and McDonald's) and the proliferation of arms, especially in developing countries, are among the leading agents of economic globalisation. A related example is the globalisation of HIV/AIDS, which has itself accelerated through the worldwide spread of economic and military interests as well as tourism. Rooted in the quest for profit, power and leisure, globalisation lacks a human face, especially among the poor and marginalised peoples and nations. Special care thus needs to be taken when we speak of 'the global Jesus' within this contemporary context of globalisation. Jesus' identity and his mission to the world are radically opposed to the central concerns of contemporary secular globalisation.

THE GLOBAL JESUS IN THE BIBLICAL CONTEXT OF PROTOLOGY (GEN 1–3)

The central biblical message is that God created the universe, 'the heavens and the earth', fundamentally good. Creation itself is God's work of love for humanity and existed before the appearance of humanity on earth (Gen 1.1–25; 2.4–6). When God finally created human beings, he charged them to continue the divine work by governing and taking care of creation. Through the ages, this charge as given in the first creation account (Gen 1.1–2.5) was often misunderstood as a mandate to abuse or exploit the earth. On second thought, it is of course unthinkable that the God who created the world with such love and care would then surrender it to human beings to destroy at will. The second creation account (Gen 2.1–24) brings out more clearly God's charge to humanity to care for creation as a labourer looks after the property of his or her master. Unfortunately, human beings did not obey this divine mandate; nor did they recognise their essentially creaturely nature. Tempted and deceived by Satan, they distrusted God and sought to grasp at divinity, thereby demeaning themselves and rejecting their own identity of existential dependency on God. However, instead of dealing with humanity as their sin deserved, God pledged the divine self to fight for them against the deceiver, by promising them a decisive victory over Satan.

This divine promise in Gen 3.15 is traditionally known as the *proto-evangelium*, the first Good News of our salvation. The rest of biblical history unfolds as the process of God's fulfilment of that promise through the seed of the woman (Gen 3.15). The history is long and protracted. It includes the destruction of a large part of humanity by the flood, the renewal of the cosmic covenant with Noah and his family and the scattering of the nations at the incident of the tower of Babel when human beings repeated their attempt to grasp at divinity (Gen 7–11). The process continues in the call and choice of Abraham, through whom God will eventually effect the promise of salvation for all peoples: 'By you all the families of the earth will bless themselves' (Gen 12.1–3). Paul interprets this passage to mean that all peoples will be blessed as Abraham was (Gal 4.8–9) – thus continuing the love-story of God's election and covenant with Israel, from whose direct line 'according to the flesh' came Jesus, the Messiah (Rom 9.5).

THE GLOBAL JESUS IN THE BIBLICAL CONTEXT OF SOTERIOLOGY

The New Testament concludes this history by declaring that in and through the person of Jesus of Nazareth, God-Word become flesh (John 1.1, 14), God personally fulfilled the divine promise of human salvation. Paul states that God in Christ was reconciling the world to the divine self, not counting our sins against us (2 Cor 5.19). From the purely human perspective, however, Jesus was a Jew, a descendant of Abraham through David of the tribe of Judah. His Jewish disciples viewed him first as their expected, exclusive Messiah. They believed his mission was to restore to Israel the kingdom usurped in their time by the Romans (Acts 1.6). Jesus himself is reported to have asserted that he was 'sent only to the lost sheep of the house of Israel' (Matt 25.24). Yet from the very beginning the New Testament also proclaims Jesus as the universal Messiah.

This is already evident in the infancy narratives. Luke sees Jesus both as a light to enlighten the Gentiles and 'the glory of [God's] people Israel' (Luke: 2.32). In Matthew's Gospel, the birth of Jesus brings wise people from the East in search of him to pay him homage as the 'king of the Jews' (Matt 2.1–2,10–11). This is strange, because normally in the ancient world, like in our world, people feared the kings of other nations. So the theme of Gentiles travelling from the ends of the earth to seek and worship the 'king of the Jews', knowing what his kingship might later mean to them and their peoples, requires some reflection. Whatever Matthew might have understood by the event, the church celebrates the coming of the Magi on the feast of Epiphany (6 January, or the Sunday after the feast of the Holy Family) as the revelation of Jesus, God's Messiah, to the Gentile world. It is thus a parallel to Christmas, which celebrates his revelation to the Jews through the shepherds (Luke 2.8–20). The feast of Epiphany also marks Jesus' baptism, where God reveals and declares him to be his beloved son to whom the audience is to listen. Epiphany thus celebrates both the completion of Jesus' revelation as God's Messiah during the period of his hidden life and the launch of his public mission at Cana in Galilee, where he performs his foundational sign through the intervention of his Mother (John 1.1–11; cf. further Okure 1998b, esp. 1463–65).

During his public life, Jesus reveals the global nature of his mission as he ministers even to Samaritans and Gentiles who appeal to him for help: the centurion (Luke 7.1–10); the Syrophoenician woman (Mark 7.24–29); the Samaritan leper (Luke 17.15–17); the Samaritan woman and her people (John 4.1–42); and the Gerasene demoniac (Mark 5.1–20). The most theologically developed episode is John 12.20–32, where certain Greeks seek to see Jesus through the help of Philip. Jesus interprets their desire as the advent of his long-awaited hour for the fulfilment of his mission: 'The hour has come for the Son of Man [this human being] to be glorified . . . and I when I am lifted up [crucified and risen from the dead], I will draw all peoples [and things] to myself' (John 12.23, 32). John's Gospel comprehensively understands Jesus as the manifestation of God's incredible love for humanity (John 3.16), the fulfilment in person of God's promise in the Garden of Eden to save humanity. Jesus' glorification (his passion, death and resurrection which John sees as one event) is the decisive victory. His rising from the dead in the Garden of Golgotha where he was buried (John 19.41–20.18) marks God's fulfilment of the promise made to our first parents in the Garden of Eden to give them victory over Satan who, through envy, introduced sin and death into the world (John 1.13, 24).[1]

THE GLOBAL JESUS IN THE NEW TESTAMENT JEWISH AND GENTILE CONTEXTS

Jesus' Jewish contemporaries naturally drew from their Jewish religion the terms that expressed who he was to them. The titles given him included Rabbi, Master, Teacher, Son of David, Son of God, Prophet, Servant, Messiah (Christ), the Lamb of God and king of Israel. The ordinary people thought of him mostly as a prophet, perhaps Jeremiah or Elijah returned to life (Matt 16.13–14). The designation of him as the Messiah emerges clearly as a revelation from God (Matt 16.16–17) or is disclosed by Jesus himself (John 4.25–26). Only after the resurrection do his disciples know for certain that he is the long expected Messiah, though Martha (John 11.27) confesses him as 'the Christ, the Son of God, the One who is coming into the world' (cf. John 1.41). The title Son of Man (generally interpreted as a reference to the 'heavenly' figure in Dan 7) is Jesus' uniquely preferred self-designation. By this Aramaic usage, however, Jesus at the same time designates himself simply as 'a human being', with no emphatic connotation of sex.

As the post-Easter proclamation spread from Jews to Gentiles, the other titles developed for Jesus included Divine Word and Reason (*Logos*), Wisdom (*sophia*), Victor (over sin, death and the elementary powers of the Universe), Universal Ruler (*Pantocrator*), the new Adam (humanity) and Saviour of the World. Jaroslav Pelikan (1985) gives an extensive survey of different approaches to the mystery and person of Jesus in Jewish, Christian and pagan cultures. The inculturation of the gospel in Gentile cultures necessitated using terminology that for the people expressed their faith in him as God and saviour for them, and which in turn enrich Christian understanding of the gospel itself (Okure 1990). Other terms (e.g. 'High Priest' in Hebrews, 'the First Born of Creation' in Colossians) were developed polemically as persuasive strategies to encourage believers to remain faithful to Jesus, especially in times of trial and persecution. The titles for Jesus in the time of the Apostolic Fathers in particular belong here and were greatly influenced by the heresies combated. Justin, Irenaeus and Clement of Alexandria developed images of Christ and Christian faith in terms of the Logos, the revealing word, and the covenant philosophy (Dupuis 1997:53–179, 280–304 and *passim*).

These developments show that we approach an understanding of God through terms that are familiar to us as human beings. The more diverse and multicultural the people who know Jesus, the more varied and complex will be the terms used to express this knowledge. In the period of the early Fathers, christological heresies and counter-definitions played a major role in shaping the titles for Jesus. Yet their expressions were still marked by contemporary Hellenistic culture. After the conversion of Constantine and the adoption of Christianity as a state religion in the early fourth century, some existing christological titles acquired political overtones, including 'King of the Universe' and 'Lord of Lords' (cf. Torjesen 1997). The Scholastics and Aquinas found in Greek philosophy, nature and their contemporary cultures the terminology and rationale for sustaining and elaborating on the universal images of Jesus contained in the New Testament and the Early Fathers. An example drawn from nature was the famous designation of Jesus as the Mother Pelican in Aquinas' hymn, *Adoro Te Devote*.

Some authors hold that Hellenistic Christianity lasted till the Second Vatican Council, 1963–65 (e.g. Elizondo 1999). Only from this time did Christianity become truly a world religion, one that expresses itself in languages and concepts of all peoples and cultures. This may explain why images of Christ have multiplied in recent years. As marginalised men and women around the world seek to receive Christ, they find in the gospels, their own cultures and personal experiences appropriate terminology for expressing their faith in him.

In African male academic contexts, Jesus is primarily an Ancestor, God being the Proto-ancestor (cf. Nyamiti 1993; Kabasele Lumbala 1998). African American theologians and Black theologians of South Africa view him as 'the Black Christ' and liberator, in song, art and writings (e.g. Douglas 1994; Cone 1997). For many Latin Americans, Christ is essentially a liberator, a champion of the poor and social justice (cf. Batstone 1991; Sobrino 1993). Some Asians compare him with the prophets of their great religions, not by using their names for him, but by emphasising that as the Logos he existed and was revealed among them before the advent of Christianity. This in itself is nothing new, since the early church Fathers spoke of Christ as the Logos and saw the good in each culture as seeds of the gospel. Still other Asian interpreters claim Jesus as the 'western Dalai Lama', 'vegetarian' and 'Buddhist' (cf. Deardorff 1994; Panikkar 1981; Boff and Elizondo 1993; Song 1994).

African women theologians, in particular, discover in Christ a friend, lover, liberator, husband of widows, life-giver, and mother and ground of the new humanity (cf. Hinga 1992; Amoah and Oduyoye 1988; Okure 1993). Yet the explicit designation of Jesus as 'our mother' goes back to Julian of Norwich and St Anselm of Canterbury. That women regularly featured among English rulers may explain why culturally Julian and Anselm had little problem calling Jesus 'mother'. For the African women, the designation of Jesus as mother derives from the cultural view of the woman as the embodiment of life, the one who gives birth to life. The continent itself is fondly called 'Mama Africa'. If Jesus is 'the life' and our source of enduring life (cf. John 14.6), it follows naturally for African women that he be also called 'mother'.

The devotion to Jesus, especially among evangelical and charismatic churches, is easily this past century's most explosive manifestation of faith in the global Jesus proclaimed in the gospel. In these circles, Jesus is seen as a miracle worker, Lord and master, victor over sin, death and all dehumanising forces, and a personal Saviour. These churches are truly global in nature, and particularly tend to flourish in Third World countries (see e.g. Anderson 1992 on South Africa). Alongside this seems to stand an increasing Jewish interest in Jesus both among 'Messianic Jews' and among Jews who dispute the appropriateness of Jewish religious interest in Jesus. Where it is genuine, this interest may yet usher in the fulfilment of Paul's faith in the eventual conversion of his people (cf. Rom 11).

The discussion on the global Jesus thus far could give the impression that no difficulties existed in the acceptance of Jesus as the Saviour of all humanity, or that all nations accept the gospel proclamation of his divinity as God incarnate in whom alone salvation is to be found. But while believers of many nations, cultures and epochs have held this, peoples of other faiths have denied it. Adherents of oriental religions increasingly contest the Christian biblical claim that Jesus is the Saviour of the world. Their traditional religions, some of which are older than Christianity, seem to them to teach an equally good or better way to God than Jesus. Even Islam, although younger than Christianity, honours Jesus only as a Prophet along with Moses and Mohammed. It rejects the Christian belief in his divinity, since Allah is one and has no son. Still other opponents arise even from within the post-Christian west, where some vilify, or at best 'secularise' Jesus in art, films and scholarship, seeing in him no more than a human being. To many Christian observers, a notable example of the latter is the so-called 'Jesus Seminar', started in 1985 by Robert Funk of the Pacific School of Religion in Berkeley, California (cf. Borg 1992; Funk 1996).

Efforts to vilify or secularise Jesus are of course not new. He was called all kinds of names in his own lifetime (e.g. 'a glutton and a drunkard', Matt 11.19), and by his own leaders. That practice will probably continue till God's restoration of all things in Christ is fulfilled. Just as in the first century Jesus was embraced as Saviour of the world by Jews and Gentiles excluded from religious and political power, so today he is welcomed above all by ordinary, poor and marginalised people – in the west and the east, and especially in the South. Like Paul, they see him, God's gospel, as having the power to liberate them from sin (cf. Rom 1.16), their personal sins, the socio-political, cultural and structural sins of their nations, cultures and churches and the unjust economic and technological structures of the so-called 'global village'.

As seen earlier, the Christian belief in the global significance of Jesus is a logical outcome of the belief that, in Christ, God has begun to restore the goodness of creation, and that this restoration attains perfection as a new heaven and a new earth (Rev 21–22). The earth, cursed because of Adam (Gen 3.17–19), will be set free from its bondage to decay to enjoy the glorious liberty of God's children (cf. Rom 8.20–21 and see Okure 1998a).

Jesus, God's agent in this work, is in the scholarly world not usually described as the founder of Christianity. This designation is given either to the apostles conjointly or to Paul. One corollary of this way of speaking is to recognise that while Jesus is the head of the church, the life given freely by God in and through him is for all peoples, including those who do not confess faith in him. Seen thus, the church that Christ builds on Peter (Matt

16.18–19) is bigger than the Roman Catholic or even the Christian church. It embraces all God's people, including those who 'have not yet arrived at an explicit knowledge of God', as Vatican Council II upholds in the Dogmatic Constitution on the Church (no. 16). Because Jesus himself is the locus of God's gathering of humanity to the divine self, he cannot be restricted to any one church set up on a partisan basis. Christ gives the church its fundamental meaning. In him, the church becomes the gathering into one of God's children previously scattered by sin, but who now worship and serve him, not their own exclusive claims to orthodoxy – even though orthodoxy (truth in the divine relationship to the world and to every human being) is an integral part of what it means to be his church.

It is ultimately in his identity as one who gives his life so that others may live (John 10.10) that the global Jesus parts company with secular ideologies of globalisation. It is also here that he becomes truly universal, the agent of God's redemption of the world from Satan, sin and death. Jesus defeated Satan, sin and death on the cross, not for the Jewish nation only but to gather together God's children, scattered by the anthropological sins – both local and 'global' – of racism, sexism and classism (John 11.52). Satan today need not be viewed exclusively as an external evil being. Satan is concretely a force that operates in human beings and derails them from the path of true self-realisation, a life of love, of sharing God-given goods of the earth and caring for all God's creatures, made in God's own image and likeness. Participation in the life of the Trinitarian God was God's legacy for humanity, created male and female in God's own image and likeness (Gen 1.26; cf. Boff 2000). A global view of Jesus which misses this point, or that of Jesus' divinity, the bedrock of the proclamation, misses a vital element in the proclamation. Because Jesus is essentially a Saviour, peoples of all nations, tribes and languages are attracted to him. They receive him in their diverse ways as God's general amnesty to the entire creation. Today even some professed atheists call themselves 'atheists for Jesus' because they believe in his message of love and kindness. Mahatma Gandhi, though not an atheist, is known to have said of Christianity that he liked their Christ but not their Christians.

THE GLOBAL JESUS AND THE CONTEMPORARY READER

The last observation challenges the interested reader in 'the global Jesus' to define his or her own way of making him relevant to his or her life. Jesus liberates us from the false self and enables us to gain the true self that God intended for us at creation. When Jesus is not confused with how human beings use and have used or abused him to further their own interests (prestige, power and authority over others), race or sex, one will find in him a friend and a love. Every human being loves life. Jesus gives his life so that believers in him may live. He offers eternal life, a participation in God's own unending life. In the biblical vision of this life, death is destroyed, the heavens and the earth are transformed, and God becomes the life principle of all peoples. No one is excluded from this divine life-giving mercy.

We recall here the situation in the former Communist Russia, where God and Jesus were seen as infringing on human freedom and self-realisation. Communism and atheism were projected as having the power to free one. To be freed from the 'opium' of religion, the people were made to reject God, Christ and the church. Yet in so doing, they still depended on other human beings for their understanding of how to be fully human. Christians who today convert to Hinduism, Buddhism, Islam or the African Traditional Religions do so because someone or their life circumstances persuaded them of the 'superior' value of these religions. But the same applies to conversions to Christianity. As human beings we are never completely free of the influence of others.

A recent conversation with a person from the formerly Communist East Germany illustrates this. The person was asked whether he knew Jesus, since from what one saw of him, both he and Jesus could become great friends. The person responded that he had no need to refer either to God or to Jesus to authenticate his existence. He was satisfied to discover his own humanity, by looking for meaning deep within himself. Neither God, Jesus nor religion gave authenticity to his life or provided the reason for his existence. The resources for realising his human potential lay deep and squarely within him.

It was observed that though he was right in his quest for self-realisation, of course he could not conclude *a priori* that God and Jesus had no relevance for his life until he had made a personal encounter with them. His position was probably based on other people's views of God, Jesus and religion. Only his own personal discovery could help him to decide whether Jesus blocked his self-realisation or helped him to realise that self beyond possibilities that he would never have dreamt of. Both the human self and the desire to realise it are gifts from God, who never takes back what he gives as pure grace. God's glory is human beings fully alive, and Jesus, too, is that glory. It was suggested to our East German inquirer that he could begin to establish a first-hand contact with Jesus by reading the gospels. The encounter might lead him to discover with regret, as Augustine did, that he took so long to discover God's infinite beauty and love in Jesus. For example, he might reflect on how his self-realisation had been affected by the positive influences of people who really loved him for himself. People who really love us do not impoverish us. They enable us to discover our true selves and potentials. This is what the global Jesus does for every human being who comes into the world. Christians are privileged to know and confess him explicitly.

Against this background, it can only be deeply regretted that, throughout history, Christians have killed their brother and sister Christians and other human beings called 'non-believers', allegedly in and for Jesus – in defence not of life but of doctrine. A key example, because of its concentrated magnitude and the horrors attached to it, is the Holocaust. But equally horrifying in their own way are the evils of colonialism, the slave trade and its entire system, the Inquisition and the many subtle ways in which Christians continue to tear down one another today, in the name of Jesus. These actions are a betrayal of Christians themselves and contrary to the spirit of the global Jesus. Instead of resorting to violence, Jesus commanded Peter, the rock on which to build his church, to put his sword back in its sheath when Peter had used it to protect Jesus from his enemies (John 18.10–11). He forbade his disciples to stop a preacher who was not of their company. By helping to liberate human beings from oppressive and dehumanising forces in his name (Luke 9.49–50), such people, in Jesus' view, were and still are his true collaborators. Jesus accepted and still accepts their ministry as part of his agenda to save. Today as we seek to understand the global Jesus and align ourselves with him, we are called to ensure that action on behalf of social justice forms a constitutive aspect of the claim to know Jesus. Ultimately we prove our knowledge and love of Jesus by participating in his saving, life-giving mission:

> Come, you that are blessed by my Father, inherit the kingdom prepared
> for you from the foundation of the world; for I was hungry and you
> gave me food, I was thirsty and you gave me something to drink, I was
> a stranger and you welcomed me . . . As you did it to one of the least of
> these who are members of my family, you did it to me. (Matt 25.34–40)

By this declaration, Jesus claims every person (his 'family members') as himself. Therefore, the discussion on the global Jesus leads us ultimately beyond the mystery of his person to the awareness that we ourselves and every human being are part of his mystery. For he is, by God's design, the ground of the new humanity and of the entire cosmos (Col 1.15–20; Eph 2.9–10). The question of his identity becomes our own question, as individual beings and as a human family. This awareness challenges us as God's children to treat ourselves and every human, made in God's own image and likeness, with a respect due to Jesus.

It also calls for deep respect for the created world. The ecological issue today is an integral part of our respect for God and Christ in creation. If every human being accepted his or her own identity as God's child, if the entire human family accepted the challenge of feeding the poor, giving a home to the homeless, sharing opportunities equally as members of a loving family, we would progressively grow into people made in God's image and likeness, thereby enacting together, instead of disputing on, the universality of Jesus. This life of mutual sharing and respect would be nourished by efforts to discover in each culture and religion the good that God has already placed there, to enrich our understanding and love of Jesus, who came to bring God's general amnesty for everyone (Rom 1.1–3).

The global Jesus is God's answer to the globalisation of sin. He is God's own victory for humanity over the anthropological sins of racism, sexism and classism with their multiple global branches. 'As in Adam all died, so in Christ [the new Adam] will all be made alive' (1 Cor 15.22). Acceptance of the biblical faith that death came to all human beings through the work of Satan calls for a corresponding acceptance that God in Christ has liberated the whole humanity from the powers of sin and death through Christ's resurrection. Jesus, therefore, whom the Bible sees as God's agent for this liberation, is necessarily a global, universal Christ, God's anointed Saviour for the world.

CONCLUSION

This study holds that the question of the biblical Jesus gains its meaning and essence within the context of the biblical story of creation and redemption. We have focused on written works, and readers may broaden this awareness of Jesus to include works of art, sculpture, songs, hymns, popular literature, even captions on the doors of private houses and vehicles. Indeed, it is amazing to reflect just how global Jesus is and has been in the life of individuals, communities and nations throughout human history till today.

In biblical history, Jesus is God in human flesh, the very God through whom and for whom the world was created (John 1.1–2; Rom 11.33–36). Human beings did not bring about creation and the incarnation; both are God's act of pure grace and love. Ultimately, therefore, human beings cannot determine the perimeters of Jesus' global significance, however much they may dispute it. They can only seek to know and accept this grace in faith within their own socio-cultural and historical contexts. Faith itself is God's grace, given for the asking. One's response in faith or lack of belief in Jesus as God in human flesh cannot change the reality of who Jesus is in himself and in God's biblical plan of salvation for humanity. Belief in the divinity of Jesus is an integral aspect of his global significance, and needs to be borne in mind as foundational in the entire discussion. Because the world belongs to Jesus and was created through Jesus, God-Word incarnate, it follows that he be known, loved and followed by peoples of all nations, languages, cultures in all ages in their diverse expressions. The Book of Revelation celebrates in its own enigmatic way the last stages of what we might call 'the divine globalisation of Jesus'. Before then each successive generation has to work out the details of this faith for itself and the entire human family. The communion of saints on earth requires that we develop concrete ways of celebrating this communion as a participation in the divine Trinitarian life.

Note

1. On the symbolic significance of the Garden of Jesus' burial and resurrection in relation to the Garden of Eden, see Okure 1998b:1497. Jesus was also arrested in a garden, Gethsemane (Mark 14.32–50).

16 Jerusalem after Jesus

DAVID B. BURRELL, CSC

As the gospels testify, Jesus was hardly drawn to Jerusalem. The turning-point verse in Luke's Gospel underscores the tension: 'he set his face resolutely towards Jerusalem' (9.51 NEB). Moreover, after his resurrection that same Gospel directs his disciples to proclaim 'repentance bringing the forgiveness of sins . . . to all nations beginning from Jerusalem' (24.47), as they are sent (in the companion narrative of the Acts of the Apostles) to 'bear witness for me in Jerusalem, and throughout Judaea and Samaria, and even in the farthest corners of the earth' (Acts 1.8). So the New Testament explicitly reverses the centripetal movement of all nations gathering to Jerusalem (in the messianic prophecies of Isaiah) to a centrifugal one, leaving Jerusalem to be a centre whose role would remain ambiguous throughout Christian history. In her masterful account, Karen Armstrong (1996) delineates these ambiguities through a history punctuated and shaped by diverse interactions with Jews and Muslims. Peter Walker (1990) provides an early set of reflections from Eusebius and Cyril (see also Walker 1994), while Robert Wilken (1992) offers textual evidence of the richly theological exchange between Jews and Christians in the context of this holy city. Frank Peters (1985) offers a rich compendium of texts from 'chroniclers, visitors, pilgrims and prophets from the days of Abraham to the beginning of modern times'.

A BRIEF OVERVIEW OF THE HISTORY

The earliest set of attitudes towards Jerusalem, evinced in Origen and Irenaeus, reflects the end of Luke's Gospel, in reminding us how Jesus' apostles, emboldened by their resurrection faith, 'preached the good news from Jerusalem to the ends of the earth'. As has often been remarked, the Romans' destruction of the Temple reinforced the convictions of contemporary believers in Jesus that they were to carry on as God's special people, preaching the God of Abraham, Isaac and Jacob to the nations. The only Jerusalem relevant to that faith was the 'new Jerusalem, coming down from heaven, adorned as a bride' (Rev 21.1). So Origen:

> Since we have been taught by Paul that there is one Israel according to the flesh and another according to the Spirit, when the Saviour says: 'I was sent only to the lost sheep of the house of Israel' (Matt 15.24), we do not understand Him as [referring] to them who have an earthly wisdom . . . Rather, we understand that there is a nation of souls, named Israel. Even the meaning of the name suggests this, since Israel is translated 'the mind seeing God' or 'man seeing God'. Moreover, the Apostle makes such revelations about Jerusalem as 'the Jerusalem above is free, and she is our mother' (Gal 4.26). And in another of his letters he says: 'but you have come to Mount Zion and to the city of the living God, the heavenly Jerusalem, and to innumerable angels in festive gathering, and to the church of the firstborn who are enrolled in heaven' (Heb 12.22–23). If, therefore, there are certain souls in this world that are called Israel, and in heaven a certain city that is named Jerusalem, it follows that these cities that are said to belong to the nation of Israel have as their metropolis the heavenly Jerusalem. And we understand all of Judea in this way . . . Therefore, whatever is either told or prophesied about Jerusalem, if we hear the words of Paul as of Christ speaking in him (cf. 2 Cor 13.3), we should understand according to his opinion to have been spoken of that city which he calls the heavenly Jerusalem and of all those places or cities that are said to be cities of the holy land of which Jerusalem is the metropolis. (*On first principles* 4.1.22, Origen 1979:194–96)

For Irenaeus, the matter was not simply transcendent: 'in the time of kingdom, the earth has been called again by Christ [to its pristine condition], and Jerusalem rebuilt after the pattern of the Jerusalem above...' (*Haer.* 5.35.2 *ANF*). Although eschatological in character, this Jesus was to rule a literal kingdom from the geographical, if renewed, Jerusalem.

Eusebius (*c.* 260–339) reflects the view of Origen, whom he personally admired. As bishop of Caesarea at a time when Jerusalem had been effectively replaced by the Roman garrison-town, Aelia Capitolina, after the successive destruction of the city in 70 and in 135, Eusebius consistently downplays the continuing theological significance of Jerusalem. Part of his motivation was doubtless to underscore the contrast between Christianity and Judaism, by emphasising the way in which New Testament spirituality looked upwards to the 'heavenly Jerusalem' rather than remaining focused on earthly realities. This attitude will be challenged, however, towards the end of Eusebius'

life by the bishop of Jerusalem, Cyril (*c.* 320–386?), who inherited the fresh
perspective of the edict of Constantine, and that emperor's personal intent
to embellish the city as befits its proper dignity. His more positive assessment of Jerusalem reflected the change in spirit: 'The "Jerusalem mystique"
was present and powerful, the potential of the city inviting, the presence of
the pilgrims demanding and the possible increased status of the Jerusalem
Church compelling' (Walker 1990:314). But bishops cannot initiate pilgrimage; there had to be other factors at work, not the least of which was an
appreciation of an incarnate Christ, in opposition to the Arians. That the
Word of God became flesh in space and time should give Jerusalem pride of
place, for it was *here* that it all happened. This contrast, or, better, opposition
regarding the status of place would continue to mark Christian theology;
holiness might attend place because of human association, but the free creator of all could hardly legitimise turf wars, as though this place and not that
belonged to God. It had rather to be that the presence that Christians sought
to establish in Jerusalem would be one consonant with imperial recognition;
it would be a monumental presence fitting an imperial religion. Abetted by
the Council of Nicaea in the early fourth century, which would be elaborated
into the celebrated formula of Chalcedon in the mid-fifth century, the iconic
status of Jerusalem mirrored the articulation of orthodox faith in Jesus as
'one person with two natures, fully human as well as fully divine'. That this
formula was an imperial one, accepted by the bishop of Jerusalem, helped
to restore that see to the original status it had lost after the Romans had
destroyed it a second time (in 135).

Yet while the histories may have focused on the basilica of the Anastasis
(resurrection), constructed by Constantine, churches only function with communities to animate them, so it was the 'church of Jerusalem', rather than
its churches, which began to elaborate and sustain the memory of this place
as holy. Jerusalem became home to Christian communities, whose memory forged a bond between *place* and *people* that allowed Jerusalem to take
its place among the 'churches' of the East, indeed, as the first, the 'mother
church'. So the earlier predilection for a 'heavenly Jerusalem' became trans-
muted into a love and respect for this Jerusalem, where the 'Word made flesh'
had lived, preached, died and risen from the dead – a place made holy by people whose presence kept the memories alive of the crucial facts shaping this
personal revelation of the Word of God. Nor was Jerusalem itself to absorb
all the 'holiness'; in fact, it was the desire of monks and nuns to populate the
desert, 'that the prophecies made about it by the eloquent Isaiah be fulfilled'
(*Life of Sabas*, Cyril of Scythopolis 1990:88) – an about-face from the earlier
set of attitudes. It was in fact their presence that inspired the name of 'Holy
Land', as Robert Wilken has reminded us. That glorious chapter was to be

abruptly truncated in 614, when the Persians took revenge on the Byzantines, slaughtering (by a contemporary account) some 66,000 Christians in the city alone, along with countless monks and nuns in the countryside. As Karen Armstrong (1996:214) tells the tale, 'Christians [who] had sharply differentiated their experience in Jerusalem from that of the Jews, now . . . went into exile in their turn [and] turned naturally to the gestures and psalms of their predecessors in the Holy City, and like the Jews they spoke of God and Zion in the same breath'.

A scant twenty-three years later a Muslim army arrived outside its walls. The caliph Omar's peaceful entrance is legendary, along with his desire to rehabilitate the ancient 'temple mount', which the Byzantines had treated as a refuse site, following prevailing Christian conviction that the demise of the Jewish temple simply confirmed the truth of Christianity. It was the Umayyad caliph, Abdul-Malik, who built the signature 'Dome of the Rock' over the rock of Moriah in 691, both to establish Muslim hegemony as well as to commemorate Muhammad's celebrated 'night journey' mentioned in the Qur'an. Between 637 and 1099, under a largely tolerant Muslim hegemony, Jerusalem became a coveted pilgrimage site, and the recorded travels of women and men fed the imaginations of western Christians regarding the land where Jesus had lived. Pilgrimage could only enhance the theme of place made holy by the presence of faithful people, turning it into a 'full-blown sacred geography [which saw] Jerusalem as the centre of the world...' (Armstrong 1996:216). When that imagination was encouraged to fuel an irredentist urge to 'recover the holy places' from an upstart faith and to restore the 'holy land' to Christianity, however, the Crusades were born. That urge was in turn fuelled by the destruction of the Holy Sepulchre by the mad caliph Hakim, which precipitated a call for assistance from Byzantium to western Christians – an appeal they would soon regret. Beginning in 1099, power was to prevail over presence in Jerusalem and the Holy Land, and often brutally so, although those among the interlopers who stayed became themselves entranced by the land and its attraction to become a new breed of local Christians, Latin by persuasion.[1]

This 'Latin Kingdom', however, was to last little more than a century. Following Saladin's decisive victory in 1187, and especially under subsequent Mamluke hegemony, the refurbished temple mount, Jerusalem's *haram ash-sharif*, became home to Sufi brotherhoods, while the city housed both Jews and Christians. Pilgrimage became expensive and often dangerous, however, due to the tenuous hold of the Egyptian political power over the countryside, and soon waned in the face of religious contention in Europe, as well as preoccupation with a freshly discovered continent by those seeking alternatives to the Silk Road. In fact, pilgrimage to Santiago de Compostela tended to replace Jerusalem as the favoured destination. Yet transfer of the city to Ottoman hegemony led to Suleiman's reconstruction of the current walls in 1536, making it possible for communities of Abrahamic believers to continue to people Jerusalem, where their memories bonded them to the city, and the city to them, in ways peculiar to each religious faith.

The novel situation of the nineteenth century stemmed from Napoleon's landing in Alexandria in 1799, signalling the onset of a creeping colonisation of the two major Islamic empires – Ottoman and Mogul – by western powers. By the latter half of that century, European powers had managed to prevail upon one sultan after another to grant them privileges and place in Jerusalem, ostensibly to receive their pilgrims. Yet in the cases where these ventures were spearheaded by religious men and women who were educators of health-care workers, they settled into their accustomed role of serving the local Christian populations, and so enhancing the education and well-being of local communities of Christians, and decisively altering the local ecology of Jerusalem. Another strand of western Christians descended on the 'holy land' with tools of archaeology, impelled to use these 'scientific' explorations to further our understanding of the Bible. In time that very archaeology would call into question the biblical narratives of conquest of the land, but the principle of using archaeology to reinforce a particular view of history and of identity had been established.[2] These Christians were less interested in the local communities, and more focused on the 'holy sites', thereby setting a pattern for preoccupation with place that could ignore people. In fact, by reducing 'holy land' to 'holy places', this biblically inspired movement unwittingly set the stage for policies towards local Christians on the part of the next ruling power, the state of Israel, designed to dispossess them from Jerusalem while assuring 'free access to the holy places' to Christians and Muslims alike who come from abroad.

Yet places cannot remain *holy* very long without a people whose memory and presence confirm that holiness. For while it is true that the Bible proclaims the holiness of the land because of the Lord's own presence: 'the Lord will hold Judah as his portion in the Holy Land, and again make Israel his very own' (Zech 1.12), the same prophet urges Israel itself to 'Sing, rejoice, daughter of Zion; for I am coming to dwell in the midst of you – it is the Lord who speaks' (Zech 1.10). Place needs people to affirm its specialness, and to confirm it with their lives. Indeed, the latest chapter in Jerusalem's history is intimately linked to the 'return' of Jews to the land – *eretz Israel* – in the specific form of Zionism, a nineteenth-century socialist utopian movement which initially focused on peoplehood, but soon came to see how crucially symbolic was the attraction of this 'holy land' to their constituency, however avowedly 'secular' their Jewish audience might have been. The initial movements of people to the land – named ʿ*aliyah*'s after the symbolic journey *up* to Jerusalem – began at the end of the nineteenth century, and continued in successive waves during the first half of the twentieth century (encouraged by the Balfour Declaration of 1917), only to become a poignant flood at the end of the Second World War when the Nazi extermination camps were liberated. The fears of local residents had found expression in a series of 'Arab revolts' during the British mandate period between the two world wars, as the hegemonic consequences of the Zionist movement became increasingly clear. In the years just after the Second World War, however, pitched battles to establish that hegemony turned thousands of local Arab residents into refugees in their own land, while the stalemate left enough territory to establish the state of Israel in 1948 – a state which world opinion quickly embraced in the wake of the genocide at Auschwitz. The 'holy land' remained so divided until 1967, when Israel occupied the rest of the land in a lightning war, begetting an immediate euphoria followed by decades of occupation contested by a series of United Nations resolutions comprising an international legal consensus.

So we are returned to the dialectic between presence and power in regard to place, and especially to a place deemed 'holy'. The Muslim caliph Omar sensed this when he took over Jerusalem, both in adopting an alternative site for worship from that of the Holy Sepulchre, and also by inviting Jews from Tiberias to return to the city. In each case, he realised that to take possession of a place which others not only deemed to be holy, but which their presence had sanctified in memory and often in blood, in such a way as to render them unwelcome, offered a needless provocation. Whoever holds the power – and place requires power if it is to be held – over a 'holy place' will soon realise that embracing the presence of those whose lives and memory make it holy is the only way to peaceful co-existence. Place alone cannot be holy, as once-monastic sites like Mont Saint-Michel testify so eloquently; a one-time monastery turned into a national monument lacks its essential ingredient: place requires presence to be holy. Indeed, the same could be said for Hagia Sophia: after its origins as a Christian basilica, transformed into a mosque when Constantinople became Istanbul, its final state as a monument inspires awe only by remembering all that it had been! Moreover, the power that holds a place fails to respect such a presence at its own peril. For in the end, presence may wield even more power than a power that tries to erase presence. And what a visitor to Jerusalem finds today is a vibrant Jewish presence, an imposing Muslim presence for Friday prayer, and Christians omnipresent as pilgrims, with fewer local Christians each year. In 1944 there were 29,350 Christians in Jerusalem, while in 2000 Christians living in Jerusalem number 10,000 at a most generous estimate. The Christians in Jerusalem make up 5.6 per cent of the Arab population and 1.7 per cent of the total population of the city, both Jewish and Arab. Whereas in 1967, West Bank Christians numbered 43,000 in the West Bank and Gaza Strip (2,000) or 3.9 per cent of the total population; in 2000, Christians in the Palestinian Territories number 50,000, which makes only 1.8 per cent of the total Palestinian population. In the same year, with respect to Israel, Christians number 130,000 or 13 per cent of the Arab population and slightly less than 2 per cent of the entire population of Israel.[3]

The diverse Christian groups who continue to reside in Jerusalem, however, are busy making common cause with Muslims to activate their presence to this city holy to them – and not merely the 'holy sites'. Jewish cultural life takes place mainly in the institutions of the new city, which testify to the way in which a concentrated and articulate presence can foster deeper understanding of a tradition. Jewish society is divided on its willingness to accommodate others' convictions regarding this city. Debate on Jerusalem as the 'everlasting and undivided capital of Israel' tends to be dominated by ideological concerns, while the facts of the matter present a city divided into neighbourhoods almost as neatly as the Ottomans separated Armenians, Jews, Christians and Muslims into the four sectors of the old city. Storied Jewish return to *eretz Israel* often focused on Jerusalem – *le-shanah ha-ba' bi-Yerushalayim*, even though many Israelis feel far more comfortable in Tel Aviv or in kibbutzim scattered throughout the land. The 'holiness' of the Western Wall, however, is shared by all observant Jews, as the ever-present rituals there can attest. What is certain is that this city will remain holy to all three religious faiths, and will be so effectively in the measure that the respective faith communities display its special character in their life and work, and especially in their interaction with each other.

REFLECTIONS ON A CONTINUING CHRISTIAN PRESENCE

How does this chequered history and divided geography affect Jerusalem today? And how can we assess the presence of Jesus there? We cannot begin to tackle these questions without reminding ourselves of the relevance of people, presence and power to place. The Jerusalem of today is a pastiche of peoples within a triad of faiths – Jewish, Christian, Muslim – whose presence to one another may only be glancing, yet the dynamic is unmistakably one of interaction with the place. So the living presence of Jesus can be felt in the diverse communities of Christians in this place, living as they do beside one another, yet within Jewish and Muslim majorities. They have always accepted that part of their inbuilt mission, one might say, is to receive pilgrims to this land. Yet those who make the effort of pilgrimage will inevitably encounter the inscription above the tomb in the church of the Holy Sepulchre: 'He is risen; he is not here!' This motif, which epitomises the faith of Christians worldwide, also relativises the place that is Jerusalem. For here, as anywhere else, Jesus lives in the communities that bear his name. In that sense, there can be nothing special about Jerusalem, as the early witnesses – Origen, Irenaeus and Eusebius – testified. Yet the fact remains that there is something special about this place!

What seems to be the case is that what makes the place special is also what makes Jesus special – indeed, so special that it took four centuries to bring it to full articulation in the formula of Chalcedon: 'one person with two natures, fully human as well as fully divine'. But formulae need always to be reappropriated in the light of shifting historical realities, and this one above all. For the full humanity of Jesus can either be eclipsed by the universality of the 'Christ-event', or in reaction to that, be affirmed in such a way as to evacuate his theandric character. So Christians need always to be reminded of the Jesus of time and space, and where better than in the land that Jesus walked, and especially the city in which he was put to death. That he 'rose from the dead', to foil the expectations of those who would have his person and subversive teaching out of the way, is of course a matter of faith. That is the faith which continues to animate those communities of Christians whose multiform presence has shaped Jerusalem over the centuries, and whose reception of each generation of pilgrims continues to make Him present to those who come seeking Jesus in this place.

Let me propose that this presence is iconic, and try to suggest how it can be so. Icons are not ordinary pictures, we know; yet few western Christians find it easy to appreciate the power their presence bears for eastern believers. It is also appropriate to use such an image to help introduce western minds and hearts into the mystery of place that is Jerusalem, since the icon epitomises the spirituality of its local Christians. An icon is so constructed as to suggest more than is presented, to gesture towards a transforming power at work in the persons depicted, and so to confront persons regarding it with their own selves at this stage in their being called to transformation. So to people of faith, icons initiate a transaction and invite a continuing transformation. To those who view them without that element of faith, they can seem hauntingly strange, at once enticing and offputting. So it is with one's initial encounter of the congeries of communities of faith in Jerusalem, many of whom western Christians have never before acknowledged – Armenians, Melchites, Chaldeans, Ethiopians, Copts; as well as the palpable presence of Jews and Muslims. Yet that variety itself poignantly displays the human condition with regard to faith: enticing but elusive, aggravating yet unavoidable. Moreover, none of the three Abrahamic faiths that share Jerusalem can dispense with time or space. If the land assumes a paramount position for Jews, for Christians the history of Jesus is tied to that land even if it does not tie Christians to it. Islam too, by orienting its daily prayer to Mecca, as well as by requiring, when feasible, pilgrimage there (and inclusively, to Jerusalem as well), reminds us where it was that Muhammad received the Word of God in flawless Arabic.

So certain places, and Jerusalem in a special shared way, are iconic for these three faiths. That is, this place is more than simply 'a place', just as an icon is more than a representation. What marks it off, of course, is the irruption of eternity into time, as in the founding events of each of these faiths: the giving of the Torah to Moses, the incarnation of the Word in Jesus, and the 'coming down' of the Qur'an. These events are unique in the way that no other historical event can claim to be, precisely because they represent (to believers) the presence of the creator in creation, or eternity in time, in such a way as to make the eternal creator subject to temporal description. It is that 'theandric' character that alone can give a place iconic status. For just as any historical event must be comparable to others, so any place must be able to be mapped in space and in time; yet just as some times serve to punctuate time itself – as creation (biblically calculated) does for Jews, the birth of Jesus does for Christians, and the *hijra* for Muslims – so some places bear the mark of God's palpable presence. Merely stating this, however, raises the spectre of a 'particularity' that threatens to send us all running for comfort into a 'universality' that renders all time and space homogeneous. Lessing's 'ugly ditch' puts the scandal of Abrahamic faith directly before our eyes, just as Jerusalem does. So we are returned, in a Christian context, to Chalcedon, and to the four-century struggle, often bloody, to craft that formula, for Jerusalem and the land it epitomises confronts us with the 'full humanity' of Jesus, and the shocking particularity of Jewish as well as Christian faith – for Jesus, after all, was not a Christian!

But what have icons to do with formulae? Very little, usually, but when the formula in question is one which attempts to formulate a community's faith, and in this case, faith in a person who is – in his very person – the revelation of God, then understanding the words themselves will require more than our intellects. The words must engage our very persons as well, and icons are meant to do just that. Yet if icons fail to do it for a western sensibility, encountering a place like Jerusalem may awaken this untapped potential within us. For just as icons call us beyond the response reserved for mere pictures, so Jerusalem continues to have an uncanny effect on its visitors. In her attempt to capture this quality, Karen Armstrong (1996) recalls us to the ways in which (by the nineteenth century) 'modernity was gradually changing religion [so that] people in Europe and the United States had lost the art of thinking in symbols and images . . . yet the mythology of sacred geography went deep' (p. 363). And among Jews facing their own modernity, 'Jerusalem was still a symbol that had power to inspire . . . secular Zionists as they struggled to create a new world' (p. 367). So a place that has been touched in the way Jerusalem has will confront our standing presumption that any place must be like any other, and open us to the 'scandal of particularity' that characterises Abrahamic faith. Moreover, in our time, this place shapes the interaction among those faiths in ways that would baffle the 'non-violent crusaders' of the nineteenth century. For the Jesus whom Christians meet here is unmistakably Jewish, even if the current Jewish presence for local Christians is more often oppressive than it is illuminating of the gospels. Moreover, the hegemonic claims of the state of Israel over Jerusalem itself have awakened in Muslims their ancient attachment to this 'third holy city of Islam', which Israel itself has effectively acknowledged since 1967, in accepting *waqf* jurisdiction over the *haram ash-sharif*, however pragmatic the motives may have been for doing so.

Here we touch, I propose, the current shape of the presence of Jesus in Jerusalem. The legacy of the nineteenth-century 'non-violent crusade' establishing a variegated western presence in Jerusalem continues to affect the ecology of the city, and through the standing institutions, the livelihood of countless of its Arab citizens. And these institutions are always more than buildings: they are staffed by dedicated women and men, many of whom are young volunteers drawn to serve in this special place, whose lives are animated by a faith which transcends Jerusalem but nonetheless draws sustenance here. Often enough, they will not possess categories sufficient to articulate the effects that the special presence of this place has on them, even though their own work and presence will go on to contribute to it for visitors who come. So once again, place and presence interact to produce a power that baffles our rational modes of discourse, much as icons do, and yet conspire to spell the charm of Jerusalem and the special presence of Jesus in the communities of Christians here. This presence lacks power today, confronted as it is by Israeli hegemony and an increasing majority of Muslims; yet that very fact shapes the current witness Christians can give. What is becoming clearer in our new millennium is that Jesus' presence in these communities – themselves legacies from an earlier century and then current political visions of Christendom – will be found in the ways they learn to interact with their Jewish and Muslim compatriots to exploit the symbolic potential of Jerusalem as one city of three faiths. If local Christians have benefited from the educational opportunities granted by institutions founded from the West, their unique contribution today will be to show western Christians how to live in an environment shaped by many faiths.

Indeed, it is precisely because Jerusalem is a city dear to three faiths that the conflicts are so sharp. Here especially will the shadow sides of faith-communities be played out: the demand that one's own *truth* must cancel out that affirmed by the other. It was that fierce intolerance, so often elicited and indeed sharpened by faith, which led the West into an enlightenment designed to circumvent these potentially conflicting particularities. Yet after passing through the gauntlet of a century in which more human beings were killed in the name of ideologies offered as secular alternatives to faith, we may be more inclined to return to those same faith-traditions to ask whether they do not also contain, within themselves, the capacity to criticise the abuses executed in their name, and thereby effect their own renewal. Here Jerusalem may offer the best test case, precisely because it always seems the most intractable. The landmark visit of Pope John Paul II (in the early months of the year 2000) to the 'holy land', and especially to Jerusalem, may give these reflections their proper perspective. He came as a 'pilgrim', yet made explicitly 'political' statements – as indeed he had to do, since Jerusalem is a flesh-and-blood reality, iconic of three faith-communities, so cannot simply be relegated to a 'holy place'. His statements were not calculatedly 'political', however, reflecting 'special interests', but clearly emanated from principles imbedded in and redolent of each of the faith-communities whose composition mirrors extant political conflicts. In that way, groups currently at odds had to come together in affirming his presence, and although each would inevitably attempt to interpret his message in ways favourable to themselves, the discourse he provided is one in which all perforce could share.

Marcel Dubois, O.P., a friend and mentor, reflects as follows on a lifetime of ministry to his Jewish brothers and sisters in Jerusalem (1999:101–05):

> While it has become commonplace to speak of Jerusalem as a meeting point among the three monotheistic faiths, in fact, considering the history and the actual state of relations among these three religions, Jerusalem rather emerges as the 'high place' of disunity. Its history represents one long path spiked with rivalries, conquests, revenge and persecutions. The city is still marked by these secular battles, in its

stones and in its hearts. The wounds of time have still not been cauterised. Today a situation of waiting which is neither peace nor war threatens to freeze into a lasting tension, a state of mutual ignorance and deaf hostility among three communities, each of which nonetheless believes in the same God and lays claim to Abraham.

One feels this standoff in an especially striking and tragic way in a holy place in Jerusalem atop Mount Zion: the building that is celebrated by Christians as the Cenacle, by Jews as the tomb of David, and is now crowned by a minaret. We need only ponder this ancient edifice to understand how broken is the human world here. For the three major monotheistic religions manifest their division in the very place where, according to our faith, the Lord bestowed the sacrament of unity in the Eucharist, and where He sent the Spirit of Pentecost to be the leaven of love in heart of each person – indeed, the very place where Love itself was manifested and communicated in a definitive way. The handsome large gothic room was constructed by the Franciscans and served as a church for nearly a century. Then it became what it still is: Muslim property used for many centuries as a mosque, as the décor testifies. Now it is an empty vessel where any official ritual is forbidden, according to the status quo (regulations governing the holy places since the Ottomans), administered by the Israeli Ministry of Religious Affairs. This tension was even more striking before the 1967 war, when the Cenacle was situated on the border dividing the city, among ruined houses and fields laced with barbed wire, between a Jordanian and an Israeli military post which regularly exchanged fire. So the 'high place' of the Eucharist and Pentecost stood as a counter-sacrament to a broken world and human divisions.

Nevertheless, as we could say equally well regarding the chasms that continue to divide Christians here, the sharpness of the feelings testifies to the depth of the realities at work. The very vehemence of attachment to Jerusalem displays the import of a perception paradoxically common to all those whom it seems to divide so radically: indeed, that perception reveals nothing less than the very vocation of Jerusalem.

Why has this perception been the cause of such tragic conflicts, and why does it remain so? The reason is as simple as it is profound: it marks the very spiritual condition of humankind. We seem to be made in such a way that we fail to perceive the richness to which we are called until we have experienced our own limits and contradictions. We only discover the homeland of which we are citizens and for which we are made through feelings of exile. Happiness only appears to us in that nostalgia which lurks within our privation and our emptiness. Similarly, we only perceive the positive reality of unity among human beings in the suffering of division and conflict. All this is especially poignant in Jerusalem. It is unfortunately true that religion has for centuries offered the pretext for merciless wars and bloody persecutions. Human beings have faced off against each other in the name of their convictions and their religious identities. In our own time, intolerant and aggressive religious fanatics pose a signal danger to world peace, so that religion appears to many as a factor of division and hostility among us.

Such a tragic error contradicts the very essence of faith, however, so it is incumbent upon people of faith to denounce this disastrous misreading by the witness of an encounter among believers animated by an authentic faith. If the differences among religions have provoked such rivalry and conflict, that can only indicate how impure was the faith they claimed, and in whose name violence was perpetrated. Indeed, faith has too often been adulterated with other causes or interests of this world, for which it offered justification and a banner, thereby falsifying itself.

Indeed, rather than dividing human communities, the truth of the matter is that the spiritual attitude demanded by an authentic faith ought to unite believers, in a place beyond the object and content of their particular beliefs, by whatever signs and rituals these may be expressed. For in the hearts of human beings, faith provides, before anything else, an essential reference to the transcendent principle of the universe and of history: the One whom the monotheistic religions call God. On the part of one who believes, faith implies awareness of the glory and the limitations of the condition of creatures; that is, their radical dependence on the source of all being and every gift. That is why every authentic faith finds expression in prostration, humility and thanksgiving. Opened in their spirit and their hearts to the transcendent principle of their being and their action, those who live by faith cannot but be open to all other human beings at the same time, whom they find called to that same recognition and the same openness. That is why the faith that inspires every authentic religious attitude is the very condition of love and peace among human beings. The fidelity of every believer to this spiritual dimension of their faith is the condition for that mutual respect among believers, and the most powerful factor bringing them together: 'everything that rises must converge'. Holy men and women of all spiritual traditions testify to this profound linkage between personal fidelity and openness to others: the very security of their religious convictions grounds their respect for believers of other faiths. Much more than in the past, and with an urgency ever more pressing and a scale as large as the world itself, our age needs to be awakened by the witness of such a spiritual attitude ...

Indeed, this is the enduring spiritual vocation of Jerusalem. This city in which the three great monotheistic religions co-exist, recapitulates in its history and its very stones the tragedies, battles and bloody events which have set Jews, Christians and Muslims against one another over the centuries. It is the place in which the contradictions and divisions that separate these religions shine forth in the most visible and symbolic way. In this respect, Jerusalem has been and remains a sign of contradiction. Yet it is also a sign of hope. For believers of the three great monotheistic faiths, Jerusalem is the 'high place' where God has intervened in the history of humanity. It is there that God revealed to us his proposal for unity and peace, and there that he has prefigured it. As the utterly unique point of contact between eternity and time, Jerusalem is called to be the laboratory of mutual comprehension and respect among human beings. For believers living in Jerusalem, in the fidelity each has to the interior light and in the joy of discovering that same fidelity among others, encounter among religions is an experience at once unique and exemplary, addressed to all human beings of good will: 'Zion shall be called "Mother", for all shall be her children' (Ps 87.5).

Nearly ten years ago, Yehezkel Landau and I co-edited a book whose subtext leaned towards showing how the very interfaith composition of this city gives it sufficient consistency to serve as capital of two states (Burrell and Landau 1992). Yet our perspectives (and available human resources) at that time were so restricted that we issued the collection without a Muslim voice! In fact, however, both our perspectives and the available resources have now shifted considerably, so no one can any longer conceive the issues in merely 'Jewish–Christian' terms, but must always pose them in a triadic fashion: Jewish, Christian, Muslim. That is what Jerusalem does to one who lives here and imbibes its special spirit. Jesus is doubtless present in the Christian communities which dot the landscape and serve its many peoples, yet the Spirit of Jesus will be found active in the ways those communities engage other faith communities to mine the resources each possesses, to bring this sacred place to the point where it displays the power of each tradition to animate peace rather than justify conflict. Will that happen? *Allah ʿarafu;* God alone knows, yet the God of Abraham has left the execution of the 'divine decree' in human hands – for better or for worse.

Notes

1. For an account based on historical documents, yet presented in narrative fashion, see Maalouf 1984.
2. Note how an author like Michael Prior (1997) relies on archaeological findings to query the accuracy of biblical accounts.
3. These telling statistics were supplied by Bernard Sabella, Associate Professor of Sociology at Bethlehem University, and serving as Executive Secretary to the Department of Service to Palestinian Refugees of the Middle East Council of Churches. See Sabella 1994:39.

17 The future of Jesus Christ

RICHARD BAUCKHAM

From the very beginning, the Jesus Christ of Christian faith has been also the Jesus Christ of Christian hope: not only the one who preached and practised the kingdom of God, not only the one who was crucified, not only the one who was raised from death and exalted to participation in God's sovereignty over all creation, but also the Christ who *is to come*. One of the earliest Christian prayers that have survived and certainly the earliest Christian prayer to Jesus Christ that has survived is the Aramaic prayer *Maranatha*, meaning 'Our Lord, come'. It was so significant that it was evidently still used in its original Aramaic form in Paul's Greek-speaking churches. Paul, writing in Greek, quotes it in Aramaic (1 Cor 16.22), and it survives, also in its Aramaic form in an otherwise Greek prayer, in the earliest eucharistic liturgy that has come down to us (*Didache* 10.6). Translated into Greek, it forms almost the last words in the Bible: 'Amen, come, Lord Jesus!', where it is a response to Jesus' own promise, 'Surely, I am coming soon' (Rev 22.20). Even in the Gospel of John, despite its reputation for emphasising 'realised' at the expense of future eschatology (where 'eschatology', in the language of biblical scholars and modern theologians, refers to God's final completion of his purpose in history), Jesus' last words are: 'until I come' (John 21.23). That this promise was not fulfilled 'soon' by any ordinary reckoning did not prevent it remaining integral to Christian belief down the centuries. Those creeds of the early church which are still widely recognised and recited as authentic summaries of Christian belief strongly affirm it, concluding the story of Jesus thus: 'he will come again to judge the living and the dead' (Apostles' Creed), or more fully: 'he will come again in glory to judge the living and the dead, and his kingdom will have no end' (Niceno-Constantinopolitan Creed). In eucharistic worship, Christians not only remember the crucified Christ and practise the presence of the risen and exalted Christ but also look forward to the coming of Christ in his kingdom. The Christian story of Jesus, which is also the story of the salvation of the world, has not yet reached completion.

This Christian hope is closely related to two aspects of Jesus that have been emphasised in this volume: his Jewishness and his global relevance. Jesus undoubtedly understood himself and his mission in the context of Jewish faith, which interpreted the world and Israel's place in it primarily by telling a story, a grand narrative or (in postmodern jargon) 'meta-narrative' of the world, its origin, its history and its final destiny in the purposes of God. The story runs from God's creation of all things to God's future completion of this world's history. This will be the coming of God's kingdom, not with the implication that God is anything less than sovereign here and now, but in the sense that God will then finally put an end to all evil, suffering and death. Good, which in history is constantly threatened and overcome, and truth, which in history is contested and obscured, will prevail when all people, including the dead, face the judgement of God on their lives. All that by God's mercy survive judgement receive new life in the renewed creation in eternity. This is not an 'end of the world' in the sense that the world will be abolished, but an end of the history of this world, which will be at the same time a new beginning for the world, both its redemption from evil and its fulfilment in endless good.

Only within this universal narrative of the world could the story of God's people Israel be adequately understood. In the Jewish world of Jesus' time there was more than one way of telling it. Different interpretations of Jewish faith entailed differing ways of telling the common story. But most maintained that the destiny of Israel, her purification from sin and the renewal of her faithfulness to God, her liberation from her oppressors and vindication in the eyes of them and others, and her relationship to other nations, were closely connected with the purpose of God for the world. All expected Israel's God to come to be universally recognised, by friends and enemies alike, as the one true God, the Creator and sovereign of the world. Some, like the first Christians, stressed the positive role of Israel as God's witness to the nations and expected the nations in general to share in the salvation that was coming to Israel in the future. As God's covenant with Abraham suggested, his descendants were to be a blessing to all the nations of the world.

Earliest Christianity was a new version of this Jewish meta-narrative, a re-reading of the story in the light of Jesus. It followed the indications Jesus himself gave of the place of his own mission and destiny in the coming of God's kingdom. His shameful and abandoned death and his resurrection to eternal life required the re-reading to be radical. Essentially Jesus and his story were seen to be central and decisive for the coming of God's kingdom in all creation. Jesus' Jewishness was understood in the light of Israel's election as God's witness to the world. Jesus and his story were the way that God himself was fulfilling this destiny of Israel for the sake of both Israel and the nations. This was also what was meant by calling Jesus the Messiah (Christ), the one title for Jesus that all early Christians certainly used. As a result, it became virtually a surname, distinguishing this Jesus from others, and was also the term after which his followers came to be called Christians. Jesus was the Jewish Messiah for all people, *the* offspring of Abraham by whom all the nations were to be blessed.

This understanding of the Messiah as the one who would accomplish and exercise God's universal rule over both Israel and the nations at the climax of history was in itself an unsurprising variant of the Jewish meta-narrative. But the cross and the resurrection of Jesus made all the difference. The cross negated any purely triumphalistic understanding of the coming of God's kingdom. It brought God's loving, even suffering involvement with his people in the history of Israel to a new depth and universality. As the Jewish Messiah for all people, Jesus died a sacrifice for the sins of all and in solidarity with all who otherwise suffer the abandonment to death he suffered. His resurrection therefore was representatively for them, opening the gates of the kingdom of God to all who recognised in him their Messiah and Lord. An *eschatological* understanding of Jesus (i.e. an understanding related to the final achievement of God's purposes for the whole world) was mandated, not only by his own consciousness of eschatological mission, but also and unequivocally by his resurrection. For the Jewish meta-narrative, resurrection was an eschatological event. It was entry into the eternal life of the new creation, beyond the reach of sin, suffering and death, to be given by God to the living and the dead alike only at the end of all history. The resurrection of one ahead of all others was not expected and, along with the death of the Messiah, therefore deeply informed the distinctively Christian re-reading of the Jewish meta-narrative. The Messiah himself had pioneered and made possible for all others the way through evil and death to the life of the new creation. Raised by God, he was now exalted to God's throne in heaven, there to reign until in the end he achieves the uncontested rule of God in all creation. This creates a meantime in which the kingdom of God is coming but has not yet come, an age in which the followers of Jesus live by faith in his hidden and paradoxical Messiahship, participate in his suffering love for all people, and hope for his coming in glory to execute God's final judgement of all and God's final redemption of all things. So identified was Jesus with the coming of God's kingdom that the eschatological future could only be understood as his future coming. Christians associated with the future coming of Jesus (in the Greek of the New Testament: his parousia) not only what many Jews expected of the Messiah, but also what the Hebrew Bible expected of God's own final coming to his people and his world to judge and to save.

A powerful Jewish objection to the Christian identification of Jesus as the Messiah is that, when the Messiah comes, the world will be freed from evil, suffering and death. As Walter Moberly puts it, in chapter 12 above: 'The heart of the Jewish critique is simple: if Jesus is the redeemer, why is the world still unredeemed?' One form of Christian response, an unfortunate one, has been to 'spiritualise' redemption in a way that is alien to the Jewish religious tradition. Salvation is reduced to what Christian believers experience as forgiveness of sins, personal justification before God, and virtuous living, with spiritual immortality in heaven after death. But the Christian tradition at its most authentic has realised that the promise of God made in the bodily resurrection of Christ is holistic and all-encompassing: for whole persons, body and soul, for all the networks of relationship in human society that are integral to being human, and for the rest of creation also, from which humans in their bodiliness are not to be detached. In other words, it is God's creative renewal of his whole creation. Here and now such salvation is experienced in fragmentary and partial anticipations of the new creation, and these are only properly appreciated as anticipations of the fullness of new creation to come. But even these anticipations are not limited to a 'spiritual' sphere artificially distinguished from the embodiment and sociality of human being in this world. Significantly, what has most kept the holistic understanding of salvation alive in the church, when tempted by Platonic and Cartesian dualisms to reduce it, have been the resurrection of Jesus in its inescapable bodiliness and the hope of his coming to raise the dead and to judge, which makes all individual salvation provisional, incomplete until the final redemption of all things. Hope for the future coming of the crucified and risen Christ has continually served to counter Christian tendencies to pietism and quietism, spiritualisation and privatisation, because it has opened the church to the world and the future, to the universal scope of God's purposes in Jesus the Messiah.

It has also been a corrective to absolutising the status quo in state or society: either the transformation of Christianity into a civil religion uncritically allied to a political regime or form of society, or the church's own pretensions to be the kingdom of God virtually already realised on earth. In such contexts the Christ who reigns now on the divine throne has been envisaged as the heavenly sanction for the rule of his political or ecclesiastical deputies on earth. Resistance to ideological christology of this kind can come from the hope of the Christ who is still to come in his kingdom. The expectation of the parousia relativises all the powers of the present world, exposing their imperfections and partialities. This is why it has often been more enthusiastically embraced by the wretched and the dispossessed than by the powerful and the affluent. It embodies the hope that the world will be different, contradicting every complacent or resigned acceptance of the way things are. It offers an eschatological proviso and a utopian excess that keep us from pronouncing a premature end to history, as a tradition of Enlightenment thought from Hegel and Comte to Francis Fukuyama has encouraged people to do and as totalitarian politics is often minded to do in justification for repressing dissent. Thus the Jewish messianic critique of Christian messianism is a necessary one whenever the church's faith in the Christ who is still to come falters.

JESUS' STORY AND THE STORY OF THE WORLD

The hope of the parousia or future coming of Jesus Christ is most at home in a narrative theology. It belongs both to the insight that Jesus' identity is, like all human identity, a narrative identity, and to the Christian understanding of the world by means of a meta-narrative. As Francis Watson notes in chapter 10 above, 'Jesus *is* his own life-story; his identity is not detachable from his history'. We should add that, for Christian faith, his story is not yet finished and cannot be while the meta-narrative of creation also remains unfinished.

That Jesus' identity *takes place* in an unfinished history that can and must be narrated has not always been as clear as it might in theological teaching. The conceptual tools with which the Fathers in the early centuries of the church developed their christology of the two natures and the one person of Jesus Christ the God-man did not easily lend themselves to expressing a narrative understanding of personal identity. Their christology was indeed derived from the narrative of Jesus' history and was in turn intended to enable an appropriate reading of that narrative, but it may too easily give the impression that it is in principle separable from the narrative. The act of incarnation itself can seem sufficiently to define who Jesus is, requiring christology to look back to the pre-existence of the divine Logos before incarnation, in order to speak of God's becoming human, but not to look forward to the cross, the resurrection and the parousia. Even when traditional christology in later periods has attempted to understand the incarnation in a way that does justice to the differences between the earthly Jesus and the risen, exalted Jesus, the interest has been in the contrast between these two states or stages: the humble life and death of Jesus, on the one hand, and his glorified reign on the divine throne, on the other. The state of exaltation itself has been perceived statically, with the result that the parousia has not been properly recognised as integral to Jesus' identity.

Yet, as we have noticed already, the Creeds do embody such a recognition. In the christological second of their three articles of faith in the triune God, they identify the Jesus Christ in whom Christians believe by summarising his story. The Apostles' Creed begins with his conception by Mary and ends with his future coming to judgement. The Niceno-Constantinopolitan Creed, a product of more developed trinitarian and christological thinking, begins in eternity with the eternal relationship of the pre-existent Son with his Father, and ends, not with his coming to judgement, but with its consequence: his kingdom without end. Such a narrative of Jesus has always been normative and living in the faith and worship of Christians, whether or not theology has always managed to do it justice. It coheres, not only with the sense that a person's story is integral to their identity, but also with the nature of a story: that it gains definitive meaning only in the light of its end, and that therefore even the provisional meaning we may find in it along the way depends on some kind of anticipation, explicit or implicit, of how it will end and what it will turn out to mean in the end. This is why the parousia is essential to the Christian understanding of who Jesus is.

Of course, the parousia cannot be narrated in the same way as the past history of Jesus. The narratives of it in, for example, 1 Thess 4 and Rev 19 are not history written in advance. This is for two reasons: the parousia is not only a still future event, but also the event which will end history and is therefore intrinsically transcendent of history. For both reasons it lacks the contingent and concrete actuality of narrated history (even the theologically interpreted history in the gospels) and can be narrated only in symbols that convey its essential meaning. Its images depict only what, in the purpose of God, must be so, nothing of what, through the contingencies of history, may or may not be so.

Nevertheless, the parousia is the end of the story which must be in some sense anticipated and articulated for the sake of the meaning of the rest of the story. The story the gospels tell is, by their own testimony, an unfinished story, open not only to the history of the church as its continuation but also to this projected conclusion, the parousia, which the gospels are able to narrate in the form of prophecies by Jesus. The parousia is the narrative prospection of Jesus' identity, as the gospel histories are its narrative retrospection.

It is by no means unusual for narratives to include projects, expectations and anticipations that reach forward beyond the time frame of the narrative itself, but in this case, the story of Jesus, there is a unique aspect to its prospection. The parousia concludes not only the story of Jesus but also the story of the whole world. Though the rest of Jesus' story is implicitly related to the whole world, only the parousia makes clear its unique character as a story which will finally include the whole history of the world in its own conclusion. This is why the parousia is that end of Jesus' story that is essential to his identity. It defines him as the one human being whose story will finally prove decisive for the story of the whole world. In New Testament terminology, it defines his identity as that of the Messiah. Apart from the parousia he could not be called Christ in the New Testament meaning of the word.

In speaking of the end of the story we are, of course, speaking of an end that also constitutes a new beginning, because it is the new creation of all things. The Creed's 'his kingdom shall have no end' is like the 'they lived happily ever after' of the classic fairy tale. It is as that definitive result that the story's end completes and concludes the meaning of the whole story. Every such fairy-tale ending, like every seemingly satisfactory end of a fictional or historical story, is implicitly eschatological. It anticipates some final ending of all history, since, without that, the meaning given to a story by its own end would always be open to revision or even reversal by the continuing course of events. Ultimately the meaning of all particular stories depends on the meaning of the whole story, constituted by its end. But in the Christian meta-narrative there is also one particular story, that of Jesus, which is decisive for the meaning of the whole story. His resurrection, as the one human person who has already entered fully into the life of the new creation that awaits the rest of reality, marks him out as this ultimately decisive person. But, since it is not yet the end of the whole story, it is not yet the end of his own story. For that, his relationship to the rest of the world must be completed by his future coming.

THE ECLIPSE OF THE PAROUSIA
IN MODERN PROGRESSIVISM

A well-known statement by the contemporary theologian Jürgen Moltmann, first made in 1965, claims that 'Christian eschatology does not speak of the future as such . . . Christian eschatology speaks of Jesus Christ and *his* future . . . Hence the question whether all statements about the future are grounded in the person and history of Jesus Christ provides it with the touchstone by which to distinguish the spirit of eschatology from that of utopia' (Moltmann 1967:17). But this decisiveness of Jesus Christ himself and his future coming for the future of the world was, of course, abandoned in the modern idea of historical progress, not only in its various frankly secular forms but also in the Christian theology that has assimilated its eschatological hope to modern progressivism. In this process the parousia as the real future of Jesus Christ himself lost any meaning other than as some kind of mythical symbol of the goal towards which human history was evolving.

The issue here is that of the transcendence of the final future that Christian faith has understood as the coming of Jesus Christ. Philosophies and theologies of historical progress of the modern period have been characteristically immanentist. They have envisaged the final future of the world as the goal towards which the historical process of the world is moving and the result which that process itself will produce. By contrast, the biblical and traditional expectation was of a divine act of new creation in which God will make of the world what it has no immanent capacity of its own to become. A transcendent eschatology of this kind introduces a radical discontinuity between history and the new creation, where a more immanent eschatology envisages continuity between historical progress and its ultimate result. Continuity is, of course, also important for transcendent eschatology. God will renew this creation, not simply replace it by another. But the continuity is given by God in God's transformation and glorification of creation, bringing to completion God's own work of creation, redeeming it from all evil, and delivering it from transience and mortality by giving it eternal life. Although this will end historical time, it is not simply what happens to the world as it will be at the end of its history. In a sense it happens to the whole of history. All who have ever lived will rise from the dead.

The distinction between transcendent eschatology and the Enlightenment's progressivist view of history is often played down when it is said that the Christian tradition provided the linear idea of history moving irreversibly towards a future goal which the modern idea of progress has taken over in secularised forms. There is some truth in this, provided it is recognised that secularisation made a radical difference. In place of hope for the transcendent God's creative and redemptive action, human activity working in harmony with some kind of inherent teleology in the historical process would bring about utopia through a cumulative and continuous progression. Humanity will be perfected through reason and education, and the world re-created through the great modern project of technological mastery and transformation of nature. Hope thus derives from confidence in human rationality and also in the inherent direction of the historical process towards utopia. Evolutionary views of the world helped very much to bolster the idea of historical teleology, as can be seen in the work of the Jesuit paleontologist Pierre Teilhard de Chardin, probably the most thorough-going attempt to

Christianise the progressivist worldview of the modern age. He understands Christ as the goal of a cosmic process of gradual 'christification' of the world. This is a cosmic christology which is more at home with the Pauline images of Christ in all things than it is with the parousia images of his coming from heaven, suggesting a transcendent rupture of the course of history. More often theological versions of modern progressivism have reduced Jesus to his historical past and his historical influence. In such views there is no more future for Jesus himself than there is for the dead in general, and such a Jesus is bound to recede progressively into the past. The future that develops purely out of history can be only for future generations.

Enlightenment optimism and dogmatic progressivism have suffered fatal blows to their credibility in the twentieth century, which, so far from realising utopian dreams, has been appropriately characterised by George Steiner (1997:103) as 'the most bestial in human history'. According to much contemporary thinking, progress has not merely failed but turned against us. Not only has technological advance fuelled the destructiveness of modern wars and genocides; even many of its most apparently benign aspects are having calamitous results and put the very future of humanity on the planet in doubt. Moreover, in the face of Auschwitz and numerous other atrocities, the old progressivist justification of the historical process, which made the evils and sufferings of the past seem worthwhile, or at least negligible, in the light of the glorious future to come, becomes intolerable. No historical future could compensate for Auschwitz. We shall return later to the postmodernist critique of the idea of progress, which sees it as an ideology of domination and oppression, promoting liberation for some only at the expense of the rest.

In a world for which the dominant modern forms of hope have failed it is time for Christian hope to extricate itself from its entanglement with Enlightenment optimism and to recover its own source and focus in the Jesus Christ who transcends his past history and ours and so is still to come.

NOW AND THEN

Is the parousia adequately understood as the completion of historical process, the outcome of some kind of incremental process of immanent divine activity in the world, such as theological versions of modern progressivism have so often assumed? Or does it represent something really new, something quite different from what will have happened hitherto in the history of the world, an event in which Jesus himself relates in some important sense differently to the world? This is a critical question not only with regard to liberal theologies assimilated to modern secular progressivism, but also in respect of the tendency in some modern theology not at all of that kind, such as that of Karl Barth, to reduce the parousia to an unveiling of what is already true, a revelation of what has already been accomplished in the past history of Jesus, new only in the sense that this is now made unequivocally known to all.

This latter view could be supported by appeal to the way the New Testament can speak of the parousia as the 'unveiling' (or revelation: *apokalupsis*)[1] of Christ or his 'appearance' (*epiphaneia*).[2] Corresponding verbs are also used.[3] But in that case we must also notice that the New Testament also, and most often, refers to the parousia by the use of the verb 'to come' (*erchomai*) and by the word *parousia* itself,[4] which in this context must mean not merely 'presence', but 'arrival'. In many of the texts what will be 'seen' at the parousia is precisely Jesus 'coming' from heaven.[5] In these usages we have, in fact, three forms of contrast between now and then: the Jesus who is now not seen will appear or be seen; the Jesus who is now hidden will be revealed; the Jesus who is now absent will come.

In the last case, we should not be troubled by the implication that Jesus is presently absent, as though this were in contradiction with the various ways in which the New Testament understands him to be present with his people now, including Jesus' promise, at the end of Matthew's Gospel, to be with his disciples until the end of the age. Presence can take many different forms and is therefore compatible with forms of absence. When I speak to someone on the telephone I am in one sense present to them by means of my voice conveyed by the telephone line, while also being in another sense absent. To collapse the parousia into Christ's presence with us already is to evade the essential question of the form and purpose of his presence to his people and to the world in each case. From the way the New Testament texts speak of Jesus' coming at the end it is clear that it is a coming to do things that he has not done hitherto: to save (in the sense of bringing believers into their final destiny in resurrection), to eliminate the powers of evil from the world, and, most often in the texts, to judge the living and the dead.

While the language of coming makes it especially clear that the parousia brings not just more of the same, but something new, we should not miss the fact that the language of hiddenness and manifestation or revelation also makes this point in its own way. What is hidden now is Jesus' heavenly glory, his lordship over the whole world which his sitting on God's heavenly throne at God's right hand portrays, and also his fellowship with his people in which their true nature as his people is hidden. This present hiddenness of Jesus' rule is what means, for example, that in the book of Revelation the beast's power can appear godlike and invincible, triumphant over the Christians whom he puts to death. The real truth of things from God's perspective – for example, that the martyrs, by their witness to the truth even to the point of death, are the real victors – breaks through to those who have eyes to see, but it is only at the parousia that it finally prevails as the truth which all must acknowledge. This revelation is more than the unveiling of what is already true, though it is that, because the unveiling itself makes a difference: no longer can anyone pretend or be deceived, those who wield power by deceit can do so no longer, all illusions and delusions must perish before the truth of God and all who insist on clinging to them must perish also. It is in this sense that Jesus, though seated on the throne of the universe, has not yet brought all things into subjection to God. The revelation of his lordship will also be its final implementation.

From this point of view, the parousia is the event which concludes history by making the final truth of all things manifest to all. This is why the language of 'revealing' and 'appearing' is used in the texts not only of Jesus, whose true relationship to the world is made evident to all, but also of all that his judgement of every person who has ever lived will bring to light (1 Cor 4.5). There is nothing hidden that will not be uncovered (Matt 10.26). The full and final truth of each person's life will be made known, not least to that person. Similarly, the language of 'revealing' and 'appearing' is used of the final destiny of those who believe in Jesus, 'a salvation ready to be revealed in the last time' (1 Pet 1.5). The parousia is that revelation of all that is now hidden, the disclosure of the full and final truth of all who have lived and all that has happened, that determines the form in which this present creation can be taken, as new creation, into eternity. Thus in the parousia, both as coming and as unveiling, something happens which, in relation to the world as it is now, will be both new and conclusive. As the New Testament understands it, the parousia cannot be taken as a symbol merely of the outcome of history that history itself will produce.

JESUS' HUMAN IDENTITY IN UNIVERSAL RELATEDNESS

According to the faith of the Christian church, Jesus is God's human identity. He is both God's *truly human* identity and *truly God's* human identity. Since this is a narrative identity, it should be possible to look at the parousia as the end of his story from both of these perspectives. It should also be possible from both perspectives to see how the end of his own story can also be the end of the whole story of the world.

Christology involves the assertion of Jesus' universal relatedness. In the history of christology a variety of concepts have been used to express this: representativeness, substitution, incorporation and participation, universal humanity, and others. All these concepts are attempts to express the fundamental conviction that this one human individual Jesus is of decisive significance for all other human persons, whether they are yet aware of it or not. Other human individuals, of course, have exercised very extensive historical influence, and in some cases, such as the unknown people who first discovered how to make fire or who invented the wheel, it might be said that they have made a difference to the lives of virtually all subsequent human beings. But the Christian claim about Jesus asserts something more than an historical impact of this kind. The claim is that in some way Jesus is intrinsically – in his very identity – related to each and every other human being.

How can this be said of a human individual? Some of the christological concepts just mentioned attempt to conceptualise Jesus' universal relatedness by denying him human individuality. The attempt is made to view his humanity as some kind of supra-individuality in which others are included. Or his humanity is in effect dissolved in the universal presence of God. Such views fail to preserve the true humanity of Jesus, human (as the Fathers said) in every respect as we are, and no less truly human in his risen and exalted humanity than in his earthly and mortal humanity. In not maintaining the true humanity of the risen and coming Jesus, such interpretations contradict the New Testament principle that our eternal destiny is to be like him.

A more satisfactory approach is by means of the only way in which human individuals can transcend their individuality without losing it: that is, in relationships. Human individuality is also relationality. There are individuals only in relationships – with other humans, with God, and with the non-human creation. Such relationships are integral to the narratives in which human identity is found. We are who we are in our relationships with others and in the story of our relationships with others.

In Jesus' case – and focusing for the purpose of our present argument only on his relationships with other humans – his human individuality is unique in its *universal* relatedness. He is the one human being who is intrinsically related to each and every other. How does this universal relatedness take place narratively? It is not constituted solely by his incarnation as human, but by the particular course of his human story. We can say that in his earthly life and death Jesus practised loving identification with others. In his ministry he identified in love with people of all sorts and conditions, excluding no one, and finally in going to the cross he identified himself with the human condition of all people in its worst extremities: its sinfulness, suffering, abandonment and death. Only because Jesus died in loving identification with all could his resurrection be on behalf of all, opening up for all the way to life with God beyond death.

Thus in his life, death and resurrection, the exalted Christ has established his identity as one of open identification with others, open in principle and potential to all who will identify with him in faith. Until the parousia his identification with all remains open to all. This means that, insofar as his human identity is constituted by his universal relatedness, it is open to all that takes place in relation to him. His narrative identity cannot be complete until every human story with which he has identified himself has turned out as it will have done at the end. The parousia as the completion of his own identity, as revelatory of the final truth of his loving identification with all, will be also the completion of the identity of all others. Their identity, the truth of their whole lives brought to light at the end, will be defined either by his loving identification with them or by their refusal to let it be so defined. For those who have sought their own identity in his identification with them, his parousia will be the revelation at once of who he finally is and of who they themselves finally are: 'your life is hidden in Christ with God. When Christ who is your life is revealed, then you also will be revealed with him in glory' (Col 3.3b-4; cf. 1 John 3.2).

Thus Jesus' identity at the end is inclusive of others, but not in a way that dissolves his properly human individuality. As the one who has identified in love with all other humans in their own stories, his story finally includes also theirs. Since his loving identification with them is prevenient but not pre-emptive, that is, it is open to all but actualised only in the living of their own lives, his own identity as the one human whose identity is found in the story of his relatedness to all others remains to that extent open until his parousia.

We may perhaps take a little further this principle that Jesus' own identity is open to the future because it includes his relationships to all things (and not only to all people). We should be more cautious than some theologians have been in speaking of the finality of Christ with reference to the gospel story of his life, death and resurrection. His story will not be complete until his parousia. We could say that Jesus in his history, Jesus of Nazareth crucified and risen, is *definitive* for our knowledge of who God is, of who we are in relation to God, of who Jesus is in relation to God and to us and to all things. Definitive, in the sense that anything else must be consistent with this, but not final, in the sense that there is nothing else to be known. Since Jesus' identity is in universal relatedness, Christian understanding and experience are not to be focused on Jesus to the exclusion of all else, but on Jesus in his relatedness to everything else. We shall know Jesus better as we see everything we can know or experience in its relatedness to him, just as we shall know and experience everything more truly as we see it in its relatedness to Jesus. Only the parousia will reveal all things in their final truth as they appear in their relationships to Jesus and only the parousia will reveal Jesus himself in the final truth of his identity in universal relatedness.

JESUS' DIVINE IDENTITY IN UNIVERSAL SOVEREIGNTY

The meaning of incarnation – what it really means that Jesus is God's human identity – appears most clearly in the way the New Testament tells and interprets the story of Jesus in two very remarkable ways. First, Jesus' loving identification as one human being with others, taken to the depths of degradation and abandonment on the cross, is *God's* loving identification with all people. Secondly, God's universal sovereignty over his whole creation, God's uniquely divine relationship to the world, is exercised by the *human* Jesus, exalted to God's heavenly throne.

In biblical thought it is intrinsic to God's identity – what distinguishes him as the only true God from all other reality which is not God – that he is the sole Creator of all things and the sole Lord over all things. But even *God's* identity for us is a narrative identity yet to be completed. Since his ultimate sovereignty coexists now with much in the world that opposes his will and contradicts the destiny he intends for his creation – failure and evil, suffering and death – God's rule remains to be achieved, in the sense of implemented in the overcoming of all evil and the redemption of the world from nothingness. God's identity as the one true God of all is at stake in the achievement of his eschatological kingdom. He will prove himself God in the overcoming of all evil and in the acknowledgement of his deity by all creation. If it is in Jesus that God's sovereignty comes to universal effect and universally acknowledgement, which is what the New Testament writers intended when they depicted his enthronement and parousia, then Jesus' own story belongs to the narrative identity of God himself.

THE STORY OF ALL STORIES

Jean-François Lyotard (1984:xxiv) famously defined the postmodern as 'incredulity towards meta-narratives'. This rejection of any kind of grand story about the whole of reality is mainly rooted in postmodernism's critique of the idea of progress as an ideology of domination that has legitimated the exploitative exercise of power: the domination of the West over the Third World, the affluent over the poor, even men over women. Through science, technology and education the West has imposed its own particular rationality and ideals on others. Economic globalisation is a new form of the same process. To the charge that the Christian meta-narrative has also served as justification for terror and oppression, including Christian collusion with western imperialism and the arrogance of modernity, the Christian response must be repentance. But the horrors of Christian history are not the whole story, and one should go on to ask whether such abuses are inherent in the Christian meta-narrative or whether the meta-narrative itself might not expose them as abuses. The further dimension of postmodernist critique that regards any meta-narrative as *per se* oppressive depends on the radical relativity of truth for postmodernism. Truth is always somebody's truth. A meta-narrative is the grandest way of imposing my truth on others by assigning them a place in my scheme of things. But for those for whom the venture of truth cannot be abandoned without self-contradiction and for whom the postmodernist assumption that the will to power is over-ridingly operative in all intellectual and other ventures is too cynical, the character of the specific meta-narrative in question also makes a difference in considering its potential for dominative abuse.

If Jesus and his story are decisive for the Christian meta-narrative, two aspects of his story should be recalled: the cross and his still future coming. Moreover, these two are connected in that the Christian story attributes to Jesus a consistent identity: he is 'the same yesterday and today and forever' (Heb 13.8). The coming Christ is the same Christ who was crucified. In chapter 5 of the book of Revelation it is the slaughtered lamb, Christ crucified in his sacrificial love for the world, who shares the divine throne and receives the acclamation of his sovereignty from all creation. It is the one whom they pierced whom all the tribes of the earth will see when he comes (Rev 1.7). Jesus' loving self-identification with all, which reached its furthest point in his death, is thus not left aside in his coming to rule, but remains permanently his identity, precisely in his exercise of God's rule. It is as non-dominating love that he is decisive for the meaning of the whole story of the world. This ensures that, although as we have stressed already he also comes to make the truth of all people and all history finally and unavoidably clear, this truth is not the expression of his will to power. Each will recognise it, even if tragically, as the real truth of his or her own life.

This eschatological revelation of the truth of all things is still to come. The Christian meta-narrative, properly understood, is not a story that suppresses all other stories, but one that leaves open the future for the inclusion of all other stories in the only one with an ending capable of being their ending too. This is because it is not, like the myth of progress, a story of history's own immanent potential alone, but a story that has already, in the resurrection of Jesus, broken the bounds of this world's own reality and promises an end that comes as God's transcendent gift to his creation, fulfilling but also surpassing its own potential. Unlike the myth of progress, it is not a story that will privilege the victors over the victims of history, for the end that comes with the parousia of Jesus will come to all history and as life for the dead. The countless victims of history, those whose lives have been torture and those who have scarcely lived at all, all those whom progress can only forget, are remembered by the Christ who identified with their fate and comes as their redeemer. The horrors of history, the tragedy and the loss, the negatives which defy any grand story of immanent meaning in history, forcing it to suppress them or to justify them, are fully acknowledged by the Christian meta-narrative, because it is a story of transcendent redemption. It does not offer the kind of purely theoretical theodicy that would silence the cries and the protests of the suffering, but finds in Jesus crucified God's loving solidarity with all who suffer and resists all premature closure, maintaining the protest against evil, suffering and death until Jesus comes with the redemptive conclusion that only God can give.

Christian hope for the future of Jesus Christ promotes the same kind of compassionate and undaunted engagement with reality for the sake of its future in God that Jesus himself practised and pioneered as far as death, trusting that his way is the way to the kingdom of God. It is neither promethean, burdening history with an eschatological requirement of achievement it cannot bear, as the myth of progress did, nor quietist, leaving the world to its fate as every dualistic spirituality must do. It neither over-reaches itself in attempting what can only come from God nor neglects what is humanly possible in God's grace. Sustained by the hope of everything from God, it attempts what is possible within the limits of each present. It does not value what can be done only as a step in a cumulative process towards a goal. It does what can be done for its own sake, here and now, confident that every present will find itself, redeemed and fulfilled, in the new creation. Most characteristically of all, it knows that only by expending life in the service of God and God's world can life finally be found secure, hidden with the Christ who is yet to be revealed.

Notes

1. 1 Cor 1.7; 2 Thess 1.7; 1 Pet 4.13.
2. 2 Thess 2.8; 1 Tim 6.14; 2 Tim 4.1, 8; Tit 2.13.
3. E.g. *apokaluptō*: Luke 7.30; 2 Thess 1.7; 1 Pet 1.13; *phaneroō*: Col 3.4; 1 Pet 5.4; 1 John 2.28; 3.2; *ophthēsomai*: Heb 9.28.
4. Matt 24.3, 27, 37, 39; 1 Cor 15.23; 1 Thess 2.19; 3.13; 4.15; 5.23; 2 Thess 2.1, 8; Jas 5.7, 8; 2 Pet 1.16; 3.4; 1 John 2.28.
5. E.g. Matt 16.28; 24.30; 26.64; Mark 13.26; 14.62; Luke 21.27; Rev 1.7.

Bibliography

Alexander, Patrick H., *et al.*, ed. 1999. *The SBL handbook of style: for ancient near Eastern, biblical, and early Christian studies.* Peabody: Hendrickson.

Allen, Charlotte. 1998. *The human Christ: the search for the historical Jesus.* Oxford: Lion.

Allison, Dale C. 1985. *The end of the ages has come: an early interpretation of the passion and resurrection of Jesus.* Philadelphia: Fortress.

1998. *Jesus of Nazareth: millenarian prophet.* Minneapolis: Fortress Press.

Alston, William P. 1997. 'Biblical criticism and the resurrection.' In *The resurrection: an interdisciplinary symposium on the resurrection of Jesus,* 148–83. Ed. S. T. Davis *et al.* Oxford: Oxford University Press.

Alter, Robert. 1981. *The art of biblical narrative.* London: Allen & Unwin.

Amoah, Elizabeth, and Mercy A. Oduyoye. 1988. 'The Christ for African women.' In *With passion and compassion: third world women doing theology,* 35–46. Ed. V. Fabella and M. A. Oduyoye. Maryknoll: Orbis.

Anderson, Allan. 1992. *Bazalwane: African Pentecostals in South Africa.* Manualia Didactica 19. Pretoria: University of South Africa.

Angel, G. T. D. 1978. 'Apollinarius.' *New International Dictionary of the Christian Church,* 55–56.

Armstrong, Karen. 1996. *Jerusalem: one city, three faiths.* New York: Knopf.

Avila, Teresa de. 1976–80. *The collected works of St. Teresa of Avila.* Trans. K. Kavanaugh. 2 vols. 2nd edn. Washington: Institute of Carmelite Studies.

Baigent, Michael, and Richard Leigh. 1982. *Holy blood, holy Grail.* New York: Delacorte Press.

1991. *The Dead Sea Scrolls deception.* London: Cape.

Baras, Zvi. 1987. 'The *Testimonium Flavianum* and the martyrdom of James.' In *Josephus, Judaism, and Christianity,* 338–48. Ed. L. H. Feldman and G. Hata. Detroit: Wayne State University Press.

Barrett, C. K. 1994–98. *The Acts of the Apostles.* ICC. 2 vols. Edinburgh: T&T Clark.

Barrett, David B., and Todd M. Johnson. 2001. 'Annual statistical table on global mission.' *International Bulletin of Missionary Research* 26, no. 1: 23–24.

Barton, Stephen C. 1992. *The spirituality of the gospels.* London: SPCK.

Batey, R. A. 1991. *Jesus and the forgotten city: new light on Sepphoris and the urban world of Jesus.* Grand Rapids: Baker.

Batstone, David B. 1991. *From conquest to struggle: Jesus of Nazareth in Latin America.* Albany: State University of New York Press.

Bauckham, Richard. 1992. 'Gospels (apocryphal).' In *DJG*, 286–91.

1998. *God crucified, monotheism and christology in the New Testament.* Didsbury Lectures, 1996. Carlisle: Paternoster Press.

Bauckham, Richard, ed. 1999. *God will be all in all: the eschatology of Jürgen Moltmann.* Edinburgh: T&T Clark.

Bauckham, Richard, and Trevor Hart. 1999. *Hope against hope: Christian eschatology in contemporary context.* London/Grand Rapids: Darton, Longman & Todd/ Eerdmans.

Bauer, Bruno. 1851–52. *Kritik der Evangelien und Geschichte ihres Ursprungs.* 2 vols. 2nd edn. Berlin: Hempel.

Bayer, Hans F. 1986. *Jesus' predictions of vindication and resurrection.* WUNT 2:20. Tübingen: Mohr Siebeck.

Benvenisti, Meron. 1996. *City of stone: the hidden history of Jerusalem.* Trans. M. Kaufman Nunn. Berkeley: University of California Press.

Bernard of Clairvaux. 1976. *Song of Songs.* Trans. K. Walsh. The Works of Bernard of Clairvaux. 4 vols. Kalamazoo: Cistercian Publications.

Black, Matthew. 1959. 'The arrest and trial of Jesus and the date of the Last Supper.' In *Studies in memory of T. W. Manson*, 19–33. Ed. A. J. B. Higgins. Manchester: Manchester University Press.

Blomberg, Craig L. 1997. *Jesus and the gospels: an introduction and survey.* Leicester/Nashville: Apollos/Broadman & Holman.

Bock, Darrell L. 1994. 'The Son of Man seated at God's right hand and the debate over Jesus' "blasphemy".' In *Jesus of Nazareth: Lord and Christ. Essays on the historical Jesus and New Testament christology*, 181–91. Ed. J. B. Green and M. Turner. Grand Rapids: Eerdmans.

1998. *Blasphemy and exaltation in Judaism and the final examination of Jesus.* WUNT 2:106. Tübingen: Mohr Siebeck.

2000. *Blasphemy and exaltation in Judaism: the charge against Jesus in Mark 14:53–65.* Grand Rapids: Baker Books.

Bockmuehl, Markus. 1994. *This Jesus: martyr, Lord, messiah.* Edinburgh: T&T Clark.

2000. *Jewish law in gentile churches: halakhah and the beginning of Christian public ethics.* Edinburgh: T&T Clark.

Boff, Leonardo. 1978. *Jesus Christ liberator: a critical christology for our time.* Trans. P. Hughes. Maryknoll: Orbis Books.

2000. *Holy Trinity, perfect community.* Trans. P. Berryman. New York/Northam: Orbis/Roundhouse.

Boff, Leonardo, and Virgilio P. Elizondo, eds. 1993. *Any room for Christ in Asia?* Concilium 1993. London/Maryknoll: SCM Press/Orbis Books.

Bonhoeffer, Dietrich. 1978. *Lectures on christology.* Trans. E. Robertson. London: Collins.

Borg, Marcus J. 1987. *Jesus: a new vision. Spirit, culture, and the life of discipleship.* New York: Harper & Row.

1992. 'Portraits of Jesus in contemporary North American scholarship.' *HTR* 84: 1–22.

1994. *Jesus in contemporary scholarship.* Valley Forge: Trinity Press International.

Borg, Marcus J., ed. 1997. *Jesus at 2000.* Boulder: Westview Press.

Borg, Marcus J., and N. T. Wright. 1999. *The meaning of Jesus: two visions.* London: SPCK.

Boring, M. Eugene. 1988. 'The historical-critical method's "criteria of authenticity":
the Beatitudes in Q and Thomas as a test case.' *Semeia* 44: 9–44.

Bornkamm, Günther. 1960. *Jesus of Nazareth*. Trans. I. and F. McLuskey with J. M.
Robinson. London: Hodder & Stoughton.

Brandon, S. G. F. 1967. *Jesus and the Zealots: a study of the political factor in primitive
Christianity*. Manchester: Manchester University Press.

Brown, Colin. 1984. *Jesus in European protestant thought 1778–1860*. Durham, NC:
Labyrinth Press.

Brown, Raymond E. 1987. 'The Gospel of Peter and canonical gospel priority.' *NTS*
33: 321–43.

1994. *The death of the Messiah: from Gethsemane to the grave. A commentary on
the passion narratives in the four gospels*. ABRL. 2 vols. New York: Doubleday.

Bruce, F. F. 1982. *New Testament history*. London: Pickering & Inglis.

Brunner, Emil. 1946. *The mediator: a study of the central doctrine of the Christian
faith*. Trans. O. Wyon. London: Butterworth Press.

Brunner, Emil, and Karl Barth. 1946. *Natural theology: comprising 'Nature and Grace'*.
Trans. P. Fraenkel. London: G. Bles.

Bultmann, Rudolf. 1934. *Jesus and the Word*. Trans. L. P. Smith and E. H. Lantero.
New York: Scribner's.

Burrell, David B., and Yehezkel Landau. 1992. *Voices from Jerusalem: Jews and Christians reflect on the Holy Land*. Studies in Judaism and Christianity. New York:
Paulist Press.

Burridge, Richard A. 1992. *What are the gospels? A comparison with Graeco-Roman
biography*. SNTSMS 70. Cambridge and New York: Cambridge University Press.

1994. *Four gospels, one Jesus? A symbolic reading*. London: SPCK.

Campbell, Roy, ed. 1951. *The poems of St. John of the Cross*. London: Harvill.

Carnley, Peter. 1987. *The structure of resurrection belief*. Oxford: Clarendon Press.

Carroll, John T., and Joel B. Green. 1995. *The death of Jesus in early Christianity*.
Peabody: Hendrickson.

Casey, Maurice. 1991. *From Jewish prophet to gentile God: the origins and development
of New Testament christology*. Cambridge/Louisville: Clarke/Westminster John
Knox.

Catchpole, David. 2000. *Resurrection people: studies in the resurrection narratives of
the gospels*. London: Darton, Longman & Todd.

Certeau, Michel de. 1992. *The mystic fable*. Trans. M. C. Smith. Religion and Postmodernism. Chicago: University of Chicago Press.

Chancey, M., and E. M. Meyers. 2000. 'How Jewish was Sepphoris in Jesus' time?'
BARev 26.4: 18–33, 61.

Charlesworth, James H., ed. 1983–85. *The Old Testament pseudepigrapha*. 2 vols. New
York/London: Doubleday/Darton, Longman & Todd.

1992. *The Messiah: developments in earliest Judaism and Christianity*. Minneapolis:
Fortress.

Charlesworth, James H., and Craig A. Evans. 1994. 'Jesus in the Agrapha and apocryphal gospels.' In *Studying the historical Jesus: evaluations of the state of current
research*, 479–533. Ed. B. Chilton and C. A. Evans. NTTS 19. Leiden: Brill.

Childs, Brevard. 1984. *The New Testament as canon: an introduction*. London: SCM.

1992. 'Christ, the Lord.' In *Biblical theology of the Old and New Testaments*, 452–84.
London: SCM.

Chilton, Bruce. 1979. *God in strength: Jesus' announcement of the kingdom.* SNTSU 1. [Repr. Sheffield: Sheffield Academic Press, 1987]. Freistadt: Plöchl.

———. 1984b. *A Galilean rabbi and his Bible: Jesus' use of the interpreted Scripture of his time.* GNS 8. Wilmington: Glazier.

———. 1992. *The temple of Jesus: his sacrificial program within a cultural history of sacrifice.* University Park: Pennsylvania State University Press.

———. 1994. *A feast of meanings: eucharistic theologies from Jesus through Johannine circles.* NovTSup 72. Leiden: Brill.

———. 1998. *Jesus' baptism and Jesus' healing: his personal practice of spirituality.* Harrisburg: Trinity Press International.

———. 2000a. *Rabbi Jesus: an intimate biography.* New York: Doubleday.

———. 2000b. 'Resurrection in the gospels.' In *Judaism in late antiquity, Part Four: Death, life-after-death, resurrection and the world-to-come in the Judaisms of antiquity,* 215–39. Ed. A. J. Avery-Peck and J. Neusner. HO 1.49.4. Leiden: Brill.

Chilton, Bruce, ed. 1984a. *The kingdom of God in the teaching of Jesus.* London: SPCK.

Chilton, Bruce, and Craig A. Evans, eds. 1994a. *Studying the historical Jesus: evaluations of the state of current research.* NTTS 19. Leiden: Brill.

———. 1994b. 'Jesus and Israel's scriptures.' In *Studying the historical Jesus: evaluations of the state of current research,* 281–335. Ed. C. A. Evans and B. D. Chilton. NTTS 19. Leiden: Brill.

———. 1997. *Jesus in context: temple, purity, and restoration.* AGJU 39. Leiden: Brill.

Collins, John J. 1995. *The scepter and the star: the messiahs of the Dead Sea Scrolls and other ancient literature.* New York: Doubleday.

Cone, James H. 1997. *God of the oppressed.* Rev. edn. Maryknoll: Orbis Books.

Conzelmann, Hans. 1973. *Jesus.* Trans. J. R. Lord. London: SCM.

Coward, Harold G. 2000. *Experiencing Scripture in world religions.* Maryknoll: Orbis Books.

Crossan, John Dominic. 1985. *Four other gospels: shadows on the contours of canon.* Minneapolis: Winston Press.

———. 1988. *The cross that spoke: the origins of the passion narrative.* San Francisco: Harper & Row.

———. 1991. *The historical Jesus: the life of a Mediterranean Jewish peasant.* Edinburgh: T&T Clark.

———. 1994. *Jesus: a revolutionary biography.* San Francisco: HarperSanFrancisco.

Crouzel, Henri. 1989. *Origen.* Edinburgh: T&T Clark.

Cullmann, Oscar. 1956. 'The plurality of the gospels as a theological problem in antiquity.' In *The Early Church,* 39–54. Ed. A. J. B. Higgins. London: SCM.

Cyril of Scythopolis. 1990. *Lives of the monks of Palestine.* Trans. R. M. Price. Cistercian Studies 114. Kalamazoo: Cistercian Publications.

Dahl, Nils Alstrup. 1976. 'Anamnesis: memory and commemoration in early Christianity.' In *Jesus in the memory of the early church: essays,* 11–29. Minneapolis: Augsburg.

Davies, Reginald Thorne, ed. 1963. *Medieval English lyrics: a critical anthology.* London: Faber and Faber.

Davis, Stephen T. 1997. '"Seeing" the risen Jesus.' In *The resurrection: an interdisciplinary symposium on the resurrection of Jesus,* 126–47. Ed. S. T. Davis *et al.* Oxford: Oxford University Press.

Dawes, Gregory W. 2000. *The historical Jesus quest: landmarks in the search for the historical Jesus*. Louisville: Westminster John Knox.

Day, John, ed. 1998. *King and messiah in Israel and the ancient Near East: proceedings of the Oxford Old Testament Seminar*. JSOTSup 270. Sheffield: Sheffield Academic Press.

Deardorff, James W. 1994. *Jesus in India: a reexamination of Jesus' Asian traditions in the light of evidence supporting reincarnation*. San Francisco: International Scholars Publications.

Denzinger, Heinrich, and Adolfus Schönmetzer, eds. 1953. *Enchiridion symbolorum definitionum et declarationum de rebus fidei et morum*. 29th edn. Freiburg: Herder.

Dix, Gregory. 1945. *The shape of the liturgy*. Westminster: Dacre Press.

Dodd, C. H. 1936. *The parables of the kingdom*. London: Nisbet.

1963. *Historical tradition in the fourth Gospel*. Cambridge: Cambridge University Press.

Douglas, Kelly Brown. 1994. *The black Christ*. The Bishop Henry McNeal Turner Studies in North American Black Religion 9. Maryknoll: Orbis.

Dubois, Marcel. 1999. 'Jérusalem dans le temps et l'éternité.' *L'Olivier* (Jerusalem) 2–3: 7–109.

Dunn, James D. G. 1994. 'Jesus tradition in Paul.' In *Studying the historical Jesus: evaluations of the state of current research*, 155–78. Ed. B. Chilton and C. A. Evans. Leiden: Brill.

Dupuis, Jacques. 1997. *Toward a Christian theology of religious pluralism*. Maryknoll: Orbis Books.

Elizondo, Virgil. 1999. 'The emergence of a world church and the irruption of the poor.' In *The twentieth century: a theological overview*, 104–17. Ed. Gregory Baum. Maryknoll: Orbis.

Ernst, Josef. 1997. 'Johannes der Täufer und Jesus von Nazareth in historischer Sicht.' *NTS* 43: 161–83.

Evans, Craig A. 1994. 'Jesus in non-Christian sources.' In *Studying the historical Jesus: evaluations of the state of current research*, 443–78. Ed. B. Chilton and C. A. Evans. Leiden: Brill.

1995. *Jesus and his contemporaries: comparative studies*. AGJU 25. Leiden: Brill.

1999. 'Did Jesus predict his death and resurrection?' In *Resurrection*, 82–97. Ed. S. E. Porter *et al*. JSNTSup 186/Roehampton Institute Papers 5. Sheffield: Sheffield Academic Press.

Evans, C. Stephen. 1996. *The historical Christ and the Jesus of faith: the incarnational narrative as history*. Oxford and New York: Oxford University Press.

Farrow, Douglas. 1999. *Ascension and Ecclesia: on the significance of the doctrine of the ascension for ecclesiology and Christian cosmology*. Grand Rapids: Eerdmans.

Fergusson, David, and Marcel Sarot, eds. 2000. *The future as God's gift: explorations in Christian eschatology*. Edinburgh: T&T Clark.

Fitzmyer, Joseph A. 2000. *The Dead Sea Scrolls and Christian origins*. Grand Rapids: Eerdmans.

FitzPatrick, P. J. 1993. *In breaking of bread: the Eucharist and ritual*. Cambridge: Cambridge University Press.

Flusser, David. 1981. *Die rabbinischen Gleichnisse und der Gleichniserzähler Jesus.* Vol. 1: *Das Wesen der Gleichnisse.* Berne: Lang.

1988. *Judaism and the origins of Christianity.* Jerusalem: Magnes Press.

1998. *Jesus.* 2nd augm. edn in collaboration with R. Steven Motley. Jerusalem: Magnes Press.

Fowl, Stephen E. 1989. 'Reconstructing and deconstructing the quest for the historical Jesus.' *SJT* 42: 319–33.

France, R. T. 1971. *Jesus and the Old Testament.* London: Tyndale.

Fredriksen, Paula. 1988. *From Jesus to Christ: the origins of the New Testament images of Jesus.* New Haven and London: Yale University Press.

Frei, Hans W. 1974. *The eclipse of biblical narrative: a study in eighteenth and nineteenth century hermeneutics.* New Haven and London: Yale University Press.

1975. *The identity of Jesus Christ.* Philadelphia: Fortress Press.

1985. 'David Friedrich Strauss.' In *Nineteenth-century religious thought in the West,* 1:215–60. Ed. N. Smart *et al.* Cambridge: Cambridge University Press.

1993. *Theology and narrative: selected essays.* Ed. G. Hunsinger and W. C. Placher. New York and Oxford: Oxford University Press.

Freyne, Seán. 1994. 'The geography, politics, and economics of Galilee and the quest for the historical Jesus.' In *Studying the historical Jesus: evaluations of the state of current research,* 75–121. Ed. B. Chilton and C. A. Evans. NTTS 19. Leiden: Brill.

1998. *Galilee from Alexander the Great to Hadrian 323 BCE to 135 CE: a study of Second Temple Judaism.* Edinburgh: T&T Clark.

2000. *Galilee and gospel: collected essays.* WUNT 125. Tübingen: Mohr Siebeck.

Frick, Heinrich. 1930. 'The hidden glory of Christ and its coming manifestation.' In *Mysterium Christi,* 245–73. Ed. G. K. A. Bell and A. Deissman. London: Longmans & Green.

Friedman, Jerome. 1993. 'The myth of Jewish antiquity: new Christians and Christian-Hebraica in early modern Europe.' In *Jewish Christians and Christian Jews From the Renaissance to the Enlightenment,* 35–56. Ed. R. H. Popkin and G. M. Weiner. Dordrecht and London: Kluwer Academic Publishing.

Fukuyama, Francis. 1992. *The end of history and the last man.* London: Penguin.

Funk, Robert W. 1996. *Honest to Jesus: Jesus for a new millennium.* San Francisco: HarperSanFrancisco.

Funk, Robert W., ed. 1998. *The acts of Jesus: what did Jesus really do? The search for the authentic deeds of Jesus.* San Francisco: HarperCollins.

Funk, Robert W., and Roy W. Hoover, eds. 1993. *The five gospels: the search for the authentic words of Jesus.* Sonoma/New York: Polebridge Press/Macmillan.

Ganss, George E., ed. 1991. *Ignatius of Loyola: The Spiritual Exercises and selected works.* CWS. New York: Paulist Press.

García Martínez, Florentino. 1996. *The Dead Sea Scrolls translated: the Qumran texts in English.* Trans. W. G. E. Watson. 2nd edn. Leiden and New York: Brill; Grand Rapids: Eerdmans.

García Martínez, Florentino, and Eibert J. C. Tigchelaar. 1997–98. *The Dead Sea Scrolls study edition.* 2 vols. Leiden: Brill; Grand Rapids; Eerdmans.

Georgi, Dieter. 1992. 'The interest in Life of Jesus theology as a paradigm for the social history of biblical criticism.' *HTR* 85: 51–83.

Gibellini, Rosino. 1979. *Frontiers of theology in Latin America*. Trans. J. Drury. Maryknoll: Orbis Books.

Ginzberg, Louis. 1909–38. *The legends of the Jews*. 7 vols. Philadelphia: Jewish Publication Society of America.

Glasscoe, Marion, ed. 1986. *A revelation of love*. Exeter Medieval English Texts and Studies. Rev. edn. Exeter: University of Exeter Press.

Goddard, Hugh. 1995. *Christians and Muslims: from double standards to mutual understanding*. London: Curzon.

Gorodetzky, Nadejda. 1938. *The humiliated Christ in modern Russian thought*. London/New York: SPCK/Macmillan.

Goulder, Michael. 1994. 'Did Jesus of Nazareth rise from the dead?' In *Resurrection: essays in honour of Leslie Houlden*, 58–68. Ed. S. Barton and G. Stanton. London: SPCK.

1996. 'The baseless fabric of a vision.' In *Resurrection reconsidered*, 48–61. Ed. G. D'Costa. Oxford: Oneworld.

Grant, Robert M. 1961. *The earliest lives of Jesus*. London: SPCK.

Green, Joel B. 1987. 'The Gospel of Peter: source for a pre-canonical passion narrative?' *ZNW* 78: 293–301.

1988. *The death of Jesus: tradition and interpretation in the passion narrative*. WUNT 2:33. Tübingen: Mohr Siebeck.

Gregory of Nyssa. 1954. *The Lord's Prayer; The Beatitudes*. Trans. H. Graef. Westminster: Newman Press.

Grundmann, Walter. 1940. *Jesus der Galiläer und das Judentum*. Leipzig: Wigand.

Habig, Marion Alphonse, ed. 1973. *St. Francis of Assisi: writings and early biographies. English omnibus of the sources for the life of St. Francis*. Chicago: Franciscan Herald Press.

Haight, Roger. 1999. *Jesus, symbol of God*. Maryknoll: Orbis Books.

Hampson, Daphne. 1990. *Theology and feminism*. Oxford: Blackwell.

Hanfmann, G. M. A. 1980. 'The continuity of classical art: culture, myth and faith.' In *Age of spirituality: a symposium*, 75–99. Ed. K. Weitzmann. New York/Princeton: Metropolitan Museum of Art/Princeton University Press.

Hanson, R. P. C. 1962. *Tradition in the early church*. London: SCM.

Haran, M. 1988. 'On the diffusion of schools and literacy.' In *Congress volume: Jerusalem 1986*, 81–95. Ed. J. A. Emerton. VTSup 40. Leiden: Brill.

Harnack, Adolf von. 1908. *The sayings of Jesus: the second source of St. Matthew and St. Luke*. Trans. J. R. Wilkinson. London: Williams & Norgate.

1957. *What is Christianity?* Trans. T. B. Saunders. New York: Harper & Row.

Harrington, Daniel J. 1987. 'The Jewishness of Jesus: facing some problems.' *CBQ* 49: 1–13.

Harvey, A. E. 1982. *Jesus and the constraints of history*. London: Duckworth.

1994. '"They discussed among themselves what this 'rising from the dead' could mean" (Mark 9.10).' In *Resurrection: essays in honour of Leslie Houlden*, 69–78. Ed. S. Barton and G. Stanton. London: SPCK.

Hase, Karl. 1876. *Geschichte Jesu: nach akademischen Vorlesungen*. Leipzig: Breitkopf & Härtel.

Hengel, Martin. 1977. *Crucifixion in the ancient world and the folly of the message of the cross*. Trans. J. Bowden. Philadelphia: Fortress.

1989a. *The 'Hellenization' of Judaea in the first century after Christ*. Trans. J. Bowden. London/Philadelphia: SCM Press/Trinity Press International.

1989b. *The Zealots: investigations into the Jewish freedom movement in the period from Herod I until 70 A.D.* Trans. D. Smith. Edinburgh: T&T Clark.

1995. *Studies in early christology*. Edinburgh: T&T Clark.

2000. *The four gospels and the one gospel of Jesus Christ*. Trans. J. Bowden. London: SCM.

Hennecke, Edgar, Wilhelm Schneemelcher, and R. McL. Wilson. 1963. *New Testament Apocrypha*. Philadelphia: Westminster Press.

Heron, Alasdair I. C. 1980. *A century of Protestant theology*. Guildford: Lutterworth Press.

1981. 'Homoousios with the Father.' In *The incarnation*, 58–87. Ed. T. F. Torrance. Edinburgh: Handsel.

Herrin, Judith. 1987. *The formation of Christendom*. Oxford: Blackwell.

Hick, John, ed. 1977. *The myth of God incarnate*. London: SCM.

Hinga, Teresia. 1992. 'Jesus Christ and the liberation of woman.' In *The will to arise: women, tradition and the church in Africa*, 183–94. Ed. M. A. Oduyoye and M. R. Kanyoro. Maryknoll: Orbis.

Hoehner, Harold W. 1980. *Herod Antipas: a contemporary of Jesus Christ*. Grand Rapids: Zondervan.

Holmén, Tom. 1999. 'Doubts about double dissimilarity: reconstructing the main criteria of Jesus-of-history research.' In *Authenticating the words of Jesus*, 47–80. Ed. B. Chilton and C. A. Evans. NTTS 28.1. Leiden: Brill.

Hooker, M. D. 1971. 'Christology and methodology.' *NTS* 17: 480–87.

Horbury, William. 1998. *Jewish messianism and the cult of Christ*. London: SCM.

Horsley, R. A. 1995. *Galilee: history, politics, people*. Valley Forge: Trinity Press International.

1996. *Archaeology, history, and society in Galilee: the social context of Jesus and the rabbis*. Valley Forge: Trinity Press International.

Hoskyns, E. C., and N. Davey. 1981. *Crucifixion – resurrection: the pattern of the theology and ethics of the New Testament*. Ed. G. S. Wakefield. London: SPCK.

Hultgren, Arland J. 1987. *Christ and his benefits: christology and redemption in the New Testament*. Philadelphia: Fortress Press.

Hurth, Elisabeth. 1988. *In his name: comparative studies in the quest for the historical Jesus*. Frankfurt: Peter Lang.

Irenaeus. 1952. *Proof of the apostolic preaching*. Westminster: Newman Press.

Jaubert, Annie. 1958. *La date de la Cène: calendrier biblique et liturgie chrétienne*. Paris: Lecoffre.

Jeremias, Joachim. 1972. *The parables of Jesus*. Trans. S. H. Hooke. 3rd edn. London: SCM.

Johnson, Elizabeth A. 1990. *Consider Jesus: waves of renewal in christology*. New York: Crossroad.

1992. *She who is: the mystery of God in feminist theological discourse*. New York: Crossroad.

Johnson, Luke T. 1996. *The real Jesus: the misguided quest for the historical Jesus and the truth of the traditional gospels.* New York: HarperCollins.

Julian of Norwich. 1966. *Revelations of divine love.* Trans. C. Wolters. Harmondsworth: Penguin Books.

Jülicher, Adolf. 1888. *Die Gleichnisreden Jesu.* Freiburg: J. C. B. Mohr.

Jüngel, Eberhard, ed. 1992. *Christ, justice and peace: toward a theology of the state in dialogue with the Barmen Declaration.* Edinburgh: T&T Clark.

Jungmann, Josef A. 1989. *The place of Christ in liturgical prayer.* 2nd edn. London: Geoffrey Chapman.

Kabasele Lumbala, François. 1998. *Celebrating Jesus Christ in Africa: liturgy and inculturation.* Maryknoll: Orbis Books.

Kähler, Martin. 1964. *The so-called historical Jesus and the historic biblical Christ.* Trans. and ed. C. E. Braaten. Philadelphia: Fortress Press.

Kaiser, Walter C. Jr. 1995. *The Messiah in the Old Testament.* Grand Rapids: Zondervan.

Kant, Immanuel. 1934. *Religion within the limits of reason alone.* Trans. T. M. Greene and H. H. Hudson. Chicago and London: Open Court.

Käsemann, Ernst. 1964. 'The problem of the historical Jesus.' In *Essays on New Testament themes,* 15–47. Trans. W. J. Montague. SBT 41. London: SCM.

Keck, Leander E. 1969. 'Bornkamm's *Jesus of Nazareth* revisited.' *JR* 37: 1–17.

    1971. *A future for the historical Jesus.* Nashville: Abingdon.

    2000. *Who is Jesus? History in perfect tense.* Columbia: University of South Carolina Press.

Kee, Howard C. 1986. *Medicine, miracle and magic in New Testament times.* Cambridge: Cambridge University Press.

    1992. 'Early Christianity in the Galilee: reassessing the evidence from the gospels.' In *The Galilee in late antiquity,* 3–22. Ed. L. Levine. New York: Jewish Theological Seminary of America.

Kelhoffer, James A. 2000. *Miracle and mission: the authentication of missionaries and their message in the longer ending of Mark.* WUNT 2:112. Tübingen: Mohr Siebeck.

Kierkegaard, Søren. 1987. *Philosophical fragments, Johannes Climacus.* Trans. H. V. Hong and E. H. Hong. Kierkegaard's Writings 7. Princeton: Princeton University Press.

Kimbrough, S. T., ed. 1992. *Charles Wesley: poet and theologian.* Nashville: Kingswood Books and Abingdon Press.

Kingsbury, Jack Dean. 1981. 'The gospel in four editions.' In *Interpreting the gospels,* 27–40. Ed. J. L. Mays. Philadelphia: Fortress.

Kissinger, Warren S. 1985. *The Lives of Jesus: a history and bibliography.* New York and London: Garland.

Klausner, Joseph. 1925. *Jesus of Nazareth: his life, times, and teaching.* Trans. H. Danby. New York: Macmillan.

    1943. *From Jesus to Paul.* Trans. W. F. Stinespring. New York: Macmillan.

    1957. *Jesus von Nazareth: seine Zeit, sein Leben und seine Lehre.* 3rd edn. Jerusalem: Jewish Publishing House.

Kloppenborg Verbin, John S. 2000. *Excavating Q: the history and setting of the sayings gospel.* Minneapolis: Fortress Press.

Knitter, Paul F. 1996. *Jesus and the other names: Christian mission and global responsibility*. Maryknoll: Orbis Books.

Koester, Helmut. 1990. *Ancient Christian gospels: their history and development*. London/Philadelphia: SCM Press/Trinity Press International.

Kümmel, Werner Georg. 1973. *The New Testament: the history of the investigation of its problems*. Trans. S. M. Gilmour and H. C. Kee. London: SCM.

1994. *Vierzig Jahre Jesusforschung 1950–1990*. BBB 91. 2nd edn. Weinheim: Beltz Athenäum.

Kwok, Pui-Lan, and Elisabeth Schüssler Fiorenza, eds. 1998. *Women's sacred scriptures*. London: SCM.

Lapide, Pinchas. 1983. *The resurrection of Jesus: a Jewish perspective*. London: SPCK.

Lazarus-Yafeh, Hava. 1974. 'The sanctity of Jerusalem in Islam.' In *Jerusalem*, xvi, 302. Ed. John M. Oesterreicher and Anne Sinai. New York: John Day.

Lefebure, Leo D. 2000. *Revelation, the religions, and violence*. Maryknoll: Orbis Books.

Lessing, Gotthold Ephraim. 1777. *Ueber den Beweis des Geistes und der Kraft*. Braunschweig: n. p.

1956. *Lessing's theological writings*. Ed. and trans. H. Chadwick. London: A&C Black.

Lindars, Barnabas. 1990. *John*. Sheffield: Sheffield Academic Press.

Loughlin, Gerard. 1995. 'Holy texts of deception: Christian gnosticism and the writings of Michael Baigent and Richard Leigh.' *New Blackfriars* 76: 293–305.

Lüdemann, Gerd. 1994. *The resurrection of Jesus: history, experience, theology*. Trans. J. Bowden. London: SCM.

1995. *What really happened to Jesus: a historical approach to the resurrection*. Trans. J. Bowden. London: SCM.

2000. *Jesus after 2000 years*. London: SCM Press.

Lyotard, Jean-François. 1984. *The postmodern condition*. Trans. G. Bennington and B. Massumi. Minneapolis: University of Minneapolis Press.

Maalouf, Amin. 1984. *The crusades through Arab eyes*. Trans. J. Rothschild. New York: Schocken Books.

Mack, B. L. 1987. 'The kingdom sayings in Mark.' *Forum* 3.1: 3–47.

1988. *A myth of innocence: Mark and Christian origins*. Philadelphia: Fortress.

Malina, Bruce J., and Richard Rohrbaugh. 1992. *Social-science commentary on the synoptic gospels*. Minneapolis: Fortress.

Marcus, Joel. 1995. 'The Old Testament and the death of Jesus: the role of scripture in the gospel passion narratives.' In *The death of Jesus in early Christianity*, 204–33. Ed. J. T. Carroll and J. B. Green. Peabody: Hendrickson.

Marsh, Clive. 1997. 'Quests for the historical Jesus in new historicist perspective.' *BibInt* 5: 403–37.

Mathews, Thomas F. 1993. *The clash of gods: a reinterpretation of early Christian art*. Princeton: Princeton University Press.

Matzko, D. M. 1996. 'Christ's body in its fulness: resurrection and the lives of the saints.' In *Resurrection reconsidered*, 102–17. Ed. G. D'Costa. Oxford: Oneworld.

McArthur, Harvey K. 1972. '"On the third day": 1 Cor 15.4b and rabbinic interpretation of Hosea 6.2.' *NTS* 18: 81–86.

McKnight, Scot. 1999. *A new vision for Israel: the teachings of Jesus in national context*. Grand Rapids: Eerdmans.

Meier, John P. 1991–94. *A marginal Jew: rethinking the historical Jesus*. 2 vols. New York: Doubleday.

    1999. 'The present state of the "third quest" for the historical Jesus: loss and gain.' *Biblica* 80: 459–87.

Merkel, Helmut. 1974. 'Auf den Spuren des Urmarkus? Ein neuer Fund und seine Beurteilung.' *ZTK* 71: 123–44.

Meyer, Ben F. 1979. *The aims of Jesus*. London: SCM.

Meyers, E. 1986. 'Sepphoris: ornament of all Galilee.' *BA* 49: 4–19.

    1997. 'Jesus and his Galilean context.' In *Archaeology and the Galilee: texts and contexts in the Graeco-Roman and Byzantine periods*, 57–66. Ed. D. R. Edwards and C. T. McCollough. South Florida Studies in the History of Judaism 143. Atlanta: Scholars.

Míguez Bonino, José. 1984. *Faces of Jesus: Latin American christologies*. Trans. R. R. Barr. Maryknoll: Orbis Books.

Millard, A. R. 1985a. 'An assessment of the evidence for writing in ancient Israel.' In *Biblical archaeology today*, 301–12. Ed. A. Biran. Jerusalem: Israel Exploration Society.

    1985b. '*ᵓBGD* – magic spell or educational exercise?' *Eretz-Israel* 18: 39–42.

    2000. *Reading and writing in the time of Jesus*. Biblical Seminar 69. Sheffield: Sheffield Academic Press.

Moberly, R. W. L. 2000. *The Bible, theology, and faith: a study of Abraham and Jesus*. Cambridge Studies in Christian Doctrine. Cambridge and New York: Cambridge University Press.

Mohammed, Ovey N. 1999. *Muslim–Christian relations: past, present, future*. Maryknoll: Orbis Books.

Moltmann, Jürgen. 1967. *Theology of hope*. Trans. J. W. Leitch. London: SCM Press.

    1974. *The crucified God: The cross of Christ as the foundation and criticism of Christian theology*. Trans. R. A. Wilson and J. Bowden. London: SCM.

    1990. *The way of Jesus Christ*. Trans. M. Kohl. London: SCM Press.

    1996a. *The coming of God*. Trans. M. Kohl. London: SCM Press.

    1996b. 'The resurrection of Christ: hope for the world.' In *Resurrection reconsidered*, 73–86. Ed. G. D'Costa. Oxford: Oneworld.

Morgan, Robert. 1980. 'Non Angli sed Angeli: some Anglican reactions to German gospel criticism.' In *New studies in theology*, 1:11–30. Ed. S. Sykes and D. Holmes. London: Duckworth.

    1987. 'The historical Jesus and the theology of the New Testament.' In *The glory of Christ in the New Testament: studies in christology in memory of George Caird*, 187–206. Ed. L. D. Hurst and N. T. Wright. Oxford: Clarendon.

    1993. 'From Reimarus to Sanders: the kingdom of God, Jesus, and the Judaisms of his day.' In *The kingdom of God and human society*, 80–139. Ed. R. S. Barbour. Edinburgh: T&T Clark.

Moule, C. F. D. 1977. *The origin of christology*. Cambridge: Cambridge University Press.

Moxnes, Halvor. 1998. 'The historical Jesus: from master narrative to cultural context.' *BTB* 28: 135–49.

Murphy-O'Connor, Jerome. 1990. 'John the Baptist and Jesus: history and hypotheses.' *NTS* 36: 359–74.

Murray, C. 1977. 'The Christian Orpheus.' *Cahiers archéologiques: fin de l'antiquité et moyen age* 26: 19–27.

Murray, Robert. 1970. 'A hymn of St Ephrem to Christ on the incarnation, the Holy Spirit and the sacraments.' *Eastern Churches Review* 3: 142–50.

Myllykoski, Matti. 1991–94. *Die letzen Tage Jesu: Markus und Johannes, ihre Traditionen und die historische Frage.* Annales Academiae Scientiarum Fennicae B/256, 272. 2 vols. Helsinki: Suomalainen Tiedeakatemia.

Neill, Stephen, and N. T. Wright. 1988. *The interpretation of the New Testament: 1861–1986.* Oxford and New York: Oxford University Press.

Neirynck, F. 1991. 'The apocryphal gospels and the Gospel of Mark.' In *Evangelica II: 1982–1991. Collected essays,* 715–72. Ed. F. van Segbroeck. BETL 99. Leuven: University Press.

Neuner, Josef, and Jacques Dupuis, eds. 1983. *The Christian faith in the doctrinal documents of the Catholic church.* 5th rev. and enl. edn. London: Collins.

Neusner, Jacob. 1976. 'First cleanse the inside: halakhic background of a controversial saying.' *NTS* 22: 486–95.

Nickelsburg, George W. E. 1981. *Jewish literature between the Bible and the Mishnah: a historical and literary introduction.* London: SCM.

Nippold, Friedrich. 1880–1906. *Handbuch der neuesten Kirchengeschichte.* 6 vols. 3rd edn. Elberfeld: Friderichs.

Nürnberg, Rosemarie. 1996. 'Apostolae Apostolorum: Die Frauen am Grab als erste Zeuginnen der Auferstehung in der Väterexegese.' In *Stimuli: Exegese und ihre Hermeneutik in Antike und Christentum: Festschrift für Ernst Dassmann,* 228–42. Ed. G. Schöllgen and C. Scholten. Münster: Aschendorff.

Nyamiti, Charles. 1993. 'African ancestral veneration and its relevance to the African churches.' *African Christian Studies* 9.3: 14–37.

O'Collins, Gerald. 1983. *What are they saying about Jesus?* 2nd edn. New York: Paulist Press.

1988. *Interpreting the resurrection.* New York and Mahwah: Paulist Press.

1997. 'The resurrection: the state of the questions.' In *The resurrection: an interdisciplinary symposium on the resurrection of Jesus,* 5–28. Ed. S. T. Davis *et al.* Oxford: Oxford University Press.

O'Donovan, Oliver M. T. 1994. *Resurrection and moral order: an outline for evangelical ethics.* 2nd edn. Leicester: Apollos.

Oduyoye, Mercy Amba, and Rachel Angogo Kanyoro. 1992. *The will to arise: women, tradition, and the church in Africa.* Maryknoll: Orbis Books.

Okure, Teresa. 1990. 'Inculturation: biblical theological bases.' In *32 articles evaluating inculturation of Christianity in Africa,* 55–88. Ed. Teresa Okure and P. J. J. van Thiel. Eldoret: AMECEA Gaba Publications.

1993. 'Jesus: der Mann, der in der Art der Frauen wirkte.' In *Jahrbuch Mission 1993,* 53–62. Ed. J. Wietzke. Hamburg: Missionshilfe Verlag.

1998a. 'From Genesis to Revelation: apocalyptic in biblical faith.' *Concilium* 4: 23–30.

1998b. 'John.' In *International Bible commentary: a Catholic and ecumenical resource for the twenty-first century,* 1438–1504. Ed. William R. Farmer. Collegeville: Liturgical Press.

Origen. 1925. *Homilien zu Samuel I, zum Hohelied und zu den Propheten; Kommentar zum Hohelied: in Rufins und Hieronymus' Übersetzungen.* Ed. W. A. Baehrens. Origenes Werke 8. Leipzig: Hinrichs.

1979. *Origen.* Trans. R. A. Greer. CWS. London: SPCK.

Osborne, Grant R. 1984. *The resurrection narratives: a redactional study.* Grand Rapids: Baker Book House.

Osuna, Francisco de. 1981. *Francisco de Osuna: the third spiritual alphabet.* Trans. M. E. Giles. CWS. London: SPCK.

Oulton, John Ernest Leonard, and Henry Chadwick, eds. 1954. *Alexandrian Christianity: selected translations of Clement and Origen with introductions and notes.* LCC. London: SCM Press.

Painter, John. 1999. *Just James: the brother of Jesus in history and tradition.* Minneapolis: Fortress Press.

Pals, Daniel L. 1982. *The Victorian lives of Jesus.* San Antonio: Trinity University Press.

Panikkar, Raimundo. 1981. *The unknown Christ of Hinduism: towards an ecumenical christophany.* Rev. and enl. edn. London: Darton Longman & Todd.

Pannenberg, Wolfhart. 1994a. 'Die Auferstehung Jesu – Historie und Theologie.' *ZTK* 91: 318–28.

1996. 'History and the reality of the resurrection.' In *Resurrection reconsidered,* 62–72. Ed. G. D'Costa. Oxford: Oneworld.

Patterson, Stephen J. 1993. *The Gospel of Thomas and Jesus.* Sonoma: Polebridge Press.

1998. *The God of Jesus: the historical Jesus and the search for meaning.* Harrisburg: Trinity Press International.

Peers, E. Allison. 1943. *The complete works of Saint John of the Cross, Doctor of the Church.* 3 vols. London: Burns & Oates.

Pelikan, Jaroslav Jan. 1985. *Jesus through the centuries: his place in the history of culture.* New Haven: Yale University Press.

Perkins, Pheme. 1984. *Resurrection: New Testament witness and contemporary reflection.* Garden City: Doubleday.

Peters, F. E. 1985. *Jerusalem.* Princeton: Princeton University Press.

Pope-Levison, Priscilla, and John R. Levison. 1992. *Jesus in global contexts.* Louisville: Westminster and John Knox Press.

Porter, S. E. 2000. 'Jesus and the use of Greek: a response to Maurice Casey.' *BBR* 10: 71–87.

Powell, Mark Allen. 1998. *The Jesus debate: modern historians investigate the life of Christ.* Oxford: Lion.

Prior, Michael. 1997. *The Bible and colonialism: a moral critique.* Biblical Seminar 48. Sheffield: Sheffield Academic Press.

Prior, Michael, and William Taylor, eds. 1994. *Christians in the Holy Land.* London: World of Islam Festival Trust.

Räisänen, Heikki. 1990. *The 'messianic secret' in Mark.* Edinburgh: T&T Clark.

Ratzinger, Joseph. 2000. *Dominus Iesus: on the unicity* [sic] *and salvific universality of Jesus Christ and the church.* Congregation for the Doctrine of the Faith. Vatican City: Editrice Vaticana.

Reinbold, Wolfgang. 1994. *Der älteste Bericht über den Tod Jesu: Literarische Analyse und historische Kritik der Passionsdarstellungen der Evangelien*. BZNW 69. Berlin and New York: de Gruyter.

Reiser, Marius. 1997. *Jesus and judgment: the eschatological proclamation in its Jewish context*. Trans. L. M. Maloney. Minneapolis: Fortress.

Renan, Ernest. 1863. *La vie de Jésus*. Paris: Lévy.

Richardson, Cyril Charles, ed. 1953. *Early Christian Fathers* 1. Philadelphia: Westminster Press.

Riesner, Rainer. 1981. *Jesus als Lehrer*. WUNT 2:7. Tübingen: Mohr Siebeck.

Ritschl, Albrecht. 1872. *A critical history of the Christian doctrine of justification and reconciliation*. Trans. J. S. Black. Edinburgh: Edmonston and Douglas.

Rubin, Miri. 1991. *Corpus Christi: the Eucharist in late medieval culture*. Cambridge: Cambridge University Press.

Rumscheidt, H. Martin. 1972. *Revelation and theology: an analysis of the Barth–Harnack correspondence of 1923*. Cambridge: Cambridge University Press.

Sabella, Bernard. 1994. 'Socio-economic characteristics and the challenges to Palestinian Christians in the Holy Land.' In *Christians in the Holy Land*, 31–45. Ed. M. Prior and W. Taylor. London: The World of Islam Festival Trust.

Safrai, S. 1974–76. 'Education and the study of Torah.' In *The Jewish people in the first century*, 2:945–70. 2 vols. Ed. S. Safrai and M. Stern. Assen/Philadelphia: Van Gorcum/Fortress.

——— 1996. 'Jesus and the Hassidic movement (Hebr.).' In *The Jews in the Hellenistic–Roman world: studies in memory of Menahem Stern*, 413–36. Ed. A. Oppenheimer, *et al.* Jerusalem: Shazar Center/Historical Society.

Sanders, E. P. 1985. *Jesus and Judaism*. London/Philadelphia: SCM Press/Fortress Press.

——— 1993. *The historical figure of Jesus*. London: Allen Lane and Penguin.

Saulnier, Christiane. 1984. 'Herode Antipas et Jean le Baptiste: quelques remarques sur les confusions chronologiques de Flavius Josèphe.' *RB* 91: 362–76.

Schaper, Joachim. 1995. *Eschatology in the Greek Psalter*. WUNT 2:76. Tübingen: Mohr Siebeck.

Schmemann, Alexander. 1988. *The eucharist – sacrament of the kingdom*. Crestwood, NY: St. Vladimir's Seminary Press.

Schmid, J. 1959. *Das Evangelium nach Matthäus*. Regensburg: Pustet.

Schmiedel, Paul W. 1907. *Jesus in modern criticism: a lecture*. London: A&C Black.

Schneemelcher, Wilhelm. 1991. *New Testament apocrypha*. Ed. R. McL. Wilson. 2 vols. Rev. edn. Cambridge/Louisville: James Clark & Co./Westminster John Knox Press.

Scholem, Gershom G. 1973. *Šabbatai Ṣevi: the mystical Messiah, 1626–1676*. Bollingen Series 93. Princeton: Princeton University Press.

Schönborn, Christoph von. 1994. *God's human face: the Christ-icon*. San Francisco: Ignatius Press.

Schreiter, Robert J. 1991. *Faces of Jesus in Africa*. Maryknoll: Orbis Books.

Schürer, E. 1973–87. *The history of the Jewish people in the age of Jesus Christ*. Ed. G. Vermes *et al.* 3 vols. Rev. edn. Edinburgh: T&T Clark.

Schüssler Fiorenza, Elisabeth. 1986. *In memory of her: a feminist theological reconstruction of Christian origins*. New York: Crossroad.

1995a. *Jesus: Miriam's child, Sophia's prophet. Critical issues in feminist christology.* London: SCM.

1995b. 'Transgressing canonical boundaries.' In *Searching the Scriptures*, 2: *A feminist commentary*: 1–14. Ed. E. Schüssler Fiorenza. London: SCM.

Schüssler Fiorenza, Francis P. 1997. 'The resurrection of Jesus and Roman Catholic fundamental theology.' In *The resurrection: an interdisciplinary symposium on the resurrection of Jesus*, 213–48. Ed. S. T. Davis *et al.* Oxford: Oxford University Press.

Schweitzer, Albert. 1912. *Paul and his interpreters: a critical history.* Trans. W. Montgomery. London: A&C Black.

1949. *Out of my life and thought.* Trans. C. T. Campion. New York: Holt.

2000. *The Quest of the historical Jesus.* Trans. J. Bowden. First complete edn. London: SCM.

Smith, D. Moody. 1980. 'John and the Synoptics.' *NTS* 26: 425–44.

2000. 'Of Jesus and Quirinius.' *CBQ* 62: 278–93.

Sobrino, Jon. 1978. *Christology at the crossroads: a Latin American approach.* Maryknoll: Orbis Books.

1993. *Jesus the liberator: a historical–theological reading of Jesus of Nazareth.* Trans. P. Burns and F. McDonagh. Maryknoll: Orbis Books.

Song, C. S. 1994. *Jesus in the power of the Spirit.* Philadelphia: Fortress Press.

Soulen, R. Kendall. 1996. *The God of Israel and Christian theology.* Minneapolis: Fortress Press.

Stanton, Graham. 1989. *The gospels and Jesus.* Oxford Bible Studies. Oxford and New York: Oxford University Press.

1990. 'The fourfold gospel.' *NTS* 43: 317–46.

1994a. 'Early objections to the resurrection of Jesus.' In *Resurrection: essays in honour of Leslie Houlden*, 79–94. Ed. S. C. Barton and G. Stanton. London: SPCK.

1994b. 'Jesus of Nazareth: a magician and a false prophet who deceived God's people?' In *Jesus of Nazareth: Lord and Christ. Essays on the historical Jesus and New Testament Christology*, 164–80. Ed. Joel B. Green and Max Turner. Grand Rapids: Eerdmans.

Stefanovic, Zdravko. 1992. 'Jacob's well.' In *ABD*, 3:608–609.

Stein, Robert H. 1980. 'The "criteria" for authenticity.' In *Gospel perspectives*, 1:225–63. Ed. R. T. France and D. Wenham. Sheffield: JSOT Press.

Steiner, George. 1959. *Tolstoy or Dostoevsky: an essay in contrast.* London: Faber and Faber.

1997. *Errata: an examined life.* London: Weidenfeld & Nicholson.

Stevenson, J., ed. 1957. *A new Eusebius: documents illustrative of the history of the church to A.D. 337.* London: SPCK.

Strange, James F. 1997. 'First century Galilee from archaeology and from the texts.' In *Archaeology and the Galilee: texts and contexts in the Graeco-Roman and Byzantine periods*, 39–48. Ed. D. R. Edwards and C. T. McCollough. South Florida Studies in the History of Judaism 143. Atlanta: Scholars Press.

Strauss, David Friedrich. 1972. *The life of Jesus critically examined.* Trans. P. C. Hodgson. Philadelphia: Fortress Press.

Swidler, Leonard J., and Paul Mojzes. 1997. *The uniqueness of Jesus: a dialogue with Paul F. Knitter.* Maryknoll: Orbis Books.

Talbert, C. H. 1981. 'The gospel and the gospels.' In *Interpreting the gospels*, 14–26. Ed. J. L. Mays. Philadelphia: Fortress.

Taylor, Jeremy. 1990. *Jeremy Taylor: selected works.* Ed. T. K. Carroll. CWS. New York: Paulist Press.

Telford, William R. 1994. 'Major trends and interpretive issues in the study of Jesus.' In *Studying the historical Jesus*, 33–74. Ed. B. Chilton and C. A. Evans. Leiden: Brill.

Temple, William. 1925. *Christus veritas: an essay.* London: Macmillan.

Theissen, Gerd. 1983. *The miracle stories of the early Christian tradition.* Trans. F. McDonagh. Ed. J. Riches. Edinburgh/Philadelphia: T&T Clark/Fortress.

1991. *The Gospels in context: social and political history in the Synoptic tradition.* Trans. L. M. Maloney. Minneapolis: Fortress.

Theissen, Gerd, and Annette Merz. 1998. *The historical Jesus: a comprehensive guide.* Trans. J. Bowden. London: SCM Press.

Theissen, Gerd, and Dagmar Winter. 1997. *Die Kriterienfrage in der Jesusforschung: Vom Differenzkriterium zum Plausibilitätskriterium.* NTOA 34. Fribourg/Göttingen: Universitätsverlag/Vandenhoeck & Ruprecht.

Thérèse of Lisieux. 1958. *Autobiography of a saint.* Trans. R. Knox. London: Harvill Press.

Thiering, Barbara. 1992. *Jesus and the riddle of the Dead Sea Scrolls: unlocking the secrets of his life story.* San Francisco: Harper.

Thompson, Marianne Meye. 2000. *The promise of the Father.* Louisville: Westminster and John Knox.

Tillich, Paul. 1951–63. *Systematic theology.* 3 vols. Chicago: University of Chicago Press.

Tolstoy, Leo. 1961. *A confession, The gospel in brief, and What I believe.* Trans. A. Maude. The World's Classics. London: Oxford University Press.

Tomson, Peter J. 2001. '*If this be from heaven . . .*': Jesus and the New Testament authors in their relationship to Judaism.* Trans. J. Dyk. Biblical Seminar 76. Sheffield: Sheffield Academic Press.

Forthcoming. *The centrality of Jerusalem and its temple in earliest Christianity.* Bar Ilan University: Rennert Center for Jerusalem Studies.

Torjesen, Karen Jo. 1997. 'You are the Christ: five portraits of Jesus from the early church.' In *Jesus at 2000*, 73–88. Ed. Marcus J. Borg. Boulder: Westview Press.

Torrance, T. F. 1965. *Theology in reconstruction.* London: SCM Press.

Townsend, J. T. 1971. 'Ancient education in the time of the early Roman empire.' In *The catacombs and the Colosseum*, 139–63. Ed. S. Benko and J. J. O'Rourke. Valley Forge: Judson Press.

Troeltsch, Ernst. 1972. *The absoluteness of Christianity and the history of religions.* Trans. D. Reid. London: SCM.

Tuckett, Christopher M. 1988. 'Thomas and the Synoptics.' *NovT* 30: 132–57.

1996. *Q and the history of early Christianity: studies on Q.* Edinburgh: T&T Clark.

1999. 'The historical Jesus, Crossan and methodology.' In *Text und Geschichte: Festschrift für Dieter Lührmann*, 257–79. Ed. S. Maser and E. Schlarb. Marburg: Elwert Verlag.

Tuckett, Christopher M., ed. 1983. *The messianic secret*. Philadelphia/London: Fortress/SPCK.

Turner, Denys. 1995. *Eros and allegory: medieval exegesis of the Song of Songs*. Cistercian Studies Series 156. Kalamazoo: Cistercian Publications.

Turner, H. E. W. 1976. *Jesus the Christ*. London: Mowbrays.

Twelftree, Graham H. 1993. *Jesus the exorcist: a contribution to the study of the historical Jesus*. WUNT 2:54. Tübingen: Mohr Siebeck.

Ugolnik, Anthony. 1989. *The illuminating icon*. Grand Rapids: Eerdmans.

Uro, Risto, ed. 1998. *Thomas at the crossroads: essays on the Gospel of Thomas*. SNTW. Edinburgh: T&T Clark.

VanderKam, James C. 1998. 'Authoritative literature in the Dead Sea Scrolls.' *DSD* 5: 382–402.

Vermes, Geza. 1983. *Jesus the Jew: a historian's reading of the gospels*. 2nd edn. London: SCM.

1984. *Jesus and the world of Judaism*. London: SCM.

1993. *The religion of Jesus the Jew*. London: SCM.

Via, Dan O. 1967. *The parables: their literary and existential dimension*. Philadelphia: Fortress.

Walker, P. W. L. 1990. *Holy city, holy places: Christian attitudes to Jerusalem and the Holy Land in the fourth century*. Oxford Early Christian Studies. Oxford and New York: Oxford University Press.

1994. 'Jerusalem in the early Christian centuries.' In *Jerusalem past and present in the purposes of God*, 79–97. Ed. P. W. L. Walker. Grand Rapids: Baker.

Walker, W. O. 1969. 'The quest for the historical Jesus: a discussion of methodology.' *AThR* 51: 38–56.

Walter, Nikolaus. 1989. 'Paul and early Christian Jesus-tradition.' In *Paul and Jesus: collected essays*, 51–80. Ed. A. J. M. Wedderburn. Sheffield: JSOT Press.

Watson, Francis. 1994. *Text, church and world: biblical interpretation in theological perspective*. Edinburgh/Grand Rapids: T&T Clark/Eerdmans.

1997. *Text and truth: redefining biblical theology*. Edinburgh/Grand Rapids: T&T Clark/Eerdmans.

Weaver, Walter P. 1999. *The historical Jesus in the twentieth century: 1900–1950*. Harrisburg: Trinity Press International.

Wedderburn, A. J. M. 1999. *Beyond resurrection*. London: SCM Press.

Weiss, Johannes. 1985. *Jesus' proclamation of the kingdom of God*. Trans. and ed. R. H. Hiers and D. L. Holland. Chicago: Scholars Press.

Wilken, Robert L. 1984. *The Christians as the Romans saw them*. New Haven: Yale University Press.

1992. *The land called holy: Palestine in Christian history and thought*. New Haven and London: Yale University Press.

Williams, Rowan. 1982. *Resurrection: interpreting the Easter gospel*. London: Darton, Longman & Todd.

1990. *The wound of knowledge: Christian spirituality from the New Testament to St John of the Cross*. 2nd edn. London: Darton Longman and Todd.

1996. 'Between the cherubim: the empty tomb and the empty throne.' In *Resurrection reconsidered*, 87–101. Ed. G. D'Costa. Oxford: Oneworld.

Witherington, Ben. 1995. *The Jesus quest*. Downers Grove: InterVarsity Press.

Wrede, William. 1971. *The messianic secret.* Trans. J. C. G. Grieg. Cambridge: Clarke.

Wright, N. T. 1992a. *The New Testament and the people of God.* Minneapolis: Fortress Press.

    1992b. 'The quest for the historical Jesus.' *ABD* 3: 796–802.

    1996. *Jesus and the victory of God.* London: SPCK.

    1999. 'The transforming reality of the bodily resurrection.' In *The meaning of Jesus: two visions,* 111–27. Ed. M. J. Borg and N. T. Wright. San Francisco: HarperSanFrancisco.

Yarbro Collins, Adela. 1992. *The beginning of the gospel: probings of Mark in context.* Minneapolis: Fortress.

Young, Brad. 1995. *Jesus the Jewish theologian.* Peabody: Hendrickson.

Zias, Joseph, and Eliezer Sekeles. 1985. 'The crucified man from Giv^cat ha-Mivtar: a reappraisal.' *IEJ* 35: 22–27.

General index

Scripture index